A SENSE OF ARRIVAL

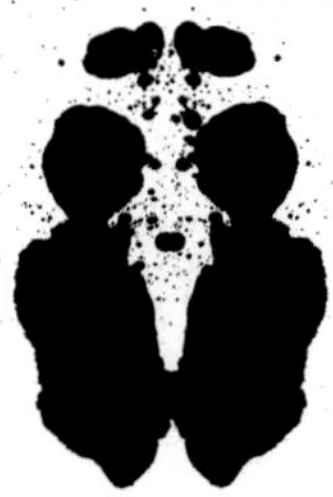

A SENSE OF ARRIVAL

KEVIN ADONIS BROWNE

Duke University Press *Durham and London* 2024

Printed in China on acid-free paper ∞
Project Editor: Lisa Lawley
Designed by Courtney Leigh Richardson
Typeset in Garamond Premier Pro and Sophillia by Copperline Book Services

Library of Congress Cataloging-in-Publication Data
Names: Browne, Kevin Adonis, author.
Title: A sense of arrival / Kevin Adonis Browne.
Description: Durham : Duke University Press, 2024. | Includes bibliographical references and index.
Identifiers: LCCN 2023057429 (print)
LCCN 2023057430 (ebook)
ISBN 9781478030928 (paperback)
ISBN 9781478026709 (hardcover)
ISBN 9781478059905 (ebook)
Subjects: LCSH: Browne, Kevin Adonis. | Black people—Race identity—Caribbean Area. | Caribbean Americans—Race identity. | Arts, Caribbean. | Arts, Black—Caribbean Area. | National characteristics, Caribbean, in literature. | BISAC: SOCIAL SCIENCE / Ethnic Studies / American / African American & Black Studies | SOCIAL SCIENCE / Ethnic Studies / Caribbean & Latin American Studies | LCGFT: Essays. | Narrative poetry. | Autobiographies.
Classification: LCC F2169 .B76 2024 (print) | LCC F2169 (ebook) |
DDC 305.896/9729—dc23/eng/20240430
LC record available at https://lccn.loc.gov/2023057429
LC ebook record available at https://lccn.loc.gov/2023057430

Cover art: *Self|Invention; or, History of a Skin Wrapped in Brown Paper No. 4*, 2020. Digital. © Kevin Adonis Browne. Courtesy of the artist.

“Sense make before book.”

—*Unknown*

for

LAYLA AND KYLE

for

EVA

MURIEL, MABEL, EUGENIA, VENA, VERA, ALEXIA

for

THE WRIGHTS AND THE BROWNES

THE JOSEPHS AND THE PITTS

THE ROCHARDS AND THE RYANS

CONTENTS

A SENSE OF ARRIVAL

NOTE

A Sense of Arrival is a Caribbean nonfiction.

It is a rhetoric of Caribbeanness whose arrival is composed as a nonfiction in the midst of an enduring catastrophe, a nonfiction whose primary function is the expression of a Caribbean Self that *comes to be.*

> *Self*, as being.
> *Being*, as a consequence of the breath.
> *Breath*, as a phenomenon that is held, but never truly held.

For me, that *self* and *being* and *breath*, which exist in spite of catastrophe, are black—a blackness whose Caribbeanness is explicit.

A *Caribbean blackness.*

I interpret arrival here as an immersive existential phenomenon—a form of status, return, belonging, citizenship, nomadism, self-exile, presence, and haunting—one that relies primarily on the vast range, complexity, and urgency of our expressive traditions:

Caribbeanness *itself* is a nonfiction.

Viewing Caribbean nonfiction as a concept and practice of rhetorical form, not merely as one of the definitive literary arts of the region, it is a Caribbean story told in a Caribbean way—that is, through the deliberative intermixing of multiple forms: prose, poetry, lyric essay, portraiture, documentary photography, archives, material sculptures and installations, and digital scans. As such, it is a meditation on the art and process of that story unfolding as a monologue that aspires to be dialogic—something that takes place between me and you, and between myself and the things I have made—which I invite you to see and, eventually, to take part in. A conspiracy of form.

In *A Sense of Arrival*, you will encounter things standing in for other things—words for images, images for objects, objects for images, images for words, words for other words, and so on. They will appear as|for other things. I have set them this way. I know you will supplant my intentions with your own whenever you arrive. You are not here yet, of course. I have to imagine you as I write. I do not know what you will look like, only that you will appear. I do not *know* if you will appear, but I must write as if you will. Know then, that as you read this, you are a moment materializing, finally. You are a dream I have dreamed. I am writing—have written—in anticipation of you.

You are not here yet, but I have written a sense of you into the very tensing of the book. I have implicated you in its grammar. What do I mean? Well, to begin with, the telling of this story occurs *in absentia*—in our absence, yours and mine. We will take turns, in fact, being absent and present in what's to come—today for you, tomorrow for me.

You are not here yet, but *You* is.

You, the audience that reach *before* the audience reach. The essence of an audience, imagined but also remembered, understood here in the way someone is addressed at Jouvay—someone who is a stranger that is, at times, yourself: when we out on the street, out in de "road [that] make to walk," and the sun now starting to come up.[1]

Maybe you on Carib Street, or on Coffee Street when it catch you.
Maybe you sprawl out in the clouds of Paramin.
Maybe you sprawl out in front of Mille Fleurs or the Cathedral.
Maybe you swirling between the police and them at South Quay.
Maybe you stop and stand up and lean up.

1 Lord Kitchener, "Road Make to Walk."

Maybe you stoop down or you skin up.
Maybe you chipping, chipping, chipping.
Maybe you dragging yourself half-dead to the Savannah stage.
Maybe you in the morning sun, and it beating you like a rhythm.
Maybe you catching your breath.
Maybe something waiting to catch you.
Maybe it catch you.
Maybe you get away.

You.[2]

You black. Black black black. But you green. And you blue.
You white and yellow and red and brown.
You paint up (but you ugly ugly ugly, and you pretty pretty pretty).
You wet down (but you don't fraid *lota* or the cold that sure to come).
You powder up (but you leave all your softness home).
You oil up (but you rough, your body grinding on somebody body on somebody wall on the road that you know is yours).
You mud up.
You stink.
You dirty—*dutty*!
You tight (because you drink).
You loose (because you drink).
You high (because you smoke).
You high (because you doh smoke).
You not too long pass Lapeyrouse.
You not too long dance in the crossroads.
You not too long drop money and make some rounds around the manhole.
You start to come apart, your form (or what was your form) dissipating
  like smoke,
  like water on the uneven asphalt,
  like rum in the blood.

Your mask about to come off, and you hear somebody—lover, friend, enemy, partner, stranger—say,

2 *You self*, as we sometimes say.

"Aye, *mas*! Ah know yuh face!"

You respond,
"Aye, *mas*! Ah know yuh face!"
Year after year.

The *You* here—who calls and responds, between being masked and unmasked, known and unknown, then and there and here and now, whose face I say I know but have not yet seen and may never see—is whom I mean to address.

I will not always know who *You* is, and you will not always know who *I* is. Even in the plain view of the page, some errant reference to *You* will lay there overlooked, like a vagrant bookmark in the gutter of the page, until a gaze is cast in its direction. In so doing, the shifting nature of audience—and author—may be disrupted and then resolved. Or, perhaps it is easier to see who *You* is and who *I* is when viewed together, conjugated as a plurality:

You is.
I is.
You and *I* are.[3]

A consideration of *You* as audience will lead to other questions:

How should that audience be encouraged to read?
What is "reading" now and in times to come?[4]
What is "writing" now?[5]
What can—or should—a "book" *be*?[6]
What must it *do*?[7]

3 Inevitably, the contraction of "you is" will occur, leaving us with "you's." It is not a plural (like "all you" or "allyuh") but the second person considered in closer relation to the verb "to be." A similar thing occurs when "I is" is contracted: we get "I's" (pronounced "eyes"). But this is not to be mistaken for the near-identical contraction of "it is," which is doubly contracted to form "i's" (pronounced "is"). This is explained more fully in the essay titled "Home."

4 Something rigid at first, something un|for|giving? But, pressing into it, maybe you will find that its rigidity will start to give, becoming pliant in your hands.

5 *Archipelagic*, maybe? Striving, in a way, toward un|knowability, such that its process resembles an unfolding of potential that may lead to knowing, then past it.

6 A *tenderness*, you could say, giving tenderness back to you as you test the malleability of thought. How tender must we be to read in times to come?

7 Dare? Imagine? Forgive?

This book is not the answer to those questions—it is, instead, a manifestation of the questions themselves caught between *asking* and *having been asked*. It is material proof of the optimism that is at the heart of every question.

Yes, it *is* possible that a reader will miss the shifting of some shapes to come. Their dislocations may elude at first as you consider their complexions, the angles and imprecise mechanics of word and light and thing, the mutual concessions of live and rounded edges, the materiality of their quiet. Some pieces may be polished, others edged and squared, fetishized for their uneven uniqueness, their offcut, their soft curves and bends along their sanded planes. Their dust, illuminated by the unfiltered light of day, may cause a tightness in our lungs, our hearts racing as we dash headlong into another shortened breath, until we can go past the hurt into something that is not hurt *alone*. The hurt (and you know what that hurt is) has done no good. I have had enough of it and long for another breath—another kind of breath.

And another. And another.

That is what I want for you, too. Though it may not yet be apparent, your place not yet set in the absented presence of this tenuous Caribbean reality, *it will be*. You are not here, but you *will* be.

So take your time. Caribbean blackness—which is as timely as it is sometimes out of time and "outta timing," as urgent as it is inconvenient—will assert itself even if the fibers of the twine and woodwork elicit no particular identification, even if the embedded dirt and sand and stones elicit no empathy, even if the threadbare edges of handwritten scrolls or coffee-dyed textiles do not shout back to what was *empire* and *colony* but whisper their indictments almost absent-mindedly on the way to some more important thing.

So take your time.
Take a breath. This book is yours.

This book—this *Sense of Arrival*—is not just yours; it is for *You*.

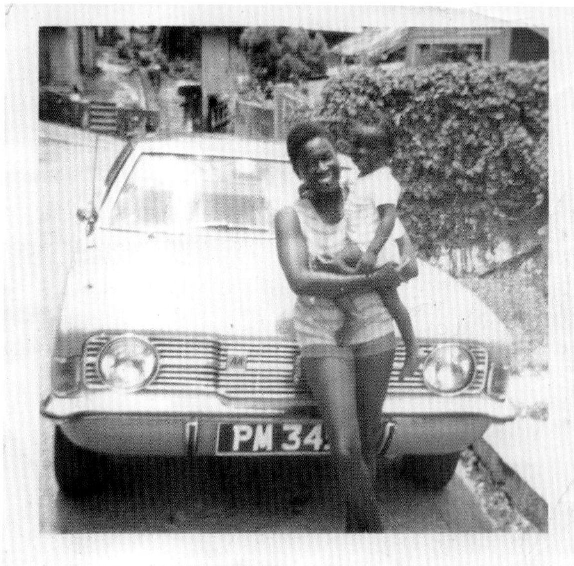

My mother and me, 1976

SENSE

When I was four years old, a child stabbed me in the forehead with a pencil.

The point, broken off, remained in my head until, drunk and high at twenty-six, I squeezed it out. Over the years, a mass developed, a consequence of that piece of graphite I had carried around in me like an idea. The point was gone, but its ghost remained—its remains have remained. Resting now above my eye, it casts its own shadow—in person, in pictures, on screens.

Searching my mother's archives for the earliest evidence of this deformity on my face, I come across an image of myself as a child. It is not the evidence I seek but what comes before it. In this image, I am not yet the altered version of myself but proof of its *provenance*, a draft of the version that later arrives. It is who I was *before*: just my mother's son, a child not yet revised at the hands of another child.

This is a short biography of memory, an essay about the act of remembering as a sensing of memory's arrival, whose wayward meanings roam in the untended garden of my past, as if awaiting some transfiguration from what it is to what it will become, before it departs from here as a thing I have imagined: a future, which may or may not be *mine*. It is also a biography about the unbelievable body—about what it is and what it is not believed to be. And about the remembering body, the remembered body. And about localizing those aesthetics—their vast referential reach—for the purpose of writing about myself. For writing about my people. It is an essay—a daring that takes place in the savage ink and dust of everyday life, in the dark nobilities of our sometimes solitary *marronage*.

It begins with the upright body, and with the seated body, and with the prostrate body. An imperfect body perfectly held. Mine.

I know the results of the biopsy before my surgeon hands them to me, but still I weigh the paper as if it were made of lead. "This one is a little tricky," I hear the surgeon say. I know what he means—it hides, appearing to be something else. Signs point, at first, to a lipoma, a fatty deposit relatively easy to remove. But no.

A second biopsy confirms it: noncaseating sarcoid granuloma. A tumor.

Attempting to remove it, he cuts again above my brow, excising it from the fat and muscle that have grown around it, sequestering it from the rest of my body. But it resists, rooting itself some distance within—in the body, a millimeter might as well be a mile. I am afraid, of course. But terror, though commonplace, is not sustainable.

Twice now, he has gone in after it. Twice I have been assured (and reassured) that it is benign—not cancer, but he is concerned that my vision may be at risk. *Again*. He shows me images of it taken during surgery. This is not the abstract presence of glaucoma that I have written about before but something more immediate, more tangible. It feeds on me.

I swallow and listen. I nod, as is the custom. As he describes my self to me, the subtle shifts of my brow, flexions and spasms that lead to smiling or crying, the sometimes cavalier confessors of my moods are all threatened by what amounts to an archive. I decide what to make of this moment—and the suspension of my mortality within it. Though afraid, I have decided not to write as if the prospect of my death were more imminent than it appears. Being black, my endangerment is a unit of measurement—how time and space are annotated and understood: when it comes to the body, black as it is, there is no difference between millimeters and miles. Miles to go—marking time in millimeters to the left or right of a nerve—the space a mark might go.[1]

Awake on the operating table in this little office in Woodbrook, I am as still as a corpse, counting my breaths. A second surgery. Soon, a third. He checks on me every few minutes. I must be awake for the entire procedure. Some things, when named—as fears, terrors, hauntings—do not always shrink away. They just grow until you cut them out.

I breathe a familiar "one today, one tomorrow" breath and the anxiety of the moment settles. Nausea eases and my thoughts give way to what I think is the nature of story, to what I would say is an aesthetic of embodiment, a sense of nonfiction as an embodied practice. Or, rather, I make way for these things, tracing with deliberation the provenance of the injury, charting a course and an outcome for a sense of arrival I had not anticipated. The aesthetic I imagine is based on the refraction of this deformity to reveal a notion of blackness that is

1 Or, in the case of a tumor, 5 by 5 mm. Its elevation varies, from time to time.

redemptive. The idea is not necessarily that the tumor itself is beautiful—it is and it is not—but that there is space for sublimity, even here.

My face, numb for hours under the scalpel, regains its feeling.
Have I been frowning all this time?

This is the problem with "   "[2] when taken from too close to the bone: covered only with skin that stretches gradually, objects abandoned in the body do not all wither into scar and symbol; some remain until they stir, growing in spite of your practiced indifference, until the time comes to implicate you—your entire body—like an accomplice in its narrative. The dilemma now emerges of either feeling what you *think* is no longer there or looking for what you *know* is there but can no longer feel. The metaphors coalesce, appearing to harden.[3]

As the blood traced the curve of the sink before swirling into the drain, I agreed with D: this moment that masqueraded as self-harm was, in truth, a sign. I noted the ironic ease with which it crawled toward the abyss, a bright red comet dragging its heavy tail down to the bottom, into whatever lay inside the drain.

"What are you doing?" she asked.

"Fuck," I whispered.

"What yuh doing?" she insisted, more the Vincentian country girl than the smooth Brooklynite who left the remains of her Rastafarian relationship to take walks with me and talk about poetry in Prospect Park.

I said nothing.

Those were the years of seeing my aunt Maureen's spirit pass up the short corridor that led to her room. After being evicted from the apartment on Washington Avenue, I moved with my mongrel dachshund back to the Bronx and the two-bedroom apartment in Co-op City I shared with my mother, who would be away for weeks working as a "baby nurse" for white families in New York, New Jersey, and Connecticut.

D and I were near the ashen point of a smoldering thing we thought was love, consecrated over a spliff she'd rolled in Bambú paper some years before. My lips—black from Backwoods—followed hers like an imitation. We loved

2 A sense of arrival, perhaps.

3 We know symbols best who have learned to eat pain and trauma as if they were delicacies, to regard them as if they were an aesthetic. To resist the seduction of *symbols* is to open yourself to the far more troubling issue of actual effects on your body. And to be opened up, as a result.

each other almost to our mutual ruin. And when she left, I would grind myself almost to dust.

But there, adhered to my fingertips, almost burgundy in the blood, a piece of graphite the size of a rice grain shone for us like a talisman. A sign, she said, of the writer I was supposed to be. I rinsed it off and scribbled my signature on a piece of paper before putting it in a Svensk vodka bottle that I had filled with water. I looked in the mirror at the small crater above my left eye. She stood in the doorway behind me, cringing as we do at signs in advance of their later significations.[4]

"Fuuuuuuuuuuuuck!" I whispered again, "Yuh seeing this?"

"What is it?"

"Me eh know nah."

I knew. But, rum-soaked and high, I forgot. It *must* have been a sign.

By 1999, having read Derek Walcott's "Hurucan" and been struck silent as a stone, I had resolved to be a writer. Not the kind I had been in years before who scribbled "hook lines" and cast them out across cramped bars and basements, hustling to make enough money to get in, or to get home, missing the unsaid point of fleeting loves, the fleeting camaraderie as we huddled like Maroons, where sidewalks were our sandbars and holes-in-the-wall our isles and inlets—but a "writer for the page." I would find a line in my own work for the word "gamboge." I would buy all the wine, smoke all the cigarettes, perfect the pitch of my tantrums. In the concrete towers of that apartment complex, I would construct a new image of myself, even if it was not me.[5]

I adjust my lips to move the cloth that covers my face.
"Are you okay?" the surgeon asks.
"Mhmm," I lie, "I'm good."
I'm not panicked, but the lack of panic, my stillness, worries me.
"Any pain?" he asks.
"Some, but I can bear it."
I lie again, more to myself than to him.

4 I thought nothing of it then, but I think, now, of the Dragon Mas and the Lagahou, whose long chains might leave their marks on the asphalt as they *drrrrrraaaaaaaaaa-aaaaaaaaaaaaaaagggggggggggggg* the chains—and themselves—from one place to another.

5 I never was able to recite my work from memory, preferring to read—one hand holding the page and, eventually, the chapbook (entitled *Bohème*) rolled back into its flimsy two-stapled spine, the other hand gesticulating to the audience, as if they couldn't see me flailing. I would grasp at the vacant air and marvel at having grasped nothing at all.

The truth is that not bothering to remember meant, simply, that I would never forget, never risk the indignity of forgetting or the greater indignity of being forgotten. I was afraid. But fear is not a method. What remains of that memory? Only a blackness, the blackness of an artifact, a memory of the black artifact of a void on my fingertips and then in the palm of my hand. Then its being lost. All of this the masochism of memory has brought back to me.

I have tried to remember the boy, but no face comes to mind, no name. For all I knew, I might as well have done this to myself had it not been for Teacher Bailey's reporting the incident to my mother (who does not remember the boy either). In this scenario, I was a text to be read.

His inscription was literary. He had, in a single focused thrust, inscribed the entirety of an epic—or its beginning, leaving me to fill in the as yet blank space of a life yet to be lived.

I moan when I feel a pinch near the site,
then at the spreading of a fresh numbness.
I've gotten another dose of lidocaine, so there was no pain, only pressure
and the nausea such pressure causes when a thing you expect to hurt does not.
The disappointment dissipates in a sigh, is forgotten in another.
I hear the cauterizer whirr and I wait
for the smell of burning flesh—my flesh—that follows.
"Don't worry," the surgeon assures me, "it's just to minimize the bleeding."
He tells me what I cannot feel or see to explain
what I hear and why I smell what I smell.
I hear the clank of an instrument on the table beside him.
(Does it have a name? It must.)[6]
"I'm all right."
"Good."

A machine breaks the silence and I groan.
"Hmm?" the surgeon asks.
"Nothing, nothing." I must have drifted off. I repeat myself out of reflex.
"Okay, that's good."

6 I think of my uncles Dave (my father's younger brother) and Collins (my mother's older brother), my cousin Andre (who knew more about Fonclaire than anyone I knew), my cousins Denise and Dionne (Aunty Lystra's children, the only ones of us to play pan).

"Can you squeeze your eyes shut for me?"
The surgeon interrupts. I squeeze my eyes shut. As I do, I remember the way Tom Selleck would raise a single eyebrow in Magnum, P.I., *and then how I spent I forget how many days holding down my left brow (in secret), training my face to do what he did without, it seemed, any training at all. I would think, later, whether it was that—and not the pencil point—that has me here, doing all I can to dissociate the pinch from the scalpel against my skin and the fading anesthetic.*
Feeling fades again into memory.

The body remembers.
The body forgets.

“ ?”

“ , .”
“ .”
“ . , .”
“ . . .”
“ ?”

"Okay, look up for me?" I look up.
"How many fingers?"
I hesitate. Is it two?
Is it a test I have already failed by hesitating?
Have I already lost my vision?
I take the chance and guess at the silhouette
I see against the blinding light overhead. "Two."
"Okay."
"Is it two?"
"Yes, yes."
"Okay, good."
"I'm going to close up now."
"Mhmm . . ."

My skin, most of my organs, and all of my bones are, according to science, at least four regenerative cycles removed from the origin of the mass in my head. Little remains. Apart from some areas of my brain, which have not changed since birth, this tumor is evidence of the oldest thing about me—my first artifact. What has regenerated time and time again as "my body" now treats it less as a foreign object than as evidence of something almost indigenous. Naturalized in the body—a trace of some former presence, an archive of a Ruin or the Ruin itself. In relation to the regenerated cells, its status is historical. Its arrival has already taken place. In matters of the heart and mind—and, lately, of method—this means I am always catching up with parts of myself. It means I am always leaving parts of myself behind.

Since these cells of the body regenerate at different rates, the stories they have to tell—whether acquired through experience or more abstractly imagined—are subject to change. Change is guaranteed, in fact, as the veracity of an origin dissolves into a more fluid story. That is, the notion that psychic, cellular, visceral, experiential memory (including the memory of experiences we may not have had) is based on a telling, listening, imagining, retelling that transcends the life of individual bodies and the spaces we take up.

An irony here is that the "efficacy" of memory relies, in part, on the disruption of the facts that precede it. The telling, then, signifies a series of shifts, one of them being away from history and toward story—toward *story|ing*. It suggests the actions of a *macumé* or, more formally, the foundational ethics of nonfiction as cultural practice. It is not a theory but more of a question in a somewhat unpressing need of an answer.

The body remembers, the body forgets.

Left long enough, the stories it tells will ascend to the "meta"—becoming a genre almost entirely about itself, sounding more like theory than the movement of blood, the binding of broken skin, the complaint of brittle backs and limestone hips worn down, the pebbled cataracts like boulders now in your Sisyphean struggles to see. And, when it moves, it will do so in parts. And when you read it, it will be as if you were reading the partial transcript of a moment, as if it were a ruptured lyric.

You will outgrow it, but it will outlast you, keeping the memory of you like an idea.

The phone rings. It is my mother calling. I'm working on an essay and think twice about answering, but she will call until I answer. So I answer.

"Eh heh!"

"My son!"

"Yes, my mother. What going on?"

Her face is growing smaller now, returning from its rounder days in America, its exiled decades of milk, its decades of honey hardened into amber between her joints, at the base of her spine and at her ankles. Her recall is sharp, in parts.

Never mind the dust, I say to myself. It, too, has been handed down, its ubiquity traced to a moment perfectly held.

"Ah make some nice cook-up with pig tail. Yuh coming?"

My mother thinks she knows me. She is asking answers.

"How yuh mean?" I follow suit. This is not a question either but an answer. With us, the answer to an answer will sometimes masquerade as a question. Unclothed, it means "Yes! Of course, yes!"

Of course, being "Caribbean" means I am already a|n im|perfect material replica of the psyche of this place. By extension, the strange logic of my methods for writing and reading is no different from the intimate, estranging logic of the place itself, its archipelagic sensibilities as apart as they are together. This is not too difficult to grasp, especially if we consider how things come to us—piece by piece, part by part, sometimes we are left to learn a lesson as if it were a song, to learn a song note by note until the song itself is ours alone, its origins unrecognizable. Consider how we learn things, even about ourselves, how we are often forced to gather the shards of our erstwhile "histories"—our pasts gathered into the present as stories we learn, over time, to tell.

They come to us in the "talk some, keep some" way of elders, and we put them together as they come—a picture, a lesson, a song, a note, a story on whose witness we weigh out our beliefs by the handful and by the pinch, by some stretch of skin, some measure of bone whose vacated cells let loose some howl, some haunting echo. An echo of a thought as it materializes, as it becomes a thing—some *thing* we sense.

It begins, at least for me,

with the upright body,
and with the seated body,
and with the prostrate body.

She calls, knowing in my response that my arrival is sure.

She has already sensed it.

"Ah coming. See you in a little while."

"Good, good."

ARRIVAL

Arrival is an eliciting and an illicit thing—
blackness regarded in a light less somber than what I
have witnessed that isn't forced to cut a path into
perfect grief, but *through* it—a taking of
liberties.

Instruction:
See the following as if to say,
"Eyes, do allyuh work. Ears, hear."
See, here, the epigraph of a coming breath.
A story of how I have come to be.
A story of the nature, motion, and affect of story *itself*.

I am thinking now of archipelagoes.

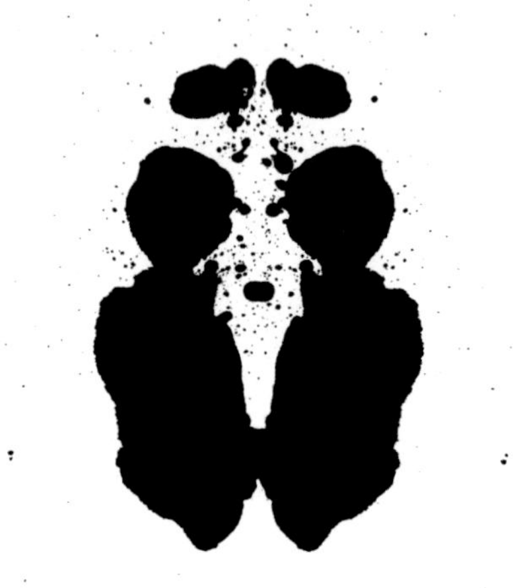

I see a turn-taking: one mouth open, the other closed; one's mouth pushed out in a *steups*, the kissed teeth of a defiant, the unsealed lips of the other. A call and a response that say one is a version of the other, that say each is a genre of the breath, a form of breathing. Less talking to than breathing with—being with. If it is also the invocation of a map, then its obvious blackness becomes an unknown, an unknowable thing whose unknowability is obvious. Reliable, even, in its blatant obscurity. To "see" it is, in a sense, not to see anything at all. A map of blackness, but not a map *to* it. No path to it that I can see. Or it is a blackness that neither insists nor refuses translation, one that does not even appear to acknowledge a need for questioning. The "question," as such, of what I see is not merely muted but moot.

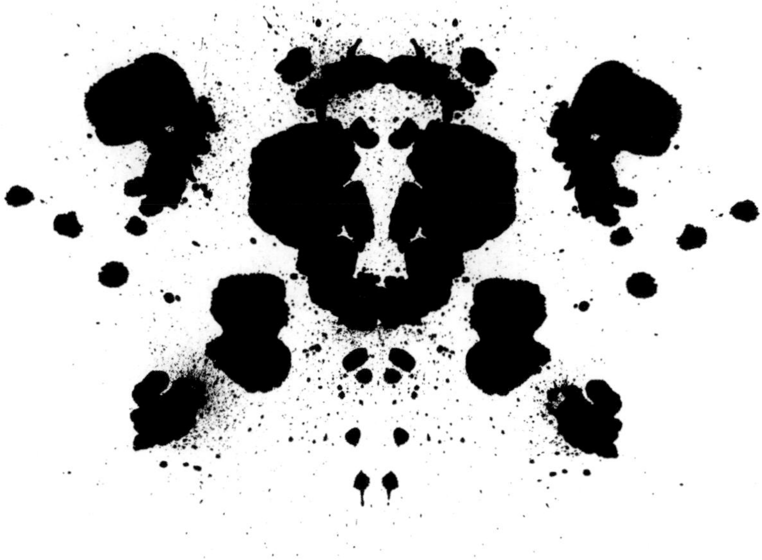

Breath is an infinite elsewhere. The splatters you see are brief testimonies of exhaled breath. Now mirrored, it is an exhalation turned back to itself—as if forced to encounter itself through imprint and reflection—masquerading as an intention that has been fulfilled: an exhalation *inhaled*. Each breath, in its deliberation from internal to external, makes space for another that is a version of itself. It is a representation of *space*, traveling. It is *shape*, shifting. Before you go on, return to the first to consider what this means for the action of monologic activity that aspires to the dialogic. Think, too, about the premium of breath in this time and in time to come. Ask who gets to breathe.

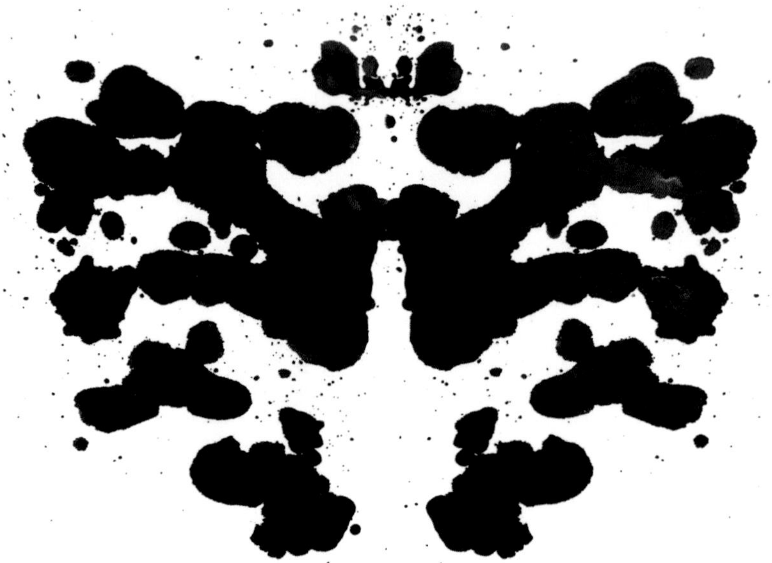

"Inquiry" is how we attempt to map the void of our unknowing. See its imperfect symmetry? Look near the top, or near its outermost lobes. Look near its base. And then you will notice that there are points missing—that they are unknown, in spite of what you know they are. Which is more confounding, more absurd, to pursue: the unknown from that which is knowable or from that which is not? Think of it as a tautology, though it is only a game for the mind, like those ring games children used to play, songs of coming and going, of mortality and of passing pleasures. Of "rings around," of "pockets full." Posies and ashes. Black death recast as text, text recast as life on the page.

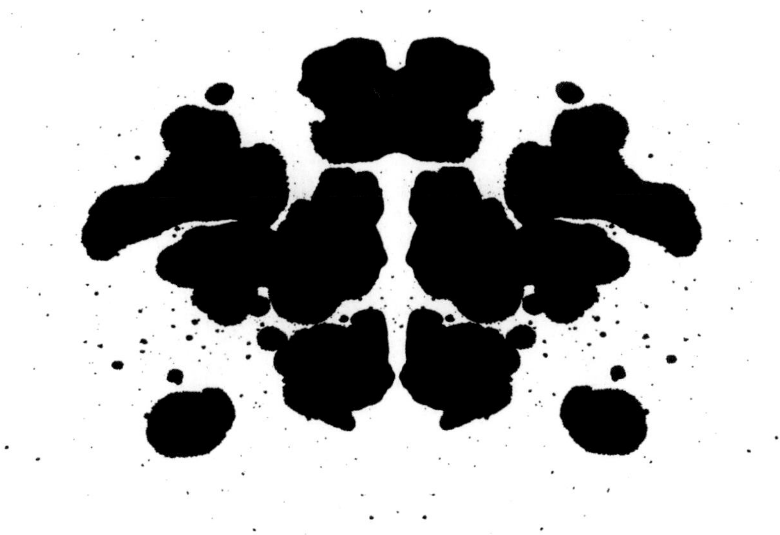

To be read simultaneously with *Blot No. 5*: One is always a reconstituted version of the other. What do I mean by this? Never mind their actual *animus*—this is an excursion, these maps a representation of an actual thing I have imagined, which I have called blackness—but think instead of the clarity their pairing might provide. Consider the ink already pressed and dried as if it were a book.

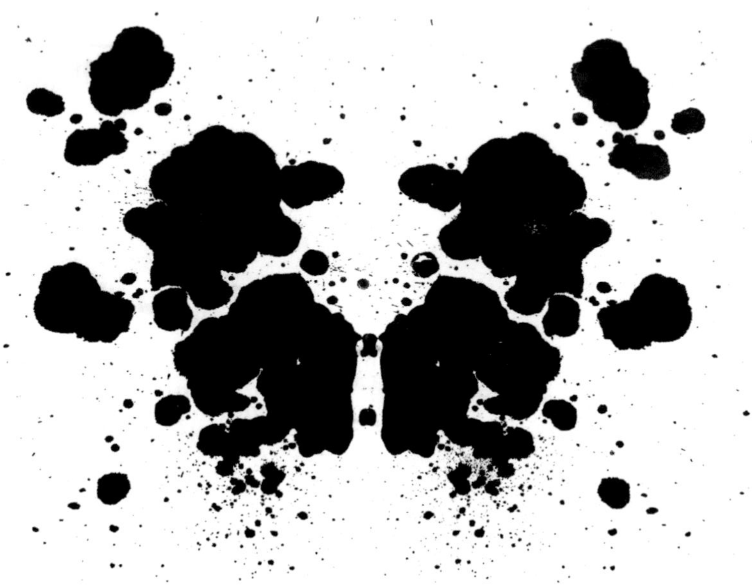

To be read simultaneously with *Blot No. 4*: The other, evidence of a variegated simultaneity. By placing some emphasis on how temporality may be rudimentarily visualized, and then infusing that visuality with the suggestion of motion or malleability, it can begin to "move." Motion is the currency. I'll take it more personally, having already done so with the imprinting of *Blot No. 1* on my skin in November 2020—it moves constantly, breathes and dries, itches and bleeds. Its motion is an action of faith. Its affect, viewed in retrospect, is a consequence of that faith.

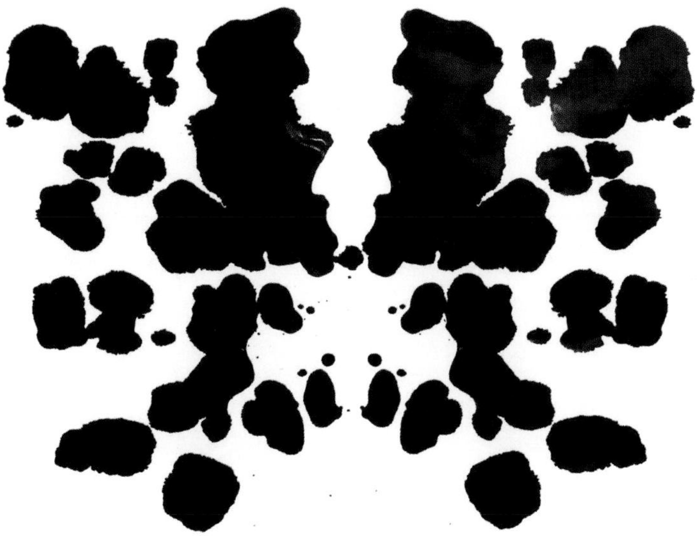

Oramaclast (n.): From *oramaclasty*, or vision-breaking; one who breaks visions, sees through|with a broken vision; one who engages a deliberative *prismatic action* for (un|re)making meanings. Also: *Ora*, the plural form of *os* ("opening[s]," especially of the mouth and cervix); and *ma*, a modifying suffix that denotes the results or effect (and more elusive affect) of an action. A way of seeing. Related, somewhat, to Francesco Grimaldi's notion of *diffraction*. (Also, *visioclast*.)

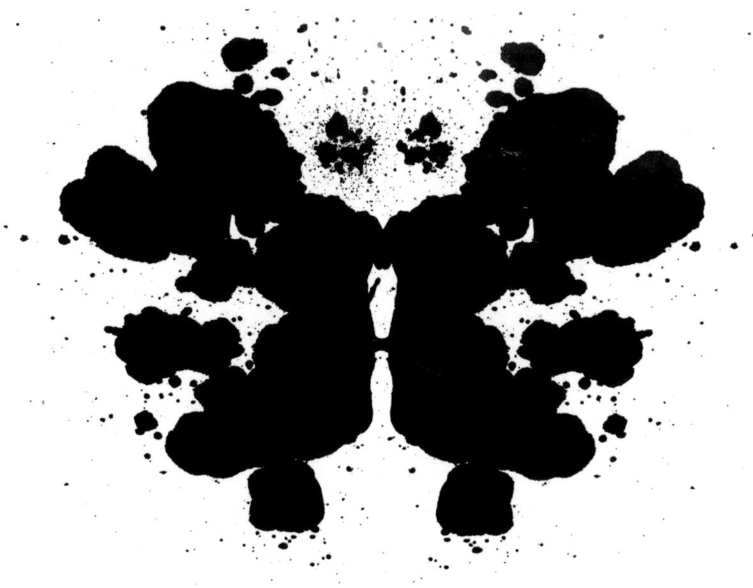

And, if you have either chance or cause to examine the dwindling coast, perhaps you will put methods of close reading into perspective.

To see what has changed, what will, and what cannot. To see what refuses, like an inkblot.

In 2018, following the death of my paternal grandfather, Radcliffe Browne, I produced this series of inkblots as an effort to articulate what I felt was an inarticulable thing: grief. Over time, their dissipating forms have come to represent a deliberate projection of methodological reflexivity: the conscious use of my breath, ink, paper, and my skin to remember, imagine, and enact the disaggregation of some typical components of a text, transforming the imaginative practice into a kind of self-care, which has been painful at times.

For the Caribbeanist and others engaged in nonfiction and the art(s) of its rhetoric, the medium—life, death, what have you—matters less than the tendency to privilege the intention and imagination, on which the faulty memory comes to feed. It is a bold wish, perhaps a little too bold for so urgent a time. There are subtler matters to consider, if you prefer. So much meaning is microscopic—*microbial*—that the question of what will become of us may have already been answered in the most minute ways, and the truth of it rests invisibly like grains on a trail, in a corner, in the archive, everywhere like dust. Left there for us to pick up, adhering itself to us as we pass.

And as we pass, *what* we find is a question of *what remains*. Remains that seem to attend and await our arrival.

BREATH

"Breathe," I say,
to the black boy of my memory.[1]
Breathe if you want to live.
Breathe.

See yuh breath and all, how it black?
See how yuh could see it? See how it not
just black.
It *black.*
Black black black
as a bounding blackbird—
the grassquit, which is blue-black.

Black like a *corbeau* black,
down to my bone and nail,
like a Cemani black.

Black
like the road *under* the road,
like the pitch *under* the pitch,
the world *under* the world.

Breathing
is the familiar action of your body's encounter with

1 And to myself. And to you.

gravity,
is a shifting of the shape of space,
is shape shifting.

One today,
one tomorrow.

Breathing:
exhalation is letting it go,
letting go is how you keep it,[2]
inhalation is letting it return,
bringing back what brought you,
calling back what has left you.

Tabanca.

Breathing, too, is the reflexive recognition and embodied practice of a concept of space. A sense of infinite breadth, of breath infinitely unheld. It is proof, too, that you cannot be held—like blackness. I know, I know that it is a provisional blackness that is both troubled and comforted by other factors, other details that reside in my blood and thwart claims of purity, strands and strings buried too deep in the earth of my history.[3] Whether for the unseasonal floods or droughts or wildfires in the spirit, I could no sooner divine a cause in one than in the other. So breathe if you want to live.

Check yuh pulse. Put yuh hand in yuh other hand. Make half a fist. Let the open fingers of the unclenched hand rest along the lines at your wrist. Feel what yuh feel. See if yuh still alive. You *are* going to die.[4] But doh frighten. What yuh feeling is just yuh breathing body saying something like:

2 The exhalation|letting go of the breath seems to become more necessary under pressure, underwater, than on land, where you take breathing for granted and where, under these everyday pressures, the arrested breath is commonplace. You already know what these pressures are. Set them aside for a moment, if you can. Rest them down easy easy, nobody will trouble them.

3 The story of my great-great-grandmother, who was very black and, it is said, was rooted in Martinique. And of my great-great-grandfather, the white Irishman who loved her and was stricken from the records for loving her. Of land taken away, doubly stolen. Of "thief from thief." Of love. Alexia and Edmund.

4 I say this between breaths as I wait for a second biopsy.

Remember, spirit.
Remember, bone and muscle.
Remember stick and feather.
Remember them, unbound.
Remember.

Here, the melodrama of an imagined death is eclipsed by the lived and remembered (and imagined) drama of my struggle to *unknow* what life has been in order to understand what it is or could be. I sense its arrival. Opting instead to breathe, I want to take a turn less grave, one that sees me move within and without the frame, inside and outside of it, to immerse myself in the practice of unknowing, to shuffle off the version of "life" to which I've been accustomed, and to go in search of spirit—in pursuit of its perfect fugitivity.

Remember "spirit"? The thing whose currency of motion is current itself? Whose dialect is light? Whose critical orthography is the cameral action of shutters and sensors? Spirit, whose reflection is conceived of moments we, being human, are often too slow or too fast to catch? The sublime, which is (for some) a thing so far out of style it may be due for a return. Yes, I know the question of spirit is a tricky one to answer, even if one is dealing with material limitations, especially because one is working against invisibility and erasure and displacement and forgetting.

To speak in terms of spirit, of what the enduring afterlife of images must entail—

to know what images, in their stillness, can yield
to feel what images of things can say of still things
to see and sound what unsaying, unsayable things
these objects in their stillness must be

—is to embrace a vision.

It is to simultaneously embrace the patent impossibility of the embrace—for how can we truly embrace a thing we cannot touch, except to want it? Want without having.[5]

5 My head hurts.
My heart hurts.
Too much sugar.
Too much salt.
Too little food.

Breathe, Black Boy.
Breathe.
They might want we dead—yuh done know that—but we cyah fraid that.
Breathe. Yuh doh have time but take yuh time.
Breathe. Because nothing cyah happen if yuh doh breathe.
Breathe. Stop reading and breathe. Stop writing. Stop making things—put that down.
Put it down.
Breathe.

I breathe.
And breathe.

I breathe in a world that shows me that I am perpetually derivative, a mythical figure in an epic of someone else's composing.[6] And though I am happy to concede that I come from something and somewhere, I am as committed to the idea that there is more to me than what I might have been, that I am more than a mouthpiece of a history that has loved me terribly and that will nevertheless demand that I make every effort to redeem both it and myself. And, by redeeming it, proclaim that I will extend its life with my life, that I will amplify its flaws with my flaws, that I will claim its benefits as my own. And in exchange, it will encourage me to stand victorious like a child on a mound of sand, declaring myself *sentient*—a self-possessed man in control of nothing in particular. A man of words, owning nothing—not even himself. The vulgarity of the *endangered* redeeming the danger—the very thing that has endangered him—is, at times, more than I can bear.

These afflictions (more recent than I would like to admit) are essentially academic. I only hope not to be an accomplice in my own demise or a sacrifice for some higher purpose. I am not the work I do, though perhaps we are conduits

6 Call it *rhetorical syncretism*, which I will say is derived from and relies on an attitude toward classicism that is as much a rejection as an embrace. I have long realized that to participate in this conversation of what counts as (a) rhetoric I must assume the role of native, convert, prodigal, and heretic all at once (de facto proof of my acuity). To be persuasively "Caribbean," I must first leave, be trained, then revert to Caribbeanness for one's "claims" about the Caribbean to have legitimacy. I would have had to drink the wine of astonishment and become drunk on its unutterable vulgarity. It is, of course, patently absurd. *More* absurd for those who wish to patent ideas in the absence of those whose lives exemplify those ideas. What do I know? My ideas turn to salt in the sun or bloom white as sugar on hand-milled chocolate.

to each other. And if I am to outrun the discipline and the discretion that may be required to keep me in check (or, at least, run at the pace of my ambition, my expanding indiscretion of daring to call this nonfiction a *rhetoric*, to call this rhetoric a *nonfiction*), then I must be content to be as much a villain as any who views the promised peace of a disciplined life as a form of heresy.[7] It may, for example, be heresy to say that I have no interest in thinking about things that do not concern me or my being, or that of my people, present company included (as always), but that is only because breathing is blasphemy in a world that prefers the tragic beauty of black suffering, of black death. As if it were a pastime. Black death as a rite of passage to all who see, whether they want to or not.

Nah.

That vein of inquiry seems to ask—to demand, really—that I ignore a great deal and identify only with the urgencies of black endangerment, that I embrace the features of a "life" that accompanies a violent death, that I reach out for and attempt to grasp what can only flourish in the ineffability of death, to die and to know a peace that no pursuit of social in|justice could match.

Nah.[8]

I going and go my own way for a while, beyond the illusory boundaries of the false freedoms to which I have previously aspired, choosing here to believe that my conceptions of subjectivity mean more than to be merely subject to an unfortunate past—one that I am duty-bound to honor and repeat at my own psychic and physical expense. Or at the expense of others on whose behalf I work, and whose attention I will inevitably seek.

I'm thinking, now and again, of archipelagoes, of a Caribbean that keeps evading me, eluding my grasp with the agility of garden lizards and river fish and yard fowls. I'm thinking: How can one ever be from a place one has never seen, or seen only in the terms others have laid down for him, perpetually imaginary? How, other than through faith, do people from the interior know they

7 In truth, I sometimes aspire to ignore the bankruptcy of discipline. But only because the legitimacy of Caribbean rhetoric—of Caribbeanness, in general—has seemed to emerge as a matter of defense against the abject discreditation of an overarching, overwhelming mainstream. It is treacherous and tiring.

8 Say *nah* until every smiling yes, every too-easy yeah, becomes the no it is meant to be, the *nah* it yearns to become.

live on an island, except to go in search of all the coasts, noting each point, except to find each peak to see each valley, to understand each plain? What is an archipelago to such a person? Isn't that how a tragedy of assumptions gathers itself like an afternoon storm, swirling in the heart? Yes. That's how "out-of-placeness" can harden into plaque, how the home you swear you love will sometimes taste like gravel on your tongue. I refuse that hardness and declare, instead, that I wish to arrive in a way that looks and sounds like *me*.

And, perhaps, like a version of *you* I have imagined.

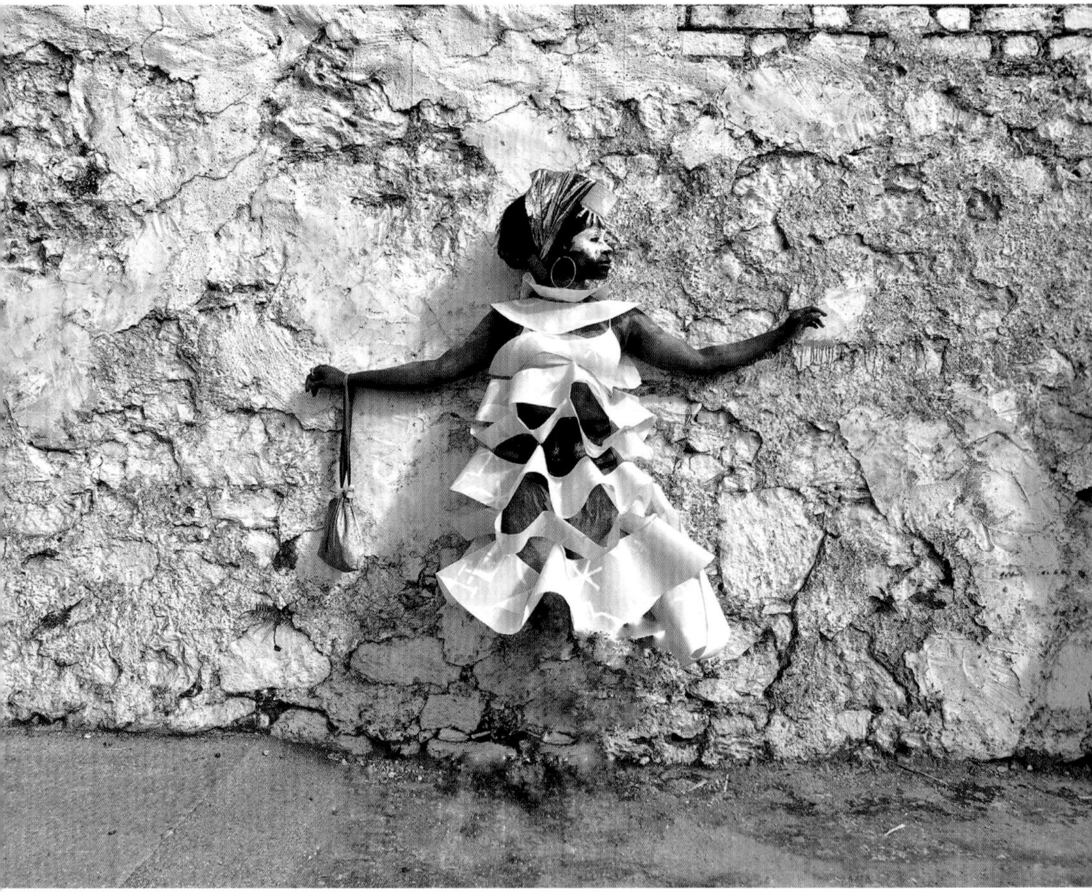

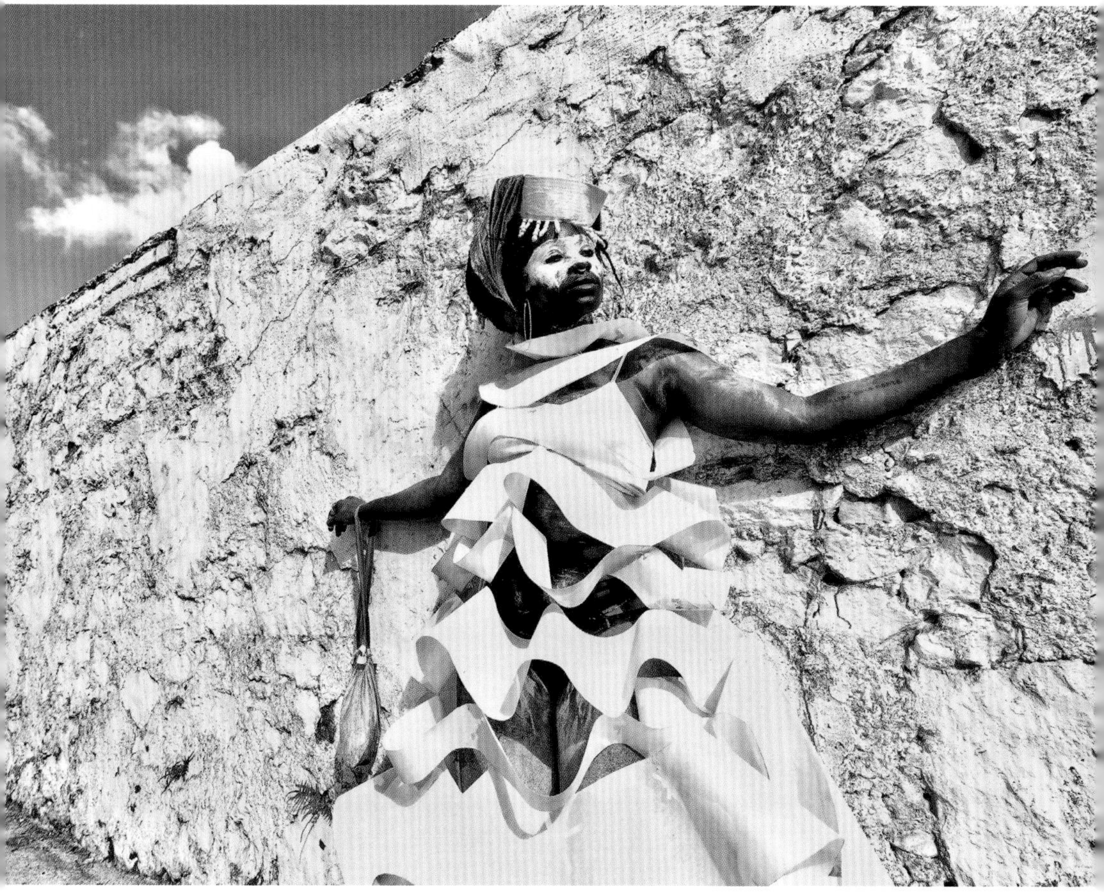

GENRE

Arrival is a genre of gathering. Mine and yours. A gathering of senses and a projection of those senses outward. Embodied and, at times, an embodiment. A bound multitude that seeks to be unbound, its meanings extending beyond the reach of language.[1] The magnitude of arrival is, of course, more than I am able to describe. In truth, I have yet to map its vast topography. Let us call it the *sense* of an arrival, then—that thing we mean to do with the articulable parts of ourselves that lead from stillness to movement through space, that thing we do that takes us off the ground, suspending us there until we are still. Not a departure, strictly speaking, but more of a levitation of presence, where what you think of as your body or your spirit has moved just enough for you to feel it. Never mind if it is only you who feels it.

The *feeling*. Not yet the thing itself, but the sense of a thing to come, and of how it will feel. The consequence of an ascension.[2] A kind of flight, however short-lived. A fantastic gasp, graceful only in slow motion, or on film, when the restlessness of touch struggles to reconcile the stillness of the body that casts its

1 Language is hampered by its inherent limitations and by our deep inability to say all of what we mean.

2 What is that consequence? Is it freedom? Freedom, even in its abstract sense, is not gained at no cost. No, it must cost *something* to be untethered from the expectation that you need to exist purely in relation to anything at all, let alone anything that would cause you to suffer for its benefit. What will it cost? What has it already cost? I'm thinking of freedom not only in an abstract sense, but freedom *from* some actual *thing*. That thing will differ, but the consideration of freedom occurs *in relation* to those conditions. Consider freedom, then, as relation—or being free as a *relating*.

shadow long against a wall, across the speckled asphalt. To sense arrival is to rise above the grounding of our contemporary sensibilities—this one in sugar, this one in salt, this one in skin, this one in cloth. It is to embrace metaphor when materiality alone will not do.[3] Not an impossible thing but a thing impossibly expansive. A sense in the only way it could be meant.

3 Consider *Lapeyrouse No. 1*. This image was an experimental reading of another image that I have not included here. I have refused to "correct" it and have the blunders do their work—part of which is the inherent difficulty one should encounter in removing or erasing even the visualized body. My failure is emphasized in its blurs and repetitions. The erasure is taken up more directly in *Lapeyrouse No. 2*. What interests me about *No. 1* are the questions of whether that erasure is an effective *punctum* and at what point its intentional (albeit experimental) affect betrays the accidental application of the concept.

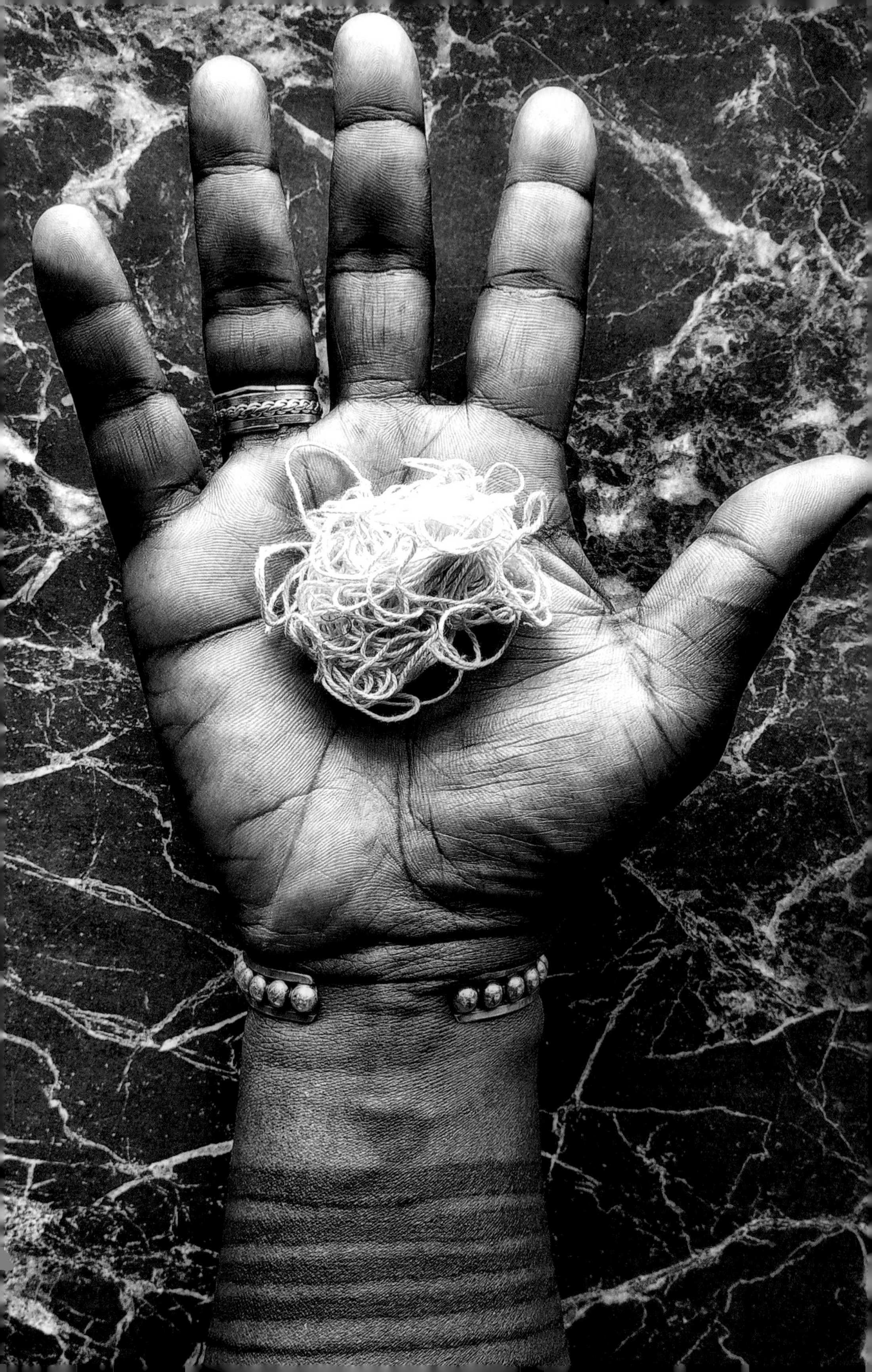

It *is* possible, though, that, however you arrive, you will learn the mystery of true solitude and will never wonder why massing exiles do not think of coming back. Or, through latent heat, you may hardly look with nostalgia toward the gallery and wave, but instead draw yourself inward and train your vision somewhere to the north, past the bordering range. Almost fleeing.

To arrive *properly*, you will need to say a few things to yourself.[4] Never mind if they are true or not. Say them anyway. Say that you will not wonder what stays in cast-iron pots, their handles pointing like dogs' ears alert to what sounds we, through habit, know so well but put neatly away for a day that blows a cold too bitter even for coats.

Put out of your mind the following:

> Ice-picked tin sprinkler.
> Yard broom.
> Three-line cutlass. Hoe.
> How quaint the blue crab looks.
> How quaint the common fowl.
> How quaint the songbirds' songs.[5]

And remember this:

> Arriving, for you, must mean that you have already left
> poui and immortelle to grow high along slow, reclining
> hills; that you have already left behind, with muted
> fanfare, the beating sun, rain as music you long to hear.
> The *cocoyea* broom, with its fork, bound with rough
> cotton, will point skyward, as you must.
> (Your turn in this sun will be different, even if it is not.
> Your faith will sustain you here, even if it does not.)

4 A breath.
5 Chaka, Hannibal, Fool, Charlie Parker, Nameless. My songbirds.

Then, having remembered, you may think of saying in a letter to your mother:

> *Forgive the nostalgia, but look how things turn, how they will persist. Adjusting grips, hard plastic handles, straps pulled up in shrugs with nervous nods, one yoke is dropped for another. But though we are no longer cast in sharp, powder-starched cotton shirts, gabardine, the instinct to leave—procession slow—is as enduring as sketches of sinew, or the Savannah, to us. I remember you. Intentions stamped and bound in sealed envelopes, and bound again in leather, are still a type of freedom for me as they were for you.*

Say these things, even if they are not true, even as the pride that was once your staying pride retreats to be indigenous to you as the spear, as native as loincloth and feather. Endangered, like letters to mothers.

Then say:

> *We no longer scale hurried stairs but rush to find our seats before we are left behind to turn to salt or ash. You know how it is here. Ash will form if you let yourself think too hard of this heat.*
>
> *I'll see you soon.*
>
> *Love.*

Memory will drift off, tumbling light like cane trash across the ground, and you will only chase it a few steps before it crumbles. You must hold yourself together, so your banded belly will not burst. Soon, the high evening sky crudely cut will swirl on the discolored argument of tides. A bare sea trembling beneath you. You will guess at what you see, forgetting your geography lessons:

Is that Grenada?
Nevis?
Guadeloupe?
Haiti?
Is it a wall, broken into an archipelago you have never seen, its mud and stone and water people rolling between them?

I will be there with you, standing here with what is left behind, or waiting for you to arrive. *You*, my people, the you I hope will stay with me until—with eyes to word, eyes to image, eyes and ears to sound, together as if hand in hand—we arrive here.

So go ahead and say your departure is complete.
Say your arrival is sure, even if you have not yet arrived.

You will.

(See? You have already begun.[6])

6 *Krik?*

METHOD

Krik?[1]

Krak![2]

Method is the materialization of intention, an intentional representation of a sense—or senses—of arrival as I have experienced it.

1 A question. A quest. A request. A call that may be interpreted this way: "May I begin?" Followed by the intervening silence—the dash that may be graceful or playful, playful and painful—before the response to a request that (according to tradition) repeats, "*Krak!*" *Begin* with a repetition that will teach us to ask answers: "Yes, you may begin." Ask answers because the asking presumes authority but preserves humility. It is not deception but deference—a recognition of the mutual power of storytellers and their audiences, the audiences to whom we appeal. Know that you have already begun, though you are not yet here.

2 A response. Remember. That is what "*Krik?*" calls for.
How long has it been? You even remember?

When last you pitch marble?
You remember playing *catch* and *scooch*
and windball cricket?
Small goal on hot asphalt? On hot sand?
The alliteration of *pelt de pan* and *kick de can*?
Remember *skip* and *hopscotch* and *moral*?
And slingshot and chow?
And then when current gone?[3]
Waaaaaaaaaaaaaaaaaay![4]
Remember: *Krik?*

Krak!

I wonder:

How must it look to inhabit the province of a lore
that one has constructed?
How must the lore itself behave?
How to stake and situate a claim in the mysteries of
impending arrival that one has wrought, to tap into the illicit
utterance of the imagined and the intended?

I don't know.

What is the nature of a work?
What must it be to operate in such a way?
(And, of course, what must we be?)
What is the nature of a work that *imagines*,
one that loves and frees,
one that forgives?

3 Whenever the electricity was cut off, we would say "current gone." The same with water.
Water gone.
Current gone.
We say it so much we believe it, and then we come and consecrate that belief with a grammar, setting it in stone with the correct tense and the correct mood. And then they would come back, the water and the current. After a few minutes or hours. Rusty, at first. You could smell the iron in it. Or the lights and them flickering on and off like an old woman waking up. They come back, like the old women and them does sometimes do.

4 With my thumb squeezed to my middle finger, my wrist flicks, and my index finger snaps at the arch it forms.

What is the nature of such a work?
What is the nature, more finely, of a work of *touch*,
of light
and desire?

What must deliberate *wanting* be to move us
beyond want,
beyond reading,
beyond the
unrequited gaze?

I don't know.[5]

To say "I don't know" is to say two things, really. The first thing is that no singular method will be adequate for the telling of our stories—Caribbean ones, generally speaking, but yours as well. This will become more obvious as you go on, but let me say now that the sheer inadequacy of words to do the work of story|ing is too well known to warrant their exclusivity here, not when a word might so easily be supplanted by a sound, when an image will do better than its description, or when the "notion" of embodiment is felt in my own bruised knees, my stiffened wrist, my numb hip and pincushioned left foot (its neuropathy creeping into its second decade), my one-too-many-times-pounded fingers. Here, the feeling is the thing itself, a sense of arrival localized in—and on—my body.

The second thing is that because this is something of a philosophy of rhetoric as a nonfiction that is essentially *Caribbean*, it will appear to resist the modes available for comprehending the logics and dynamics of its undisciplined framing (as vehemently as it will appear to resist attempts to resolve its disciplined unframing in retrospect).[6] I say "appear" because it will not be resistance but more of a subtle disregard of the normalized legitimacy of unworkable frames. What have they done or *could* they do? Have they yet enhanced my understand-

5 September 2021.

6 A friend is fond of saying, "It have things for people and people for things." The chiasmic reference resonates. Together, we limn the affective resonance of thingification with the play of words, its re|inversions evoking the ongoing tensions of representation and address: in this case, the *who* of this address and the *of what* they may be constituted.

ing of myself or merely confirmed my abiding unbelonging? You already know how I would answer that.

Typically, I would keep the anxiety of these questions private, as I've been taught to do. But, having scoured the gorge of my own short history for proof of greater failures than this experiment is likely to be, I find a thing worth knowing: the greatest success of the Caribbean is steeped in a series of minor existential failures that cascade like the river that burst in Bagatelle. I don't know what I want to know, only that I want to know—and that what I know and want to know are not enough.

I refer here to an attitude toward method that may inadvertently highlight the fundamental inadequacy of my own methods for accomplishing all of what I have set out to do, along with my inability to mold them to serve my needs. But it is not an attitude that treats *inadequacy* as a type of futility or as a rationale for inaction—for, if one were to follow the rationale of the unadulterated inadequacy of method, one could arrive rather quickly at the conclusion that it is better *not* to do the work than to attempt and fail. But what failures are more spectacular than any number of Carnival costumes that languish on Ash Wednesday, or of panyards whose players sometimes turn to rust? What loss is sweeter than the amputating sugar, the exploding salt? None, I think.

To do this particular work in this peculiar way is to recognize that the methods could never be enough because they operate in service of a sense of reality that, *in spite of* the implied objectivity, will be entirely subjective. They will be, as I am, unable to approximate the dream of freedom.

No single method will suffice. Nor, for that matter, will any combination of methods.

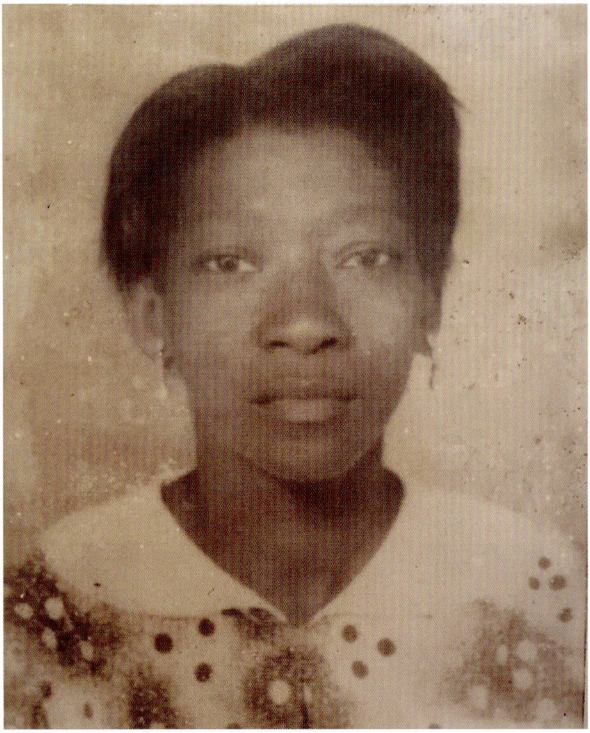

ARCHIVE

1. My mother's mother, Muriel Sylvia Wright née Pitt (1912–1959), was beautiful.
   a. My mother and her sisters Evelyn and Jeanne (Dolly) call her "Mother," a formality that is also a tenderness.
   b. I call her "Mother" because they do and because she died before she could become a grandmother, a tenderness that is also a formality.
2. As we plumb our archives for fragments of our pasts, what *feels* like a desecration can also be made tender. It can be remade as *tenderness*.
   a. a picture frame is dismantled, its rusted nails pulled out and thrown into the yard to become dust (finally);
   b. its decades untouched are now undone;
   c. its decay is hastened and interrupted—in its transformation, in my hands, into a troublingly ir|retrievable past that has also surpassed us to become a haunting of a time that never was (and could never be);
   d. an impossibility.
3. A tenderness and a hope—a hope for a memory of a thing that could never be.
4. The desecrating impulses of inquiry can be softened into *disturbance*.
   a. disturbance further softened into *haunting*;
   b. haunting softened even more, until it is tenderness.[1]

"Archive" is an addendum to an early draft of "Method."

1 How tender they must be for the work you have to do is for you to know: what is yours is yours.

I've attempted this tenderness in my treatment of her archival image, hinging what I feel on what I cannot ever know. I realize this may appear counterintuitive. But in terms of an approach to truth[2] not taken exclusively through fact, and as I consider the virtues of an ostensibly undisciplined method (that is, resisting the dangers of becoming codified into an "undisciplinary methodology"), I know only that I want to make space—

in the mind, with insistent memory,
    but also with forgetting and imagining
in the body, with sure and trembling touch,
    but also with light and sound
in rooms, on roads, with objects and within them,
    but also in their absences, their negative spaces,
on beds or beneath them
—for something un|familiar.

My sense of arrival originates in the turbulence of vernacular intention that sees me beginning after things have already begun. And though I sometimes find myself bristling at the notion of arriving too late, this is where you might say the story|ing of us resides: in the absented presence of our "coming to be"—present because we are obviously here, absent because we can so easily miss its happening, as if it has already happened.

But it is here, nevertheless.

Right here. The existence of the archive confirms it.

We already know that all work that falls within (even beyond) the scope of humanistic inquiry will, at its core, be self-indulgent. Once begun, it exists in the afterlife of its maker's imaginings. We understand this because we know beginnings and endings, *befores* and *afters*, how we wish for things to occur that we have never seen and then we wish for others to come back because their stay was too brief, their departure shockingly swift. Archival work is a deference to the very notion of afterlives—no archive exists of *a life to come*, except in the repository of the imagination. When it comes to nonfiction, the archive takes us

2 Truths, if I come upon any at all, will take shape here in the negative space of the page, in the too often unsaid areas of an image, in the unlightable shadows and interstices of stained and polished wood, in a web recently abandoned, in the scouring of stormwater-driven stones in a grate outside the capital, in a ball of thread found in an old drawer next to Aunty Marjorie's old Singer sewing machine in San Fernando.

further, reminding us that it is not a matter just of fact but of the truth of a matter we may never know: when regarding the archive, there can be tenderness.

As you can imagine, the notion of lives and afterlives applies to created things—images, ephemera, works of art, texts—just as naturally as it can be applied to the many acts and abstractions that comprise what we think of as the Caribbean Imaginary. And it is an afterlife as much to the living as to anyone mired in the elsewhere of some other existence—dying, dead, remembered, unremembered, and so on. If I could, I would delve headfirst into the labyrinth of what that Imaginary might fully extract from these creations (and vice versa), but time is short, and I am running out of it—I'm unambiguously mortal, you understand. Let it be enough to say at this point that if we are willing to compose ourselves, we can move beyond the limitations of custom and customary form, going further in, further out, and in between to consider the different forms such compositions can take, archival or otherwise.

As nonfiction and as nonfictional method, archiving is an act of claiming that can undo the debilitating politics of accesses and divides (whose archives? found where? held by whom?). *You need not die*, the archives remind you. You are already the afterlife of every thought you have ever had (or things you did or did not do as a result of those thoughts), the afterlife of every image you've ever taken. Of every object you have ever handled, too—their shifting shapes and moods, their obstinate fluidities, their forms both inside and around language, sounding and suturing the fissures, binding the failures as if they were bones and meaning itself were flesh, sinew, and skin. We need not die. (How fortunate to know this while we are still alive!) Afterlives notwithstanding, my point here is that the very engagement with the archive hinges on the fact that we—writers, readers, makers, seers—all arrive at a thing that is already here, already inhabited.

With archives and archival representations as troubled as ours, it is easy enough (though never as easy as I'd like) to begin this work in darkness, with what may feel like dark understandings, with hurts that look and feel like hauntings (but may not be).[3] At times, the pathology is more pronounced, as our engagement with the archives—even those we think are ours—can occur beneath the weighted veil of reverence: reverence for the archive meant here as a hypercorrected expression of "care" that is derived from a sense of un|authority. By this, I mean that the vernacular archivist is radically un|authorized—we are com-

3 But *are*.

pelled to resist engaging too intimately with the archive or with its fragility and its fraught representations. This is not the tenderness I mean. In my view, the ironic fetishization—not of the archive or of the act of touching it, but of wanting, almost desperately, to touch—is hegemonic, as archives are endowed with a talismanic significance that often precludes intimate engagement. Archival work involves risk—that is, the inferred risk of performing archival work, wherein the archivist may be inclined to treat their inquiry as a form of desecration, simultaneously ascending to the level of heresy as the archivist descends to the level of heretic.

I want something other than that to be the case—with archives of Caribbean blackness and with blackness more generally—but you know this already.

For now, it is enough to say that this desecration can be violent, but its symbolic revisions—the rearrangement of representations and meanings that emerge in reflective practice and|as deliberative relation—can also be gentle in their deployment, if not also in the appropriation of their logic, their design, their mechanics, and their coding, though we may have had no hand in their genesis. But we may return, at this or that moment, to un|make them by hand—to destroy them entirely.

Am I fomenting revolution here? An uprising from the recesses of the archive? Yes, insofar as that revolution is the intentional and enacted turning away from the myth of a desecrated archive, an archive "desecrated" by our touch. Until that revolution occurs, it may be necessary to resituate the impetus for archival practice primarily with the archivist who proceeds in relation to not only the representations we encounter but also the representations we design. That is, what we are inclined, not forced, to make of the archive.

MAS

Every Carnival—
in which Mas is embodied,
from which it extends,
beyond which is *Mas*[1]
—is always your last *and* your first.

Dedication: For Rasheed Hosein, a Midnight Robber

1 In which
a horse is not a horse
its rider not riding
a dragon is not a dragon
the absence of fire counterposed by a fear of water
a devil is not a devil
though their skins are blue
a baby is not a baby
its mother not a mother, its father not its father
a woman is not a woman
a dead man is not yet dead, his hell contrived
the cemetery in his hat emptied of its graves and mourners
its diggers
its mortal bearer.

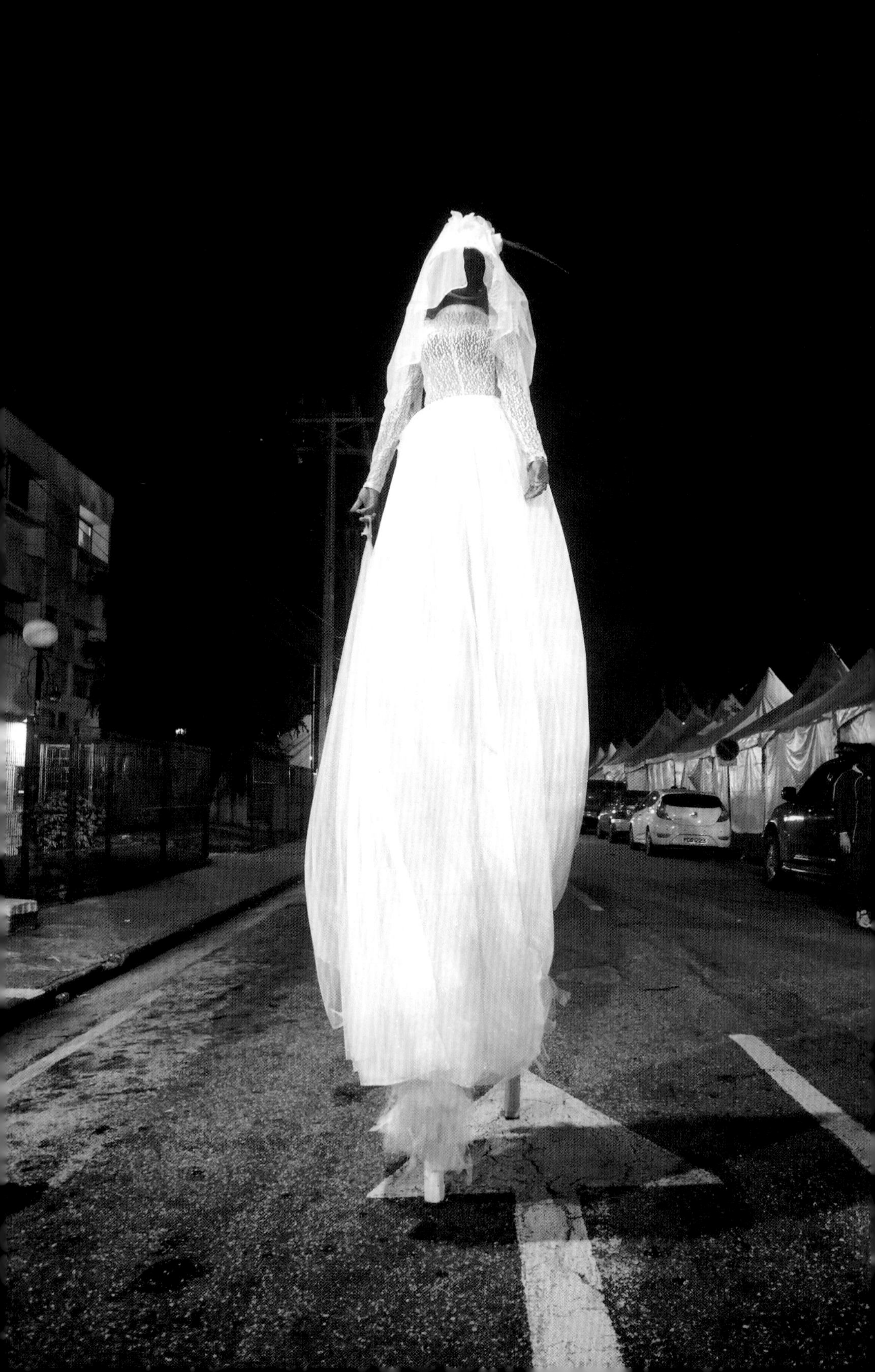

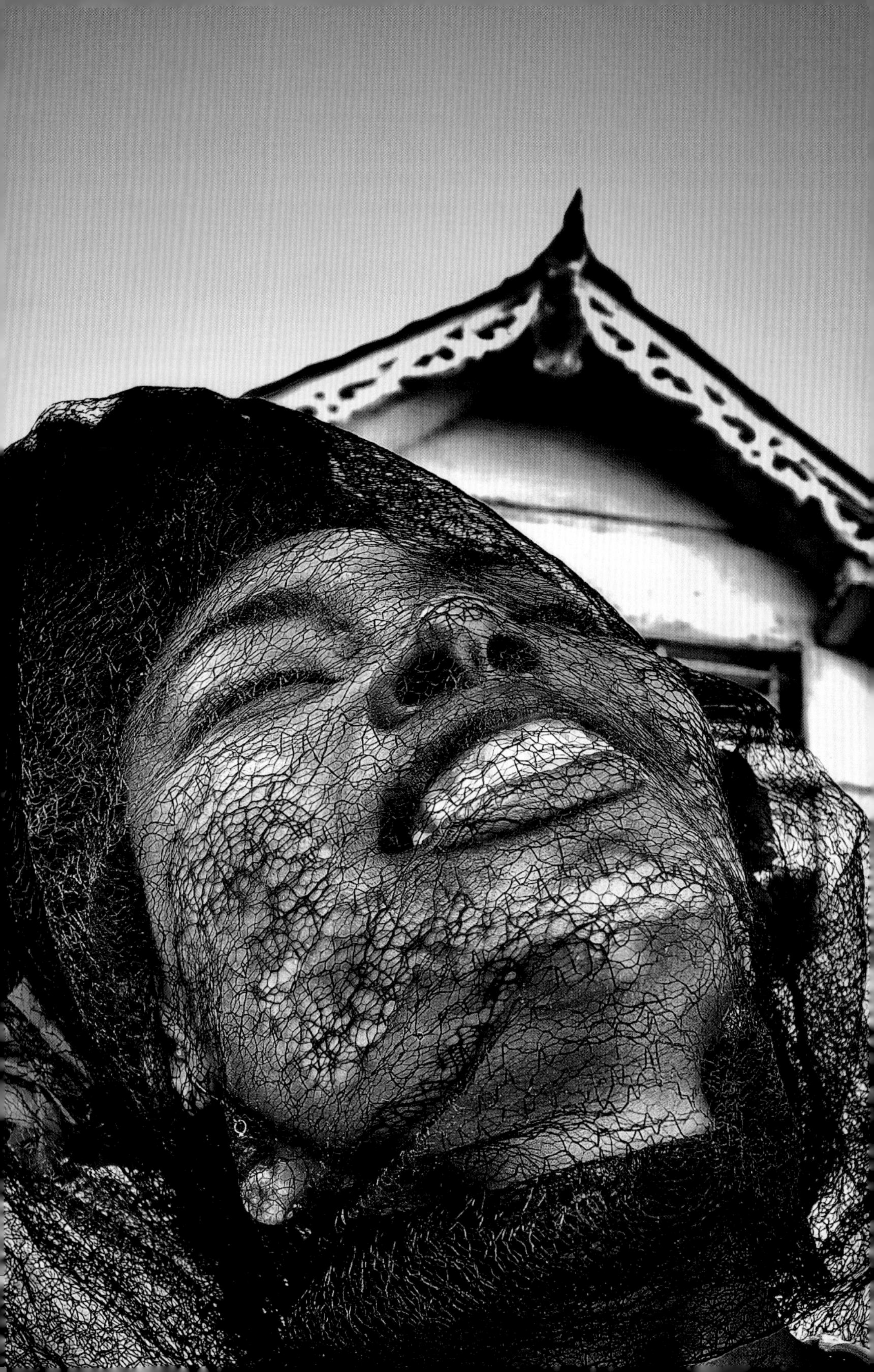

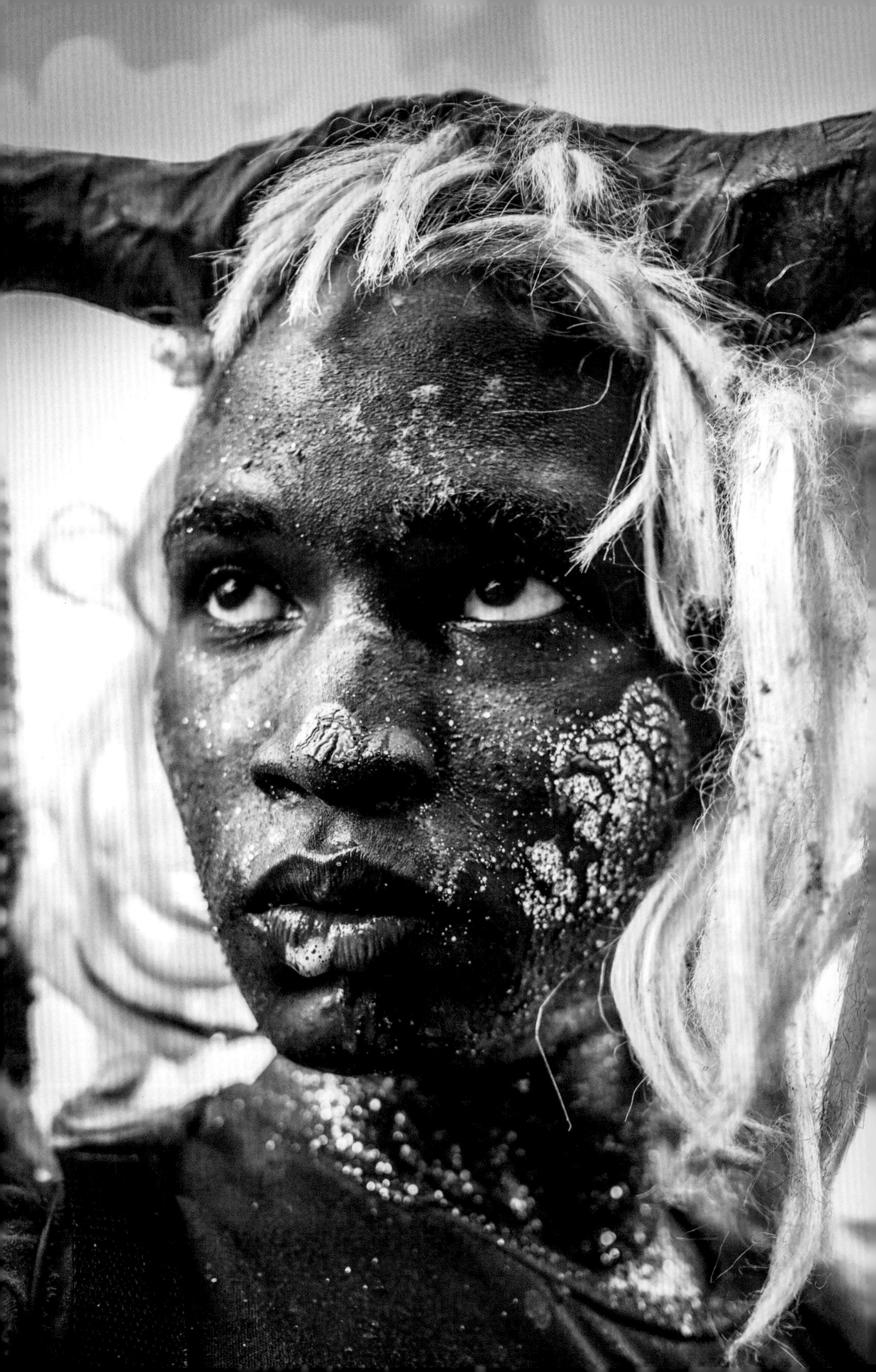

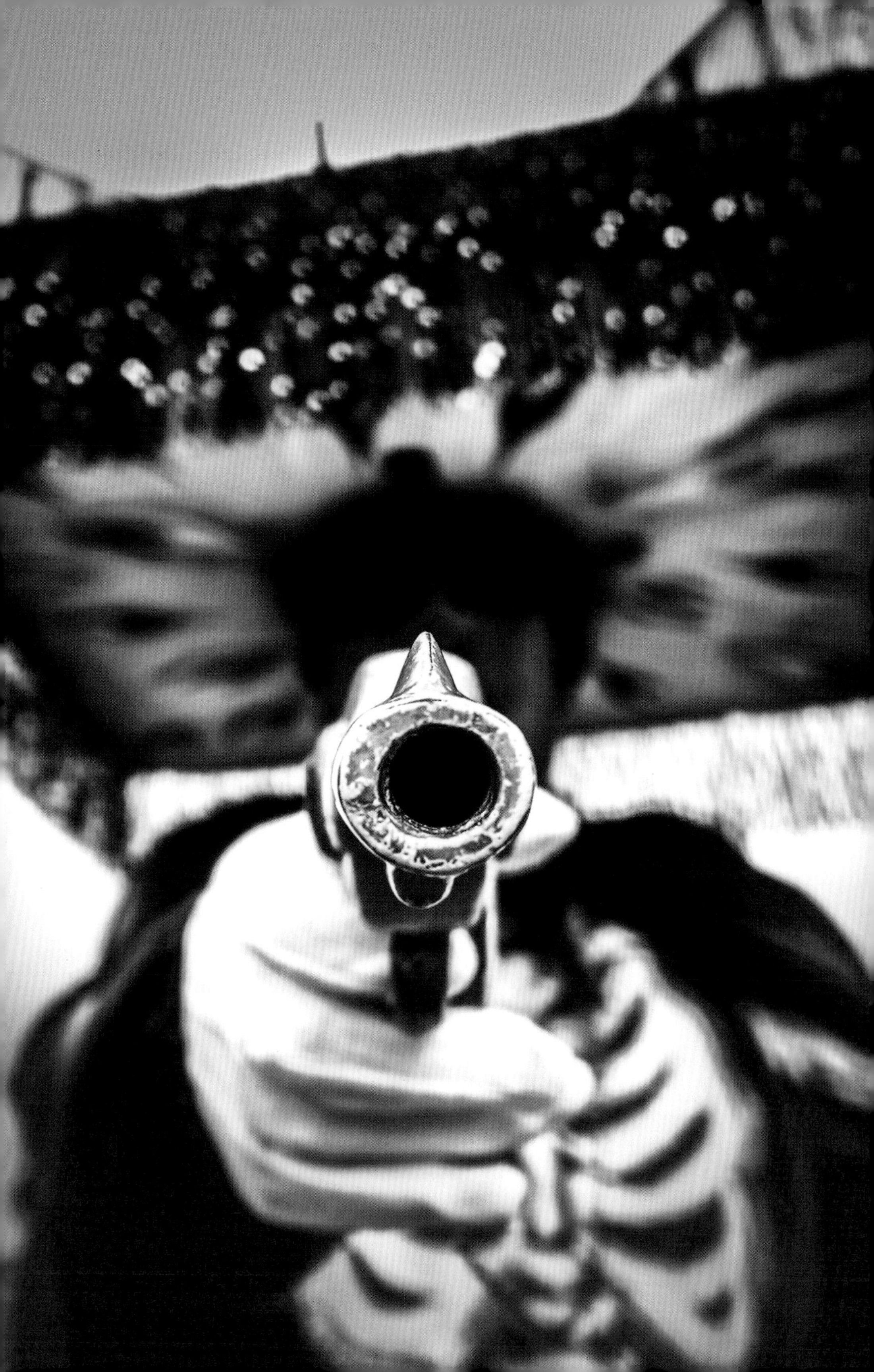

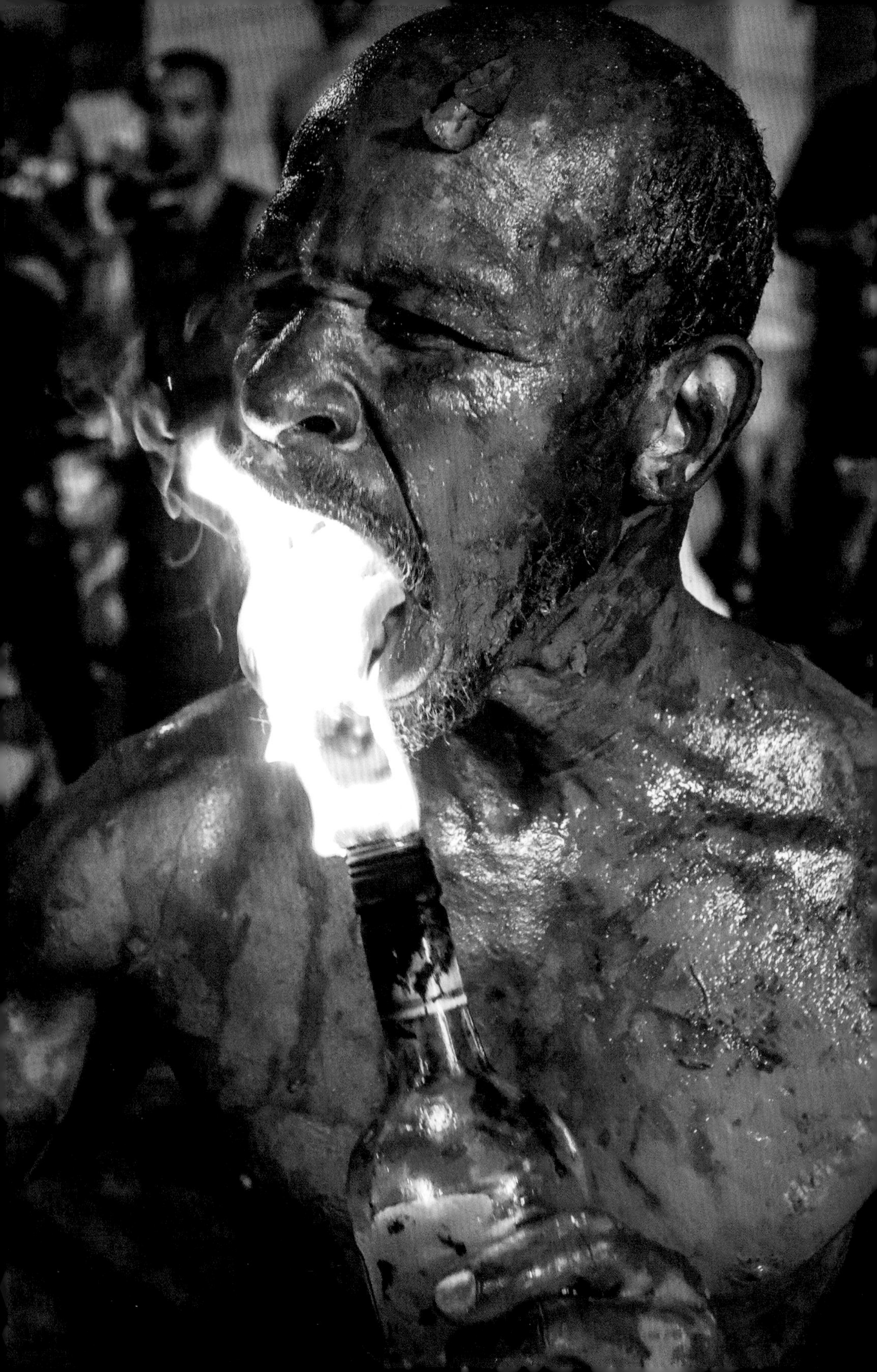

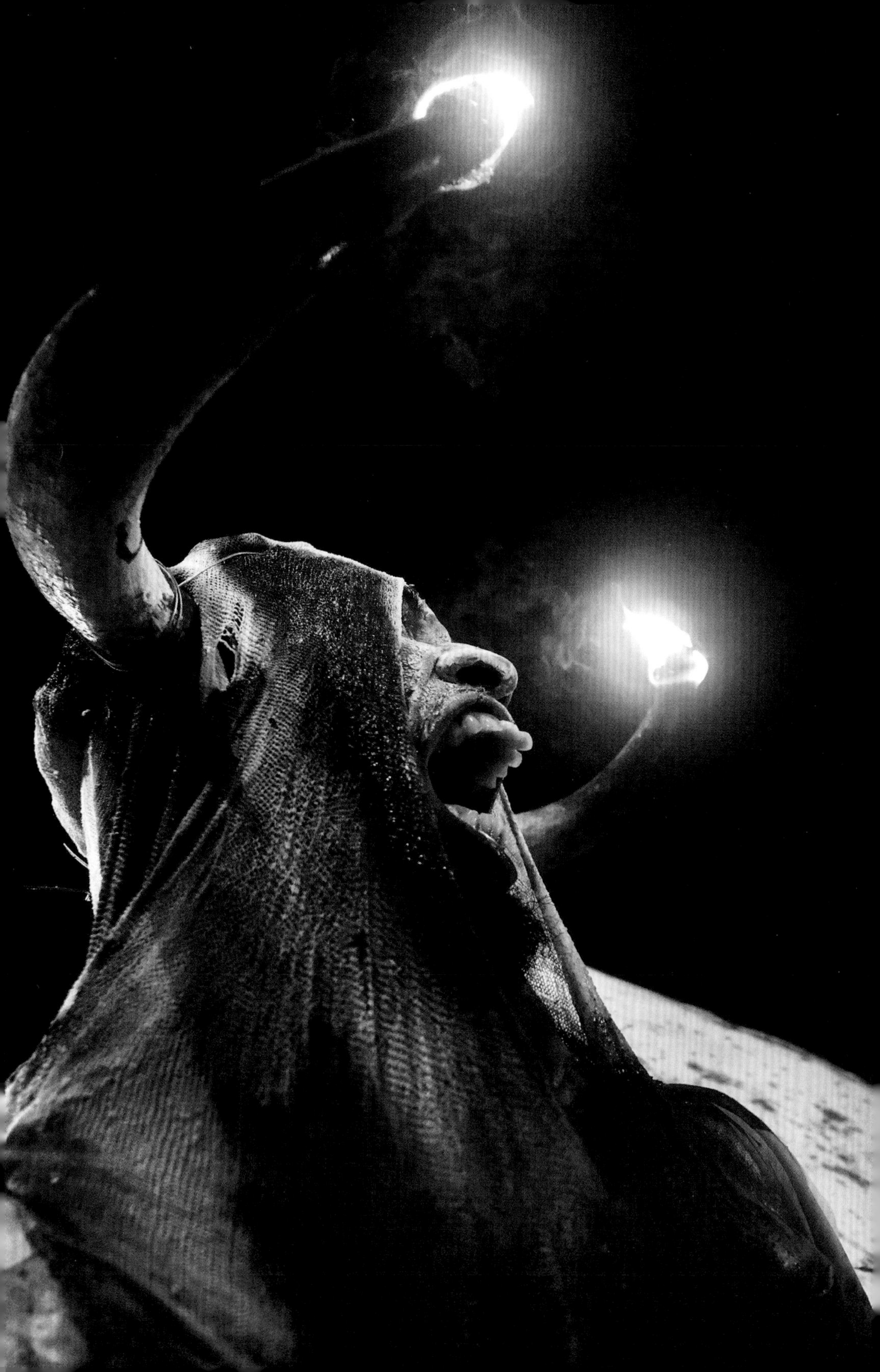

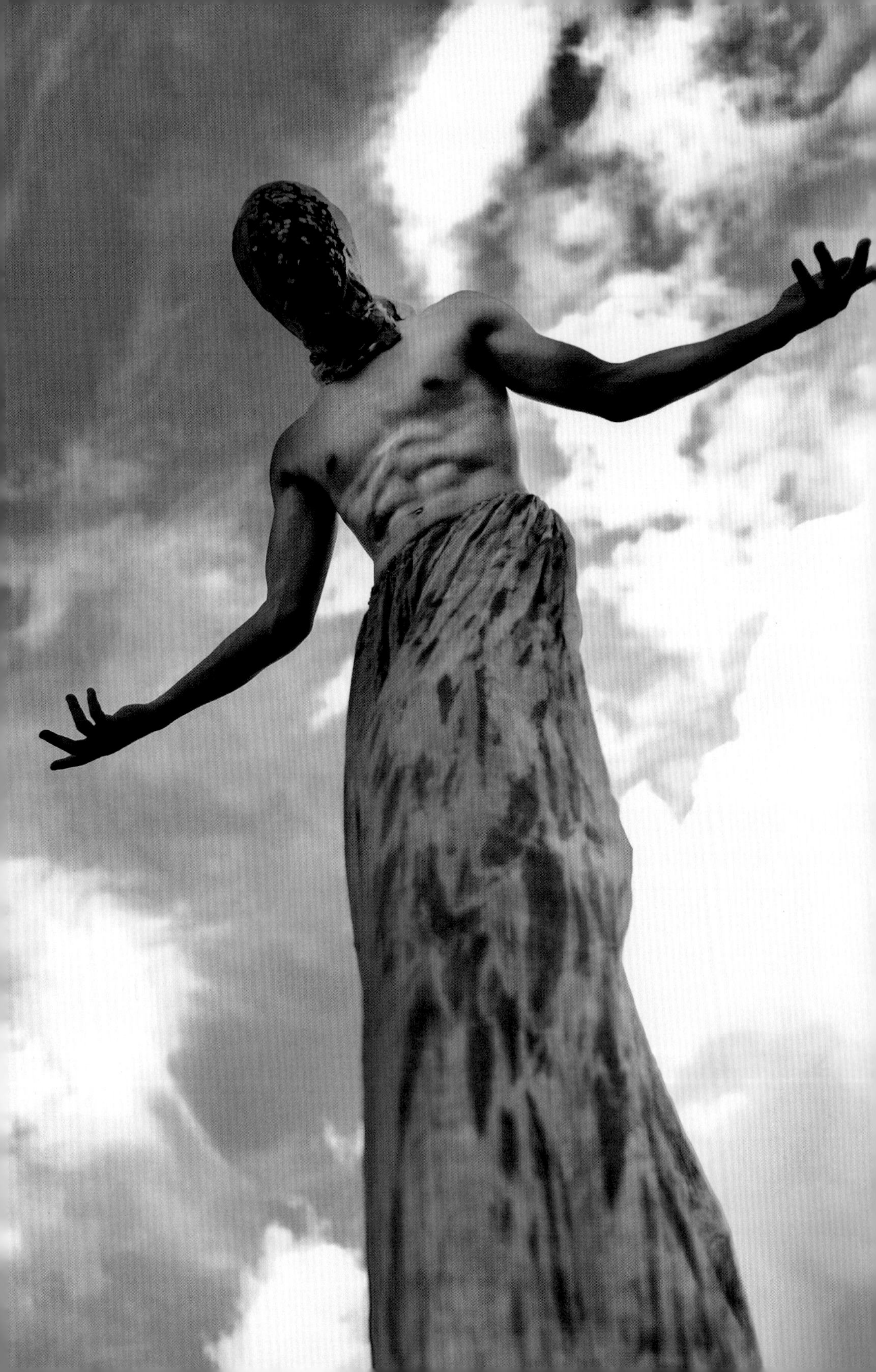

RHETORIC

No larger than a songbird.

A semp.[1]

A Matelot stone.
A rum glass with water.
Calabash.
Ixora.
A brass bell. A bone. A cigar.
Rose water. Florida water. Olive oil. Vermilion. Mud.

There is blood everywhere,
but doh frighten, *doux doux*.
There are Carnivals, too—
Jouvays to save yuh soul, and Midnight Mas
to shake all them jumbie and them
that could hear yuh breathing.
Doh frighten, *doux doux*,
go ahead and breathe.

Breathe *for spite*.

1 And, also, others: chikichong, picoplat, twa-twa.

[Then]

Dream in the dialect
of fever grass and vetiver,
of mauby bark and zebapique.

Dream in the diffusions
of soursop and verveine,
in the contortions of orange peel,
in the grated cocoa skin tea.

The grains and petals will stay on your
tongue and on your lips.

In perfect, unknown yellows, I have had cause to enter, here and elsewhere, through the threshold of my opaque traditions, into and through the blackness I know and do not know.[2]

A blackness I know.
A blackness I do not know.[3]

Imagine a half-buried prism, which you will feel compelled to call one thing but which will be other things. To see, you will have to prise it from the grip of the field in which you have come across it. You will have to dig it up to feel anything but silt, to see anything but sunlight through the mud that has caked its facets and its edges. Light will appear, at first, to lose itself inside of it, and you may get tired of looking for your reflection in it. Rest, then come back. When you wake, know only that those whose compass needles stitch other horizons will not know, at first, what it means when you say that, for a southern people, the ethos of the North is a story of the West, even as the setting sun performs its daily tumble back to an East we may never see.

Try to remember what this means.

2 Or perhaps, *douen*-like, it is the other way around.

3 The caimate has a purpled discourse, you know—it can talk to the cocoa, their blackness bound in white like Shouters.

Between the sea grapes and the sprouted almond seeds that seem to scorn the blackened sand, the sable nuts and boulders, the ants, the tumbled manchineel tree, the cast-off shadows of fronds that bow and shake like single-minded worshippers in the aftermath of a sermon, an answer comes in the form of a question: Is Caribbeanness—which is part of the vast corpus of black, brown, and indigenous rhetorics of the Atlantic—a thing built purely in the mind, or also on the bent and broken backs of people forced to howl through a glass-filled throat at some familiar in|justice? Is it the embedded sickle of a parenthesis that cleaves—and cleaves *to*—the word like some ancient *tabanca*? Is it the sickle's soundlessness, the stride of a dash?

Or, do *we* compose it, writing relentlessly to an unreachable horizon? Existing beyond the reach of that horizon, where hate and terror still stretch toward us, are we our own? Do we at least belong to ourselves, our meanings sacrosanct? Are we ours to behold? What is rhetoric if not what we find in the pale plumeria of a child's fingers before they prune with water and appear to age, in the yellowing almonds of his eyes and teeth like a ripening carambola, in the purpled cocoa pods of his mother's pursed, uncursing lips, each infinite in their asymmetry?

At its heart, Caribbean nonfiction is a rhetoric, a *materialist art of discursive being*. At every stage, it asks: What is *Caribbean* about us, and about this rhetorical tradition of ours that anyone (but us) should consider it, in whatever form it takes or is given? Is it ours at all, this nonfiction we—or I—dare to claim? The vulgarity of these questions may be more easily detected in their comparatively less adorned form: I might ask, for example, Who are Caribbean people, that anyone, even we ourselves, would be inclined to study our ways of rhetorical meaning?

It should go without saying that, as with all things related to us, I would prefer if Caribbean rhetoric were not defined by the kinds of indignities so many of us have had to endure, our arthritic gyrations in deference to power. Will the time ever come when we will be taken on our own terms? Has it ever really been the case that those terms have not come connected to something hard-won, to some dull, aching loss? Perhaps. I may have missed it and would blame my own myopia for the oversight. Rhetoric, as I understand it, is a response to necessity. Having determined what was necessary for my own explorations of the field on behalf of an (at times) elusive conception of "a people," I may have neglected other things. Nevertheless, I view this thing we do very much the same as it has always existed: in a kind of obscurity. I confess that I prefer to plumb and sound that obscurity, where I believe the greater breadth of these traditions resides.

And yet, in spite of what I think should be, I am inclined to ask: Where in the field of Rhetorical Studies *does* the question of Caribbeanness land? Nowhere? Or do we only inhabit the imagination as *Nowhereians*, consigned to the imaginary as the term itself is consigned to this essay? I realize I'm being a bit provincial here, but having seen Caribbean rhetoric inadvertently weaponized, I have to wonder: To which camp can it be said to belong?[4] And, having found no satisfactory answer, do I now dredge up the litany of offenses collected over the years like dust on my psyche? Do I sound each of the bones I have come across like an ancient flute until the burned and buried walk, until the drowned emerge to testify? Do I dare confess, even now, to its pleasures?

Yes.

For some, the contemporary iteration of this tradition has been forged in the various crucibles of Caribbean conservatism that still embrace the scourge of colonialism and its derivatives—enthusiastically, at times.[5] You already know that I want something other than that to be the case. (I know I have to disturb the dead to do this.) These attitudes are entrenched, their proponents often intransigent and deceptively endearing.

A case in point: Some years ago, Edward Kamau Brathwaite told a joke. Growing up in Barbados during World War II, he had heard of Grantley Adams sending a cable to King George VI as the onetime and sometime Mother Country faced Germany:

Go on Big England, Little England is behind you!

That was the joke—the apocryphal "joke" of colonialism that had made its way into our bones and has haunted us all ever since. The scourge of colonialism that has always seen us fighting to be heard and seen, fighting to hear ourselves,

4 If you are a Caribbean rhetorician—or a rhetorician with cause to imagine freedom and enact it in your work—let me tell you now that you belong *exactly* where you are, until you decide or are caused to move to where you wish to be. Frame it, perhaps, as a syllogism. Say: Freedom is everything. To imagine freedom is to imagine everything. We have either imagined everything and have thus imagined freedom, or have not (and have not). We will, having imagined it, come closer to knowing than not knowing, closer to knowing that we do not really *know* anything. The act is as Socratic as it is Caribbean.

5 A call for hangings as a deterrent to the rise in crime is far less jarring when uttered in an accent we recognize—or "recognise"—as our own. It is as if we ourselves have said it: "Bring de hangings back!"

to see who we really are. We are still mired in our loyalties to "the Crown."[6] That we do this at the expense of our inherent complexities, and in spite of our similarities and differences, should come as little surprise. Models of that dynamic abound, our "progress" and deeper "progressivism" notwithstanding, our efforts at individual freedom resonating as if the "basin" of the Caribbean were a hollow gourd and we were like so many disaffected tambran seeds bouncing around inside of it.[7] Call it the *inescapable situational reality*—or call it everyday life—the navigation of which we tend, as a matter of course and culture, to view as a norm, aided by the fact that we continue to negotiate the intransigence of *empire* and *colony* at great existential risk.

As it is with us and our unbelievable bodies—hollowed by the legacies of racism, colorism, classism, sexism, a menagerie of bigotries and environmental encroachments—the ostensibly chimerical Caribbean reality that we have inherited is at times too restless to identify, its character too nebulous and unruly to fully embrace or name. Though, at daybreak or when we go in for the night, we call it "home."

6 Trinidad and Tobago became independent in 1962.

7 Barbados is newly independent. In her inaugural address, newly appointed president Dame Sandra Mason proclaimed the new "ship of state" as vessel *Barbados*. Embracing the archaic reference as a vehicle for the future, Mason invokes reversion and mimicry as much as any aspirational progression. This "vessel," we've learned, is bound for the *metaverse*, placing it simultaneously out of reach of our contemporary preoccupations with space and yet securely situated in enduring conceptions of place and power—the futurist impulse securely lashed to what I would say is the deeply pessimistic decadence of power's promise. For me, the true perversity of the comment is filtered through the tidalectic screen articulated, as fate would have it, by Brathwaite himself in *The Arrivants* (1973). To truly embrace what the metaphorical vessel might imply in the articulation of an imminent futurity—that is, activity that would result in what Brathwaite has described as the "submarine" actualization of Barbadian prosperity and wider Caribbean unity—we would have to be submerged within the greater metaphor of the Sea to be embraced by it. This is idiosyncratic, but the image of that embrace is troubling to me, because whether enacted by volition or involition, it would involve a kind of *disembarkation*: a going, or throwing, overboard.

Who goes? Who throws? Who is thrown? And how?

In every scenario, there is floating, there is swimming, there is sinking, there is drowning. And then, maybe capsizing. Then, a wreck. These metaphors conspire.

If that chimera were a great beast—a Leviathan—we would be lodged in its gut, fueling the intensity of its lore, or a mass of grinding stones in its craw, our *selves* ground almost to dust in the tumult of "belonging."

Or, as we consider what it would mean to exist in this archipelago of ours, perhaps we could imagine being embedded in its spine, our separate and connected islands like vertebrae[8] that we inhabit, unable to embrace the scale of the thing, leaving us at odds to disrupt the affect of its reluctant motion. Along the way, we may find ourselves bearing a range of existential discomforts.

A cramp, perhaps.
A piercing pain.
A borrowed revolution.
A coup. A carnival.
A Carnival! A Mas!—perhaps the queerest thing about us.[9]

And what is the comfort of these things, of what use are they now? If nothing else, they remind us that the fate of the Leviathan is already assured. And however transgressive it may seem to acknowledge the intransigence of power, of dominating discourses and the systems they sustain, Caribbeanness and its myriad appeals, whether public or hushed, are oriented here toward nothing less than our human concerns—that is, I mean to concern myself with the fact, and the consequence, of what it means to be human.[10] This concern, as I see it, is rhetorical—nonfiction the vehicle in which it arrives.

Borne on the currents of our submarine and subterranean unities, we navigate the vagaries and the deeper tempers of this scourge as if it were an ocean, dancing at low tide as if we do not expect some new catastrophe to crest and

8 Of course, the affinity for symbolic vertebrae is amplified, closer in memory than imagination, nearer to feeling when you recall grinding a piece of geera chicken neck, or chicken-foot souse. On your tongue, a hint of seasoned marrow from the oxtail or the pigtail. Symbols have their limits.

9 A Carnival, that troubled archive of acts and intended acts: rituals crafted at crossroads, new prayers, old prayers. Preceding its repeated memory, you find it as a thing that has already happened, a herald of its own promise to arrive—pretense is lost in the euphony, and we are left to gather ourselves in the fleeting taxonomy of beautiful dangers. Amid this litany of things that are not what they are (for metaphors are not what they are, but what they appear to be, or are named as being) a concept masquerades as memory. What are these things to us if they are not what they are?
We will see, eventually, whether that is the case.

10 What is less than the human? Nothing.

break—and break us. As if where we are and where we find ourselves were a singular origin, as if origins are even possible now. Of course, they are.[11] The story of how this art has come to be, how it is practiced, and how those who use it are able to construct particular versions of themselves—as citizens, for instance, but also as humans—is not only a Caribbean preoccupation. Who, aware of their own unfreedom, actively wishes for its continuance? Not me, certainly. Not you. This truth is borne out in story.

Rhetoric, from whatever thread it is traced, is grounded in story—story that repeats, story|ing that exists to tell the story of itself. This is to say that rhetoric in the Caribbean is indigenous. Here from the beginning of us. *From morning*, as the expression goes. We do not arrive at rhetoric only now but have done so continually, and we have taken our time in doing so. Our arrival at this point is more than a question of practice; it is also the enactment of a philosophy of intent, for embedded in the *what* of "what we do" is *why*. The *why* may be considered the unsaid *how* of "how we have come to be." Which is to say, we are *intentional*. Our expressions appear derivative—so derivative, it can be argued, that we have long made a *pidgin* of the most intricate devices, long naturalized the subtle and caustic categories of vernacular expression, seeing them less as *rhetoric* and more nonchalantly as "who we are" and "what we do"—with language, with light, with whatever we come across or bring across. Note our strange capacity to dismiss ourselves, to deny with full voice that we do what we do: the things we do so well, what we do "without thinking." It's so "natural" that we do not name it "rhetoric" but revel in its sobriquets, if we bother to name them at all.

But call it *rhetoric*.

If it appears to make an argument at all, it would be for its tacit indigeneity, too busy being a thing in itself to be overly concerned with mastering the specializations of its classical cousin. It is, as the old people would say, "too own way," which I read as a deliberate *owning* of the way an idea, for instance, might be expressed.

11 In *A Map to the Door of No Return* (2001), Dionne Brand has written that "too much has been made of origins." We can argue that too much has been made of some and not enough has been made of others. But, in general, we understand that the discourse of origins—emerging in the overarching discourse of dehumanizing ecologies of patriarchy—can hamper those whose origins have been and continue to be so deliberately obscured. I wonder, though, if enough has been made of arrivals—of *coming to be*.

Note calypsonian Raphael De Leon's description of an arrival in "Papa Chunks" (1995):

> When I was born everybody made a fuss.
> In order to touch me this they did, of course.
> Put on their gloves and touch me very light.
> Silk cotton mattress for me to sleep at night.
> Bathed me in milk. And, as a towel was too rough,
> they rubbed me with a sweet little powder puff.
> [Chorus]

De Leon, also known as "Roaring Lion," recounts a particular origin—not just his own but that of an alter ego, a *second* sobriquet, "Papa Chunks."

"Chunks" is an abbreviation of "chunkalunks," a term of endearment.[12] It may be compared to the use of "baby" to refer to a baby and to an adult. In the latter case, an adult referring to another adult as "Baby" is not an irony but a tenderness, a loving that requires no rationale. By supplanting "chunks" with "baby," we find that "Papa Chunks" becomes "Papa Baby," which not only evokes the title and thesis of Hortense Spillers's seminal "Mama's Baby, Papa's Maybe" (1987), but also resituates De Leon|Lion|Papa Chunks as godhead—that is, as self-creator, both father *and* child—in the world of the song, which exists in the imagination and, thus, enables him to transcend the existential and epistemological limitations of the body. We can speculate ad infinitum, though it helps to note that all these moves are to enable De Leon|Lion|Papa Chunks to be a "*Doux Doux* Man"[13] and sing calypso, eschewing the practices of law, medicine, and eventually education. *Choice* maintains.

This is a narrative of an ethos—a story|ing of its emergence—that he admits to hearing through gossip, later entreating the listener to repeat the chorus he and the listener have inherited ("Sing it out loud!"). By casting himself as an audience to his *own* self-creation, De Leon|Lion's self-referential mytheme of a "choice birth"—that is, a birth by choice—suggests that some deliberate kind of Obeah had to be working. The dynamics resonate, for me, in the sonic rhetoric of the silk cotton tree and the sighing brass, moving through the forms and features of studios and soundscapes to what resides in the tenor of his lyrics, in

12 Also, "choonkaloonks," "chookaloonks," and "chookalooks." A derivative of the latter form is "cookolooks," which is sometimes abbreviated to "coco" (the penis).

13 A "sweet man," a charmer, a lover.

the marrow of the bass: an origin that turns inward to greet—and then define—itself, going its own way.

In this rhetorical tradition, "situation" is subject to transcendence from what is *known* (or thought to be known) to what is *unknown*. This is not too much of a leap. All of what we claim or speculate emerges from an unknown—an unknown that is sometimes sacred and sometimes profane—a *me eh know nah*. In my considerations of what Caribbean rhetoric ought to be, at least for the purposes of enabling the imagination and enactment of freedom, I embrace what I don't know as the grounding of my Caribbean intentionality. That is, I embrace the *esoteric praxis* of not knowing to explore the *materiality* of Caribbean rhetoric as a phenomenon that can be not merely observed but also seen, not merely touched but also felt. The Caribbean itself is part of this exploration—a *material nonfiction* symbolically presented as a series of discrete, inhabitable truths, however unreal we might appear—and the author of that idea is the biographer of a moment, its advent, its being, and its afterlife.

That said, the Caribbean story of rhetoric cannot depend on any one genre for its telling (have I said this already?). Even the staunchest specialist would step out of their crease to concede at least that. Each, they know, would feed and be fed by the other. We are often mistaken for one thing or another, and I think it is because the question, What more is there to us? will always demand more than a single genre could report.

I am thinking here of an archipelago as method.

Having chosen to engage nonfiction from the standpoint of rhetoric, I realize the irony in the implicit reference to *invention* (that is, self-invention as a way of being in the world) and the explicit reference to *discovery* (even if it is self-discovery) of a world I sometimes think I know. But my rationale for this approach is simple: relevance gleaned purely from contention is bound to be short-lived, its yield unfulfilling. The symbolic power of these moves hinges on a familiar discourse—"belonging" to a "field," "staking one's "claim" in an ideological "province," and so on. Together they reinforce our subscription to a model of power that moves but hardly yields. Similarly, we see the postcolonial faux-imperialist capitalist pretensions that churn at the gut of our Caribbean sensibilities, and we are often at odds to navigate them without losing ourselves in the deeper, more sinister implications of un|belonging. Thus, we are often consigned and confined to the discourses we intend to resist.

If we can agree, however, that *contention* is not required for relevance, or for ethical approaches to contemporary cultural rhetoric in general, then perhaps we can agree that there may be something more to be said about the various mechanisms of vernacular expressivity as rhetoric—that is, *how* this or any situation may be weathered—as well as the splendor and depth of these traditions. These traditions not only equip their adherents with the basic tools of argumentation for negotiating passing controversy but also endow us with the more technical instrumentations of spirited thought that enable us to see and be seen—*seen* as if for the first time by those who are inclined to look.[14]

Caribbeanness is not simply rhetorical; it is a rhetoric. Origins aside, I have long proposed that Caribbean rhetoric is not merely a matter of persuasion, or even that its logics and mechanisms are oriented solely toward the eventual negotiation of troubles and a troubled reality, but rather that it enables its adherents to see their—our—way *through* the complexities of Caribbean being to whatever there is on the other side of it. This is what Caribbeanness enables, and it is toward this archipelago of ours that I cast my gaze, obliged to discover its rhetorical resonance in matters of arrival. This archipelago of hours that is also the passing of our time and everything in between. This archipelago whose meanings demand a closer consideration of the ethos that has come to define it—and us.

14 Think of this as a differentiation between what is *urgent* and what is *exigent*.

ARCHIPELAGO

To be read "as if":

To see yourself in relation to the Archipelago,
you have to see yourself as separate from it.

The separation is discursive:

There is the archipelago.
Then there is *you*.

It is true that you would sooner see yourself out of
breath—separated from breath—than see yourself
outside of the archipelago.

But even together, you are not

one and the same.

Dedication: For LB and KB, water signs

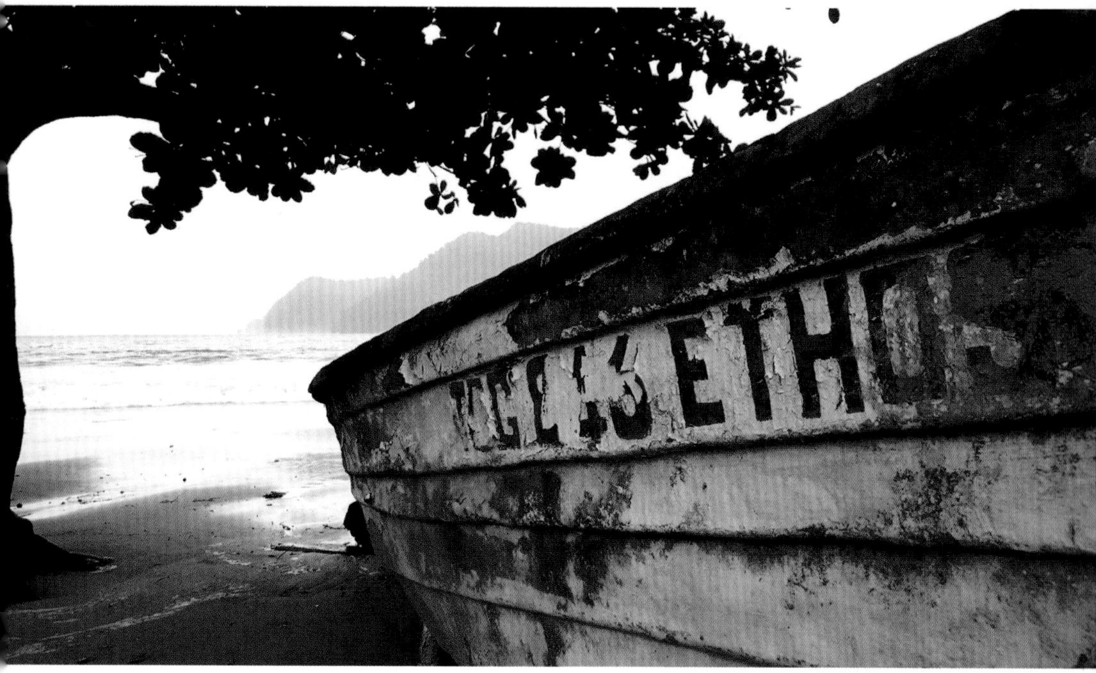
ETHOS

On the north coast of Trinidad, *Ethos* is a fisherman's boat, abandoned and rotting on the shore, subjected to and inextricable from the climatic tempers of this archipelago of ours. What is rhetoric when *Ethos* is a boat, when tides no longer matter to it, yet it is held by the binding sea that is part of its memory? What do memories of salt and sand, the cliché of a palm, do to it? What does it become when an almond has taken root on its shallow hold? Does its story fall away and build like a polyp just offshore, or stay to languish in the congregation of barnacles that gather and dry up at the keel and stern? Maybe something else?

I suspect it may be something else for you too. You may find that your spirited resolve to know things will start to come loose the nearer you are to the reality of this place, closer to the idea(s) of being (from) here that crystallize on your tongue or in the corners of your eyes. You may find that even your once-pained walk changes, the embittered swagger of your assumptions easing into a stroll. You become simpler, and the spirits you try to hold now hold *you* in memoriam. They sing you like a hymn. They hum you like a lavway whose words you used to know. This may be what it is: a desire to arrive at an untranslatable idea. To craft it. To *live* it, really.

Like life.

Life, eh? What is it at all?

Well, it's an image. A photograph, of course. A word, which is an image made of sound. An archive, as you've seen—proof of life. What else could it be? Could it be a catfish's partial and intricately studded skull loosely bound in a tangle of wire (and then freed from it), or the relief of constellations and the imprint of negative space that, in its bones, appear white? Is it the crucifix underneath?

Could these things be life? A story of Caribbean life told as a nonfiction? A story|ing of ethos itself, of what holds and is held by it?

Could it be a headboard made by hand, or the house—the *attitude* of the architecture—that its fabrication precedes or follows? Could their existence in the world as "headboard" or "house" or some other simulacrum of a handmade reality serve as the before- and mid- and afterlife of Caribbean thought and effort, or do they supersede thought and effort, extending beyond the grasp of an inevitable *after* as they become even more deeply entrenched in their own perfect presence, their *nowness* and *hereness*—confirmed by sight and scent and touch—fully realized? Are they evidence of the persistence of imagination once it has been corrupted to form an illusory memory?

What is it at all? Is it the breath?
If it is the breath, then breathe.
Breathe, even if it is not.
Is it a "form" of life?
Black. Caribbean. Life.

What is nonfiction when ethos has appeared to run aground, abandoned at the tail end of an archipelago, a still life of all its comings and goings that have all come and gone, its beginnings already at an end? I will argue that it is the materialist art of our Caribbean being in space and time, a nexus of spatiotemporal thought and articulation that, though grounded, nevertheless stands as a relation to the archipelago, a relating of its troubled meanings—and our relating within and, crucially, without it.

That is, what *being (from) here and there* might mean and how those meanings come to matter for us.

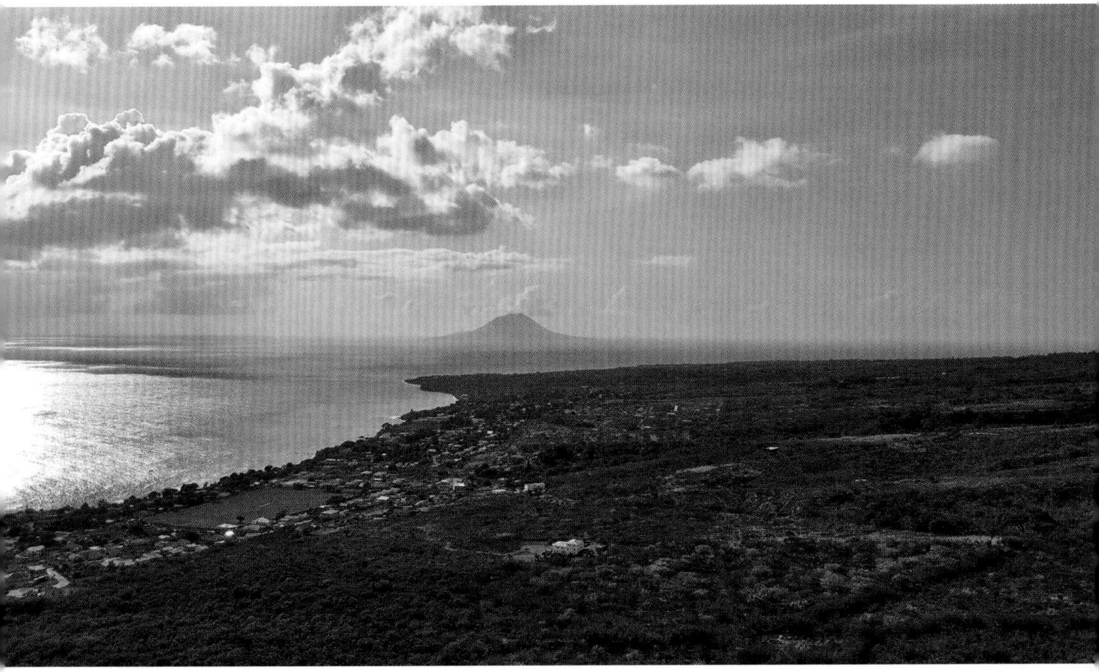

Between what we know of its etymology (Greek for "chief sea," the Aegean Sea, specifically) and its common use (the Aegean Islands, then a collection or cluster of islands), we find that, from a visual interpretive standpoint, the basic logic of an archipelago appears to resolve itself. The rhetoric of the archipelago is therefore inherently topographic—that is, it invites a consideration of *topoi* and the subsequent *graphic* composition of "place" and what the emplacement of those topoi may mean to us. But its duality also suggests the inevitability of a psychic void, a kind of nothingness that results from the interaction of two disparate entities—the *surrounding* sea, the *surrounded* land—with one acting as a natural counterbalance to the other. We find that, as both the *thing that holds* and the *thing that is held*, the archipelago is inherently oriented toward resolution: a duality that moves toward singularity, fragmentation that aspires to a wholeness that we call *Caribbean*.[1]

We could also infer that the reference to an archipelago as resolution is grounded in discursive self-negation, that it is inherently pessimistic. Inherent and inherited. This is how some of us can (still) fix our mouths to say there are no people here, or that nothing is made here—the archaic anti-reformationist claim that the Caribbean is an unpeopled place, that the Caribbean being is a nonexistence. That it is *unreal*. We never really have to ask "What is it if not what it is?" because we already know it is real enough for us to gather like dirt and, under its pressures, crystallizing into something like story, into a sense of Caribbean being that will appear to undo itself, binding us as it unravels—or as we try to unravel it to unbind ourselves.[2]

We who say it (or think it) know better. We know, for instance, that (as far as the actionable work of complaints is concerned) the rhetorical unrealness of a place cannot address the full index of catastrophe that is ours to contend with. We know that it cannot quell the politics of forced migrations into and out of and back to the region, or quiet the turbulent grammar of belonging. We

1 The Bahamas, in somewhat of a comparative formulation, derive their name either from *ba ha ma* (Taino for "big upper middle land") or from *baja mar* (Spanish for "shallow sea"), which describes the shallow waters that surround the islands. This archipelago, because of its low elevation, is the most susceptible to rising sea levels—the negation of land by sea, an engulfment. (Strauss and Kulp, *Sea-Level Rise Challenges*.)

2 Thankfully, it is never that *we* are also unreal. *Too* real, perhaps. But never unreal.

know that it will not absolve us of our many contempts and denials, that it will not save us from our rupturing governments, our ruptured borders, our corrupted land, our deep conservatism, our devalued dollars, our devalued lives, our enduring anti-blackness.[3] It cannot stem the tide of trafficked narcotics, of trafficked weapons, of trafficked bodies—black, bleached, bronzed, beautiful, perpetually endangered. It cannot untell the lies of our persistent dis|unities, but let us say it is a place as unreal as any other. Let us say, too, that it is no more unreal than America, or Europe, or Africa, or the Middle East. As unreal as the cages, camps, prisons, and the precarious spaces in between them, that have been built for holding their exclusion in place—built, that is, "exclusively" for holding those who learn the grammar of their un|belonging at the border or at the checkpoint, or at the barrel of a gun, with broken treaties, with unbreaking walls. Places as mercurial as the people who fill those spaces—my people as well as yours, wherever they may be or wish to be.[4] My point here is that, in spite of our familiarities and deeper affinities for being where we are and where we come from, the tropic figuration of the archipelago solely as a "place" is insidious for a people who want to be free.

The index of catastrophe is thick and deep, but we shouldn't have to be faced with imminent doom in order to write ourselves into a preferred being, only admit to the sheer inadequacy of what being has become. Let us say, anyway, that it is true: it is not a real place, this place that sometimes causes dreams to be dreamed. Let us suspend our dis|belief enough to say that it is unreal. Because to do so would be to know what it is to sense arrival. Arrival that is imagined until it occurs. A *sense* of arrival as an episteme—a way of knowing—of Caribbean being that is yet to be.

It is an appeal to a people whose apparent defiance of the literal is, in truth, the expression of an ethos that is *literary*. By which I mean that as far as a sense of arrival is concerned, *archipelagic thought* is perhaps best suited as a method for reading nonfiction as an embodied rhetoric and reading the archipelago itself as a point and means of subjective departure. This occurs when we envi-

3 In passing, I wonder about the grammar of belonging. What is that grammar when love of country is punctuated by the interminable ellipses of potholes, the exclamation of direct and indirect hatred that can be felt as a jolt to the pelvis and the spine?

4 What is any place viewed through the idea of what it *ought* to be? Only the refracted version of an idea through which the seers might see themselves anew. Besides, no place that eats its young could ever be real.

sion our engagement with the archipelago as a reconfigured relation in order to imagine and assert ourselves *beyond* the boundaries of place.[5]

There *is* a logic to our despair—a strange and estranging logic—to our too-easy grasp of the inherent pessimism of a singularity that consumes and is consumed by its apparent plurality, leaving us stranded to contemplate the affect of existential abandonment before we get ready to begin again—from nothing. From nothing, yes, but also on the only terms possible: ours. *Our terms* because, in the absence of all other things, no other terms would exist. What else could remain in the presence of a thing that appears to resolve itself, its elements reduced to nothing? *Nothing.*

But that is not all there is to ask.

We could ask: What could be, or happen, or take place?

And the answer changes: *Everything.*

5 "Through Wynter:
Here, There, T|here, Elsewhere, Nowhere, Now|here,
and Other Iterations"

On a scale that is both grander and more granular than this, we are reminded by Sylvia Wynter that this archipelago is one of an infinite number of archipelagoes produced as a result of the human encounter with the West, the West's constitution of the human, and its leviathan systems of oppression—otherness, wretchedness, homelessness, criminalization, poverty—that create "captive populations" of people (Wynter, "Unsettling," 321). That is to say, we are not black just in the Caribbean sense but also in the more expansive sense of being already implicated in the extant operation of the West, which functions as the incubator for an infinite constellation of sites where these unhumaning systems are perfected, part of "the lumpen archipelagoes, and their locked-in and 'captive populations' as the now [and, for me, still] primary embodied bearers of the antonymic sign-complex of the abject" (Wynter, "Rethinking 'Aesthetics,'" 259). The "repeating island," as Antonio Bénitez-Rojo has called it, therefore sees its form become *even more* diffuse than its postmodern interpretations alone might make it—and, simultaneously, more materially embedded as "culture" and "society" and, of course, "the World." The categorical repetition—archipelagoes upon|within|between archipelagoes—not only results in what we know as "the World" but also necessitates the gradual dissipation and reconstitution of what we know as "the subject" existing in relation to it and to other subjects, as well as what I call the *infinite arrival* of those subjects—you and me, for instance—at one archipelago or another. One can therefore imagine not just "genres of the human," as Wynter has termed it, but also continent|al genres of the archipelago, of which this is one. My attention is localized, but it does not ignore this broader complication.

We could ask, more pointedly this time: How can we resolve the mystery of our presence, of being lost where we "know" we belong, but to imagine an elsewhere for us to be, to see where we are as essentially a nonplace—a *nowhere*—in|to which we are simultaneously bound? What binds us and what are we bound to do? How can we unbind ourselves from the archipelago, or from anything else that binds us? We could ask (and ask), but see how the persistence of the archipelago relies on the sufficiency of the unreal, on our ability to maintain it infinitely as a means of traversing the unreality we have learned to embrace? See how its logic of inherent resolution doesn't just undo but models—and mocks—the very coalescence we crave?

Coalescence of the *individual*.
Coalescence of individuals as *a people*.

That coalescence is the collective rendition of an internalized desire to *be*, the externalization of which has been interrupted, held in suspension, almost perpetually in the offing, because (the argument goes) it occurs in a place that is not (yet) real, a place whose being has not (yet) fully occurred. It is a trope of perpetual loss—of losing and of being lost. An idea. A culture. But it is not *just* that.[6] It is also the essence of our contemporary mytheme of Caribbeanness, the one we make for ourselves—and *of* ourselves—about our resilience, our contradictory presence, our superhumanity because of where we come from, our fragmented wholeness.[7] The mytheme of place—our "being (from) here." A boat will only take us part of the way toward understanding this—to the horizon, perhaps, but no farther.

6 Have we perfected (better than anyone else, anywhere) the aspirations of being in a place we cannot all reach, making versions of ourselves that outdo the dreams we dream, to dream all the more perfectly? The dream, for some, is still the illusion of empire, the concession to a version of statehood and citizenship that can only be sustained as brutality, as terror. Never mind that it is an empire that has long lost its relevance (and we, the need to oppose it with any more passion than it actually deserves).

7 I have long been struck by the idea that the racist trope of black superhumanity is fundamentally *unidimensional*—that is, oriented toward receiving. To be superhuman is to possess the singular ability to receive, to react as opposed to act or (worse) create. Struck, I suppose, by the fact that the worst thing that can be imagined about us is our ability to endure pain, a fact made far worse—which is to say, far more obscene—because it requires no imagination at all nor demands it of us. In that matrix of whiteness, we are infinitely unimagined and unimaginable. Does this bind or unbind us? I will come back to this.

Of course, the imagining of—if not the desire to be—elsewhere is essential to the Caribbean psyche, for to inhabit the unreal place of the archipelago is to yearn for what we (are led to) believe it could never truly provide: a space for us to be, in spite of our being here. We are, as Édouard Glissant has described, *errant*.[8] The errantry is, like the archipelago itself, an enduring tendency of the Caribbean consciousness, an *artifact* in our psyche, an abjection we keep among the early relics of our infinite arrival, an heirloom of subjugation, a memento of hurt expressed as a presence. What is more Caribbean than that?

Perhaps nothing.
Perhaps everything.

The archipelago appears to present us with the fluid fragmentation of meanings that are secure(d) in their apparent contradictions—almost indigenous. But in terms of arrival, it is a relation that is, for all its inherent tension, a self-contained phenomenon that does not require our presence. We know this, however implicitly. We who declare the unrealness of this place understand that *our* presence is, in reality, incidental to the existence of the archipelago—at best, a disruption of its essential being. Whether we are here or not makes no difference to what it is: a thing engaged with itself.

From the time we arrive, we are already exiled from the archipelago. We are already exiled—united by our exile—within it. In it, but never of it, our psychic connections to it notwithstanding. And yet, as eager as any society to participate in the bacchanalia of the Anthropocene, we are bound to destroy it, as we strive to affirm its literary unrealness with the literal consequence of *us*. The more real the archipelago is, the more susceptible to us it will become—until it is unreal, a *place without us*, which is the inevitable outcome for a people who think they have *no place*.

The pessimism is tacit.

8 "[In] the poetics of Relation, one who is errant (who is no longer traveler, discoverer, or conqueror) strives to know the totality of the world yet already knows he will never accomplish this—and knows that is precisely where the threatened beauty of the world resides. Errant, he challenges and discards the universal—this generalizing edict that summarized the world as something obvious and transparent, claiming for it one predisposed presupposed sense and one destiny. He plunges into the opacities of that part of the world to which he has access" (Glissant, *Poetics of Relation*, 20). What part of the world is that for us?

But this also means that the workings of the archipelago are incidental to our self-creation, that its operation may be viewed as a backdrop and how we see ourselves suggests not only our tenuous relation to the archipelago from a point of exile, but also a critical reorientation of our gaze toward a future. This is a future in which we—our bodies, minds, spirits—have not only discovered ourselves but also left the archipelago to recover from and resolve the effects of its own unthinkable past in favor of something yet to unfold. That is to say, the future *itself* is an unreal place because it has not (yet) occurred. What's more, it will *always* be unreal because it may *never* occur—the future can only arrive as something else, the present. Is this also pessimistic? From this refracted perspective—in which to suggest the Caribbean is unreal is to refuse the limitations of memory and to opt, instead, for the limitlessness of the imagination, our imagining of a version to come—I would have to say it is not.

It is not just an artifact here, not some languishing *Ethos*, but a statement that masquerades as fact in order to articulate an idea until our enactments make it true: to suggest that the Caribbean is unreal is to imagine *a place that cannot hold us*—and to make things that reflect our understanding of what we have imagined. We cannot hold what we behold, nor can we truly be held by what withholds us. The self can barely contain itself. How can anything else contain it?[9]

I see this as our nonfiction coalescing, *taking place* in the theoretical nothingness of the void created in the relational tension of historical and contemporary notions of the archipelago.

We might want to ask: What is more persuasively Caribbean than a sense of un|belonging, of not|belonging where we are? Instead imagining an "elsewhere" that we know is only a substitute—a placeholder for the void we think we know, this nowhere of ours—where some might argue that standing is impossible? I don't know, but I would say that, for me, it is more a question of realizing the potentialities of Caribbeanness than acknowledging its obvious disappointments, more a consideration of being that is not yet "being," because it is in fact an anticipation of a coming transcendence.[10] A sense of being *yet to be*. Caribbeanness *yet to be*. Our selves projected away from here into the future. To say

9 I might also be asking: Who are we in the absence of sovereignty, in the void produced by a notion of sovereignty that will never include us? Who are we beyond the faulty grip of "place," beyond the lecherous hold of "nation"? This is living. *Black life* regarded at scale.

10 The "elsewhere" may be freedom or death or some other in|comprehensible inevitability. We will come to that, in time.

this place is unreal, therefore, is to imagine, while awake, our inhabitation of a version of it that is still left to be seen.

The pessimism is also utopian.

Or, perhaps it is not pessimism at all.

It is optimism playing a *mas*.

It is futurism with an accent.

Archipelagic thought as I understand it here—as negation and resolution—is not merely a question of liminal space, but a questioning of liminality as a viable construct for and expression of Caribbean being. As such, I see Caribbean people—those who inhabit and are inhabited by the archipelago—as a collective *liminality*, or an infinite combination of liminalities. The expression of Caribbeanness, in other words, is the result of an embodied liminality existing with|in exile from the voided space of the archipelago. We who declare that we are nowhere declare simultaneously that we are *now here*. To be Caribbean, then, is to announce infinitely that we are *here* in every time, present in every situation, in every *now* we inhabit.

Nowhereians.

In terms of conscious relation, *we* are the essence of what may be considered an *archipelagic encounter* playing out interminably, contradicting and resolving ourselves as if we were metaphors, requiring no explanation past the acknowledgment of our presence—almost indigenous. *We* represent the active negative space of the void (indeed, because you is and I is, and because the void *is not*), and we shift our shapes as a necessary consequence of motion with|in it. You think you have escaped it by saying it is unreal, or by refusing to name it and instead taking its troubling existence for granted, but its unrealness holds, maintaining its integrity in spite of your refusals. And maybe we are more human because of it, more *Caribbean* because we are essentially *unable* to truly be in the place we conceive, cast as it is into the future. This, to me, is an archipelagic encounter as much as any. I am not concerned with the archipelago solely as an ontological preoccupation but rather in our ability to read it and understand who we are and who we can be. I mean to affirm our Caribbean *presence*, not just our presence *in the Caribbean*. Our *Caribbean being*, not just our *being in the Caribbean*.

Embedded in these articulations of the Caribbean's unrealness, and our concomitant desire to be real in spite of it, is a question: Can we see ourselves here, in this place? The answer, dressed as it is in this crocus bag of pessimism, would appear to be no. Not on our own, anyway. Whether we like it or not, we need each other to resolve the matter of seeing ourselves here. The binary—you, me—dissolves. "Seeing ourselves," then, is relational because it is not by seeing *ourselves* that we prove that we are here but by seeing *each other*. Indeed, our difficulty achieving this only further affirms that nonfiction is the art of what is left to be seen. An act of faith, if you like. That faith is further tested when, in the absence of someone to see (or see us), we are inclined to imagine, or to see what we imagine coalesce into an imaginary in which to ground ourselves, our intentions, and our meanings. Our fragility in that state will persist until we discover for ourselves what cannot be discovered *by* ourselves. Until what we have imagined is given form—*made*. A consciousness materialized.

This is not a theory, unless by "theory" we mean the capacity of thought to do what the body cannot do alone, or what a lack of resources—time, money, access, opportunity, and so on—might otherwise prohibit: a concept of ourselves that we have conspired to inhabit, one we have imagined together.

An approach to nonfiction as an *archipelagic philosophy of rhetoric*, if we can call it that, calls to mind the conceptual notions of rhetoric (and philosophy, to a lesser extent) as bearing a classic (and classically performative) reference to Greek traditions. Others have their traditions, of course, their influences, all with their implicit and explicit elitisms and entitlements.

But we are not *Aegean*.[11]

In truth, Caribbean rhetoric is no more Greek than my English is *English* or a nation is "home" to those it despises and (yet) consumes. No more than the *rolling calf* is a calf or the *lagahou*—the creolized *loup garou*—is a wolf. There

11 *Archipelagic*, yes. But Greek (however we may be named or middle-named) we likely will never be. This—saying what should, by now, go without saying—is the danger of being preoccupied with origins, for it leaves us in the Caribbean susceptible to our own versions of injustice, seen in the treatment of refugees that move with—and sometimes against—the normal transnational flow of people throughout the region. Some examination will reveal the comparatively wretched state of black refugees who may not be "pushed back" in the manner we see in the Aegean Sea but are certainly not welcome when they arrive. Haiti has long been martyred in this regard, left to suffer its own wretchedness. As if that wretchedness were not also our own.

are no wolves here to speak of, only pothounds that turn to dust along the roads that lead to the flood-prone capital.

This may all make better sense to you than it does to me. My concern is not what the archipelago prohibits but what it enables. If we cannot see ourselves here, we have to imagine what being here might (actually) mean, what those meanings might yield, what that yield might do. It is undoubtedly one of the predominant tropes of Caribbeanness, a situating construct of the Caribbean psyche—the afflictions, too. But we are laden with paradoxes here—there is one in every portrait, in every yard, borne in every vein of stone, in every fissure, in every scrap of wood, borne between the binding of that wood with wire, in what bending brass will utter, its sigh at the weight of an unhandled blade. Paradoxes in and of—and out of and into—the water.

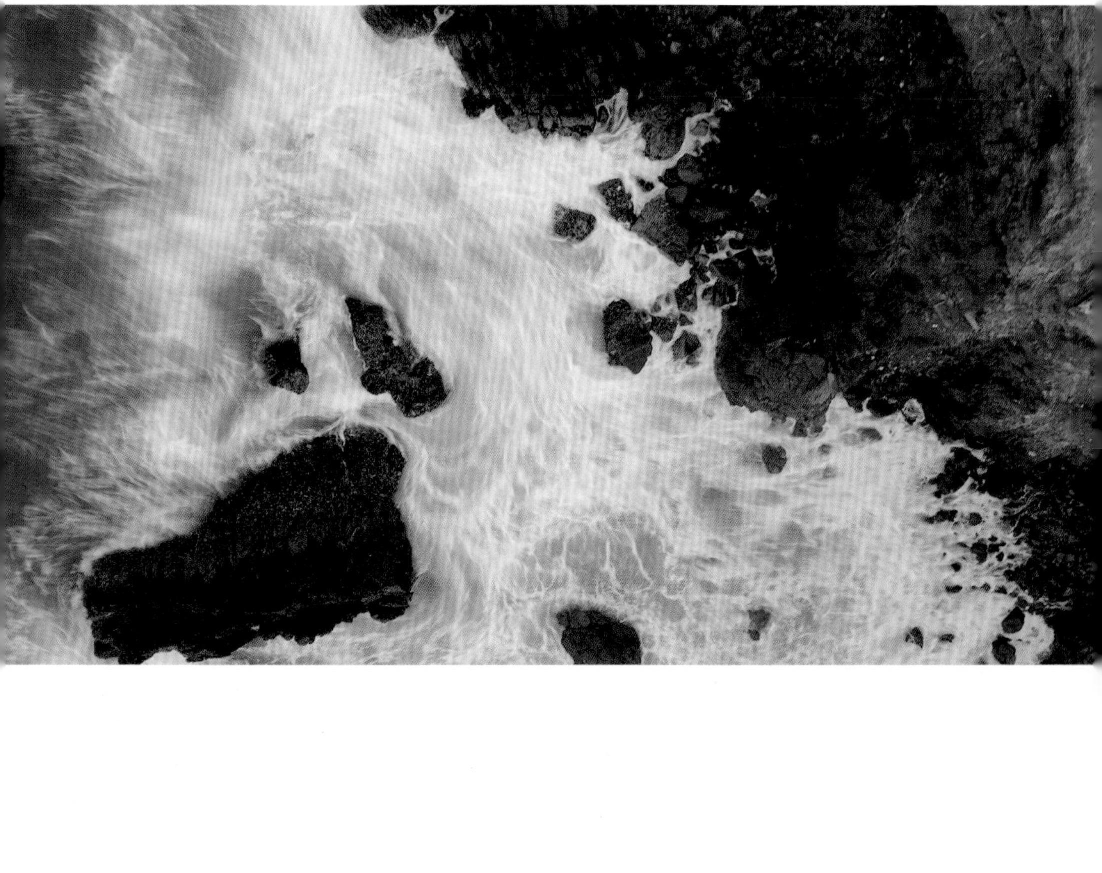

See?

Even when I imagine a void, my mind wants to fill it, to speak and make some substance of the silence, my observation of it already undoing the nothingness its initial resolutions suggest.[12]

To claim that this nonfiction is *archipelagic*—which is to say, that it is in some way characteristic and peculiar to our grounded spatiotemporal (rather than only shifting geopolitical) realities—is to even more emphatically situate my ironic "exploration" of arrival *beyond* the immediate reach of traditions that, for all their inclusivity, have yet to account for me or you. If you cannot readily imagine the archipelago, imagine the synecdochic life of a Caribbean mind and its struggle to navigate the vicissitudes of mainstream thought, its diversities valued most for their unthreatening homogeneity.

Archipelagic thought, experienced as a sense of arrival that is resolved to be Caribbean, is also a coming apart:

> an unhinging of a familiar door
> a doorway haunted by the absence
> of a door—its jamb empty
> an unhinging of the hip and shoulder, an opening
> the isolation that precedes an embrace
> an embrace to come
> a holding to come
> the mouth opening but not speaking
> the enunciated breath, before the word
> the thing to be said before it is said
> the mouth seeming to come unhinged at the jaw
> rearticulating what will be more than a cry uttered
> in response to a hurt
> a thing that occurs *before* the cry:

12 Like with you: you are not here, but I believe you are on your way, helping to fill the emptiness of the page with (let us call it) vision.

> a cri de coeur—like the sound a *douen* might make
> before it moves in the bush.[13]

These moments of dissipation and cohesion take (their) place in the nowhere of the archipelago—not just the unfulfilled moment of eternal loss but the emptying of it and its refilling.

Using the archipelago as frame and as method for reading Caribbean spatiotemporal being and transcendence, rather than merely a place we might all have wished to escape from, we are able to go beyond the apparent nothingness of archipelagic space—the space undone by means of its own reflexive design—and see that the imaginative act of being (here, Caribbean, black, and so on) is not merely revolutionary.

No, to presume subjectivity where subjectivity seems to have no "natural" place is to engage in the divine blasphemy of narrative self-invention, of self-assertion, the enactment of self-creation.

What I am attempting here is to articulate the unarticulated and the inarticulable—the unsaid and the unsayable. I am attempting to see blackness as the art of touch and sound: the *beforelife* of sound, which is the breath, and the *afterlife* of touch, which is how the breath as well as the moving body will encounter the phenomenon of arrival. That is, *life*, or what is seen as life, existing as|in a kind of *suspension*. A suspension of disbelieved bodies, like in a Carnival. But done well enough to move past the stark and subtle immediacies of our despair, arrival will unfold as an art of black thought in the form of light and the lightness of touch disabused of their secrecy, not burning like sugarcane or capital cities, not roasting but turning fragrant like cocoa in the sun.

13 I will try to be as careful as I can be when I think of and refer to the *douen* and to things like it—magical things—because they inherently justify *not* writing (about them or anything else) and thus forestall my articulation of the knowledge I wish to pursue. I am neither the archetype of the magic I have encountered nor the one most equipped to explain all of its mysteries. I will navigate according to my limitations, leaving opaque what demands opacity, leaving settled what needs not to be stirred, calling only what needs to be called (lest an answer comes of some careless invocation).

But, to the extent that its rhetorical appeal is like that of a creolized jeremiad—that is, one that eschews a Messiah in favor of a Mas—I will attend to what occurs in the spaces it and those other(ed) things inhabit: regions somewhere *past* the point of declension whose borders line the promise of doom like a limbo pole or a *diametre* (that discerning line), with you or me crossing into it from time to time but returning until it is our time, our turn to go through like the *jamettes* we are.

A blackness to come that is *archipelagic*, measured in grains that collect like islands, nations, protectorates, outer departments—

one
by
one,
one
by
one
at the back of my
neck

—the "*graine graine*."

These are grains I must count with the obsessive compulsion of the *soucouyant* caught at daybreak in the frame of his own door, with his secrets and his old, unanswered prayers embedded in the architecture of a single window.

Grains on a photograph of my mother that is the visual epigraph of my own unbridling, its silence punctuating its deeper silences.

Grains on black skin in white light.

Grains I count until I lose count, forgetting my place.[14]

This archipelagic sensibility will appear, in the beginning, to offer little comfort, as we think of yet another thing that does not require *us*, a system that can undermine the urgency of our many appeals, or cast doubt on our claims to understand what we arrive at, let alone what we bring, let alone what we hold—

14 Grain: a unit of measurement for time and space. It did not feel very much like it at first, but I feel it now: time is running out. I look at my mother, her skin more like paper every day, it seems. I look at my children too, and I know I am running out of it, each of us outpacing some kinder euphemism with the fleet-footed agility of lost youth.

I am in the furious afternoon of my life—the furious afternoon sun, you understand—which is why I turn feverish and launch headfirst now into what will look and feel like a manic state until the inevitable lull, the ebbed tide that will look so much like peace, chaos receding to reveal a bit of freedom in the surf. A stillness, perhaps, that I can share. Also, "   ."   (as in preferring to say nothing,
or preferring nothing be said).

hold, as to and by oneself,
like and unlike in and on a boat,
a branch,
a basket,
a bassinet,
a bed.

let alone what we carry—
carry, as with oneself, as with the voice
through air, ground, water,

to be carried like water,
be carried away like water,
be carried away
by water—
and brought back.
be carried away
from water—and
brought home.

But try to remember what is happening.

Arrival: to be carried, brought, born|e.
An end in itself.

Arrive, like an archipelago,
already resolved by the time you encounter it,
already resolved by the time we encounter each other
and are ready to begin.

Begin again where|ever you are.
Or *here*.

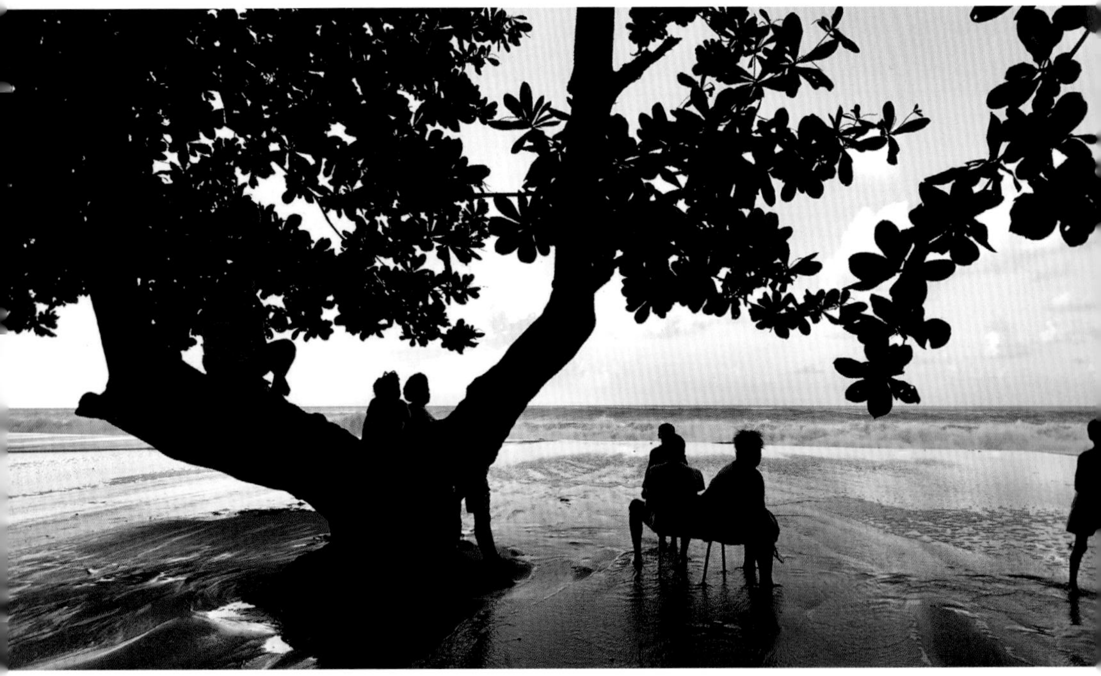

Near the water. Or, in it.[15]

15 Or, if possible, as water *itself* on its way home.

CARIBEA

Remember, you may have come from the deep,
but you can always drown in the shallows.

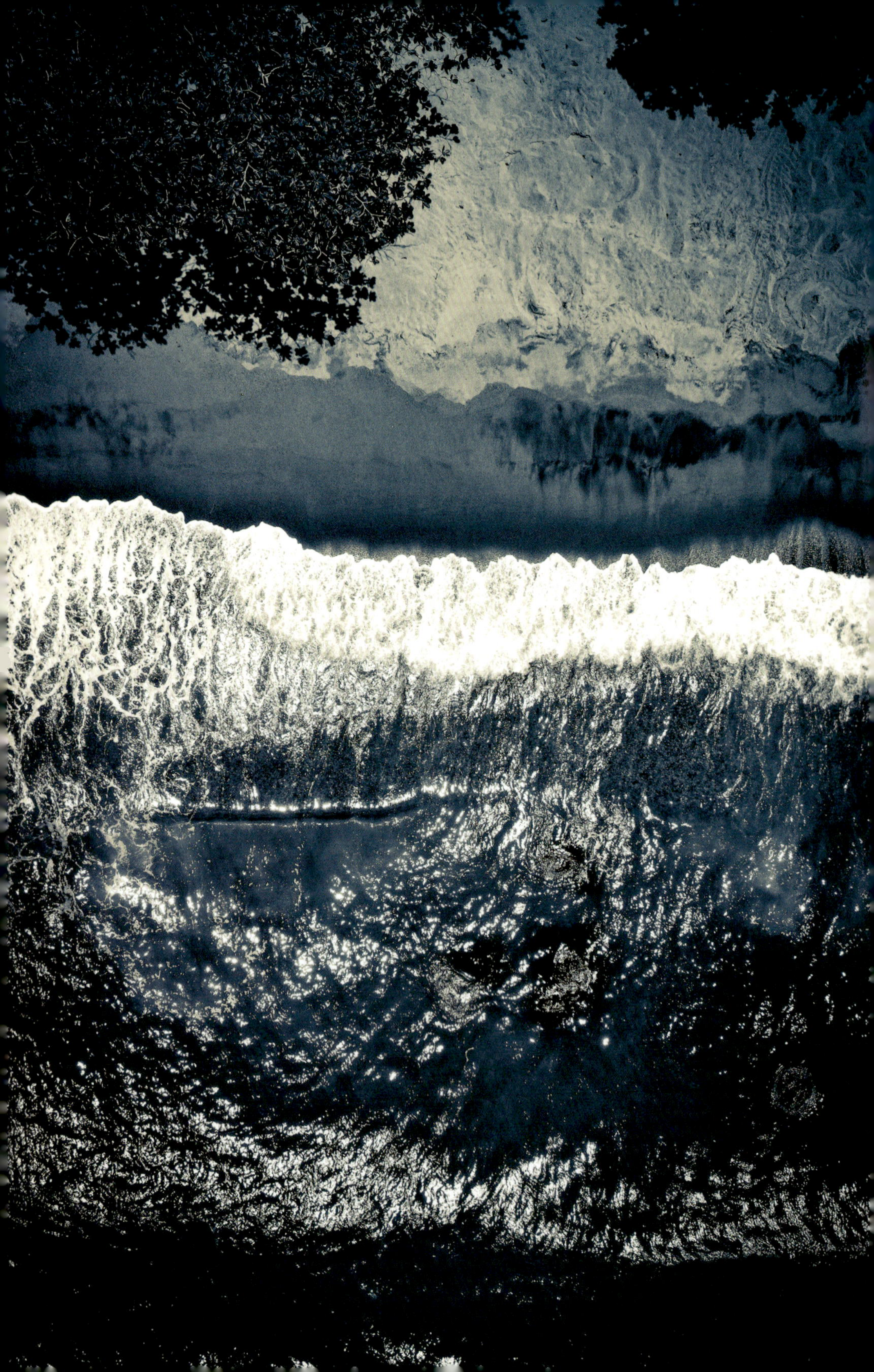

In Syracuse for the spring, I note the timbre of these narratives, remembering the driver who didn't know where Trinidad is. "Ten degrees north of the Equator," I said calmly, maintaining my five-star rating, "nearer to Venezuela than Jamaica." He has never traveled, wants to but does not have a passport. My dialect of degrees and lines is foreign—doubly foreign in my not-quite-American tongue. "What's stopping you from getting it?" I ask. "Nothing." I think, there is an empire in that "Nothing." I know he doesn't realize it. "Sometimes," I respond when he asks if the weather is nice. Sometimes nice. I go the rest of the way in silence, thanking him as I get out. In temperate, distempered America, we melt into a single island, learn to ignore the absurd scale such an island must possess to possess us all, to never overflow its borders into the catchments of Brooklyn, Boston, Atlanta, Miami. We almost forget the uninhabitability of parts of Vieques and Culebra, the long inhabitation of Guantanamo Bay, almost forget the currents of this sea pulling us back to that perfect tropical island that does not exist, back to a home we no longer know but are unable to forget.[1] I almost forget.

Later, in my office, I go back to that conversation, wondering:

> Where is best to drown?
> Is it worse to drown or to be "feared to have drowned"?[2]
> What is the favored language of drowning? Spanish? Kweyol?[3]
> Whose black tongue breaking, whose mouths broken open
> like a wreck, on which shore?

1 Vieques (N 18°07'29.8956", W 65°26'31.6428") and Culebra (N 18°19'01", W 65°17'24") are still contaminated with unexploded US military ordnance. I read somewhere that a child was burned with white phosphorus. The bombing has stopped, but the burning has not stopped. Naval Station Guantanamo Bay (N 19°55'03", W 75°09'36") is described on its official website as "the forward, ready, and irreplaceable U.S. sea power platform in the Caribbean." Irreplaceable. On April 27, 2023, Vectrus, a defense subcontractor, was awarded $41.3 million for base operations support. This is how the "irreplaceable" is maintained.

2 On December 6, 2020, an unnamed vessel departed the Venezuelan city of Guiria for Trinidad. Eleven bodies were recovered, and nine remain missing—feared to have drowned. On January 12, 2021, another unidentified boat left Nouadhibou, Mauritania. More than a dozen passengers, all male, died. This boat was one of at least eight that left the African continent and drifted across the Atlantic bringing their dead ("Adrift").

3 In "Haiti I'm Sorry," David Rudder sings, "They say the Middle Passage is over, how come crowded boats still haunt our lives?" Released in 1993 on *The Gilded Collection 1986–1989* album, the song is part of the soundtrack to the years I spent without my mother, in the care of my aunt Marjorie.

Whose bodies thrown overboard?
Whose birds?
Is it better to die in Arabic?
Or to live, while Arabic, in English?
How is the weather? Is it nice?[4]

Instead, I say nothing, unsure of whether my silence was tact or condescension—or cowardice.

4 When I say to the border officer at JFK that I've come from Trinidad, he responds, "Nice." I know he means the weather. *Weather*, for him, is a metric of escape. He registers no imprisonment in the sun. No trauma he is bound to consider. "Welcome home," he says. "Thanks." He knows he doesn't have to be cynical. He knows I'm not from here.

BOCAS

Can the cartographer be the place, writing him-
self as|into place (as into being)? If we understand
that the map—the cartograph—is an annotation of
objective|object-filled space, am I obliged to view myself
at the confluence of place and memory and imagination?

Or am I obliged to view myself—that is, to view and be
viewed—as a map, as some entity inseparable from the
text, or as a set of disparate entities?

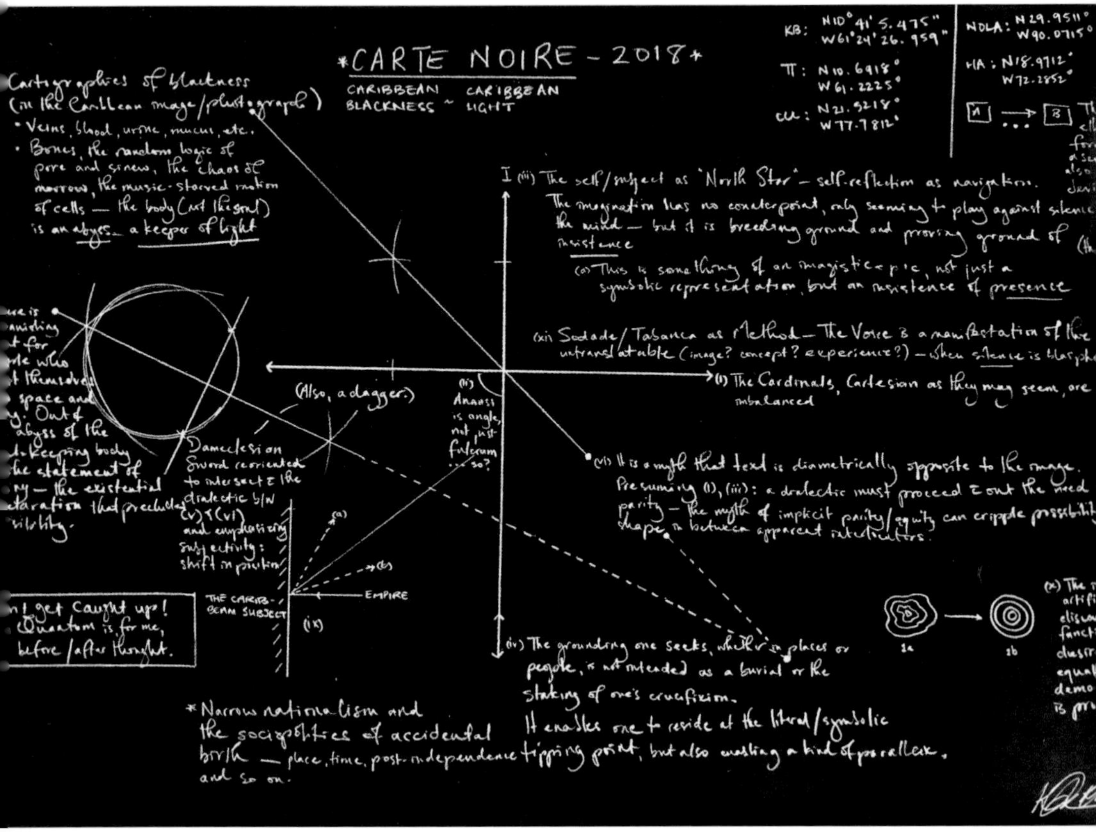
CARTE NOIRE - 2018
CARIBBEAN BLACKNESS ~ CARIBBEAN LIGHT
KB: N10° 41' 5.475" W61° 24' 26.959"
TT: N10.6918° W61.2225°
NOLA: N29.9511° W90.0715°
HA: N18.9712° W72.2852°
Cartographies of blackness (in the Caribbean image/photograph)
• Veins, blood, urine, mucus, etc.
• Bones, the random logic of pore and sinew, the chaos of marrow, the music-starved motion of cells — the body (not the soul) is an abyss — a keeper of light
I (iii) The self/subject as 'North Star' — self-reflection as navigation.
(i) The Cardinals, Cartesian as they may seem, are imbalanced
(Also, a dagger.)
Damoclesian Sword reoriented to intersect the dialectic b/w (v) & (vi)
THE CARIBBEAN SUBJECT
EMPIRE
(iv) The grounding one seeks, whether in places or people, is not intended as a burial or the staking of one's crucifixion.
*Narrow nationalism and the sociopolitics of accidental birth — place, time, post-independence tipping point, and so on.

Bell No. 1, for Noel

Again with sight.
Again and again with sight.
                                                                        And again,
                                            as you alone might imagine.
And again, of course, like breathing.

Like the outgoing breath, love is not unlike vision,
the act and affect of having seen that accepts light
and sends it back to where it has come from, back to
its erstwhile home. Waiting for love is
commonplace. Natural as breath.

Again, you wait with expectant sight to see:
        What come
        What gone
        What pass you
        What you pass

                is the visitor you send hastily away
        so you can hasten the waiting, and breathe
        the soft, labored breath of your longing for
        something old as if it were something new.
        Longing to see it approach again, and leave,
        so you can see its form dissipate like an
        expelled breath, like the expulsion of
        thought: of what I think of what I see, of
        what I feel for what I see.

        Sometimes it is nothing.

Here, the dissolution of ideas is commonplace, the dissipation tidal.[1]

(I will soon begin to panic,
so let me leave off of sight
for a moment.)

I think, instead and again, of a maelstrom—
what a boastful word
for a person
who has never seen one.

This is a word for sailors, or those who have sailed,
for those who have been sold—not for those who
have never sailed, who trawl anchorless for memory.
A word for those who know maps and their
unlanded catastrophes: cartographers.

I have made miniatures, of course, born of thrashing
about in waters that listen and speak, but have no
answer for desperate mothers who take out their
breasts and rend themselves on the shore, calling
until their drowned children answer at the surface,
their bodies an echo of the sound they no longer
make, the breath they no longer hold, for brothers
who bawl and try to throw themselves from cliffs,
who eat sand—we know, those of us who have
pretended at drowning until we come to know it
intimately, that the Sea (like History) is monologic.

1 We had spent most of our energy consuming each other in the rented house in Buccoo the year I almost drowned at Store Bay. *One last dip*, I had said, taunting the sea, whose waves swelled as the water pushed toward the shore. Having nowhere to spread, the waves crested but barely broke the way the waves might do at Swallows or Castara.

Bell No. 2, for Cudjoe

Here is an imagined captain: "I could tell you if you
want to know. Real[2] men find their death in them
waters, oui. Even some partners of mine and all,
who swear they know the sea. How long I have to
wait for this rum, for me to tell the story right?"[3]

Before we descended like aimless *corbeaux* to the
shore, we might have understood what it was that
drove the people inland—further in, with sanded
skins, from Chacachacare.
(Is that Maracaibo or Macuro, my love? Yes, my love.)

Looking out from the road to La Fillette, casting
imagination over the indelicate hump behind us, the
Northern Range became the stone-axed rim of a
chasm cut deep enough for history to make a
catacomb of its people's memory.

Bocas.[4]

Angry swell that only seemed to make the islands,
broken off the tip of Trinidad. Crumbs from
unleavened bake left on the counter. Serpent's
Mouth. Dragon's. Mouths open to swallow
pirogues—bows pointed skyward like the broken
aristocracy, sterns half-sunken, undignified, for the
drowning poor—their displacements.

2 A unit of im|measure: *many, plenty, countless*.

3 Pirogues' captains are uncommissioned but are named Dionne, Curtis, Cleve. No astrolabe. No compass.

4 N 10°45'00", W 61°46'00"

Remember the imagined captains,
the dreams of a crew:
Are these the ones who lost the belly, and too many
stubborn stubborn brothers, to it? Are mother and
daughter also swallowed? Open your mouth for
them, now.

Open, like the Bocas.

For those who longed to mourn: your paid lovers,
your unpaid family, your diluted blood, your found
bodies, your bloated immigrants, your shelled
martyrs turning back to salt, bones rebellious with
age, scattered and gray in silt and salt and thirst for
the decisive end of breath.

Everybody knew, those waves rolling a rhythm
as steady as the mile markers that looked (to the east)
like Scarborough. Crown Point. The impossible sight
of Speyside, Charlotteville, Tobago, from the boat at dusk.
Ask the cartographers, they know. There, like
instinct, present like a macumé or a stone lodged in
the heart.[5]

Smokers who flick hard with every drag before the
ash could grow never rush to talk about lunatic
waters. Who know, with nods and dancing smoke,
clothes ever damp with pity, that tide is both syntax
and mood? Loss is literacy. Language, the
architecture of love. Love, care of the ruined. Like
old men who laugh, embers jumping off their
tongues like the rock divers at Macqueripe, hurdling
twice-broken and unset fingers like dogs hunting in
the bush?

5 Who is *everybody* here?

The Sea.

This Sea: impatient enough to raid its own vaults, not
given to lingerers or crowds, a ruthless mimic of
time bored with itself, wagering on the exhausted
stroke, mother and father to orphan and widow,
leaving its shore bound with grief for pole, sorrow
for tackle, with hands wrung around like *douens*.

And what to stand with brush to color, or anxious
poet's hand, or glassed, flattering eye to marvel at,
then? The quiet efficiency of the water, its
unceremonious taking, black bodies glistening like ebony
weights? Some distant romance of men, their own
gods, casting nets wide for dolphin, flailing as
Gasparee slept in spite of their noise? Had they not
trawled some days ago for vagrant dead when they,
too, sank and surfaced?

Where had mothers, like salted pillars, wished to
hide, before breasts held fast beneath blended cotton
brassieres rushed here to burst, blue-black, wild and
untuned, from them—wrinkles cut across their
chests like drying muck—calling their children to land?

To Land.

Whose hip is that?
Whose pelvis have you learned to wear
like a mask?
What is this shade of blue? It is, of course, the blue
in which my mother, terrified of the water, stoops
and washes herself, in which I turn away and try to
make a meditation of the frigate birds.

Bell No. 3

There is no other question, no upsurging from my
gut as I, half-swallowed by this place, cast my vision
north to Chacachacare with its iodine vials crushed
underfoot, its bullet-riddled partitions and petitions
of who want to do what to whose mother and
daughter and son, its whispers of Venezuelan boat
men who dock in secret and trek to the reservoir, its
whoooop
whoooop
whoooop
whoooop
whoooop
whoooop
whooooping of the early roosting *corbeaux* behind the
doctor's house.

ICACOS

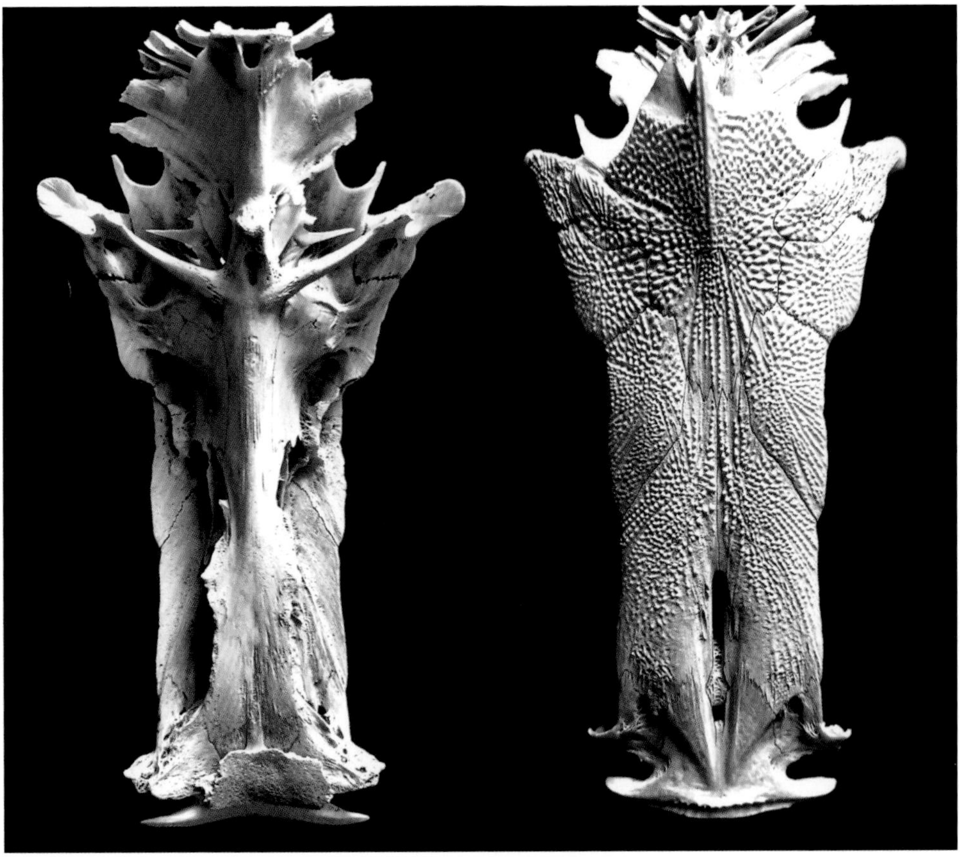

The stillness
of formerly moving parts and the suggestion
of movement that occurs elsewhere (having once moved),
of light hardened into bone,
of an action desiccated and immortalized,
the picture of an object long vacated

by the eye.

PALO SECO

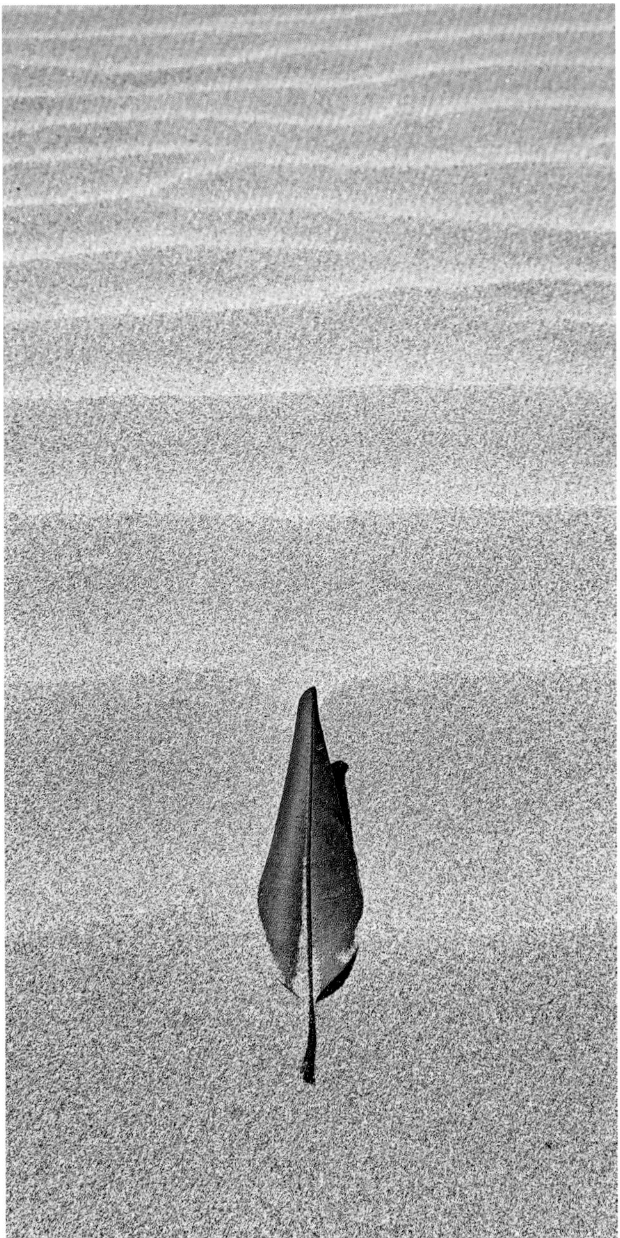

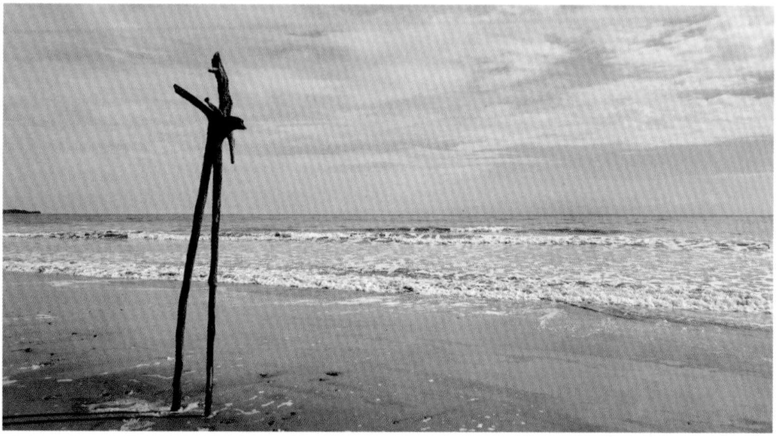

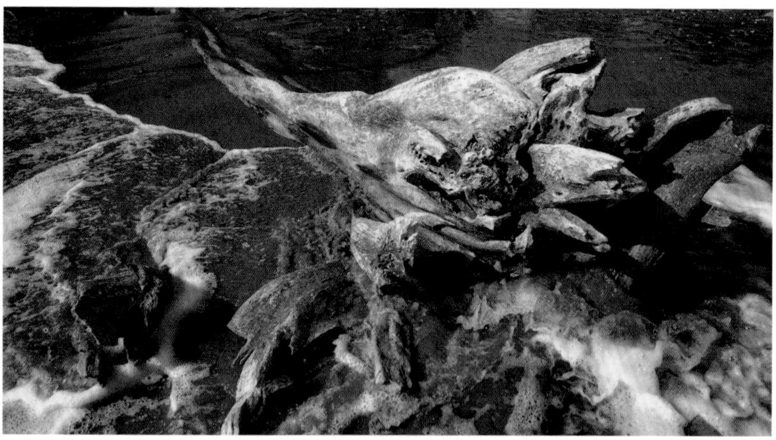

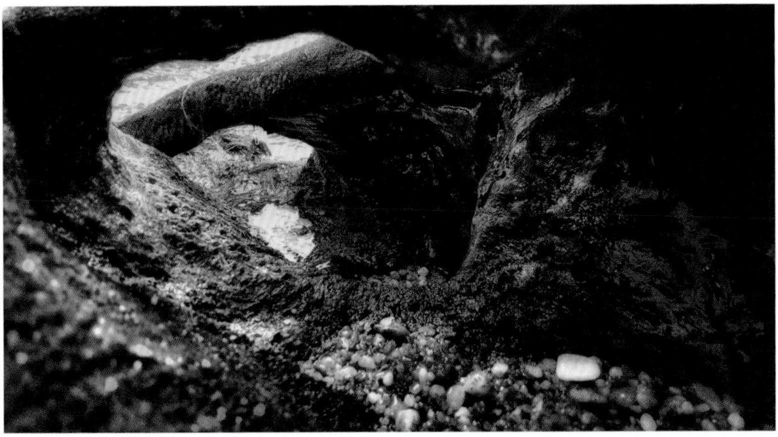

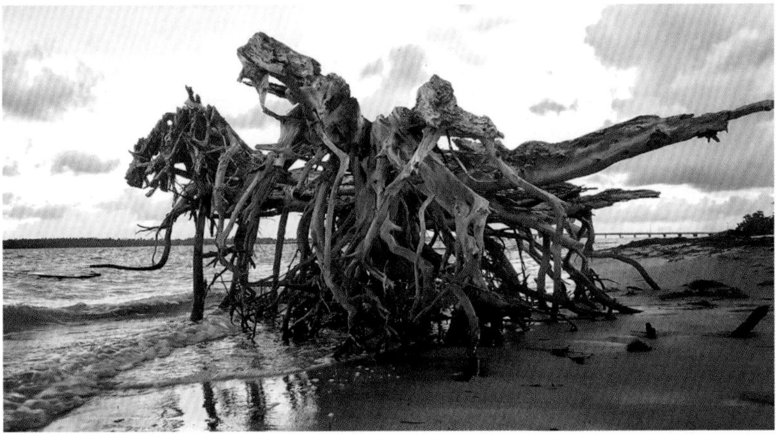

MAYARO

Black children will
punctuate the pages of the sea like bookmarks.
Silhouetted bathers staining the water's edge

like an oil spill, or the flotsam at Mayaro,
where the last of the palms are unlit torches
bending, blowing toward the ubiquity of a wreck.

I had walked for years along the bared teeth of the sea
and, once, sat to understand the fury of the breaching seabird,
washed my face where the wrinkled mudbanks of the Ortoire shine.

Later, I wrestle only with a cerulean thought:
The keel will always be perpendicular to the horizon.
Upturned, its inversion demands a righting for the upturner.

You are always midway between bow and stern that say
I cannot be measured with astrolabe or compass.
Alive, not yet in the wake.[1]

Dedication: For my brother Nicholai, who died on May 1, 2023, in Midland, a small town in Texas. He was forty-one. He was my father's first son with his wife Lynette, whom I called Aunty Lynette. He *was*.

1 Reprise of an earlier reprise:
What happens when there is water and a boat but no wake? What is lost (and loss) in this too fluid grounding? What remains? What must "captain" and "passenger" be, from what can their meanings be derived but the silence?
Here, *you* is: Intent. Direction. Motion. Consequence. *Wake*. Poetry crawls through the mangrove of the brain, punctual as the leatherback.

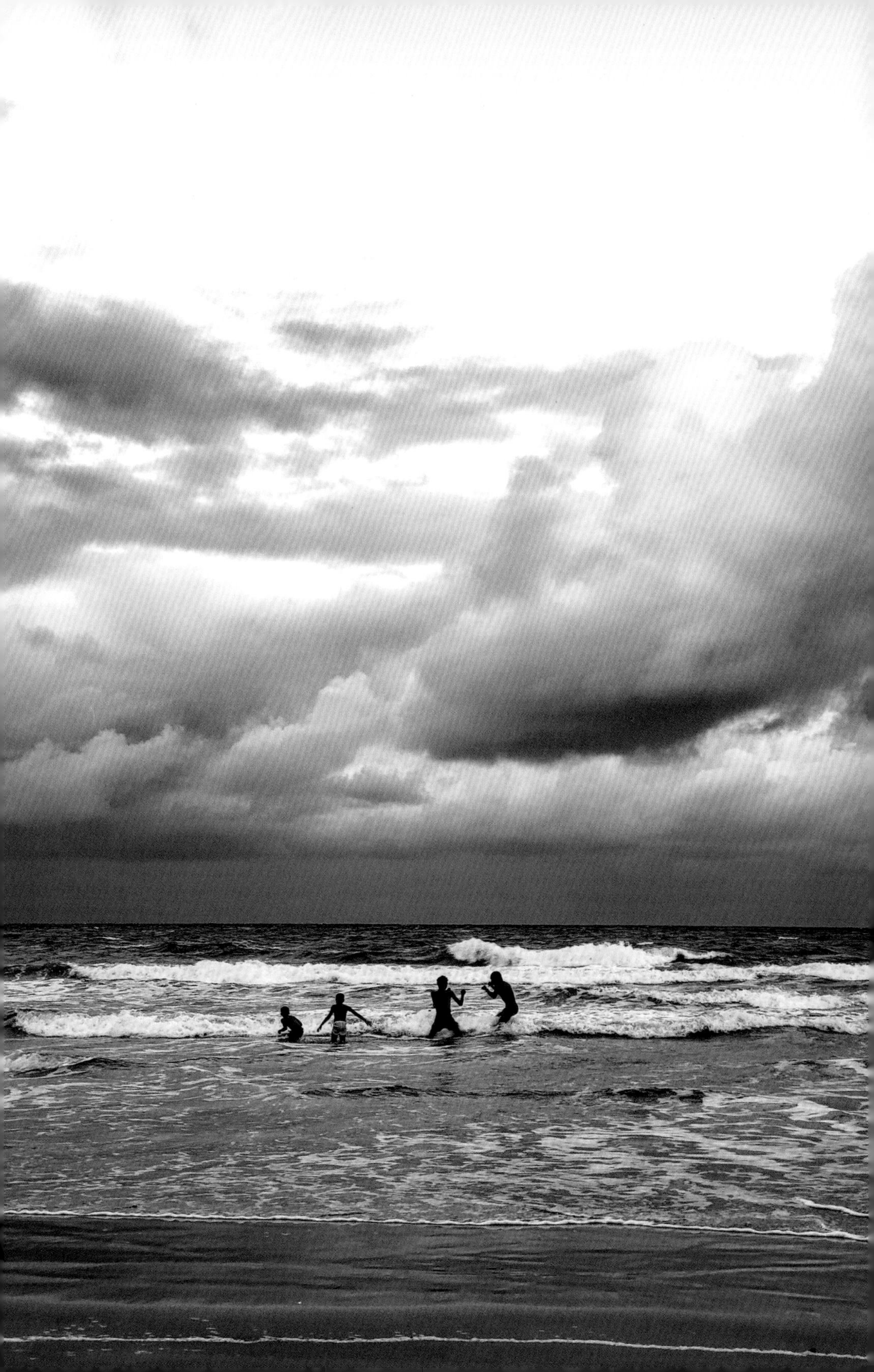

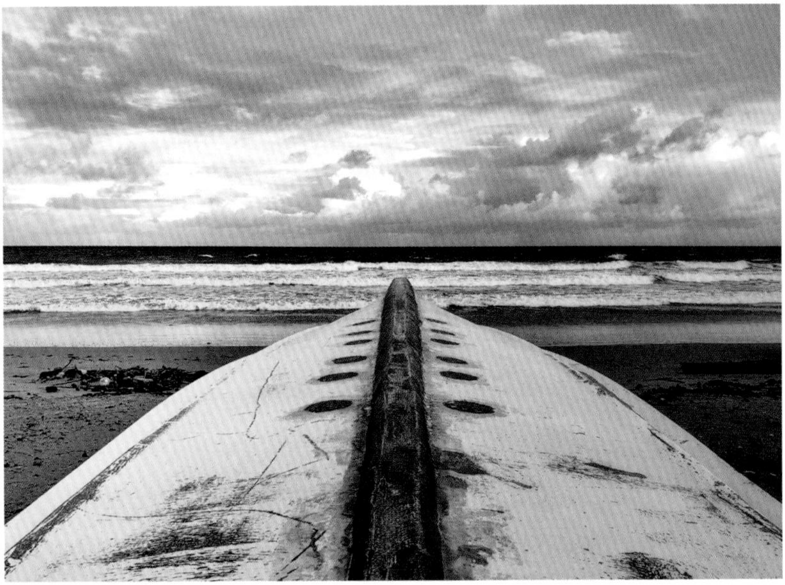

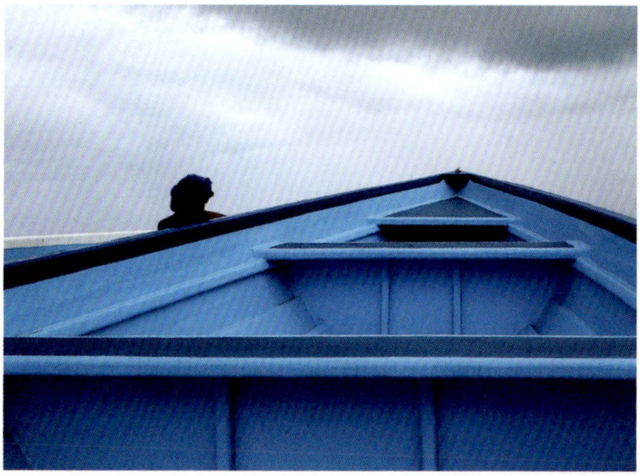

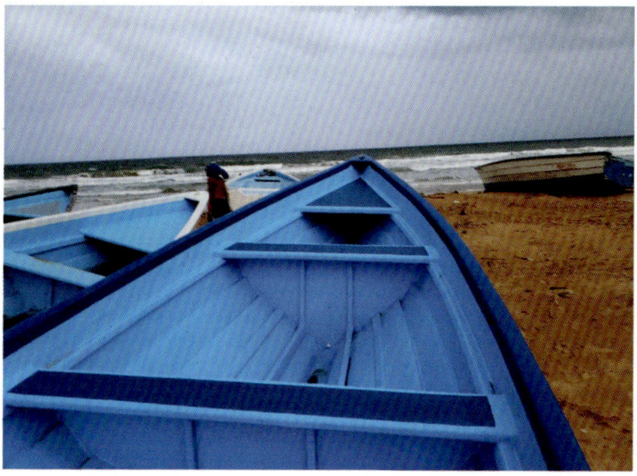

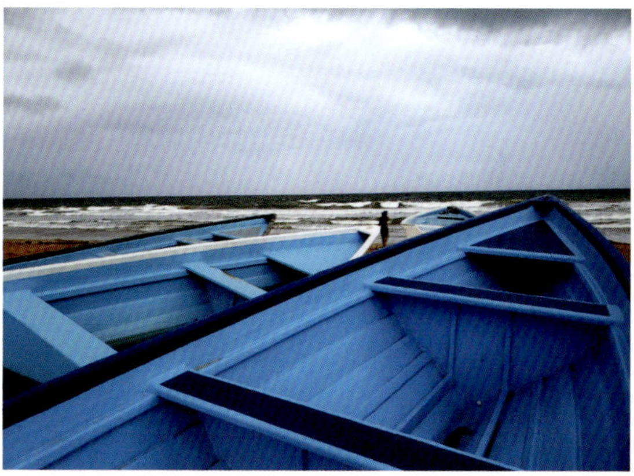

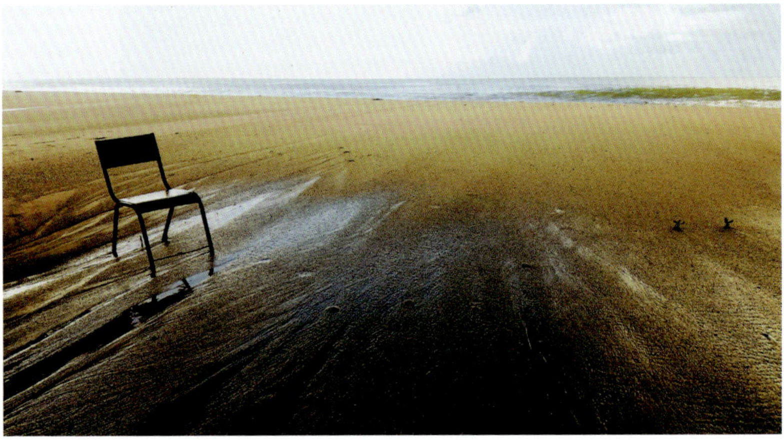

BASSE-TERRE

Art form ruin
Form art ruin
Ruin form art
Ruin art form
Form ruin art
Art ruin form
—a poem[1]

As I've come upon them here and there, it has occurred to me that our ruins are not ruins at all. Rather, by allowing us to "discover" evidence of an erasure that has already happened, they appear intended to evoke a sense of empire's endurance, its inherent self-contempt. At least, as it has been imagined by those who have inherited the memory yet strain for the experience of what it was. (Some of us are "independent," after all.) I am thinking of places whose enduring meanings rise or fall to the apparent "prestige" of ruin. I wonder what is the fate of a society that rises and falls to matters of status—the granulated patois of Caribbean "class"—that it has internalized but may not be as cohesive or as stable as it promises to be. Ruin, in this sense, is an invention designed to ensure the absence of intimacy. It effectively outlasts the performative "rejection" of imperial rule in our declarations of independence, along with the illusion of "nation" and "country." As such, it is possible to read ruin as a defiance, an expression of the tacit refusal by the "sovereign" or "self-determined" state to accept that it—and, perhaps, its citizens—remains in the hold of an empire that considers itself eternal.

1 *AA-BC-BC*, essentially.

For the sake of style, I will call it the "seduction of the patina" of ruin, but by every reasonable measure it is a matter of failed aspiration, a version of Caribbean life viewed only as a thing that exists in service of the greater thing—the sense of a "national" identity presented as a synecdoche of empire's obstinacy, of its tendency toward ruin. Ruin of others. Ruin of itself. So what you (as citizen, exile, scholar, or tourist) happen to see in this or that building poorly kept is not only a pretended rejection of empire for the sake of keeping up appearances, but also the ironic embrace of it—an embrace that is expressed in the simultaneous refusal to change, the rejection of aging, the literal oldness of its leftovers in a more local form, the inevitable dissipation of its form interrupted—*preserved*. An embrace that allows those appearances to come apart.

The ambivalence of empire toward its colonies is now the ambivalence of that (former) colony toward itself, viewed as it is through the imported lens of an empire whose self-contempt yields nothing but ruin—a self-contempt deteriorated into the absence of a self. What you see, then, is the enduring tendency of our creolized sensibilities to be represented as the bones and shells of things, as stains on the material consciousness of our "built heritage." Ruin, here, is more than the celebration of heritage, or the remembrance of that misguided aspiration to the inevitable rot of empire, not merely to what Empire might once have been. It is also a reminder of what we, in this unreal place, *could never possess*.

Sometimes, on account of their age, empires are measured by their ruins—measured eventually by the inevitability and scale of their ruin, but that is another story. This is not the unfair thing. The unfair thing is that while ruin is the absence of intimacy, intimacy is *not* the absence of ruin. Ruin, in fact, is intimacy's singular promise. This is the case especially if it is a colonial building, an old, unkept house for example, with its fretwork dangling like drunkards' teeth, its siding scarred like untreated lepers—their former parts unknown—then all the better. A government building, whose finials once looked like sharpened whalebones but now lean blunted by disregard, after the pipes and planks have gone, after being gutted of its employees and their covered shoulders, their closed shoes, their forgotten lives delivered in triplicate, triply forgotten (and forgotten).

A Brief Inventory of Perpetual Ruins:
A brick.
A rusted nail evicted. A phallic bolt fixed.
A pickaxe undone by stone. Stone.
A pot.
A pothound (this one alive, for now, though we know his fate).

Also,
An empty form strewn across floorboards like a metaphor.
An empty form of a building, its painted skin removed, its shingled roof and copper wires gone, on whose floor an empty form blows.
An empty form of a man bending like an archipelago behind the infant stroller (also empty) stops to empty himself against a wall near Lapeyrouse, at the overpass on the Southern Main Road, by the post office in Sangre Grande.

Also,
Some errant "piper" almost electrocuted for his trouble.
Some family installed on a corner like a monument—the minor monuments of its aging children.
Some archaic fixture standing dismantled at the junction—his and her and their apathies preserved in sun-and-rain-beaten skin.

Everywhere in every ruin is the absence of intimacy. It is *abject*. This is true whatever its era, whether it was filled with objects or with empty space, whether filled with people or their memories—or memories of them that linger in the objectified abstraction of stone and petrified wood. In the absence of the quarried boulders built up with bone and mortar, an insurgent army of nuts and bolts, nails and spikes. How they warm and stay warm even after the sun has set. Whatever they may be, I know this much: I have never seen an intimate ruin.

Of course, any preoccupation with the impermanence of intimacy is academic —it is not supposed to matter to the person who feels it: the lover, the child, the aging mother of mine, the aged man who will crumble and fall between his grandchildren's fingers like gravel from his own unpaved yard. It cannot matter to them that intimacy will end, that it *must*. Because all things end. Love (which I have said I am after in this book) will end as well, perhaps even before I find it. That is left to be seen. But the certainty of ruin—which is also the certainty of change—is a certainty that counteracts the illusion of permanence. Ruin itself is impermanent, intermediate, but it will nevertheless outlast intimacy, even the insistent intimacy of our visitations, our insistent witness. It insists on what must be: an inevitability. Even in our latter-day forts—such as the one in Basse-Terre, built and abandoned in our brief lifetimes—the insistence on our passing resounds: this is its design. This is where I see its value in my consideration of artistic method.

Regarding artistic method—that is, a way of making, and of making my way to and through the things I make—I see the ironic embrace of ruin as an expression of aesthetic and rhetorical agency, a deliberative grasp of the present, of things as they are, through which a deeper sense of presence may be grasped, as well as what it may ultimately be able to endure:

> Ruin of the image with digital tools—the tools themselves that hardly ever come to ruin.
> Ruin of the artifact by environmental means—sun, and wind, and rain.
> Ruin of the archive with the desecrating touch.
> Ruin of the work by design or distress—the performance of distress that can sanctify, even if it is at the expense of the thing made (that bears the evidence of that distress) or at the expense of the maker (who appears not to, though we know he must be).
> Ruin of your—and, at times, my—visit to the islands with talk of Ruin.
> Ruin of the ruin by building on top of it and letting that building rot—rot anew—into a ruin.

Ruin that is bound to occur because it is *bound to* intimacy—to the experience of it. The living and the dying know this.

What does it mean to live in a state of ruin? It means, first of all, to recognize the implicit contradiction of "living" in "a state of ruin." To sit (not unlike a ruin) with the obscenity of the idea. Then, considering (as we have been attempting to do) the notion of Ruin as an invention that can be revised, we see that while it can certainly be read as a localized expression of an imported desire (a need to be seen that overshadows wanting to be understood), it can nevertheless be revised for a somewhat more provocative approach, which is neither imperial nor colonial (a need to see that undermines merely wanting to understand, and then to act on what one has seen).

Bringing myself as close to ruin as time and space will allow, I contend with its imagined sovereignty. I am not yet beyond being seduced. But, held in the plaited arms of these islands' noises, I take a moment to ask, What do I know of empire that I have not read, or learned to covet, or coveted of my own freed will? What is there to know of myself and my people that only ruin can teach? What have I dared to make (of) myself, to ruin with intent? Am I ready yet to dismantle the frame of this nostalgia, to pick apart the beams and boards, its brittle bones that look so much like mine? The time will come for me to say. The time will come when saying will not be enough. For the moment, I know only that ruin is the absence of intimacy, and that there is no intimate ruin, except what may exist in the gaze, the witness, and the act: the gaze turned tenderly to witness, and witness turned necessarily to act.

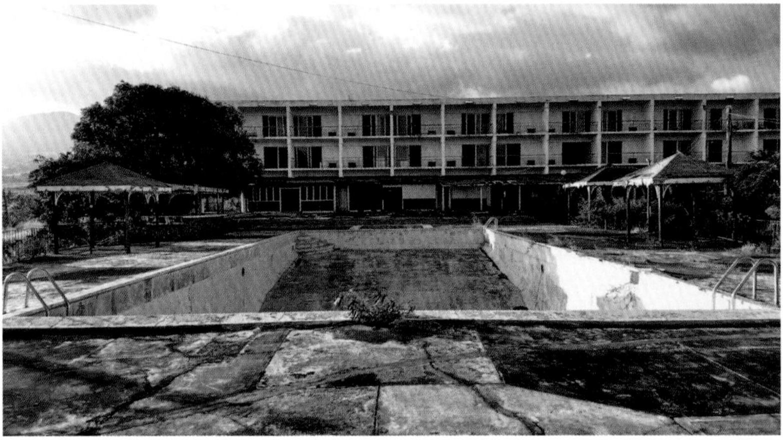

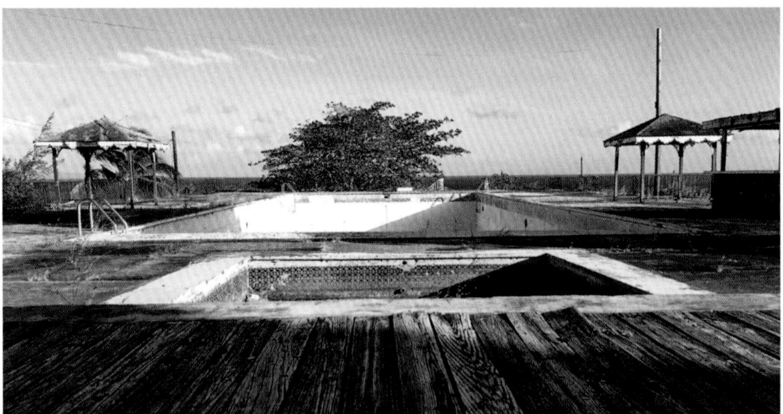

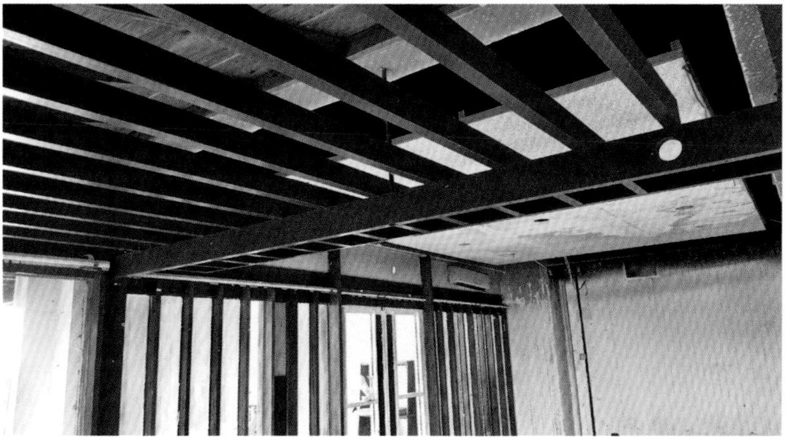

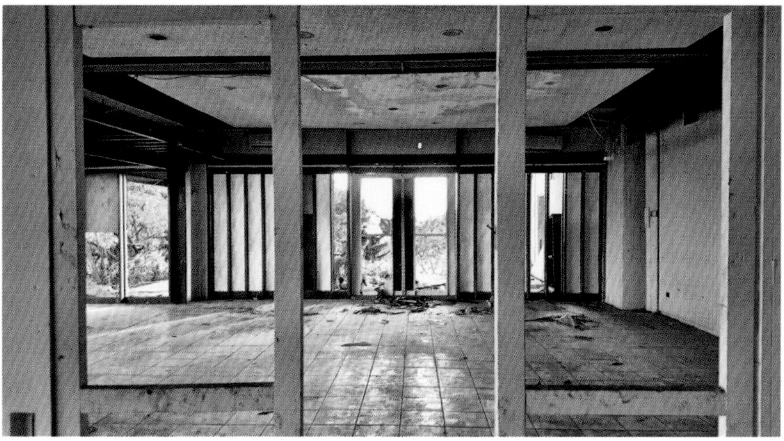

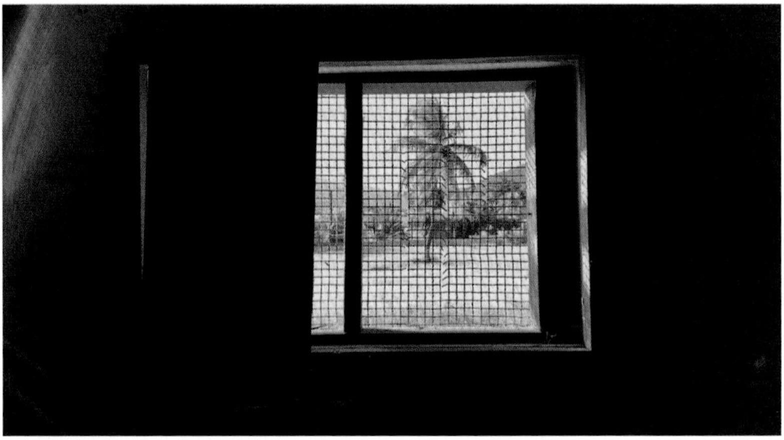

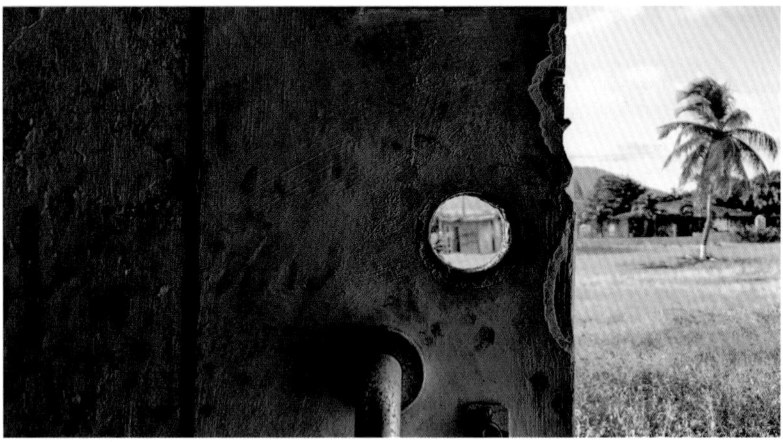

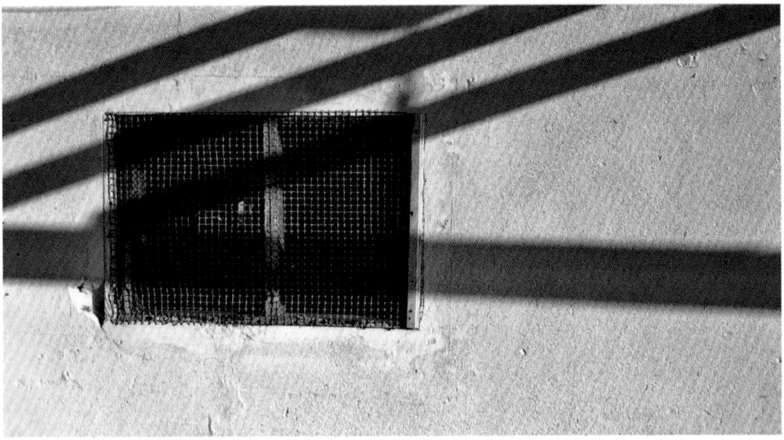

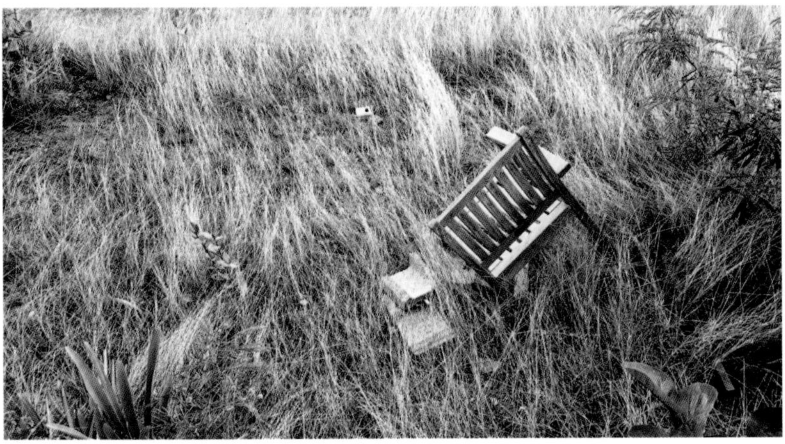

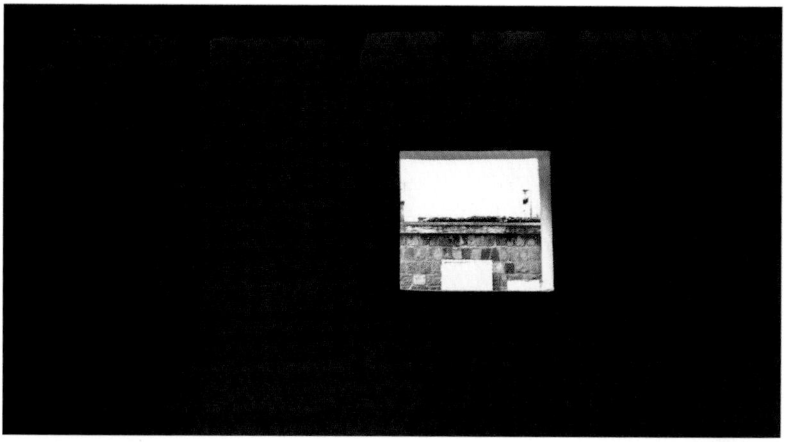

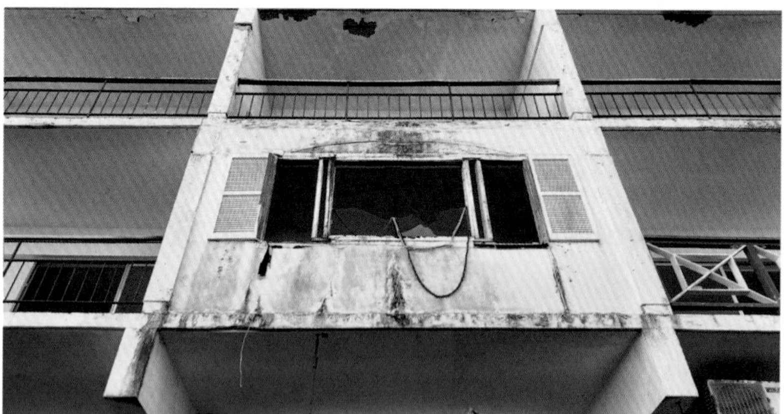

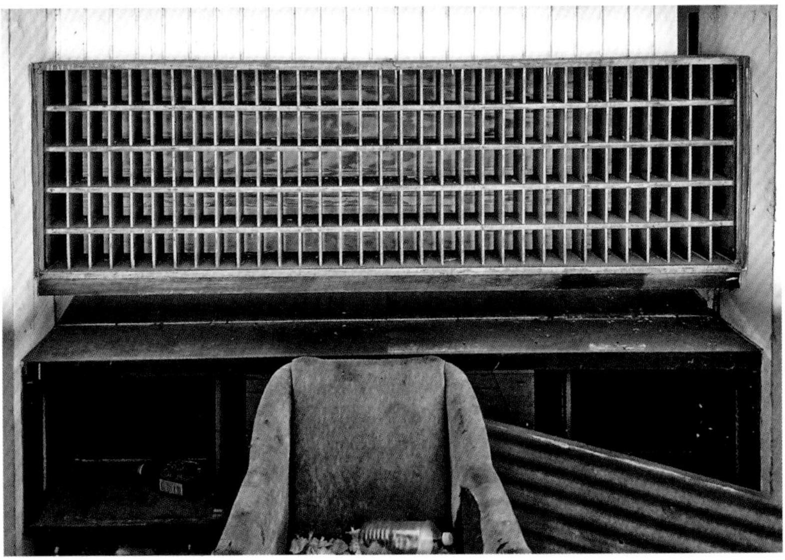

HOME

Go.
Come when ah call yuh, eh.
Whey yuh gone?

"Home" is what you feel it is,
and i's not just what you know it is.[1]
What that mean?
It mean i's a tautology.
It mean i's a *douen*.
It mean i's bound it bound[2] to haunt you.
You cyah go where it cyah find you.
You cyah run from it,
and it cyah run from you.
I's yours.

1 *I's*: Pronounced "is," as in C. L. R. James's *Minty Alley* (1936). My use of it here is epistemic and temporal, for in the transition from "it is" to "i's" to an enunciated "is," there is a tenuous subjectivity that imposes itself (an "I"), while simultaneously troubling the obstinacy of an overtly objectivist referent (the "it")—softening it, balancing it.

2 I will not explain this repetition. It is bound within itself, a binding doubly bound ought not be explained. There are bindings and unbindings throughout.

And once i's yours, i's yours.[3]
And it going and walk with you,
and it going and talk to you even if you doh talk back.
And it going and follow you[4]—till you pick it up.

3 Say this a few times. Say *it's* as I say it here, without the *t*, as if it were a softened, somewhat more balanced *is*. The orthography, you notice, is subtle enough to be misread as orthography *alone*, but it is orthography *masquerading* as orthography *alone*—it is far more, with a complexity that resides in the ironic expansiveness of the contraction. Notice, too, that the pronoun is not supplanted; rather, the "it" is impli(cat)ed in the "I" as the subject becomes embedded in the verb, such that the mercuriality of being, we are reminded, is bound to|with|in the doing: *I is. I's. It's. It is. It is I.**

Then there is, as you may recall: *You is. You's. You're. I's you.*

4 Note the "going and" as process *and* intention: *going to*. It is temporal and spatial, in that the intention to occupy a particular space in the future is *both* a question of *when* (are you going to?) and *where* (are you going to?).

* "It is I, as in, 'I have arrived.'" Contraction here is a diffusion that discloses: an "I" that one may, if so inclined, "see"—an "I" that declares "I is" in lieu of a more refined "I am." How do its subsequent iterations remake what I might have thought, what I might have intended, or what you or I might have or might still see? The fact that James removes the "t" but leaves the apostrophe redirects the tone and tenor of the contraction, making it more of a deliberate address to the reader than a reference to the sociolinguistic peculiarities of the respective characters in the novel. That is, the *apostrophe* functions more (faith)fully, more expansively, as a rhetorical device for addressing who or what may not be present at the time of the address—at, say, the moment of conception or composition—but whose presence is nevertheless anticipated. An arrival that is sensed ahead of its advent. For James, this trope|tropic action is the narrativistic counterbalance to the more familiar trope of migration—em|immigration in the offing—that makes it all the more complete, for it is equipped with a sense of arrival that precedes both the impending departure and the arrival to come.

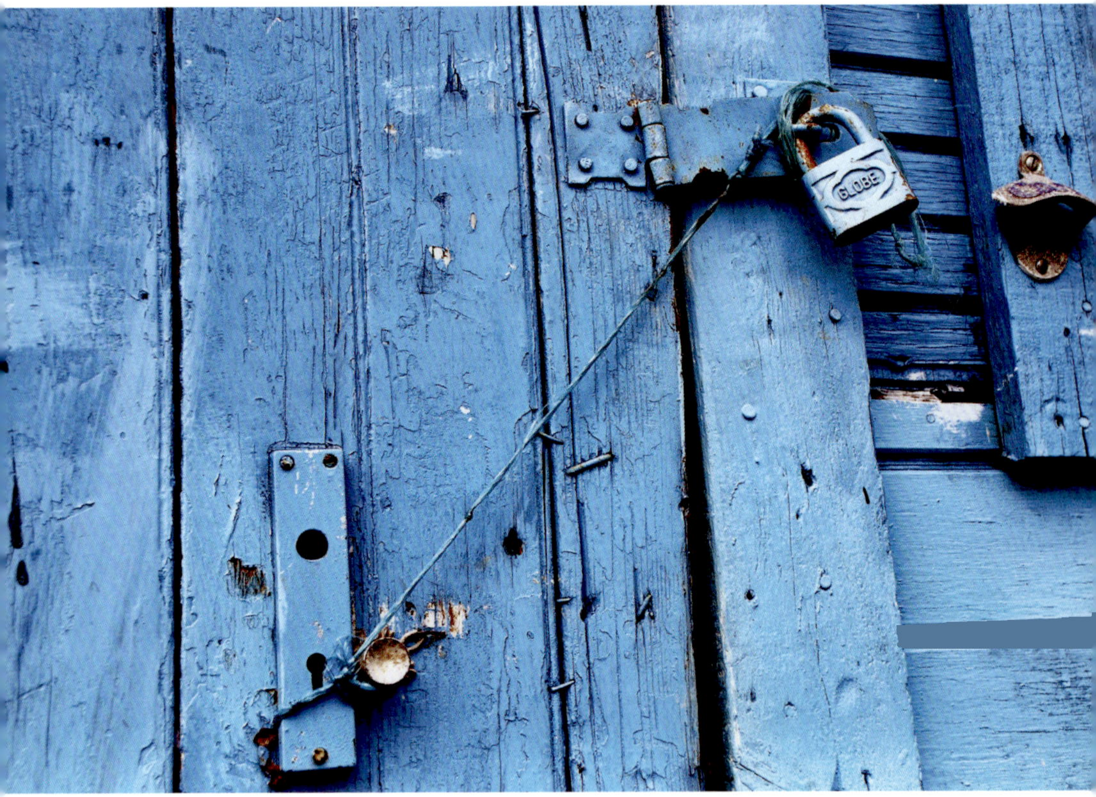
GLOBE

Sometimes i's a house, sometimes a room,
where each pyrrhic victory was once chronicled
with matchsticks laid out like natives on the unsound table
between us,

where we argued like gods, over them, imagined
gutting the gilded empires
that hung on a gesture of hidden hand and twisted brow—
a Jack, hung like a bobolee for his carelessness.[5]

Time, engorged, bursts.
The stillness passes
too near amnesia—into panic.

Where are you, that we no longer
see the same egret dancing on the water-bison,
on the perpetual mud of its skin, its heavy mystery of flesh
in slow motion?
Or the ones that attend the bushfires like pundits
at the pyres on the creek, or cross the highway like embers loosed
from the flickering lights at Point Lisas—
or is it Pointe-à-Pierre?

What happened that we missed
our islands growing smaller beneath our feet,
our mothers nursing us only partially?
Now, not at all—we grow and forfeit
the first inheritance.[6]

5 Not for the carelessness of his King and Queen, whose earlier rounds pass unthreatened.
6 But we know better than that:

a place without memory can have no mother,
a place without memory can have no children.

Mothers are born of memory—children are borne by it.
A place without memory will not know what to do with its children.
It will eat them. It must. This is how it thinks it will survive.

(We are in its belly, in the recesses of the gut,
churned up and half-digested, only thinking
we have survived its swallowing.)

And sometimes i's a place of innumerable emptinesses, most deeply felt in your distance from it, or what you say is its distance from you. Even gone, you are here—"home." It has been said that you are "home" when you no longer cast your eyes toward river boulders as if they were bodies—you will already know they are.[7] You "home" when you become so inured to the barrage of local hostilities that the noise of that barrage and the sound of burning bush and falling rain are the same thing.

When you fear a little less the phrases of "last" things: last drinks at the bar behind the funeral home, last dips in waves that swell into the bay, last looks of leaving lovers. When the throng of black(ened) bodies bounding down the hill toward you like Shadow's Abyssinia cause no fear, you here.[8]

When you gone past the futility of your escape, past the acceptance of it, past the default of your sometimes belonging, to realize just how shaken you is, to feel the cartilage between your arthritic self-denials wear away. When the cascadura causes no anxiety, you here.

I's what you feel it is, not just what you feel you know it is.

7 This familiarity, though it is an extension of the kind of particularity Édouard Glissant invokes in his notion of "archipelagic thought," this granular attention is nevertheless *unbearable*. For, between the philosophy and the geography that define the perimeter of archipelagic thought are the bodies embroiled in both the symbolic and material experiences they inhere—the bearable body of a child is unbearable.* Our bodies can no sooner escape this feature of the archipelagic encounter than our imaginations can be bound by it.

8 Mighty Shadow, "Pay de Devil."

* This morning, May 10, 2022, at around 10:54, the body of toddler Kymani Francis was found in the Guapo River, after wandering off. A neighbor reported seeing him roaming. A *neighbor*. Memory is how we keep the gruesome record—a place without memory can have no children.

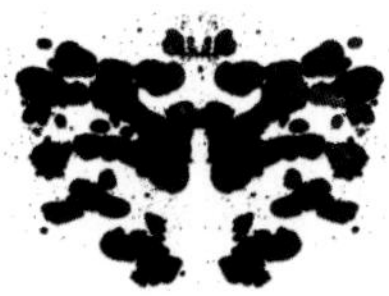

ONUS

History and its ruination are the cost
we have paid for the privilege of telling our story.[1]
So, let us begin again, some distance inland.
Not with *By whose or what authority do I . . . ?*
as we are known to ask, trying to avoid
the unavoidable strain of thinking for—
and about—ourselves.

1 *Whose* history?

Some years ago, looking south from the porch of the house I was renting in Maracas Valley, I imagined that the lights I saw on the blackened horizon ended just past the city of Chaguanas, edging perhaps into Chase Village.[2] I glanced through the open window behind me. The philodendron in the glass jar on the sewing machine was climbing slow and wild toward the ceiling, its rooting stones dark and mossy. Years would pass before it would deign to bloom. I stretched as Millie Jackson's cover of "If Loving You Is Wrong" (1974) blasted like a barrage from one side of the valley to the next, its location lost somewhere in the bush. I looked south again before the horns went out, before her insistent "I don't want to be right!" subsided and mixed into "Midnight Train to Georgia" (1973) by Gladys Knight and the Pips. Perfect silence soon after, then (soon after that) a repeat of them both.

Turning to go in, and with the air heavy with the remains of some earlier fire farther up the valley, I recalled William Blake's erotic[3] illustrations in John Gabriel Stedman's memoir of his military exploits in Suriname. Stedman's job—his duty as a soldier—was killing maroons, black people who dared to free themselves.[4] I learn years later that Stedman's *The Narrative of a Five Years Expedition against the Revolted Slaves of Surinam* (1796) was not intended as an abolitionist text, as it had come to be known; its words were revised to align with what the author called the "beautiful horror" of black death, the horror of whiteness normalized with shot and blade, with gavel and rope, with whip and chain. However whitewashed, the familiar invitation to the cruel spectacle of History bleeds through.

2 A bird's-eye view will call this Central Trinidad, the ostensible torso of the island—or, if you see what looks less like an island and more like a discarded boot from a Mas costume, it would be the upper ankle. From where I stood that night, it was as far south as I could see, so call it south.

3 . . .

4 Black freedom, for some, is a terribly illicit thing.

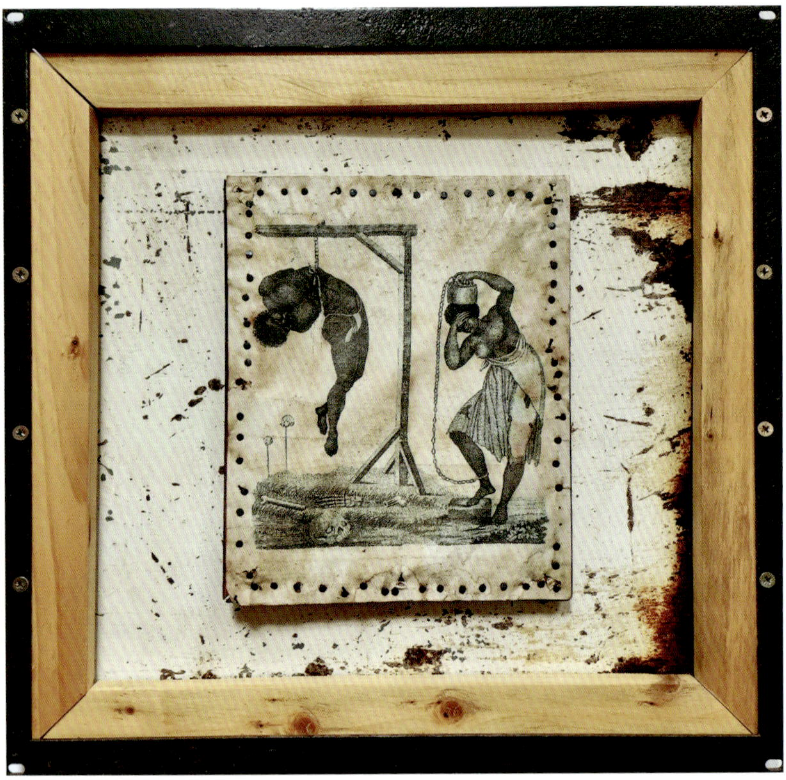

Regarding the pornography of black suffering and its canonization in the early art of this region, you will have to know for yourself whether or not there should be tenderness in your questions of black representation, whether or not your distance will save you from what you see and remember—or see and forget. As you do, consider the indelible *inhumanity* of whiteness that is always an all too certain horror, one so abject that even the negative space—here appearing to be grounded on the block, compartmentalized in the architecture of the scaffolding and the rope and the chain—is also conscripted into the service of its violence, its cascading violations.

Inside, I recalled the monstrosity of Thomas Thistlewood's self-described "methods" of punishment and sexual violence against black people in Jamaica with an intensified horror. Another colonial nonfiction. Another nastiness.[5] Think, momentarily, of his calculus—when, for example, the difference between a human and its inverse was determined not merely by skin color but by the position of the defecating body and the body being defecated on|into—then tell me the path I must take through this nonfiction that does not ultimately lead to my ruin. What (other than the abject refusal of this shit) should any one of us wanting freedom do? Do I separate classic black beauty from the subjection of blackness when they appear more respectably in the neoclassical style of Brunias or the later lithographs of Cazabon?

It is not a question, in such a case, of what one would prefer, when *preference* for the bound body would be essentially a discursive impossibility (except as a "preference" for the body to be bound). Rather, reading through these calculi to that of Stedman's confessions and Blake's engraving, and reading them all as a foil for my critique of their story in *Onus*, I wonder if the question is whether an inconceivable (impossible) blackness that we encounter in the hold of whiteness can ever be truly held by it.

Regarding the pornography of History—the art of violent remembrance—maybe the question is also whether any engagement with them can emancipate the archivist from the hold of particular tropes, traps, and narratives.

For me, the answer to both questions is *nah*.

This is what *Tabanca Onus* is: a *nah*. It holds a self-reflexive refusal, which is what the sentiment of *tabanca* insists for Caribbean people: a denial of *what is* in spite of the virtual impossibility of *what might be*. Here, it is a dream whose expressive energy is unharnessed from the historical representative and simply

5 A catalog similar in content is found in C. L. R. James's *Black Jacobins* and will not be reproduced here.

left to be whatever it will. *Art,* in this instance, is made of what remains. At times, it is the painful proof of what has been lost. Loss can be as seductive as patina. Terror, a charm.[6]

Tabanca Onus, in spite of all it attempts to frame (and frame), aspires to a lasting emptiness. Not a refusal of the factuality of the text or its historical representation—we know too well what has happened to us, what has outlived every archive to be as present in the body as slug and blade, as fresh in the mind as birdsong. So, as an artifact corroborated by other accounts of like brutality, its factuality is hardly subject to refutation. What I mean is that it endures and protests, arguing (as we might argue) to be seen:

See it and see despair.
See ourselves in despair.
See ourselves as art hung.
See ourselves as art—
hung by the ribs, hung by the neck, hung on a wall.
See ourselves driven into the soil—
driven by our own hands into the soil, like a pike.
See ourselves as a pike, driven to death,
the inevitability of death.
Buried. Out in the open.

I say, *Nah.*

Seeing, if it is to be anything meaningful to us, must be something else: a kind of deliberate unbelieving if not a move to believe the unbelievable bodies you see on the page, in the frame, and in the mirror.

See, instead, every nail—about fifty.
See them as prising open the frame that
looks like an open box, in which the myth
of our innate savagery and our supernatural
ability to survive it are said to be contained,
disciplined to death.

6 If I take too close to heart the fact that this place is not intended for black life, I would have to conclude that it is a place whose people would prefer that we were dead or had not existed in the first place. It would also mean that I'd be a specter in a stage of development, a human-shaped prototype of a ghost in a machine designed for our eradication. My black Caribbean life is a daring that leans, like a gesture, toward *sublimity.*

> And see its distress, the distressing I have
> deliberately caused. Its defacement. See
> that, too.
> See its *mise en abyme* as a prelude to a later
> framing of *tabanca*, its cruelty redirected to
> other|ed ends, of ends to come, in which
> the framed is reframed, and the (as yet)
> unframed is framed in advance of its later
> framing.[7]

It is a seeing whose subjections seem to be lost somewhere in the bush, or grow slow and wild before our eyes. A seeing that refuses the ease of spectacle. I'm thinking of that line "the best thing I ever had" as I note how casually—how "naturally"—we are directed to regard the distinction of sex and gender in this image, forced to regard the obscene complementarity in the spatial arrangement of their bodies and to compare the brutalities perpetually applied to them.[8] To look, and to see, is to behold and be held by abjection, distinctions of abjection repeated like islands, genres of pain eroticized and unbelieved. Seeing that refuses.

I admit my anxiety, which sees me grasping almost desperately for the inherent brutality of the archive for the *least* of what it can provide: proof of us, of us having been, of having stayed, of having run, of having been caught, of having been . A line in the litany of us. To me, the disruption of this affinity portends a coming absence, an emptying however temporary, of what can feel like love leaving in its realization a void we must now be inclined to re|fill. This is a form of *tabanca*. For we are also inclined to ask *With what?* and not always have an answer.

I cannot say what you will use to re|fill what you have emptied, but speaking for myself, I begin by imagining the very action of that emptying—that is, the deliberate *inversion* of the image—basing my re|reading on what it now appears to yield:

7 In truth, neither will be frameable in the end. This is one of the conceits of Caribbean nonfiction, an unfolding question of its in|exteriority and its ex|interiority.

8 One may see in this complementarity a precursor of Blake's logic in his depiction of Albion in *Milton: A Poem in Two Books* (1804–10).

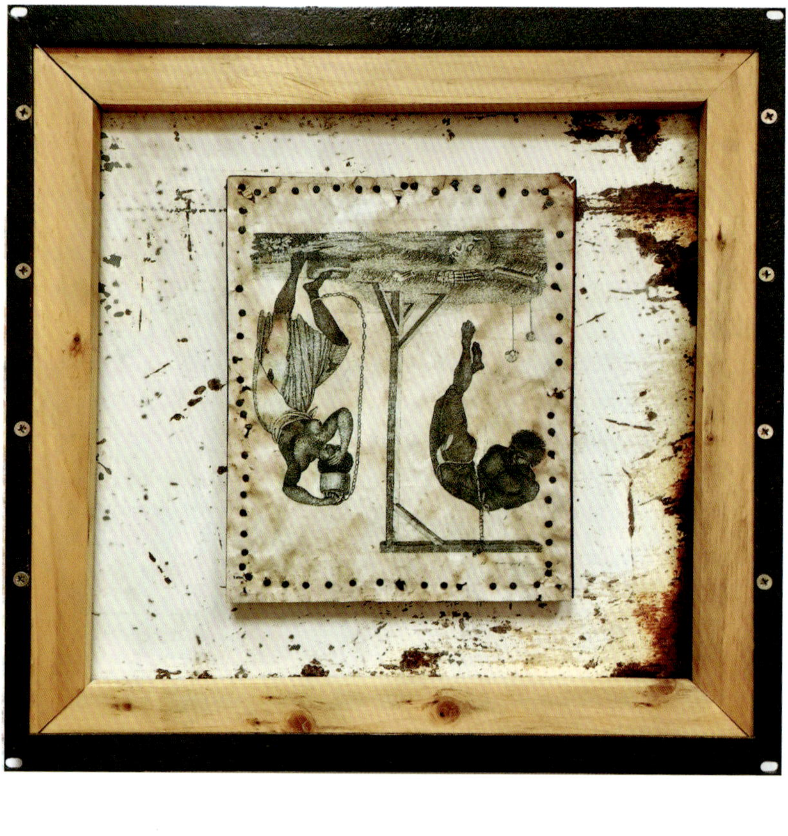

the obvious defiance of gravity—gravity as law, gravity of "law";
bodies oriented upward—
the head un|weighted,
the torso un|hooked,
the spirit un|anchored,
the ankle un|shackled,
the frame un|hung,
heads and shoulders and spines—
bending upward,
turning toward
the surface, surfacing,
see an eventual ascent,
see escape, a self-freeing, an unholding;
an uprooting, too—
not just making a hell of the hellish and wretched
earth with the inversion of the world into an underworld,
but overturning the very notion of an underworld
by undoing the world itself.

We are left, even in this preliminary stage of refusal and inversion, with a world that is not ours, but "his and hers alone." In this I see a repudiation of paradise, its loss, and a repudiation of the artist himself, of his gothic preoccupations.

If the question of *nah* requires an even more basic algebra, then see it at least as their bodies leveling out, a standing unbelievably upright and unbelievably at rest. Arriving at the moment of abject refusal, we see what the visual representation of Caribbean nonfiction ought to be, where it ought to go, or from what and how it will actually emerge.

Whose history? the art will ask at first.

And then:
What is the cost of the unbinding you seek?
Who do you mean to free?
Who strains now—with weighted waiting
—for an answer?[9]

9 You may encounter the full expression of this unbinding, as I have, in Laura Facey's sculpture *Redemption Song* (2003), in which the pair seems to have returned from the inversion that saw them emptied of their most explicit traumas—the hook and scaffold, the weight and block, the rag and bone—to find the kind of rest in art that they did not have in life. The absence of those things only amplifies their presence. Theirs is a public rest, their nude bodies of polished bronze open to the air, the opened eye, their freedom a three-dimensional stillness to be witnessed; freed of the impulse to run, we witness the end of their fugitivity. It is also, for me, a disruption of the chronology in *Onus*. Completed almost two decades earlier than *Onus* and three years after the release of Bob Marley and the Wailers' release of the single after which it is named, Facey's *Redemption Song* circumvents the process of inversion. It doesn't negate the necessity of inversion per se or undermine its inevitability (we cannot be redeemed by the very system that condemns us) but rather introduces a prophetic* sensibility. Its "redemption" is a foreshadowing of a redemption to come, an emancipation to come. We know that it's still to come because it hasn't happened yet.

* *Prophetic*, that is, rather than being subject(ed) to a simplistic linear anachronism.

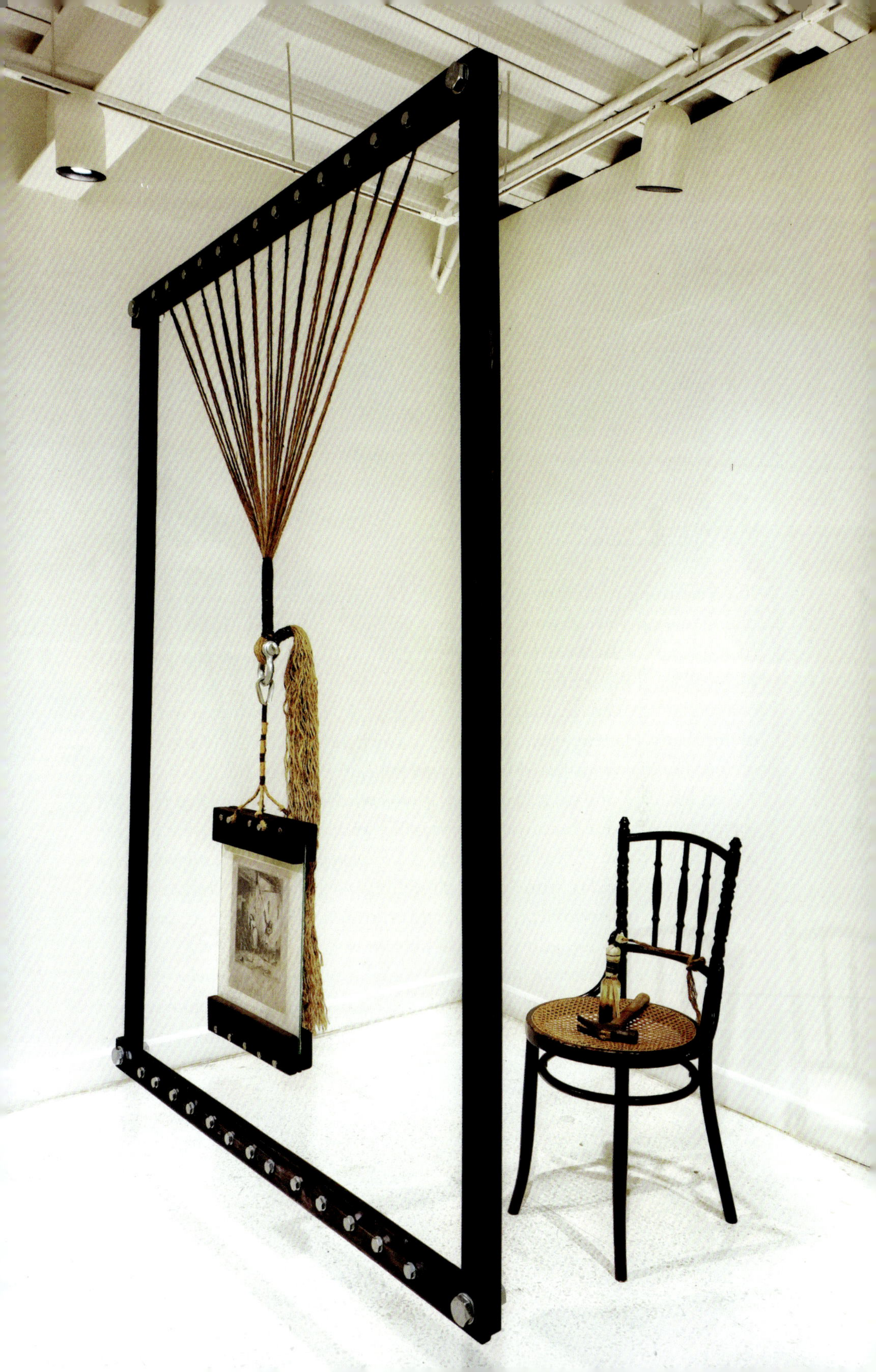

CONSCIENTIA

Trinidad, 1801–1802

If it is anything at all, *Conscientia* is a shared sentence, an interaction I imagine taking place between two Caribbean women—Louisa and Thisbe—whom I treat, provisionally, as archetypes of a feminism that asserts itself as intimacy taking place at the confluence of revolution—where, in the immediate afterlife of one that is American and one that is French, we find ourselves in the midlife of one that is Haitian, in the beforelife of black independence. Writing mostly out of a familiar emptiness, I have arrived long after their interaction has begun and ended, catching what little there is to catch, binding what I can from the shards and strands of archival memory they leave behind. It is, as far as I can tell, a conversation of bearings between a *subject suspended* and a *subject held in suspense*. I have made a witnessing—a listening in, opting in the long aftermath of accusation, imprisonment, torture, and execution to believe what I could not possibly hear or see, what I cannot possibly know.

For me, it is opting to believe the unbelievable body—that is, believing bodies no longer here to be believed. Women's bodies. It is also a conjuration of space, in which we may be present to witness the suspension of subjection—the suspended subjection of History itself—as a sense of arrival.

Louisa
is who you see
is accused
of conspiracy to steal from a man.

Thisbe
is who you do not see
is accused
of poisoning the very dominion of Man.

Who you see is:
accused,
beaten, imprisoned, tortured.
Freed, sold again.

Who you do not see is:
accused,
hanged, beheaded, burned.
Not freed, but free.

Who you see is formally known as:
"prostitute"
"thief"
"victim"
"girl"
"child."

Who you do not see is formerly known as:
"nurse"
"conjurer"
"victim"
"poisoner"
"woman."

Who you see is
a hanging body

Who you do not see is
a hanging body

Who you see,
historically framed,
is known formally
for her form.

Who you do not see,
outpacing History and frame,
is known for being formerly known
for her formlessness.

They appear, in this iteration, as two Venuses in what amounts to a single act played interminably between one and the other—a Caribbean liminality materialized.[1] Each, a flesh-and-bone contemporary of the ubiquitous bodies of Blake's catalog of scars and sketches, will suffer the letter of the law in ways I can only (but doh want to[2]) imagine, their womanness taken apart and dispersed, their form dissipated.

As we make our way into this work, we first witness the interaction between them as a set of frames that builds outward—from the historical record to its final assemblage, swinging back and forth as touch or shifts in mood and tone dictate. We cannot hear them conspiring but are nevertheless implicated in the meaning and the nothingness that fills the space between them. And, as the symbolic representations of their bodies take the place of a preceding emptiness, illuminating the secrets of *exterior bodies in interior space* and *interior bodies in exterior space*, we come (in our own time) to mean|ing with them.[3] And what, if anything, does this mean to us?

1 After and with Saidiya Hartman's "Venus in Two Acts" (2008). That "untimely story told by a failed witness" is one of the loci for a meditation on the ubiquity of the enslaved woman in the Atlantic and "takes place at the limit of the unspeakable and the unknown" (1). And though we know their names, I suggest that these women have remained unknowable, a factor that may be relied upon for their eventual liberation—or that may even constitute the nature of that liberation. Nameable, yes, but unknowable.* Their stories are relayed in V. S. Naipaul's *The Loss of El Dorado* (1969) and have the rhetorical function of framing what the author views as the larger, hitherto forgotten narrative of the British attempt to undermine Spanish power in the region, with a focus on Port of Spain, Trinidad, which had been ceded to the British in 1797.

2 And yet must.

3 As this notion cools, I will refer dually to an *in*|exteriority and an *ex*|interiority. It is, in part, an outside looking in and an inside looking out, fused by the simultaneity of the | that is bridge and partition.

* Or, perhaps they are as unnameable as a "Sable Venus," who is both anonymous *and* eponymous in the crafting of that historical gaze, immortalized by Thomas Stothard as the frontispiece to *History, Civil and Commercial, of the British Colonies in the West Indies* (1801). Immortalized in service of servitude, her blackness a grand obscenity. Obscenity in print. To say her name is to say, "Voyage of the Sable Venus from Angola to the West Indies." The only name we know. A title conferred. A grandeur said in full. A crime that repeats, like islands.

To stand as witness to the sadism of empire and tend as best we can to the wounded past from which it oozes, we learn that we must be frequent visitors to its monstrosities, lest they come back to us (as they were designed to do) in the form of what we know as "history repeating itself."[4] Caught as we are in the ceaseless back-and-forth of these repeating histories, we encounter something of a false (that is, manufactured) choice: we must either engage the atrocities with the forensic certainty of a fact we have never seen, yet whose archival affect we know and whose historical consequence we are inclined to believe—

arriving,
arriving,
and arriving again
at the beatings,
the rapes,
the mutilations,
the murders

—or act as if they had never occurred at all. Forgetting the hurt can be as violent as remembering it.

And yet, to understand the hurt by translating it into words or some form of action would be to emphasize the impossible act of "speaking on what you know." The problem is you only think you know. Indeed, all you know is that you and your words, images, and objects (as your ambassadors) will strain and ultimately fail to deliver the full weight of your unbearable meanings. The "choice," such as it is, is not a choice any of us should have to make. Each step taken is weighted and chained, hooked and hung. By the time we arrive at what it proposes, it is all already too much.

Too much, by which I mean it is unbearable in two ways:

1. the unbearable is|as *unspeakable*:
   the history as record is hard to look at; and
2. the unbearable is|as *unseeable*:
   the past is impossible to see.

4 As an art of interpretation, nonfiction proposes the creation of a history that does not merely repeat itself but longs *to be repeated* in different ways by those who encounter it. Its repetitions have no "history" to speak of but are instead arranged to be treated with History as *counterpart* rather than mere *counterpoint*.

Insofar as nonfiction, rhetoric, or the rhetoric of Caribbean nonfiction are concerned, the articulated thing—what is said and done—is only appreciable as a foil for what cannot be articulated. This only appears to be a dilemma until we understand that all expression is fundamentally apologetic—a constant re|wording and re|working against the grain of its inherent inadequacy. And mine. Any articulation that follows can *only* be a projection of what you or I have imagined, existing in the tension of the interstice—that is, the tension that emerges between these two points, represented here by Louisa and Thisbe but as easily shared by those who have known the abject irrationality of pain.

To imagine the worst thing that can happen to them is to test the limits of my own capacity for evil, demanding an identification with the perpetrator as much as with the victim. Hoping to align myself eventually with the brutalized, I must share my empathy, however momentarily, with the accuser, the brute, the jailer, the torturer, the executioner, to consider what it means to embody the worst of what history had made of them.[5]

To stand in witness of this work is also to confess: to say what I have seen and not seen, and (to a lesser degree) to say what I have done and not done. But it is to confess more specifically to the limitations of the body—my own as much as anyone else's. Confess to what I cannot say and cannot do, what I have not seen because I could not see and could not possibly have seen. These limitations are amplified as I attempt with *Conscientia* to see the unseeable, to articulate the unspeakable character of what I think I have discovered.[6]

5 My use of the past perfect is meant to be optimistic, though it may appear naive. Is it a repeating history or a single one, still ongoing? A matter of time passing, but not changing, of history constantly making and remaking? And are they still bound within it? Bound and wounded within it, within the memory of it, within its vulgar repetitions? Christina Sharpe reminds me that "there is no set of years in which to be born Black and woman would not be met with violence" (*Ordinary Notes*, 331). The abjection jars because it is familiar. So familiar that one can begin to see the soft curves of a truth beginning to take shape on the horizon of this note, the implicit shame of its indictment quivering in the latent heat until it settles into view: if there is one thing that is known beyond a doubt about women is that they are not believed. I struggle to name a time when this was not the case, denying its abjection as if it, too, were a woman. I am writing here against the tide of my own patriarchy, my own anti-black impulses, inlaid like veins of fool's gold in the sea stones at Macqueripe, or the veins of white quartz in the ones at Matelot.

6 The work is already an articulation that is not merely intermediate but an intermediary space through which the im|possibility of our own belated arrival may be resolved.

Seeing the work itself, there is, at first, what you cannot deny:

> a recognition of the rope that, though unraveled, still
> tethers you—holding you together like an old gate,
> like an affinity, a *tabanca*.
>
> It is not the gold-threaded cords that rim the
> officers' caps, their scarlet lanyards, or tassels that
> hang from the horses at the changing of the guard,
> but the frayed parts—the strands that remind you
> of hair blown loose in the ceaseless storming of an
> empire you could never know.
>
> Imagine arriving (and arriving again) at what it must
> mean to never know and yet claim, or to know and
> yet deny, to know what is from what is not.

Here, arrival is a suspension and a swinging characterized by a waiting, a waiting to see, a waiting to see what will happen when that arrival occurs, a waiting to see who will arrive.

By which I mean:

here:
a waiting

and there:
a waiting to see

and here:
a waiting to see what
will happen

and then there:
a waiting to see who
will arrive[7]

7 See, in these repetitions, the inherent refusal to settle on a singular meaning, expressed in its "swaying" from one meaning to another. I am waiting, marking time and space for you. As I do, I make a game of hardened words, as if they were more pliable than they are: wait is *weight*; weigh is *way*.

In rhetorical terms, and in spite of itself, *Conscientia* is also an *unbinding*. It is a study of form that has already dissipated, evidence of an arrival to come, offered as testimony (on behalf of myself and my people). Though held (together) with rope and wire, wood and bolt, and glass and paper, bound with oil for water and salt for sugar, it is already taking its leave of us and our reason, already coming apart. Like us. See how with the inner frame its sides appear open to offer the illusion of escape? See (though I am neither jailer nor executioner in this scenario) that I have made for myself a promise of freedom, to which the imprisoned might aspire? See its broken promise that (at its outermost framing) reminds us that it is bound in ways we do not see at first, then cannot unsee?

Held together in the aftermath of my turning hand, my twisting fingers, a pull and push of sand and paper, an infinite knot, do you see what its meanings mean? It is held in the indelible afterlife of masculinity, preventing it from doing what I think it wants to do. Here, liberation is suspended as a matter of design, which you encounter as art and as a literal consequence of an arrival—a mattering—to come.[8]

This is the rhetorical work of art as Caribbean nonfiction: that it will cause us to witness its mockery of hegemony—the ubiquity of order and of violent design held in suspension—while waiting to come apart and be undone, or to be taken apart. It is a violence that repeats, a healing that repeats, a work that wants to be unbound. (Or, bound in name but unbound in practice.[9] Or, perhaps it is I who want it to be unbound. But, as always, at what cost?)

8 You will arrive at matter in a material sense. But you will also arrive at *what matters*—matter symbolically rendered. You will do this without ever having to ask what either of these arrivals *mean*. You will know by the time you get here.

9 I'm also thinking here about the performance work of Jamie Philbert, whose ongoing transmedial study and articulation of the unbound black woman's body is both a haunting and an embodiment. This transmediality is observed in Philbert's *Bound* (2022), where we find that the former aspect (haunting) enables the latter (embodiment), while the latter sanctifies the former, with the artist and the audience suspended between one state and the other. Existing at the intersection of choreo-ethnological dance, digital photography, spirituals, and cosmogony and presented in a series of video clips, this is a work of deliberative self-possession. Performance and reception are combined for an experience that transcends the artist's merely making an argument and the audience's need to be persuaded. Argumentation itself is suspended. In particular, Philbert invokes the West Central African martial art of *kalinda* to lend coherence to her transmediality, while enabling an unbinding from the constraints of restrictive expressive traditions seen, for example in Philbert's performance of *Patterns of Freedom* (2023).

This, too, is the work: having implicated myself in the violence of this scene that is not mine to resolve, nor its weight mine to carry, I am as complicit as rafter and pulley in the motion of this narrative and in its repeated repercussions. For it is also evidence of my unadorned willingness to trade, however uneasily, on the symbolic, material, and ideological currency of masculinity to produce a transaction between myself (as subject) and the image|object (as the subjects at|in hand). The presumption of the symbolic actions of art as a form of nonfiction—its inherited|inherent conceit—is based on the recognition that though I make a place for this work to do what it will|wants, it is not my place to say what its subjects say, nor report with any presumed clarity on what the unavoidable opacity of these frames so perfectly obscure.

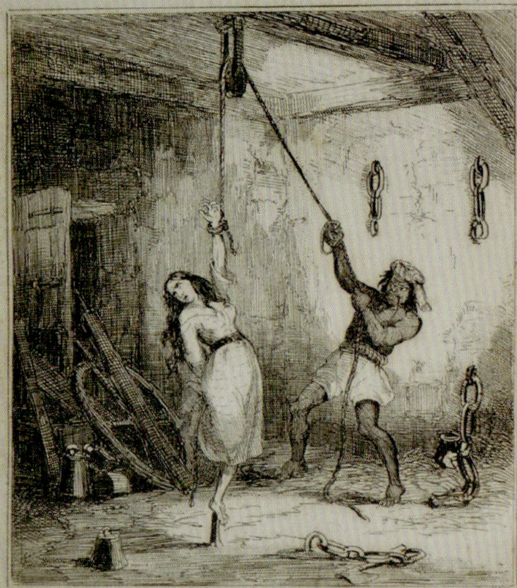

The Torture

It troubles me and is sometimes hard for me to look at. But I will sit with it until it stops moving. Then, I will attend to it as it moves me, tracing the back and the forth. It will settle, eventually. I know that. This admission yields nothing new. I have always been bound. I am black, before and after all, and the vision of an unbound version of myself is always on the horizon, my blackness like a prophecy of its own infinite arrival.

But *Conscientia* is not just about what troubles *me*.

Nor is it about the centrality of desire—the pedophilic desire for a fourteen-year-old child, or her purchase, the dowry of however much or little one would pay for a child. Nor is it to establish a hermeneutics of subjection couched in the want of a black woman's body that breeds myth in the broken minds of men with power (and men without it). Nor, for that matter, is it the frame I have made for its display or the frame I have made to hold the frame.[10] The work is not what I have done but knowing what I cannot do. The work I must do is not the work I have made but what this thing I have made demands: a nonfiction grounded in a rhetoric of black Caribbean aesthetics and poetics.

By which, I mean a kind of Obeah.

My own black hands have been trained
  to hold the rope,
  to hold it as if a woman's weight were a burden,
  to hold it and witness its motion, its coming stillness,
  to hold it burdened by my own bestiality, tethered to the haunting,
  to the pendular action of punishment and crime,
  to the pendular action of the body.

But my interpretations of arrival and my efforts to articulate them go beyond my complicity. They are transposed from the symbolic representations of archival bodies onto my own, making me a presence in the process of making things that move—and move us. No one has summoned me for this purpose. I have come of my own volition to see what I cannot see: an end to the invisibility to which I and my people are accustomed; to understand the enactment of an object-oriented intentionality; to limn the *obscurae* of hauntings that yield the subjective intention of this work I say is mine to do.

10 In 2017 and 2021, respectively.

Forgetting that not all Caribbean things are mine to claim, nor their stories mine to tell, I had sought and claimed what I ought neither seek nor claim, clung so tightly to it that I had not noticed that it was I who was bound. But, having implicated myself, having actually constructed the scaffold to support my self-haunting and, eventually, my self-possession, I start to see something out of reach: Louisa and Thisbe, certainly, but also the possibility for a more general unbinding.

Thisbe's torture was meant to horrify and coerce, her pain foreshadowing the less fatal horror Louisa would face on the *piquet*. In turn, Louisa's torture by suspension foreshadowed Thisbe's execution and beheading. I realize that, in *Conscientia*, Thisbe's horror is not merely precedent to Louisa's, not merely her counterpart in suffering as occurs in *Onus*, but more of a mythological counterpoint to the scandalization of their historically comparative tensions. *Conscientia* mythologizes. On her own, each woman is an archetype of refusal that is greater than the crude sum and subtraction of their parts at the hands of men, at the convergence of three empires on their bodies.

Relieved, as it were, of the tension of comparison between one and the other, they emerge for us already dissipated and reconfigured into a tense of the irresolvable profundity of Caribbean women's meanings, a futurity that evades capture and conjugation, eclipsing even my own understanding of what it means to free myself. Theirs is an intimacy of witness that cannot ever be known, one that exceeds the monstrosity of the scene and moves from the material to the ethereal before our eyes.

So if it is anything at all, *Conscientia* is a conjuration.

An Obeah.
An Obeah that unbinds.

And what is this unbinding?

It is the transcription of a series of negative spaces I have dared to construct to tell a story I cannot know: a story|ing of witness, in which the unsaid resides, in which its being undone is an echo in the bone, a story|ing of the repeated re|liability of witness|ing in the absence of
evidence.[11]

And what is the cost of this unbinding?
Nothing. Nothingness, nothing more.

11 An incantation for who you do not see:

Thisbe, the *witness* who is also the *accused*.
Thisbe, the *witness* who is also the *witnessed*.
Thisbe, whose very name is a declaration of the inhabited body we never see.
Thisbe, whose witnessing is foregrounded by an arrival that is impossible to replicate.
Thisbe, whose unknown witness, unknown memory, unknown experience outdo injustice itself.
Thisbe, whose haunting is labial, a curse in the grammar. Subjunctive. Declarative. Undeclared.
Thisbe, whose unbelievable body had long been consigned to the grave, preceded only by her testimony, what she witnessed known only to whom she witnessed and who witnessed her.
Thisbe, whose work is done and, inversely positioned, leaves me darkly now to do mine.
Thisbe but like a drink of water.

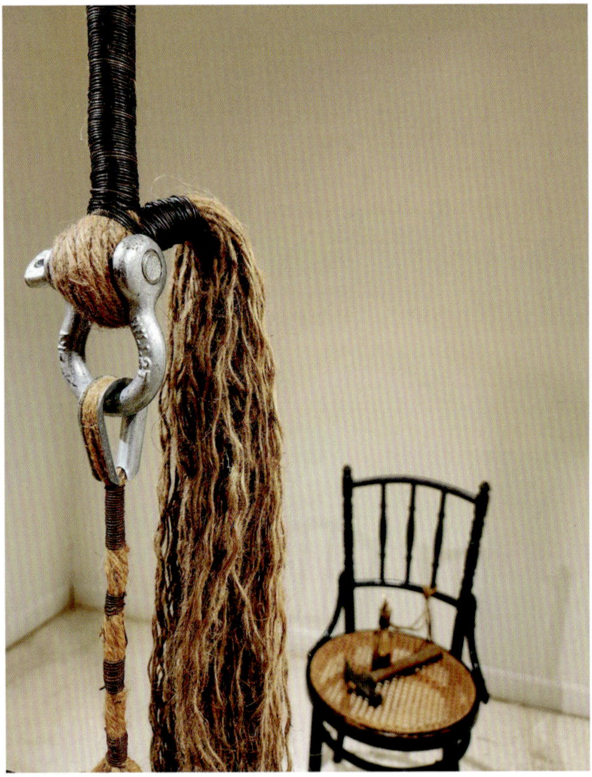

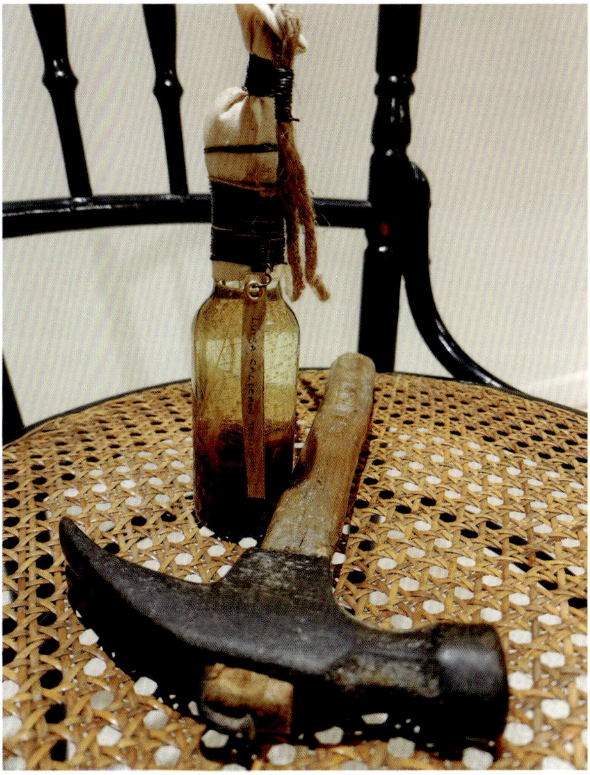

The inherent affect of witness does more than simply affirm complicity or the omnipresence of History in the apparent intimacy of a ruin (or the deliberate ruination of intimacy, which is worse).[12] It also demands a suspension of the subject at|in hand and the meanings its subjections produce. You see it in the ironic "desecration" of an archive and the subsequent re|construction of a frame for witnessing what exists *beyond* its violent insistence. A *disbelieving*, if you like, which I have said is a privilege of unbelievable bodies. This is not as abstract a notion as I sometimes wish it were: polishing the wooden frame of a work like *Conscientia* hurts. The hurt and the memory of hurt invoke the essential ruin of the scene—its unutterable depravity that yields, in my own body, a feeling as immediate and lasting as my muscles' mishandled memories of illicit touch as a boy. They are as real to me as any haunting, as real as any dormant truth that stirs like the stains and burn marks on the bolted frame, not fully masked in fragrant oil, not fully bound within the wire-corseted frame of the conscience.

In *Conscientia*, I have attempted to thread a needle with neither needle nor thread, which is to say I have attempted to do an impossible thing: attempt to grasp the impossibility of representing witness, which is underscored by the additional impossibility of representing the intentionality of unbelievable bodies and the objects that hold them. I cannot know what was intended, even in my observations of what was committed. What is more is that I have, till now, persuaded myself that I can attempt to make an impossible thing possible with the materials I have gathered

12 There are no intimate ruins, but you can take on the guilt as if it were a deep violation, a transposition of your desire and your depravity toward the representation of this body—of women's bodies. You can love and hate yourself in equal measure.

:

a plank of wood,
a pane of glass,
a coil of wire,
a ball of twine,
a jury of bolts,
a sheet of paper,
an image of a girl, soaked in coconut oil,
an image of her testimony,
stripped and soaked in oil and sugar that will not dissolve,
an image of her invisible interlocutor.

Some arrivals will be more than you or I can bear.[13]

Knowing this, I enter a conversation that has already passed, passing in and out of it as if it were an open window, as if the secrets of interiors and exteriors tell each other's secrets in the space in between. I say these *must* have been convened for a particular purpose that exceeds their place in a particular space and time: absolution, when no absolution could be possible, when no solace could be attained. How could there be? Remember, this is work that asks (softly, at times), "What have you done?" It asks this of all involved, though only what I have done is mine to contend with. Only what I have carried all this way is mine to set down—gentle gentle—so I could concern myself with something else to come.[14]

And what is that "something else"? Here, it is the emphasis on what is left to be seen: Louisa and Thisbe no longer the accused forced to see the other, but in a position to see us as we can only try to see them. To see them as we would hope to be seen: free.

It is hard to look at—*yes*.

Hard to look at, impossible to utter, utterly impossible to see, except perhaps when filtered through the multiple frames I have made and those that have preceded them. Or, when seen through the frames you have made by|for yourself, you see through them, through the filters, through the *obscurae* and the obscurities, through the redactions that compose it—through it all to see Louisa on the *inside* looking out, seeing Thisbe, who sees her back from *outside* the frame, where no one can frame her, or any man put his hand on her. Where, finally, the "drink of water" to which her suffering had been compared can do what all water is meant to do: return to its source. And we, as witnesses, will wait for it to arrive.[15]

13 Something ruptures in my thinking on this point.
I know why: it's because I want the essay to work, to do what I want it to do, and it will not. It *refuses*. I must do what it needs me to do. It is absurd to think this, I know—I must either do what it needs me to do or have it help me do what I need to do. But i's like I cripple my own self with these turns, thinking I *know* what I mean when I say that something is more than I can bear. I hear my mother's "Hm!" and her "What you know about this? You only *think* you know," reminding me that *only* he who feels it knows it.

14 How perfect is my conceit that I will fail to remember this?

15 You may already know this, but avoid the tendency to seek redemption (here). The discourse will bind you. What binds you cannot save you. See it, but know that freeing yourself from it is an impossibility, though freeing yourself may yet occur. You need not concern yourself too much with what cannot be done. Instead, craft your own redemption, even if it is out of memory, even if it is made of old, discarded things.

TEXTUS

If asked, say, "Here is what I have made." See how its binaries and obvious bidirectionalities are framed, its inherent dualities forced to ricochet, rebounding and repeating, its rippled alliterations as they encounter the border, bouncing back against what it was that sent them. See an end in itself, an infinite arrival. See how its descent and ascent take you back to *Onus* and *Conscientia* for a more subtle display of rage and sorrow and peace, suspended between coming and going. Comment, in passing, on the time you took a mouthful of linseed oil for the glass of wine next to it. Recall its taste and muse on its cooling effect on the color and texture of sanded wood—its sensuality.

For clarity, offer a list of themes:

> Sea: because your fear of drowning is drowning's first
> cousin, and you still haven't let go of your loss; keeping
> it like a land-borne mariner so afraid of the water you
> would make a perpetual tide, like the one at Mayaro;
>
> Boat: maybe a ship or some pirogue picked apart by
> rock and water in the memory, of a hold for blacknesses
> bound head to head, foot to foot, the echo of somebody
> thrown from it, who too easily could have been your
> niece, her husband, their child who, fresh from Caracas,
> calls you Chocolaté and you call Dulce de Leche, their
> precarious bodies given "leave to remain";

Archipelago: the ritual of repetitive motion for a thing that will not move unless you move it, the ritual of sanding and sealing and staining and staining and sanding as a prayer and myth and incantation, oiling as anointing;

House: the shingled or galvanized sheets, the louvers and jalousies, the Demerara windows over the sink, the door and jamb, the floors, the collected and collectible things (the living and dead among them); a building, a building within a building, the public turn of your privacy, its gutting like a herring whose bones you mimic;

Time: the hours that are not ours;

Coffin: your own or your memory of one you might have glimpsed being made on Corsbie Lane or Henry Street behind one funeral home or another, their prominence for you as a boy;

Crucifix: for blackness, wherein the witness—you, as witness to this act of making—may reclaim not just the theme of the riddled body but see it sanctified in another, see it borne home in another, then harbored and housed and kept and comforted, then held in the place made for it—sea, boat, house, coffin, for instance—where some new mourning bird will break the silence;

Blackness: holding space for these themes, holding you along with them; a space you have made; a space you have taken up.

But later, as you speak more privately of method—of how the fumes and sanded dust remind you to breathe, as you clear your throat and scrub the ebony stain from your skin to see its residue collect like parentheses beneath your fingernails, as you miss the mark you only see after you think you've done it all and it is shown to you (because you haven't looked at yourself in days and think you've been working alone)—I want you to speak of it as you would of love and of what comes after it.

Not just of your hands as if you remember making love and seek through memory to craft a correlation between *here and there* or *now and then*, but as if you only half-remember what your hands could never re|create and (as a monument of her absence) never try.

Not just in terms of an untranslatable "fit," or of being and learning to be inside and outside of each other, noting with soft attention the easy rearrangement of space around you, the "fit" of limbs and of perfect skin, dark and warm and light as sandalwood, of pains and pleasures exquisitely mirrored with arched and bending backs, breathing each other in like light, but to speak, more specifically, in terms of time—the *archipelago of hours*.

Of how it may be composed of things between you and whom you might have loved—fashioned by hand and mouth into a fleeting "Now" that is always the "Always" of a love that cannot last.

Your staying was always your leaving, ordained in the ungodly hours—and what we make is love, a presence that is also an absence as we learn to forget where we are and what our bodies do, lying still as stone, where every touch is a departure from touching, every departure a promise to return, every kiss a memory of a kiss, every memory of a kiss a promise of kissing to come, which may never come. Take note of where you are, of what you feel, of what you will leave behind.

Textus is a catechism. But it is more than that. It is how you prepare yourself to make something, how you prepare yourself to arrive again at a thing that cannot love you back, something you know you must leave. Speak of method, then, as an *archipelagic encounter*, the way you begin to address the inevitability of your absence.

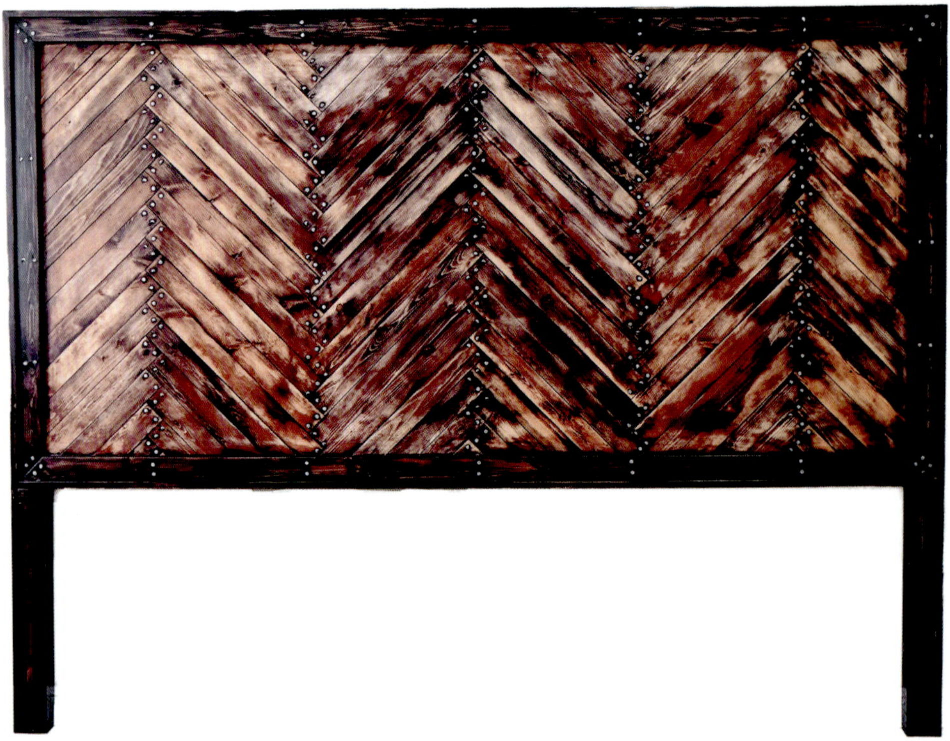

Speaking of loves and absences, consider the beloved. Consider the "coming" you sometimes say as a sounding of love before and after its throes, but also the "coming back" and the "coming to" that sometimes come before leaving.

Consider that the "coming" is not merely the symbolic action of arrival as departure and return, of leaving and coming back, but a *spatiotemporal grammar*—that is, the passing of your time and space together as a series of deliberate re|turns. It at once provides the certainty of an extant *now* and the promise of a *later* to come. Or, a *now to come* that is recursive, based on the repeated acknowledgment of a shared desire, which is itself defined in the provisions one makes for appeasing the other either *now* or *in time to come*:[1]

To make the promise, the beloved has to be present, but it is a presence that functions as antecedent to an impending departure, a foregrounding of the beloved's absence—that is, as an absence to come that is itself the necessary antecedent to a promise of the beloved's return, having neither left nor returned. An arrival, in a sense, that has already begun. The gesture of *beginning here* is the beloved's—yours, or mine. The *reception* of the gesture is also the beloved's—mine, or yours. It is an end in itself. Of what little is said, or at first appears to be felt, more will be surmised. More is yet to come. You have begun because, in a way, you have been here from the beginning. I have sensed your arrival from the beginning.

So, this is how the story begins.

Textus is a blackness composed in|from a state of mortality, a symphony of perpetual motion composed of my syncopated rebellions, rising to a crescendo. I am only too aware of where I must go to locate the sheets on which it will be composed—sheets and their odd and cruel and gentle prepositions

> through which I am filtered as black;
>
> on which intention is painted, the blackboard black
> for chalky lines and rough notes, cleft and sharp;

1 Things one may say:

A|h going, but a|h coming back.
A|h gone, but a|h still here.
A|h gone (that is not goodbye),
And a|h still here (that has not yet left).

with which we practiced our hospital corners, bisecting the angles, flattening one side, then the other, then back, then back again, then too slow, then face down, then sit up, then pull up, then mountain climbers, then breathe;

beneath which I laid still as the surgeon cut and cauterized above my eye to find the tumor that might have poisoned me, music that my mother loved, music that I loved, my burning flesh, my threatened brow, my threatened eye;

in which I lay heaving, with nowhere and with no need to run, listening to my sandalwooded lover hum Nina Simone's "Sinnerman" (1962) to me, loving with uncertain wonder, learning "Ne me quitte pas" (1965) so I could sing it word for word, note for note, breath for breath, before leaving, before coming back;

in which I lay, being left, to think of the inconvenience of my blackness, its uncomfortable beauty, the enunciations of its mysteries, as I remember humming "How Could I Leave" (1976) by Dennis Brown. We talked, you and I, about his play on "leave" and "live," that it was the heart of that song, the essence—the true sense—of what it meant for us to stay together for as long as we could: to leave as a misguided appeal for staying, to stay as an attempt to live.[2] (Then, eventually, to stay apart.) *Tabanca*, here, is a genre of arrival that unfolds not merely as consequence, but as inevitability. Both the staying and the leaving are "ordained."

Before parting again, we will linger on the single affirmation of that line: "I don't know just what I'll

2 The original, sung by the Sharks, is titled "How Could I Live." Its date is unknown.

do." We will muse at its repetition throughout, his insistence, "I really don't know just what I'll do." I will prefer to think he knows everything *but* what he will do. Casting his vision into a future (in) which he has (been) left behind, what could he possibly know? I cannot say, but I think it is comforting that he does not know. I am comforted because I have made a choice to read his not knowing as surrender, as something that is markedly other than a threat adorned in domesticated sound.

How could I leave?[3]

He never answers his question, but stays in it, seeming to prefer the infinitude of possibility that attends the not knowing. The infinite possibilities of her subjunctive moods. Of course, it is only a proposal he makes. The "you" to whom his appeal is made has not responded. It is unclear|unknown whether she arrives at all, whether she leaves. I am comforted further, then, as his not knowing is resolved, in a way, in the acceptance of what may never be.

I think of this recursive "now" as I sit half-naked at the edge of my own bed, twisting to look back at *Textus* that, for now, is only a headboard. Adrift on the memory of its making. What form(s) must our blackness take, how urgent must the transformation be? How to claim it in the midst of our long unbelonging? I should say that I think the memory is both sea and ship, that it is roof and house and coffin. There is a wave in every stroke, a strip of blackness adjoined with every pounded head to another. I have made a thing, and I have made nothing—as much an archipelago as a Nowhere that I or an idea of you may perpetually reside, its repeating narratives perpetually composed.

3 Too easily.

In *Textus* you may see a blackness that is an anagram of the senses at its disposal. Blackness that exists in the orbital echo of the opened eye—the art of sight at the site of being seen—and of touching and of being touched.[4]

4 Not blackness that emerges as the self-fulfilling prophecy of white angst, shame, desire, or terror—which are the same thing, especially when their one-and-the-sameness is projected onto our skins and our psyches—that either proactively or retroactively commits itself to the negation of the black self, let alone what prophecies those black selves may actually be able to fulfill.

BLACKNESS

Blackness is a swallowing whole.

It is already whole—a hole, too.
You gather its disparate parts
only to find that it has swallowed you.

You will have to base
what you know on what you do not know,
grounding all of what you attempt in what you cannot do.

True talk doh lie.
Talk true. Doh lie.

There is nothing so blasphemous in this broken, upturned world

as blackness.

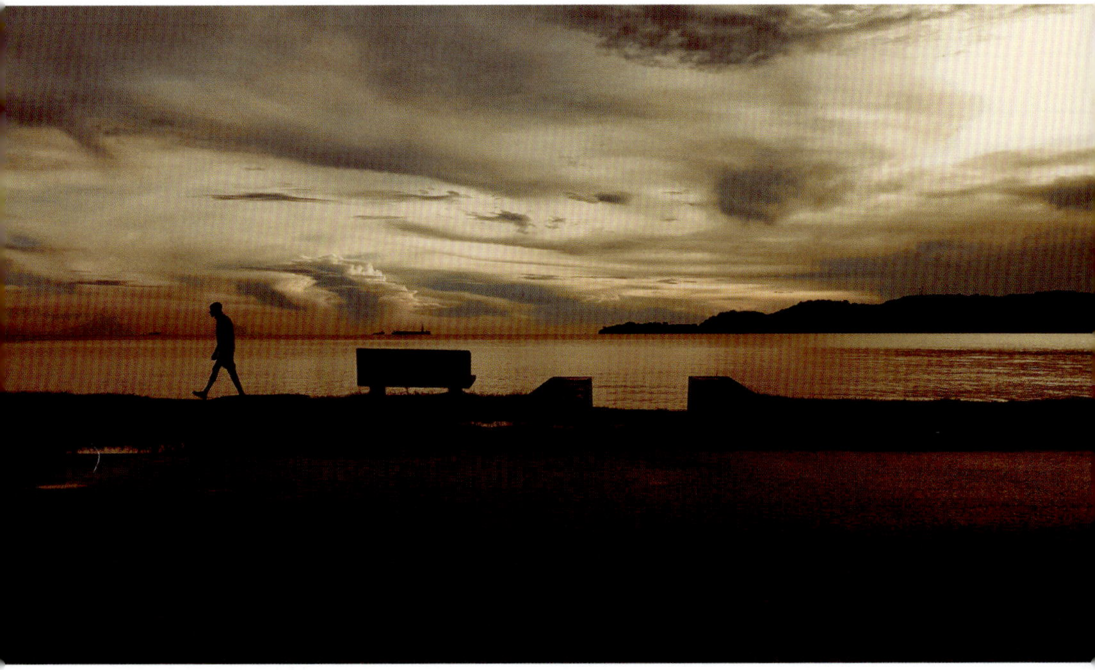

So when I say "blackness," I also mean to invoke an ecology of being that is black, a sensing and enactment of blackness in spite of a long genocide. I mean to invoke the art of sight, of seeing and of being seen, of touching and of being touched. Blackness is the beforelife of sound, which is the breath that precedes utterance; the midlife of light, which is the paradox of fugitivity and witness in the image; the afterlife of touch, which the breath and the brain recall as a memory of texture held in (and beneath) the skin. Here, nonfiction is black thought, the coalescence of shade, form, and texture as *being*.

I have used that expression before: "in spite of."

To live "in spite of" is not the same as living "out of spite." Black life is often framed as life that is lived out of spite, in (mostly) violent opposition to the "normal" and the "civil" and the "proper," as if the very notion of black life were so objectionable, so offensive, that it could only be perceived as an existential attack on whatever else passes for "real," "actual" life. In the audacious expressions of a desire for equality, justice, autonomy, sovereignty, decency, in the audacity of expression itself, we find that blackness is the offense, the spitefulness that we learn and learn to believe exists at our core—an abyss that, as you might expect, is *black*. To live "in spite of" this is not simply to deny that black life is an offense but to refuse it outright and, by refusing it, go beyond the boundary that has been drawn for how that black life may be expressed.

Sometimes that boundary is drawn for us, sometimes we draw it for ourselves, with self and being and breath perpetually endangered as a matter of course. Blackness that is perpetual *only* in its endangerment.

Not here.

Here, *self* and *being* and *breath* are evidence of a future that is black, their particular futurity defined by their blackness. Blackness is all these things—and more. And, because they are also Caribbean, they are not black *exclusively*. My own multiple origins bear this out, however subtly. Constructions of race and the persistence of its divides and enactments aside, Caribbean blackness is viewed here as a sensory and sensual phenomenon, an ecology of being that limns the abstractions of sheer complexity and shared complexion, manifesting as an articulation of intention that precedes consequence, the "I mean to" that precedes the "I mean."

Here, blackness is a way of seeing that is no more a mystery to me than herbs cooling in the cup on my counter, the steeping that sees me infuse the water with my diffusions of black and brown and red and orange. It is no more mysterious than a watercolorist's brush that, her wrist stiff with the monotony of hair and grass and rust and cloud, is now left to let the water work its way through the bristles.

Then,

> egrets' feathers best done in the afternoon light,
> blue herons, in their entirety, at morning,
> *corbeau*'s feathers as yet uncaught.

I would say it is a perfect blackness I want to inhabit, a *sight unseen*. But these are early days.

Working from and in the dark, from and in the shadows, I am oriented not just to the expectation of "light to come" but also to the way my eyes adjust to seeing in the dark—an evolving ability to see what darkness remains and what it means. My blackness is as black as what I have seen, as black as what I have not seen and have gone in search of, as if I were blind—or courting blindness as if it were mine to claim.

When I have cause to consider seeing blackness and my failing vision in more literal ways than this, I deny it. I lie to myself about what that might mean (beyond its obvious inconvenience to me) as an interpretive device. For, what is it but the silencing of vision, the sometimes gradual, sometimes sudden marginalization of sight, the degeneration of seeing, the breakdown of looking?

Denials aside, I would say that it is the ability to perceive the *adjectival* and *adverbial*—meanings that exist at|in the periphery of being. It is a hypersensitivity not only to the potential nonexistence that defines everyday black life—life lived under threat—but also the *potential* of a life *yet to exist*, a tendency toward *hypothesis*, a growing empathy for the imagined and the unseen. Are you unseen? I am, sometimes.

Asking you to imagine with me means I have embarked alone in the hope that you come along with me—or, more importantly, that you will take this work with you. What you know right now is more than enough to make it through this.[1] We always overdo and are outdone by the very meanings we create, by the inability to actually achieve the perfection of a thing we have designed. The inherent imprecision of language—its implicit logics of intent, meaning, and outcome—always falls short on our tongues and pages and screens. No words

1 Love, you learn, is always at a higher octave, a descant that resides all too briefly in the throat of your distant beloved. So is hate. So is fear. Imagination falters too, as it moves from symbol to idea, idea to word, word to act, and so on into absurdity.

can embody the precision of meaning that we struggle to reproduce in real life. But what you know is enough.

By inviting you to imagine with me, I'm also inviting you to ask with me, to wonder what there is beyond the limitations of opposition. We may be beset by opposites, but we need not be mired in opposition. We may argue about the virtues of oppositional engagement in terms of the creativity it allows, but the truth is I would be pleased if it were only something other than what I have known, some different relation, some way of seeing solely for the pleasure of discovering some new thing about our ways of seeing. Some new way of articulating blackness—as art. As an artist.

So yes, it may be that, as you regard the silhouetted figure of an unknown man walking along the foreshore at Chaguaramas, the first thing that will come to mind is the minimalism of Alberto Giacometti or the very black blackness of Kara Walker or Kerry James Marshall. I am slow to make these connections.[2] But as I regard him, none of these comes to mind at first. Instead, I am drawn to what I think is a doubled anonymity, to what I will later call a visual discourse. I am drawn to the easy interplay of his opposites—a shadowy unknownness, a Calibanesque unknowability. This will be an idea to which I return from time to time, calling it *rhetoric*. But for now, its qualities seem too obvious to name. And yet, for all I *think* I see—his black hyperpresence—I may never know who it is that walks along the foreshore, whether it is intent or indignation I see lodged in the space between his heel and the ground, whether he is walking at all. Perhaps it is because I will never know the inner workings of this scene—its *anatomy*, if you like—that I have not yet named it anything other than blackness. Blackness that is anonymous only because I have not named it, because it is unnameable.

You may see, in that same silhouette, the Bwa man retired from the *gayelle* of Alfredo Codallo's *Kalinda* (1950s), his forward lean oriented finally toward home. The reverence of the bandleader in John Newel Lewis's *Drawings from Nobody in His Right Mind* (1974), his feathered headdress and hatchet cast off sometime before entering the frame, left only with his blackness. You may end up there if you have known carnivals. You may think of a lone Moko Jumbie on the wharf. You may remember, regarding the white-sanded skin of Colin Gill's retrofitted series of humaniform walkers, that sometimes black skin *is* the mask whiteness wears, that black skin is sometimes the mask. A seeming blackness,

2 For me, it is sometimes Marshall's *The Wonderful One* (1986).

a blackness that is seamlessly anti-black—its black anti-blackness so complete, so infinite, as to be unimaginable. Perhaps a gathered shadow of Che Lovelace's *Creature* (2006) after its engulfing flames go out. The *Returning Dragon* (2006) after its scales have fallen off and the encroaching water, which is its bane, comes to claim him in the yawning breadth of the frame.

Though we know these are not the same man.

We find, in fact, that he is just a man. We find that as black humankind, he is enough. Stripped of color by the very light he interrupts, he is also a shadow of a man, a facsimile or signature or inkblot of the man he is in this moment.

Cloaked and naked,
he is his own shadow,
his own walking simulacral specter,
his own inverse,
his own reflection,
his own opposite.

I wonder what it means to be that kind of a man, striding out of the formal pretense of metaphor into a frame of his own making, striding out of the frame I have made for him. I wonder what it means to *be* the evidence of my own freedom—and to know its art as one of living. A blackness no one can name.

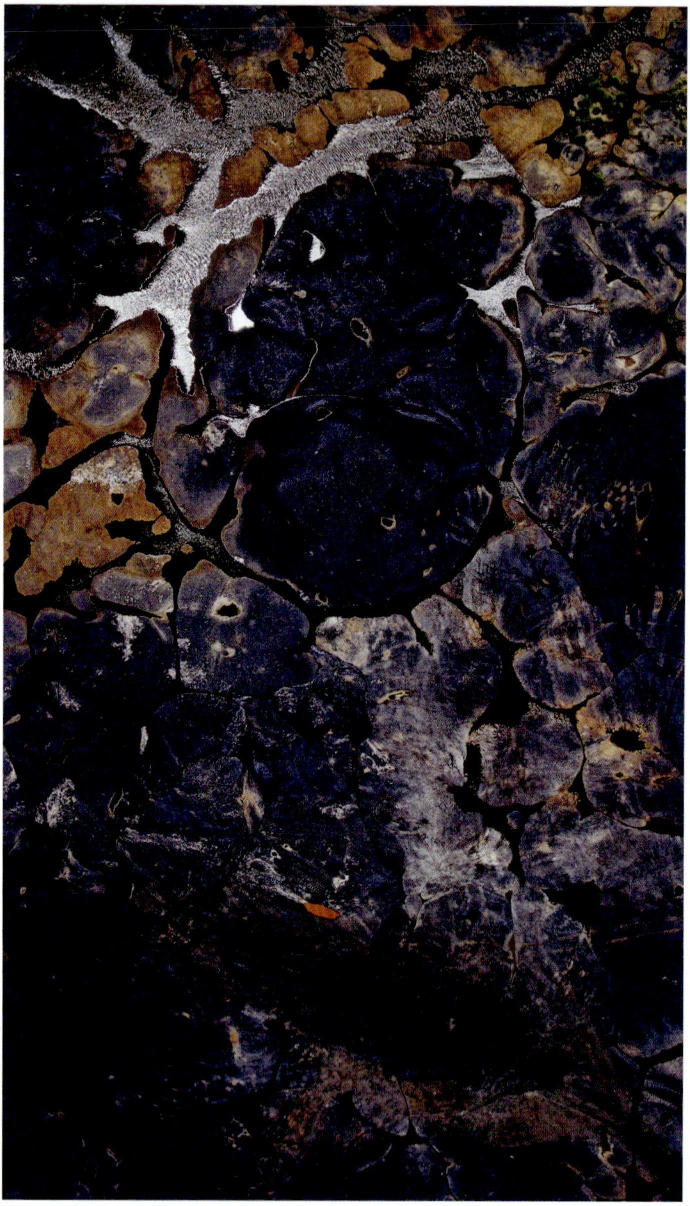

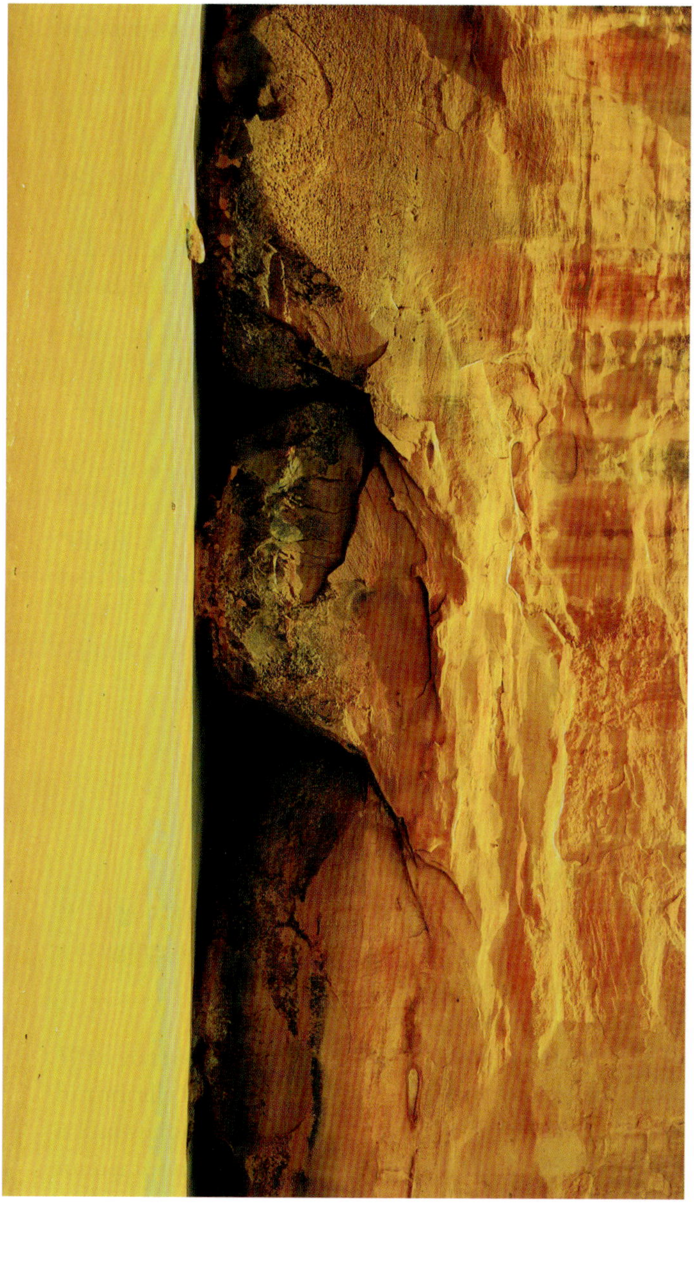

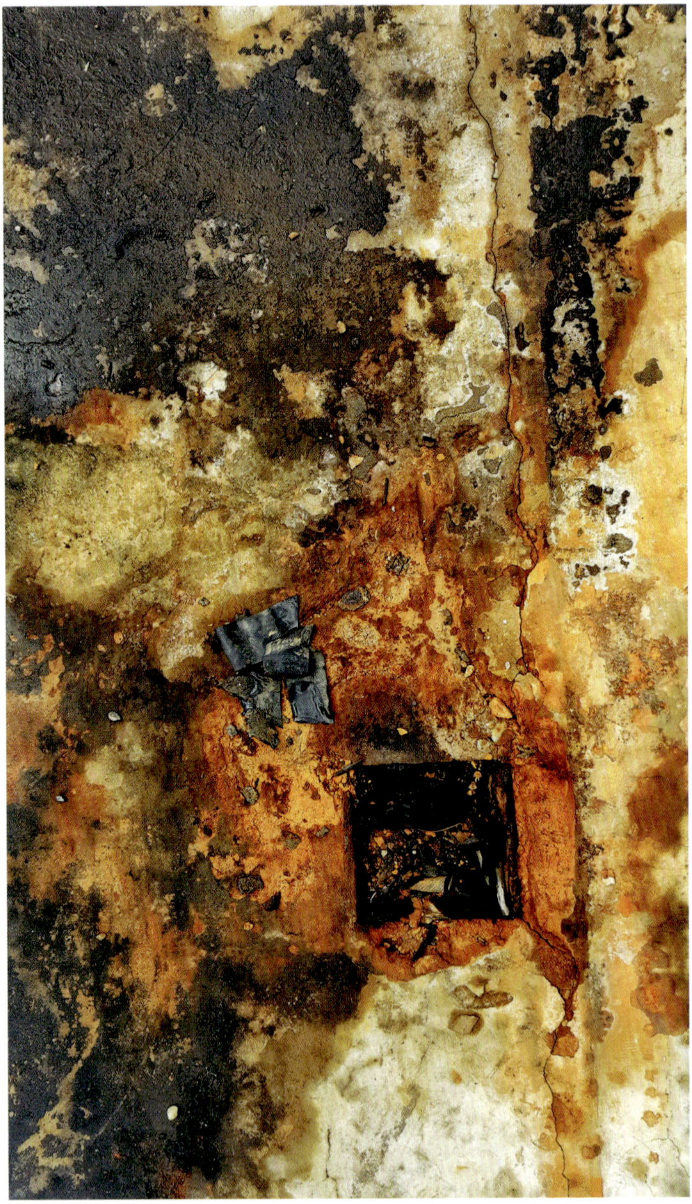

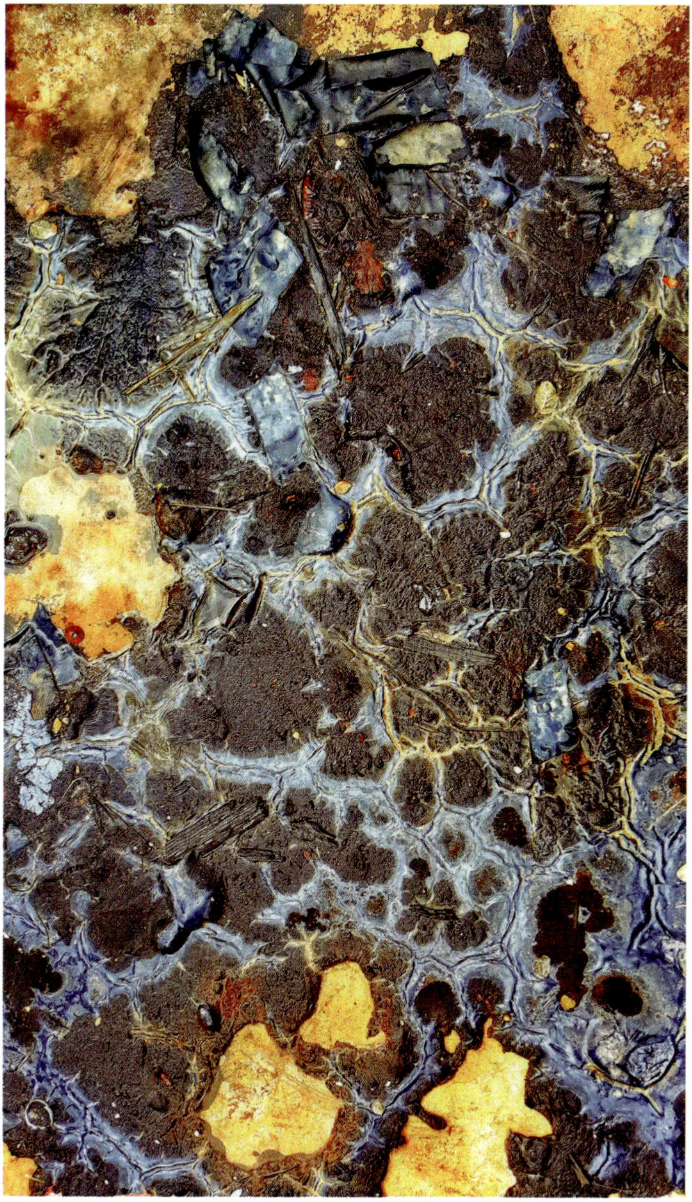

SHADE

My blackness is as black as what I have seen, as black as what I have not seen.

My blackness is blue and brown, gray and golden.

Stretching like a house cat to the west, the Northern Range is still cloaked in mist and Sahara dust that drags itself across the island from the east. I've just crossed the Caroni River, whose muddy water does a half-hearted run-walk as it winds its way to the coast. On some days, this is a land of bridges, on others a land of rivers. (In the rainy season, even the drains pretend they are yawning deltas.) I have just passed a collection of stalls laid out along the road like an abandoned scaffold—a ruin—where buyers bargain for the lives of crabs bound together with fever grass and unnamed vines. I'm in Trinidad. Crabs know no barrels here. Barrels are for other things: for aging rum and finite oil, both crude and refined, like us. Barrels are for the hammer, the fork, the rubber-tipped stick.

Yes, barrels here are for the *peem* and the *pom*:

> The *peem peem pom*
> The *peem peem peem peem pom*
> *Peem peem pom peem peem peem peem peem peem pom*
> *Peem peem pom pom*

This is sound beaten out of emptied barrels. From this hammering, the eventual crescendo—say, in A minor.

I'm stopped at a light. A middle-aged woman and young girl walk hand in hand. I think, the child could break away at any moment, but she does not. What keeps her? Crossing the road, hands loosely held, each is an archive and a prophecy of the other. I see in them an embodied tense, a history and futurity that captivates and frees. I'm looking east, toward Arima, Sangre Grande, Manzanilla, Africa. Toward doors of no return that I have never seen. To the east now, and thinking of insurrections. But between me and the East of these insurrections is Piarco airport. The airport interrupts the notion of an insurrection (fight) with a means of escape (flight). The resulting stasis is archipelagic. Between myself, the blacknesses of Africa, the indigeneity of Piarco, and the things that interrupt the insurrection: light. I look to the East of my grandparents and imagine insurrections, my attraction—more, lately—to blacks that are perfect browns, deep blues, purples. Blacks that depend, for their varying depths, on nothing but light and heat and sound alone. Blackness like chiaroscuro in practice, shadow shaken off like the blackened gossamer dust of a moth many months after being consumed.

The colors I see are not seen at all but memories of how the eye remembers: the shock of light that either ripens or decays from an invisible whiteness to a graying blue to brown and sepia that mock the shapes of passing cars. They are an action and a consequence. Call it the *palette of memory*: memoir, visually compiled.

Light coalesces into an image. In that image, darkness is a grammar, a dialect of light in need of transcription, making the phenomenon of meaning no less than the telos of light. This is seeing as prismatic action: a matter of the specificity and universality of light in its contribution to the life of the vernacular mind, their combined reach, and the rhetoric they produce, whether singularly (as with the portrait) or collectively as with a nation or region or that of a wider, formerly dispossessed consciousness that amplifies its universality as a means of becoming and returning to itself, viewed across the expanse of, let us say, time and space.

We wear this place like a *mas*. And this place wears us like a *mas*, and like the weather, filtering what we think we see: light, gathered into an image of ourselves we wear like blackness—sensed but also seen. Unmistakably black.

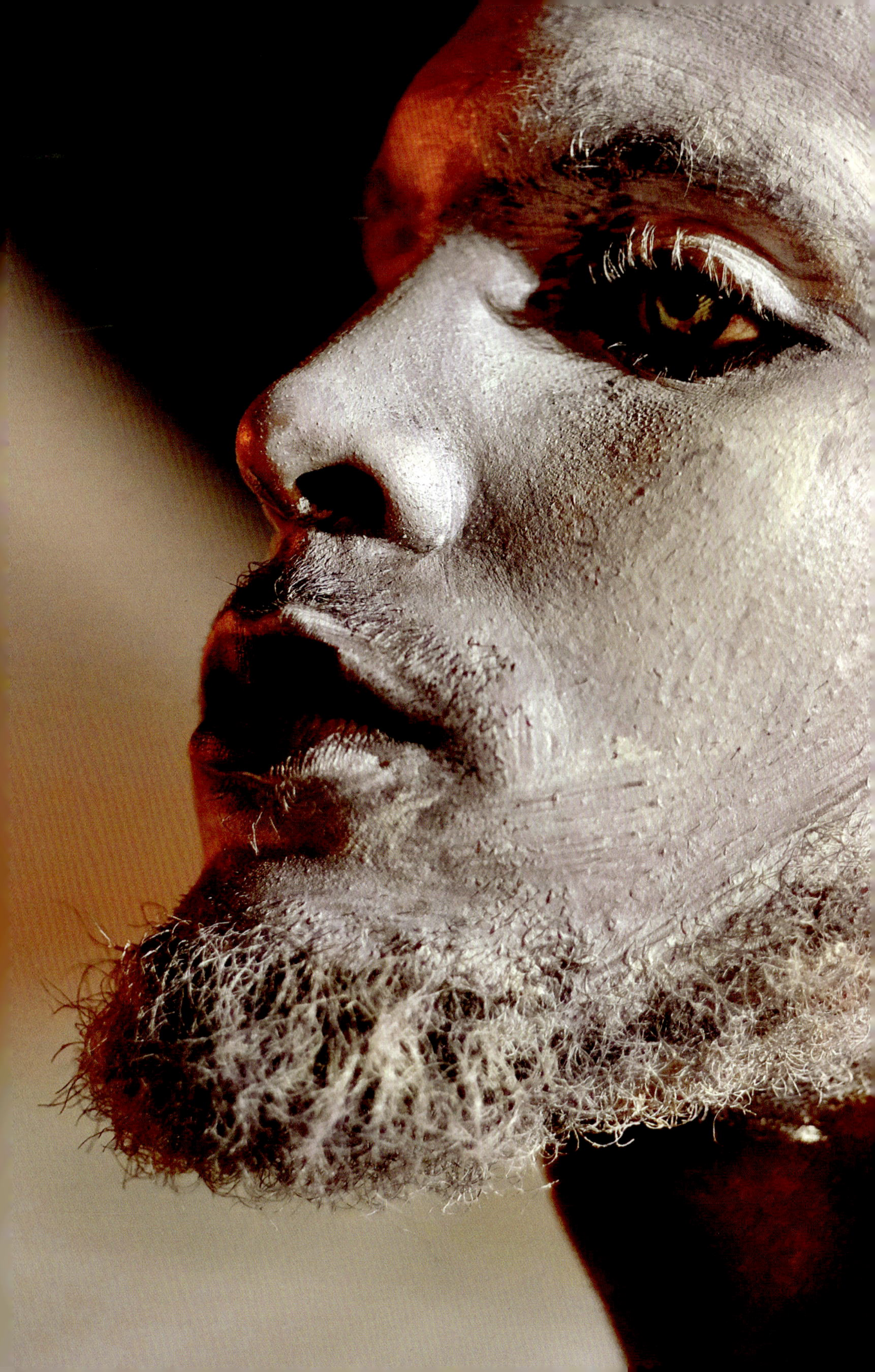

FORM

Chaguanas, Trinidad
May or June 2021

M and I sat together talking a few months after she had a double mastectomy. We were thinking of what more we could make of our collaboration that saw us nude and entwined on a small mattress in an art gallery in Port of Spain, almost as still as stone, except for our breathing, the rumbles of breathy laughter at our ribs and shoulders that no artist could detect, the talk we talked that no one could hear. *Black Life Drawings*, part of an exhibition I had done.[1] One of the artists, a slight Indian woman whose charcoals begin as eviscerations before finding lines to hold what we find out cannot be held, asked if we were lovers. We laughed and drank as we dressed and hoped for a vaccine (which came later that summer), observing protocol as best we could, but still a little tense, as if we could see ourselves living and dying in the *clink* and glint of emptying glass. The talk, this time with gin, brought us to this series.

1 *No Words* (2021), curated by Marsha Pearce.

The series brought me to this thought about re|invention and motive:

> If it can be said that we craft ourselves into unknown things, or shape our knowing to fit into unknown spaces, performing without a script, improvising with our already threatened breath, what can we say is the nature of the thing that propels us, sending us into, through, and out of the existential epistemological void where we and what we make take form?
>
> What (is) shape, what (is) space, what (is) breath but where invention takes place, repeatedly?

Then, a year later, to this revision on a matter of *form*:

> Call me X. That would be best. Like a man without a name. Or, to be more precise, a man whose name has been stolen. You talk about history... well, that's history, and everyone knows it! Every time you summon me it reminds me of a basic fact, the fact that you've stolen everything from me, even my identity! Uhuru![2]

2 Césaire, *A Tempest*, act 1, scene 2.

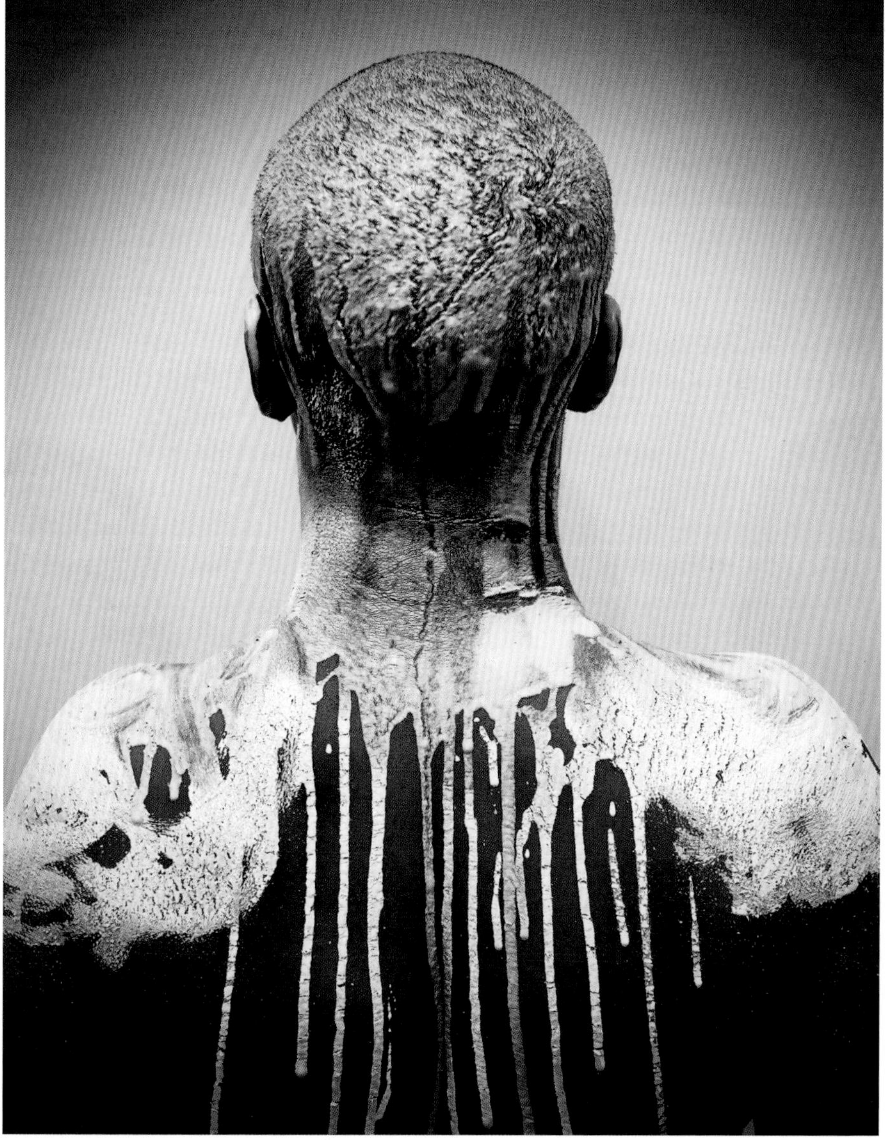

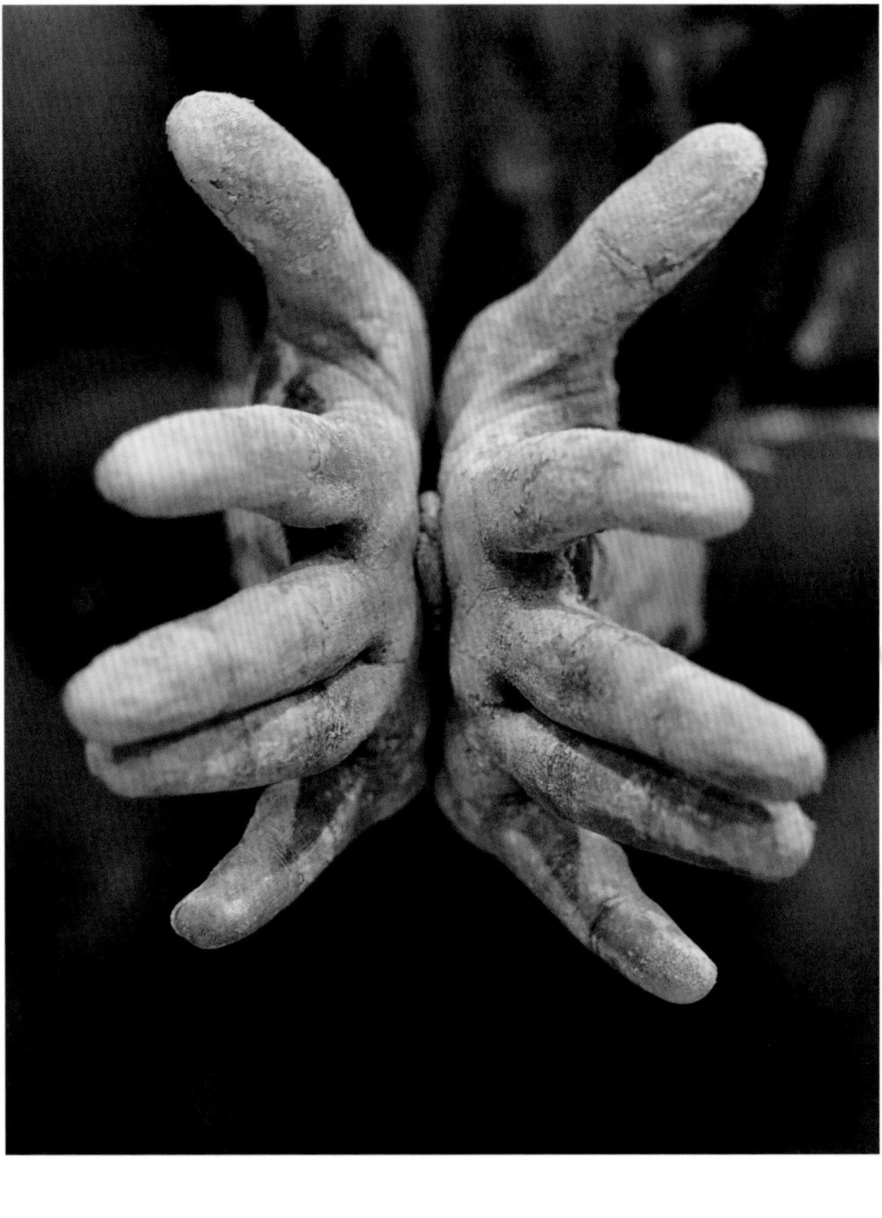

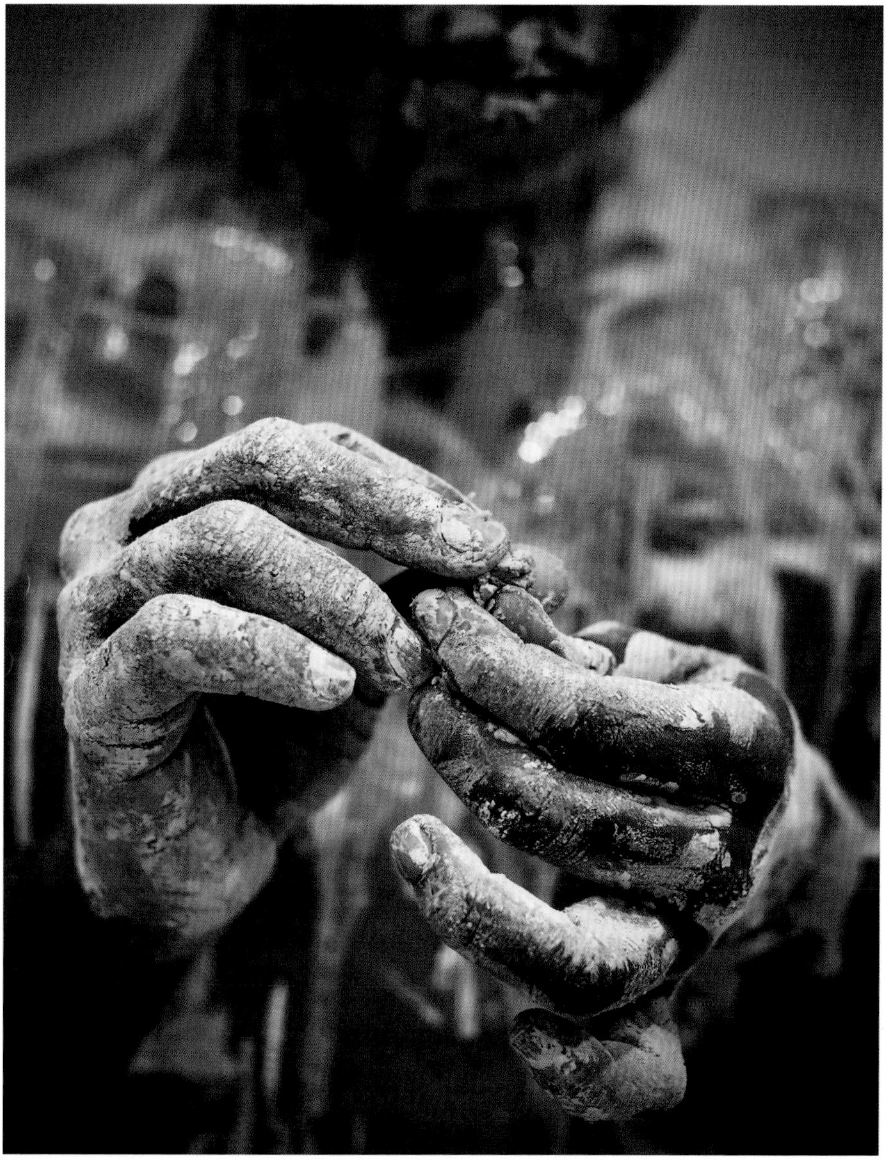

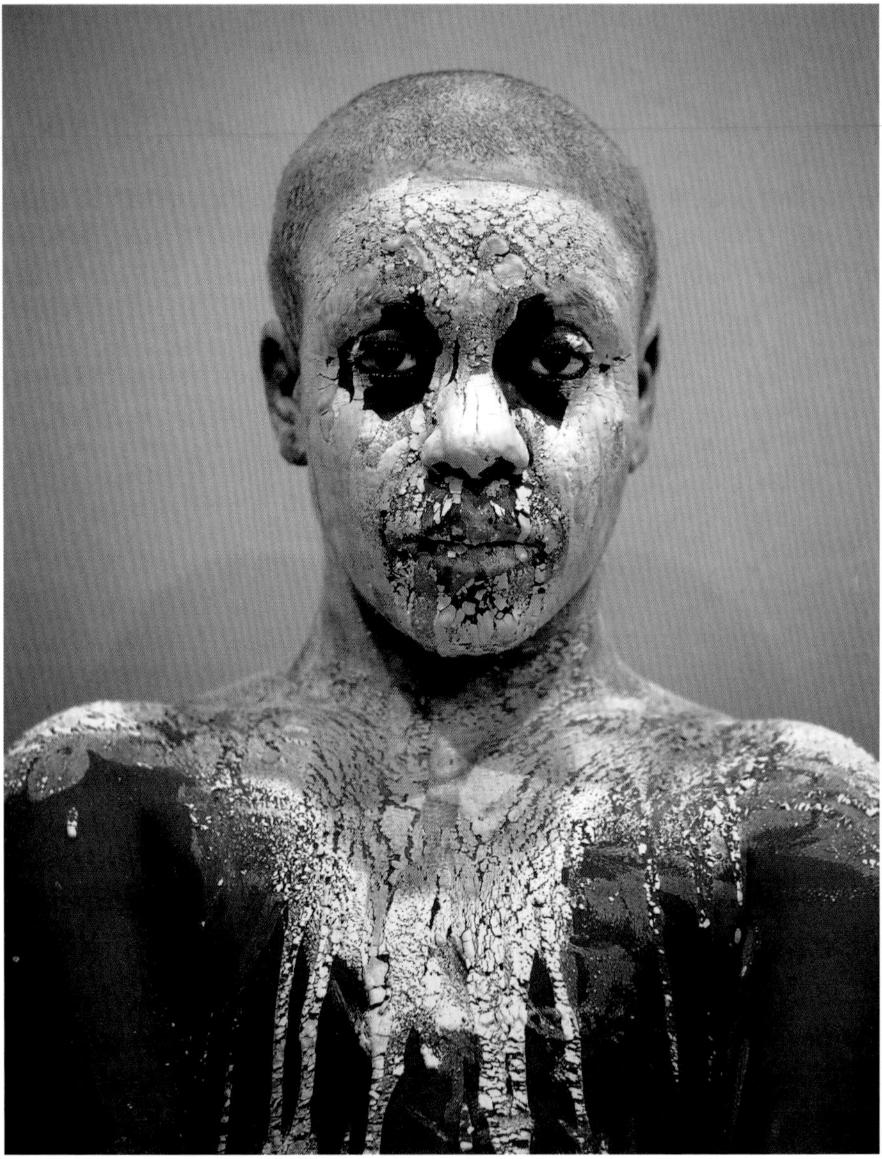

Echoing Caliban's declaration in Aimé Césaire's *A Tempest* (1969) that he no longer wishes to be called Caliban, the contemporary Caribbean subject is invited to consider the alternative to a system of historical identification that is no longer viable for him and, in doing so, to consider whether it ever was or could ever be.[3]

There is a resonance in t|his shift, in the threat to dissolve into the ether, queering himself into a *they*. Or, if not to dissolve, then at least to exist outside the reach of familiar definition—savage, indigenous, immigrant, citizen, enemy, monster, and so on. I do not think they, having deliberately dissolved from *he* into a more diffuse *X*, will ever be fully out of reach. But for this reconfigured Caliban|X to be reached, and possibly regarded if not understood, one will have to stretch beyond what one has thought or known. That shift—in the very shape of their consciousness, from Caliban (nominal) to "Caliban" (self-referential) to "X" (indeterminate)—is algebraic.

3 That echo is undoubtedly what I have observed in Césaire's method of re|making Caliban as|in a Caribbean image. In doing so, Césaire also endowed Caliban with a degree of subjectivity observable to a reader—the explicit sovereignty of his declaration is unmistakable. As such, we can reasonably presume an impulse whose echo would reach beyond the boundary of the play, or of that which the playwright may have initially set. Another thing, I am not so concerned at this point with dissecting Caliban|X's rationale, nor with indicting Prospero, Césaire, or the reader for the incidental misnaming—or, if recast as more identifiably transgender or non-binary, deadnaming—that occurs in the wake of that early declaration and continues to the end of the text. It does bear saying, though, that the echoes of t|his transformation are relevant for how one might sense arrival as re|invention in response to the cascading context of repeated loss. How far was Caliban intended to go? I cannot say, but I am moved by the sheer breadth and pathos of this notion.

That is, in the effort to figure (or re|configure) the formal conditions of one's humanity, one is carried *from* a being that appears to embody a mythos of monstrosity *to* one who (recognizing the inherent flaws of that monstrous configuration) has chosen to exude an alternative mythos with greater deliberation: to be an embodiment of the unknown that elects to transform himself into an unknown that is consciously embodied—a dissipated form. He sheds his form. Put another way, what we recognize as Caliban—that is, "Caliban as form"—is shed for a being we do not, and cannot, know.

A being we, thinking we know the text, once knew.

A being *formerly* known.

By the end of this, perhaps Caliban|X may be as unknowable as ever, perhaps more so—as I said, I am not overly concerned with Caliban|X beyond the specificity of their transformations. The shapes of these shifted conditions for encountering the human are what concern me more. The *conditions* are reconstituted for those who wish to regard their intrinsic humanity with a greater sense of possibility that may be felt, if not altogether learned or *formally* known.

Quickly, before I doubt and discredit myself, I say:

There, right there, in that echo,
in that space between what is coming and what is going,
what I propose and struggle to conclude,
what has already come and already gone,
is that sense I mean to explore.

Returning now, less quickly:
I say this only because we move from one shape to another.[4]
Not only shape, but also our subjection of those shapes to time and the various directions such time(s) may take: we move from time

to time.

4 When I say "we," I mostly mean you and me.

Say, as with Caliban|X, who goes from being *formally* known to being *formerly* known. He (now they) would have been freed, in a sense, from the initial concern about who "Caliban" was in a prior form (having vacated the shell of a name to care and be cared for on different—unknown and unknowable—terms). They have freed themselves. I see a relation here. Not just between them and Louisa and Thisbe but throughout.

We have a similar concern, too: the matter of *care* simultaneously redirected toward ourselves and toward others we do not and cannot know. That concern is for us to be freed, in a way, from the version of ourselves that isn't "ours" at all.[5]

Reading along and reading ourselves into Césaire's dissipation of Caliban's form, we are cast into that same unknown space of the imagined self, where the "formerly known" exist—and thrive. What else could the purpose of Caribbean being *be*, but to help us find ourselves in the entangled matrices of meaning derived from an inherited form—naturalized and unnatural—to commune and dissolve into and between the limbs and beams of our current social order? Perhaps this is too abstract (reading it aloud has not eased its discomfort). I hope, in any event, that we are close enough to the end of empire, or will find ourselves far enough past its ravages and reapings to imagine an elsewhere for ourselves with less anxiety, with greater clarity.[6] Close enough at least to find ourselves as we wish to be found before an arrival we may not be inclined to sense.

5 *Whose* it is, I don't know.
What can the dispossessed possess beyond the constraints of nation?
What can the once-owned truly own?

6 My optimism here is obvious. I know that empire is like language, or like the weather that precedes language—we are never truly "beyond" it, never "outside" of it. Aside from utter oblivion, no scenario exists in the aftermath of empire's impositions that has yet made room for its impossibility.

By which I mean death.[7]

And what does it matter, really? Not much, except in terms of a *mattering to come*, that aforementioned and approaching arrival—the one we sense as blackness.

7 Leroy "Black Stalin" Calliste died this morning. He was my neighbor on Turton Street and an icon in the world of calypso. A great, black giant. Both formally and (now) formerly known, I think he would know what the "once owned" could own. The newly dead know what the living strive to know—and what the long dead cannot—before they die. They say things the living refuse to heed. Perhaps it is only in the afterlife state (*post vitam*) that we will understand his thesis on self-determination in "Caribbean Unity (Caribbean Man)" (1979). His turns are subtle (from "we" in the chorus to "their," for example), and yet the too-easy tripartite appeal—to man on behalf of woman and child—is a sublimity that longs for greater exegesis. In days to come, I will dance with hundreds in the street as we move through San Fernando. And I will think about my grandmother, Muriel. In sun and rain and sun again, we will dance. His burial will move us all, huddled around the hole, to reach for a piece of earth to toss in. Later, vandals will desecrate the grave. A year after that, it will occur to me that the song redirects Caribbeanness away from the absurdity of patriarchy, away from the Caribbean man's "ambition" to be perceived as something other than what he is and, instead, toward a more inclusive appreciation of a humankind that is united but not unitary. *Caribbean*, finally. For Black Stalin, man is not "the measure of all things" but part of a larger idea. Framed as a Rastafarian treatise against "nation" in the illusory sense, the song demands a recalibration of political and civic ambition that challenges us to be more than we have been. In the appeal to a "common intention" is a conception of Caribbeanness that begins in the long afterlife of conquest and genocide, falters in the shorter afterlife of "imported" federations, and is now briefly revived in the new afterlife of a giant. After one has resolved, as best as one can, the false binary of "nobody or a nation"* as a direct consequence of colonialism,

* This is Derek Walcott's grounding gambit in "The Schooner *Flight*" (1977).

the illusion of patriarchy as the path to self-determination will finally be worn of its pretense,[†] and we may finally be ready to emerge, or to bring about the emergence of a version of *us* that is different to what we've been accustomed—call it an emergent "somebody" *formerly* known as   .[‡] All of that will come. But, standing there in the street with his daughter, at the quiet epicenter of a death that has rattled the island, we talk only about the easy movement of his spirit, its detachment from this place of labor and its move to something else—to peace.[§]

Mourning can sometimes be so vulgar. How we rush to claim the dead we might hardly have known in life. As if death and the open ritual of its happening are the only true acts of belonging.

† A "pretense" because we already know that the debility of everyday life that ends in death is all that is required for the argument and the calypso and the poem to wilt into prophecy—even as the calypsonian and poet, no longer alive, (de)compose (still). Walcott's "The Spoiler's Return" (1981) comes to mind.

‡ Caribbean, Antillean, West Indian, nation, etc.

§ Detached, as it were, from the body. A car pulls up, disrupting the quiet of our talk.
"Allyuh having anything tonight?" A wake.
"No," she says, hardly turning to look. "Not tonight."
"Okay, thanks. I thought it woulda have something."
"No, no, not tonight."
"All right then, good night."
"'Night," we reply.

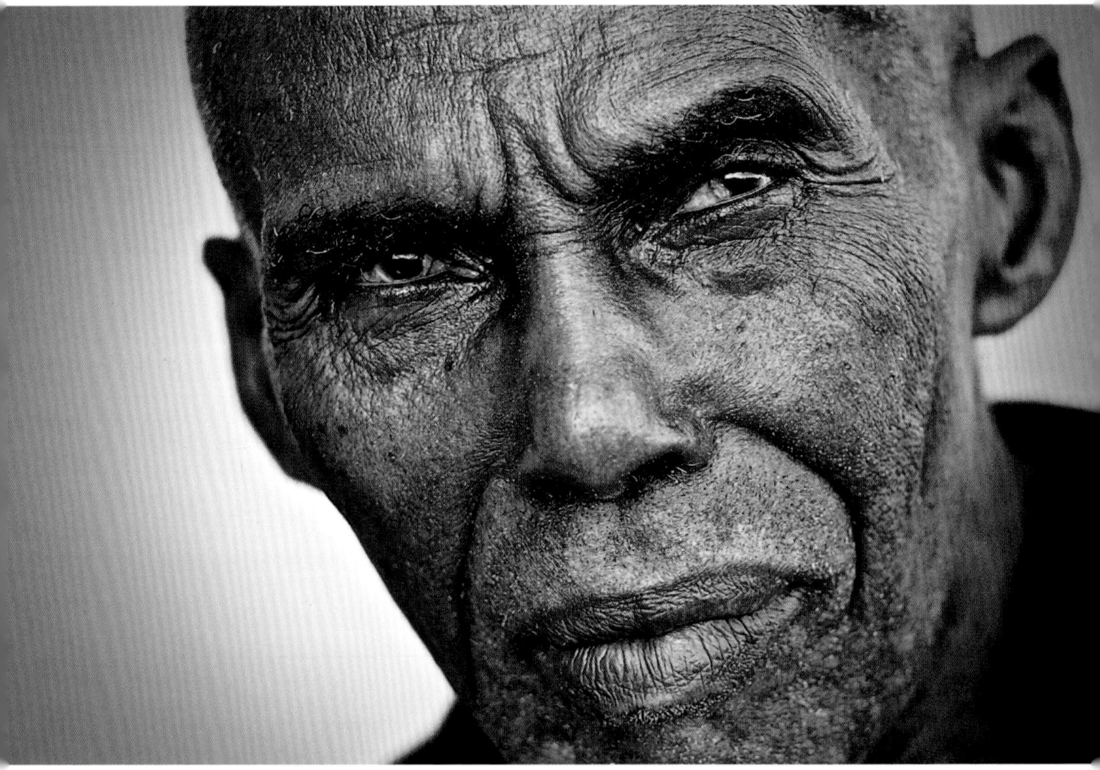

TEXTURE

When this face loses favor,
and this hand its urge to groom and cure,
and when the razor leaves ashes on this savaged chin,
not yet killed with age—though

my unsteady skin grows loose,
my heart wearing out its welcome—
I might wait with less argument
for those half-eaten moons, for clouds that stay too long.

When alabaster eyes turn to jaundiced,
bloodshot stone, the private epoch
turning homeward to memory—
a house of bones that will come to know the coming disregard:

a strand of hair painted over.
My mildewed wall is more than metaphor.

Frame (Erin)

"I look like myself," he said when, finally, I held the framed portrait I had brought with me from Boston to Trinidad. The sequence of events that led to me leaving and ending up here in Erin seemed to bear no practical logic: I had photographed him in Erin, a village in south Trinidad, where he and my grandmother had lived after his retirement, and his children and grandchildren (I am their first) would visit on occasion to mind the orchard, pick peas and sorrel, and trap and hunt. Soon after I took the portrait, I left Trinidad for Boston, promising to bring it back to him. I photographed him in silence—a shared silence—entering a space for what I saw and knew but could not name to make a portrait of a man whose name I knew but whose face I couldn't know that I would see: my grandfather's.

His portrait is a visualized silence.

Breath (Note)

I lived in Boston for almost two years. Beacon Hill. On my campus visit to the university where I'd spend that time, I stayed at my host and her partner's home, a beautiful walkup not far from the train station—the T. I would end up living there the whole time. I had been there a couple of months when I was invited to Thanksgiving dinner by the president of a local university, a black man. I shared the news of my dinner plans with my host, who said, "Oh, how lovely! I should send you with a note that says, 'Don't poach him! He's ours!'" *Whose*, I had not bothered to ask. I still have not asked.

I suppose I should have expected it. She had visited my previous institution the year before and thought I would be a better fit at her institution. The practice, called "poaching," is one of the implicit violences of a profession that refers not only to its "fields" but also its "markets"—being "in" the field and "on" the market, one is prepositionally situated within a discourse of property, and of being bought and sold. *Owned*, in a way. We all note the irony, even as we craft our applications and dossiers, frame our job talks, and train ourselves to grin in an enduring Dunbaresque mask that bears the brunt of what we cannot bear ourselves, or what we try (and often fail) to bear. A mask we wear to get the job we sometimes do not want, to do the work we think we need to do. For some of us, of course, the pretense is carnivalesque—a *mas* we play to live the lives we cannot, to say what we otherwise would not. I'd been warned to expect worse. *Boston*, they said.

She laughed—lightly, pleasantly. I was silent. I knew there was no malice intended, and she was horrified and ashamed when I told her what had had me so withdrawn all those weeks afterward, my interactions wooden. Was it the new year? Was I missing home, my family? Was I depressed? I was working on my second book at the time. Was it that, the garden variety brooding of a humanist in the grip of his "work"?

Anything but what it was: *just* a joke.

A joke more akin to the banality of whiteness and its tacit impositions on the mind and body—on the black bodymind's ability to withstand the implications of white supremacy that treats the multiple myths of black inferiority as normal. As normal as the weather. As plain and unrehearsed as a breath—not like the heavy breath the embattled black body must learn to hold out of habit, but the easy, unthreatened breath.

And there it was, my reason: it was envy.

In my silence, I wished I could breathe with the same kind of ease.

Silence (One day, Congotay!)

Leaving Boston, I thought little about the everydayness of my own fugitivity, less about the deeper reality of black fugitivity in America—like I didn't think too much of the half-hidden passages of the Underground Railroad that made a temporary haven of this neighborhood that was legacy to neither of us. I thought little of the disabling practices inflicted upon us—the historical "us," the "us" of the present day and days to come.

I am—we are—always imperiled.

What I coveted was the ease of breath. How mundane that must sound.

But give me that, as well: the *mundane*.
And give me the unclutched purse, the unstretched lip,
the unsuspecting brow, the unbegrudged compliment,
the unquestioning gaze.
Give me the unviolent joke, the unheld breath.

How to say "give me" without appearing to beg?

Or "watch me take a breath" without appearing too aggressive?

Or "take a breath with me" and have you join me in that conspiracy?

How to say "the unbound breath is mine as well as yours" without some question of the legitimacy or the logic of my claim, without asking who gets to breathe?

You say, "Give me the unbound breath. Give me or watch me take it. Watch me take a freedom that is free. Watch me take my life as it were a portrait." Freedom is sometimes loud, often violent. This is how it is sometimes, but not always. Sometimes it is quiet, sometimes silent. Sometimes it is like an unbound breath: an illicit thing, particularly for those of us who feel we have none—no voice, no breath, no freedom. But we know it is always worth the trouble. Shouldn't we always be willing to free ourselves, to steal ourselves away from unfreedom?

I imagine if my hosts told the story of my departure, they would say I left like a thief in the night. And I did. Silent as a thief in the night, though the only thing I took was myself. *I* was the only thing I needed to take with me. And is that not what it means, after all, to breathe with deliberation? I left, grateful for the lesson in how I saw and might be seen, taking only the silent freedom of an unbound breath.

This is portraiture.

Portraiture, as I understand it here, is as close to freedom as the camera will take you, as close to catching the breath as is possible with glass and light. Breathing, one soon learns, is essential to the quality of a portrait. Not the obvious fact of one's breathing to stay alive, but rather the *style* in which one breathes. The freer the breath, the better the portrait. Hold your breath too long and the camera shakes. A similar thing is true of the one who gives the portrait as the one who takes it: the held breath is heavy, it shakes the body, the face changes, becoming tense, uncomfortable. The portrait is best when the breath you catch is an outgoing one—a laugh, a scream, a sigh, all of these are best in the exhalation. The breath is not so much held as caught. This is a technical matter, but not only that.

This portrait of my grandfather is also an exhalation—his and mine—an act whose intimacy is located as much in silence as in the light. Portraiture may be many things, but here it is the alignment of silence and light, the catching of an outgoing breath, the beforelife of a coming departure. His portrait is not only the material result of light or the catching of a breath, but also the visualization of the texture of a coming silence—his and, eventually, mine.

Portrait (Voice)

> "Hello, this is RB. You just say what you have to say, and I'll get back to you."[1]

By the time I was bold enough to go in search of my grandfather for the stories that have made me, making the pilgrimage to the faraway land of my childhood, I could barely hear his voice. I had to decode the tremor of his lips and the curve of his fingers. I had to examine his brow for the nuances of miniature moles, reading his eyes like some silent picture book. I had to learn for myself that love on my aging grandfather's face would sometimes look like heartbreak. Trying not to lose my own breath as I watched him drift off, mouth gaping, into a shallow sleep, recounting some inaudible dream, I looked for what I could no longer hear.

To see, in general, is to share space with the seen, to make space for seeing and being seen, to direct the path of light, to shift the shape of space. In so doing, the portrait may find its form in the signifying work of the eye and its relation to light as it passes through the lens. But when photographing in silence, you learn that hearing is also a form of looking. Listening, its more deliberative form, is how you learn to see. In this way, his portrait is simultaneously an imaging of texture *and* an imagining of the voice.[2] As much for me as for him.

For me it was a chance to know (and then report) the feeling of moving through space, and of bearing his likeness with me—bearing what looks like him, him in his absence—paying less attention to myself than to the framed portrait I'd promised to bring back for his birthday. Would I break the glass and scratch the portrait? Would I damage the frame? Would it fit in the overhead compartment? Would I have to unwrap it at customs? Would the customs officer even bother to check that I had just been in Trinidad less than a month before? I wonder what these officials look for when they examine the emotionless unportrait in my passport, flipping through before they stamp and initial its pages.

1 Radcliffe Browne, outgoing voicemail message. June 12, 2019.

2 Only later would it come to signify something more theoretical: the materiality of an extant symbol and the symbol of an expectant materiality—breath and texture, respectively.

For him, I want to believe it was a visual transcript of an expression—a visualization of his own silence—that he could see clearly enough to say, "I look like myself." Yes, grandfather of mine, "Grampadaddy." I know what you mean. *I look like myself*, too.

He became what I think we hope to become in the end: old, a giant growing gradually smaller in the eyes of his grandson and growing greater still. Growing smaller in the eyes of the world but growing greater still. Grander, in a way, past his indiscretions and failures, past my grandmother, Vena, whom he would outlive but not outlast. RB, my grandfather, like a ruin languishing in the house they had built, sitting still enough for the ants to walk all over him, too weak to send them scurrying. *My* grandfather, as if no one else had such a thing of their own. How long had it been since you'd seen yourself?[3]

His death interrupts the arc of my inquiry.[4]
What now? Silence.

Silence (Breath)

Breathe, Black Boy.
Ah breathing.

Yuh breathing?

3 I remember asking, but either he didn't answer, or I didn't hear him. I think the latter is worse.

4 What does all this talk of the unhaunted camera mean now that his absence is literal? What should it mean since I can no longer photograph him and know so little of what I saw? What can my musings yield? And what of breath and life now, in all the inevitable stillness of the portrait? I don't know.

Ah breathing, ah breathing.

Ah say ah breathing![5]

Breath (Frame)

Framework is breathwork.

What now in this newer, more permanent silence, in the now one-sided breath?

Do I go in search of his tools to do what they were meant to do, or use them to make the meanings *I* intend, to tell a story not even his portrait could refute? Do I now craft an interpretation of "my people" or make new space for the hollowed holds I have made, inviting them in? Yes, eventually. To engage the objects that have outlived him would be to come into contact with the afterlife.[6] How else to touch the dead than to touch what they have touched, than to project into my own present and passing future a sense of what has come to pass in the life of objects that were once owned? How to see the dead, other than to take them in, their stories too easily misremembered with age, their imperfections too easily beautified with time?

Take them in, like breaths, like the portrait of a single aspiration.

Take them in and try not to panic when they threaten to leave you.

Take them in and let them out—as laughter, a scream, a sigh.

It may be argued, here or elsewhere, that the camera is designed to achieve the opposite of haunting—unhaunting, enlivening, and evacuating itself for

5 Okay, good. Yuh alive.

6 Is it too morose to say it is an afterlife we will all inevitably share, and that these objects will likely outlive me, as well?

some escape. If nothing else, it is a report on the effects and the more subtle affects of light. And while the eye may be part and particle of the universe, the vestibules, chambers, windows, and tunnels that extend as an intentional vision from the eye of the photographer—and which comprise the camera's mechanics—are only for temporary stays, not meant for things to last on their own, without the eye.[7] The camera may be haunted, but it is not essentially a catacomb. That revelation, though it will be useful at some later point, does little now, as I consider a visual practice that holds no promises for me, except that (in the absence of words) it would have to do for the promises I make and try to keep.

Frame (Epilogue)

We do not keep every promise we make to the old. But I was compelled to make the pilgrimage in that way, ignoring practicality to parse for myself the abstractions of "legacy" and "burden" with a semblance of something literal—to move my self from "there" to "here" with what was at first an unwieldy object but became easier to manage, lighter, at every stage of my return. We do not keep every promise we make to the old because we know they will not outlive our ability to do what we have promised to do. But I was compelled.

What those promises will yield is a story yet to be told—a portrait that remains to be seen. For this we may be grateful and relieved that there is still some life left to live in that story yet to be told, that there is a future. Until, of course, there is only the stillness of a life that *was*. Perhaps then we will have time enough to consider the stillness of this portrait that sits in Erin waiting, like its subject, for a more satisfactory frame.

7 Is this an inadvertent endorsement of the necessity of theory as a foreground to action? Only the theory of intentionality as a common sense—the capacity, that is, for thought as commonplace. Put another way, what good is a theory if it does not attempt to undermine inequality by making things common among us?

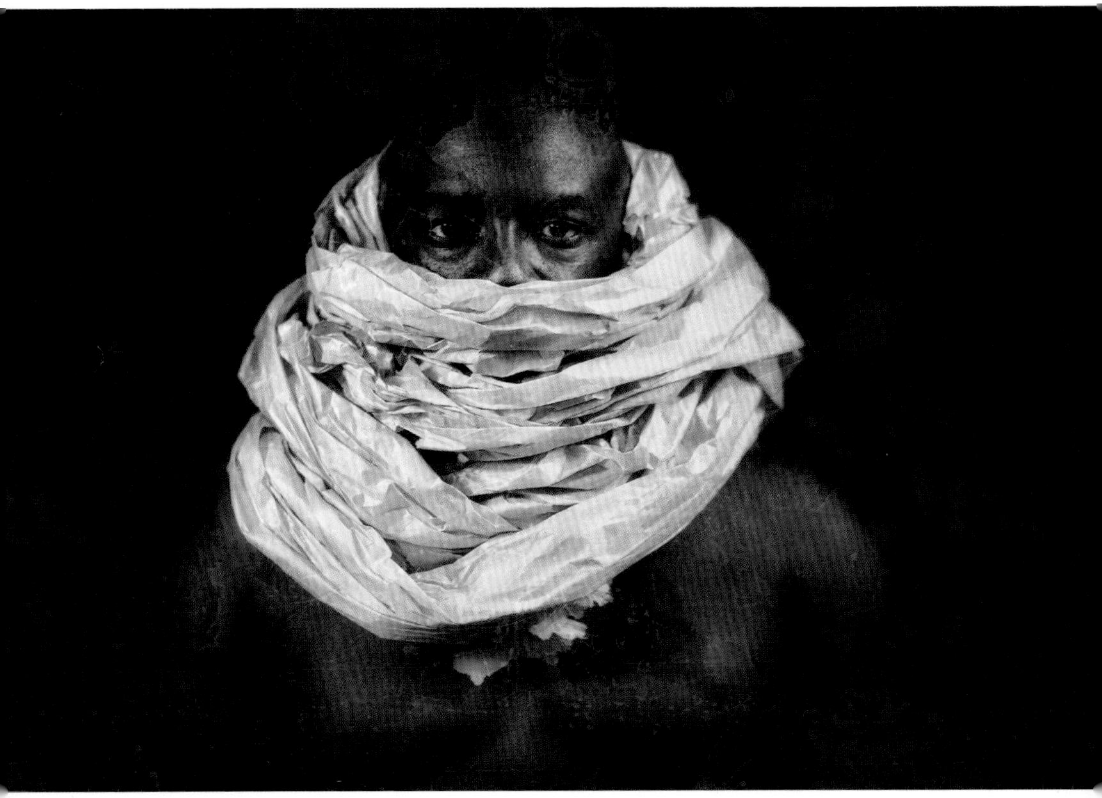

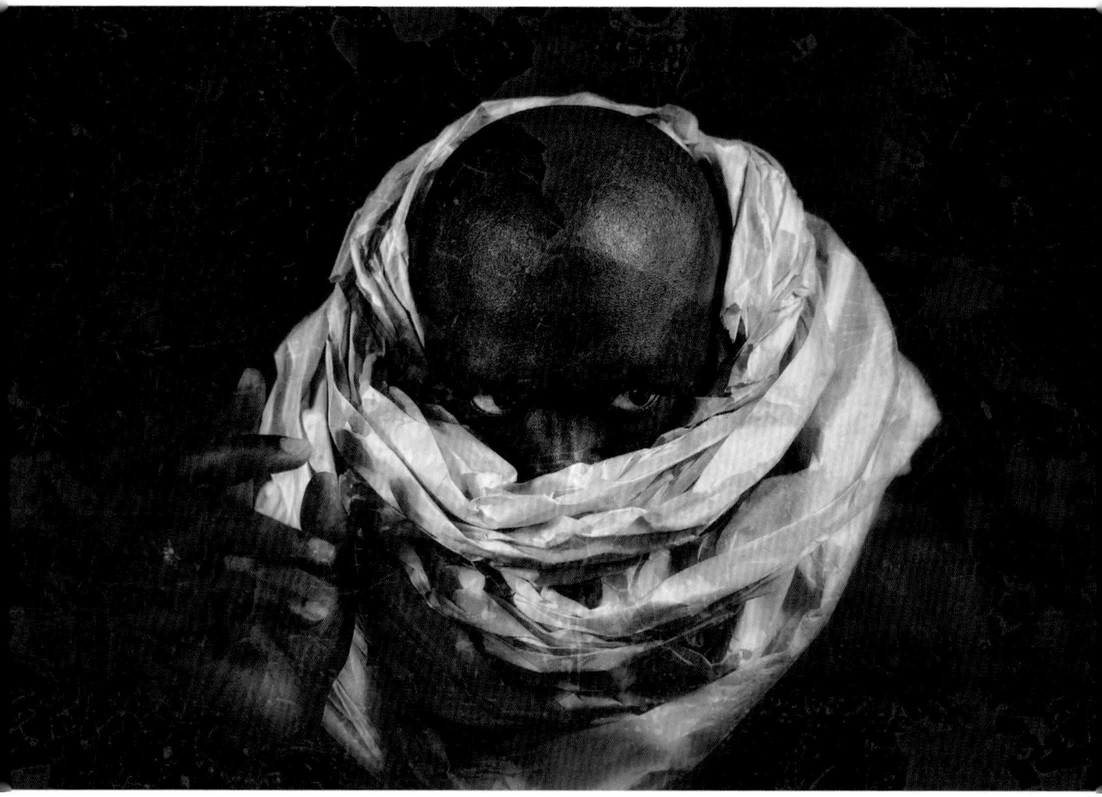

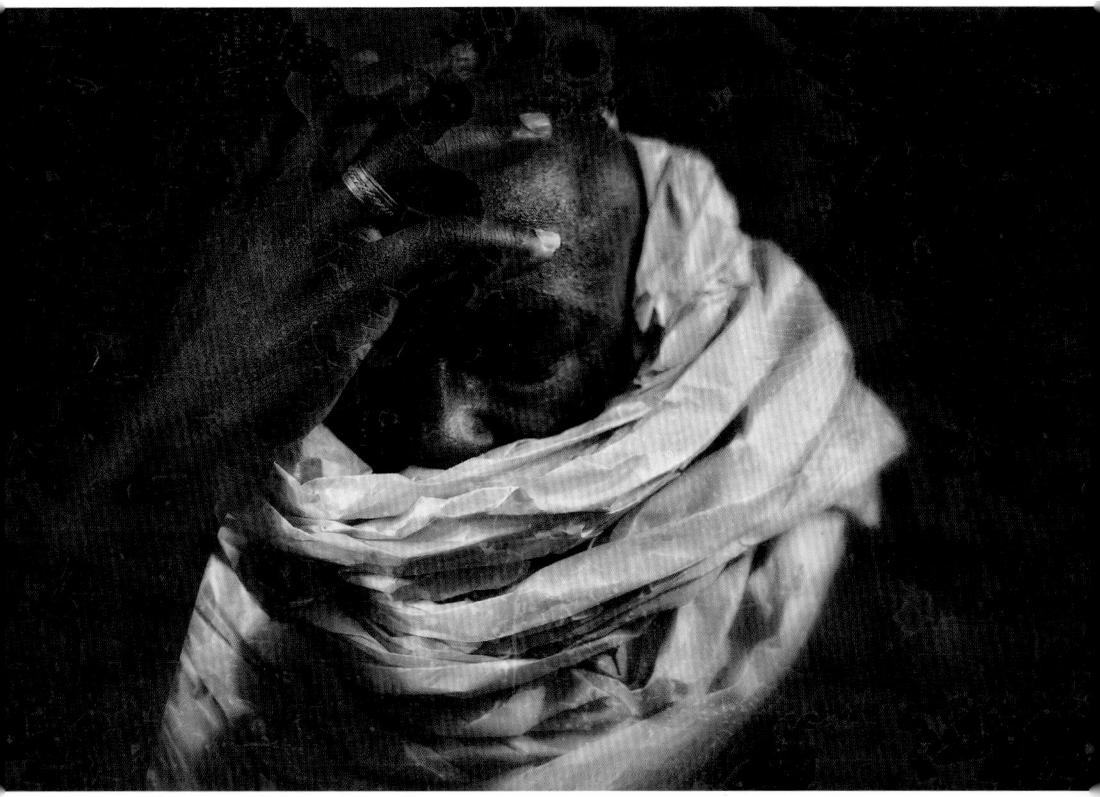

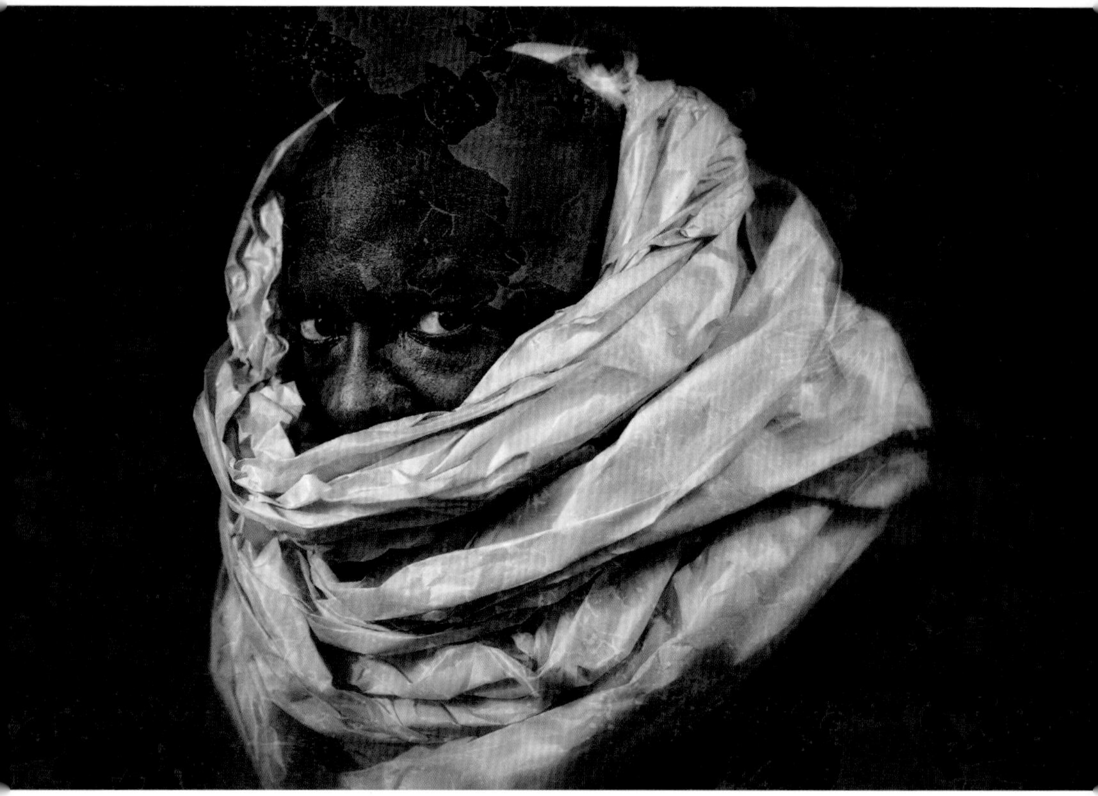

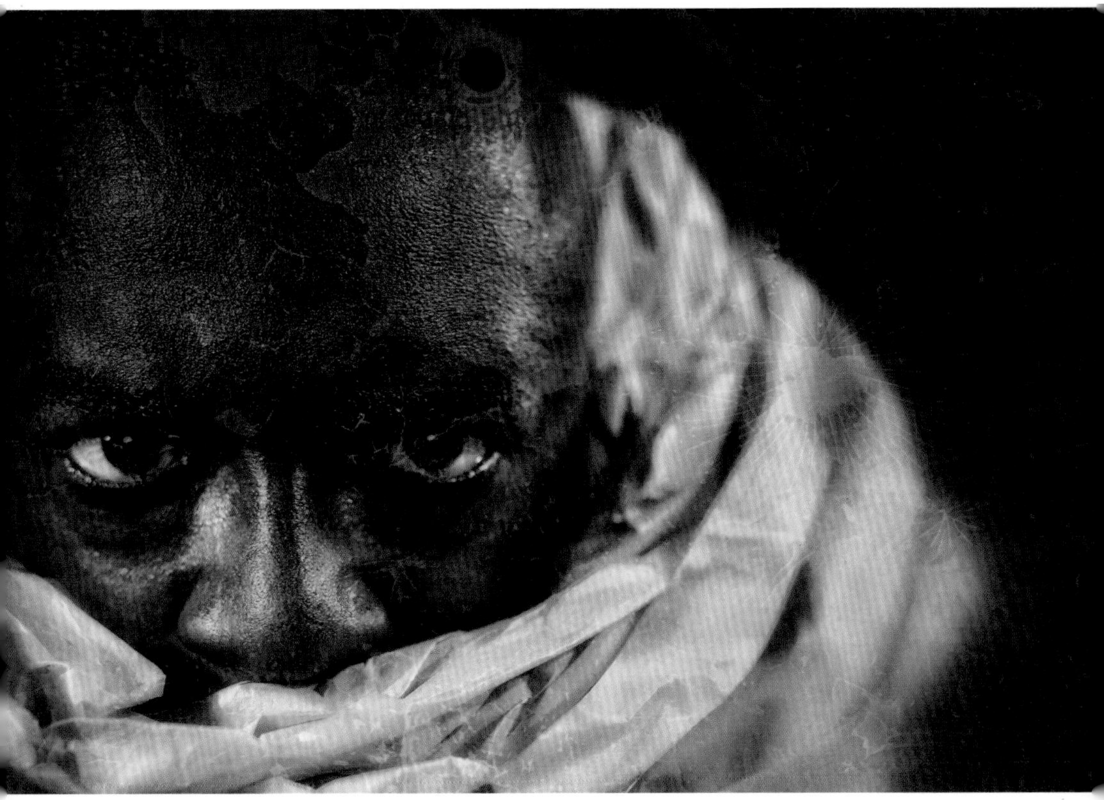

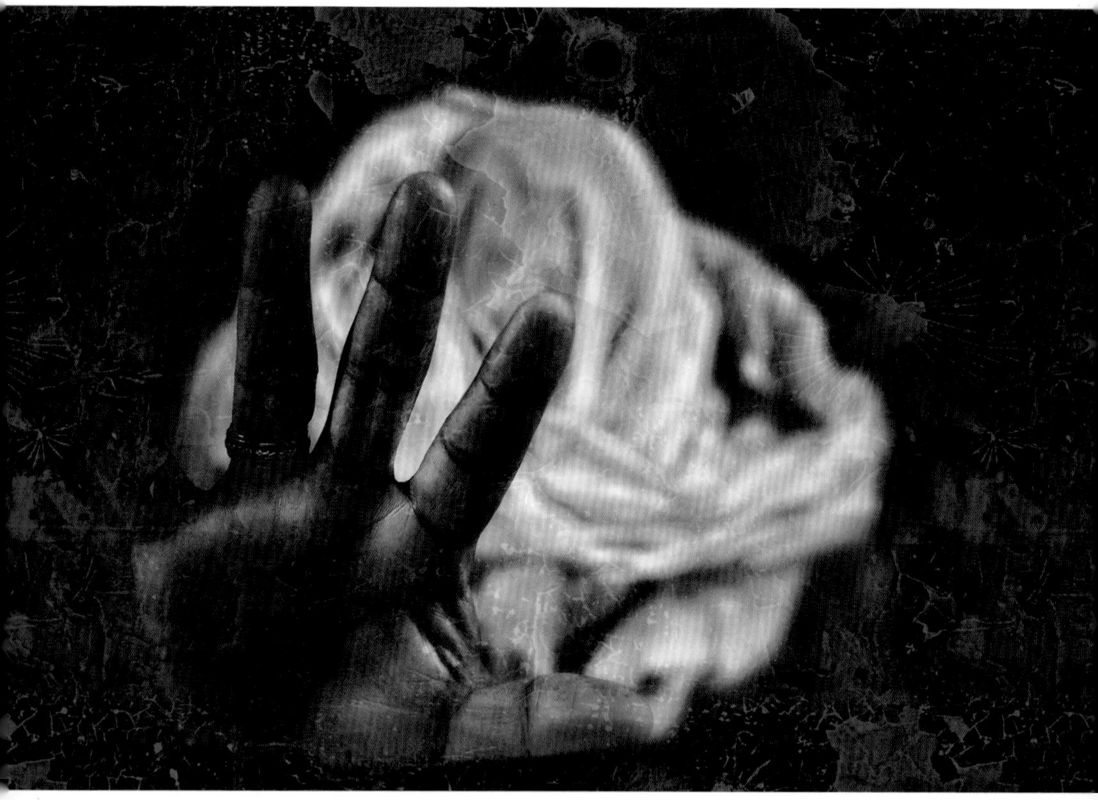

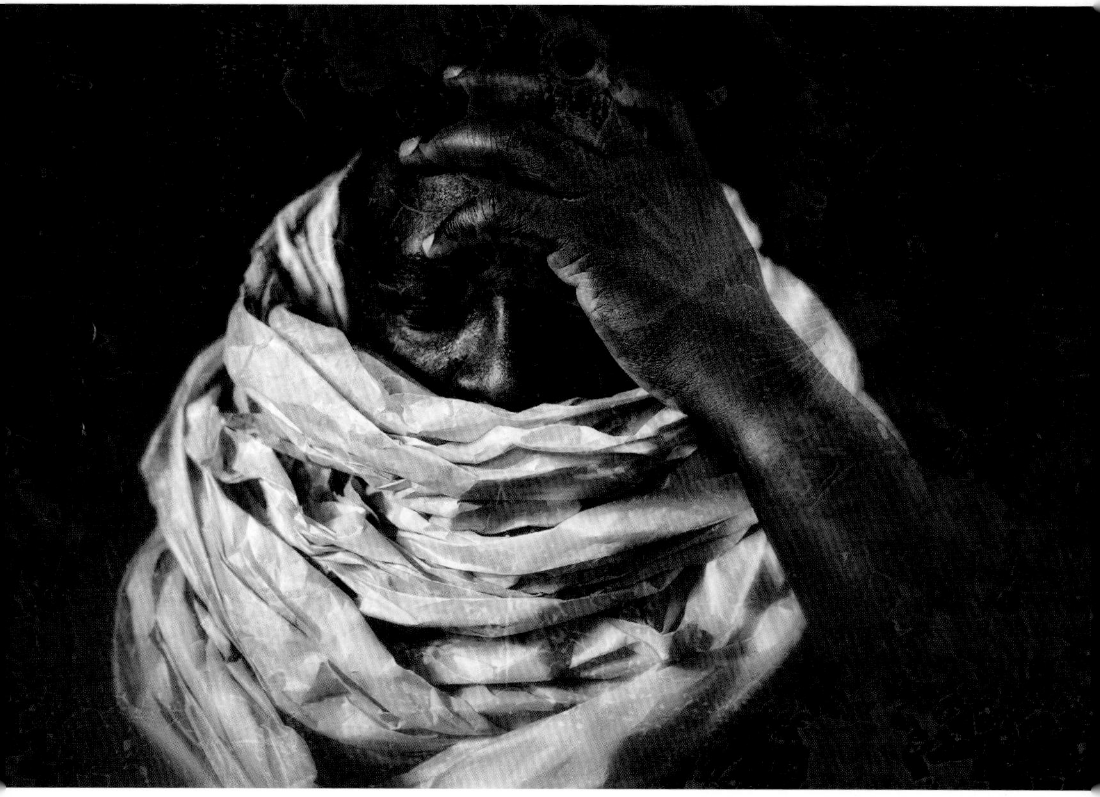

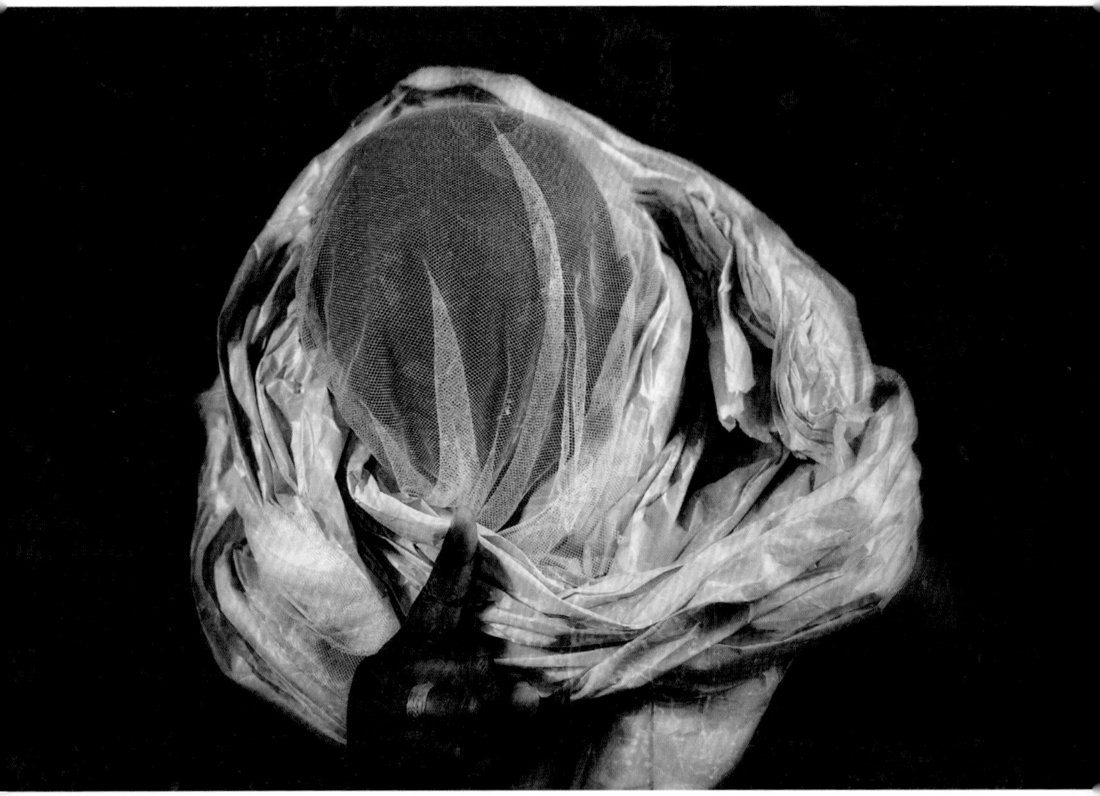

SELF

Do you ever feel yourself becoming an archive of the promise that was made when your portrait was first produced? Was there a shutter, even the *sound* of a shutter to alert you that this transformation had (already) occurred? This is the dual affect of fugitivity and futurity in which the black portrait is read—in which, more specifically, photographer, author, and reader are obliged to consider the portrait as a visualization of black being.[1] The portrait, as such, is also an undoing—it undoes itself.

For me, the self-portrait is an invention that challenges the implicit presumptions of a "self" that is subject to portraiture; the concomitant province of that self and its implied subjectivity within and beyond the parametric contexts of its frame(work)s; and the consequences of its identification and subsequent revisions for both the story and the teller of the story.

The ethos of the self-portrait is an ideal that exists beyond what may be possible for me, such that its liberatory functions may supersede that of any subject it is intended to represent. Call it the *urtext* of a fleeing self. Each version is its original. A *reproduction* but not a copy. Its resonances are recurrent—*fractal.*

Consider the autobiography of self-portrait, that it is like an invitation you have written yourself to an event you know you cannot attend. In spite of your inten-

1 In *Listening to Images* (2017), Tina Campt offers a moving synthesis of these terms. Their relevance is superseded only by their importance as a reminder that the discourses—indeed, the vocabularies—of blackness are conjugated in (and their meanings filtered through) a grammar subject to our design. Our grammars reside and thrive in the broader ecology of black thought.

tion to do so, its existence offers the promise of your attendance but prohibits your arrival. It is a promise you cannot keep. In fact, you are the only one who cannot attend the event, except as an absented guest, and only after the event has taken place. To regard the self-portrait is to orient yourself exclusively to the past.

Taking for granted that the existence of the image is an invitation to reflect, I am concerned at times with the physical and metaphysical poetics of the self-portrait as a form of vernacular "self-imaging" and the role of such an image in the process of creation—that is, the creation of a "self," as well as the simultaneous creation of an instance wherein the newly created self is *undone*. The inherent "creativity" of such works of imaging may be reflected upon as a matter of degree—*how* creative it is can be a matter of some debate. That, too, is nonfiction, albeit from the perspective of writing in the medium of light, for it is concerned with the way(s) a self-portrait makes *and* breaks with|from its meanings to mean anew. And whether that can actually be witnessed, notwithstanding the "evidence" of the self-portrait that is proof as much of the success of a creative act as its inherent failure.

The self-portrait is an *impossibility*. It has no self. That is to say, in terms of its extant materiality, the symbolism of its gathered materialities, and the apparent materialization of its gathered symbols, the self-portrait is evidence of a visual alchemical argument, the confluence of which results in a statement of subjective intent that can only exist in the absence of a self—a self in absentia.

There is, even more plainly put, no such thing as a self-portrait. Except, of course, what the conceit of naming makes of it—what the photographer attempts, and fails, to make of this particular genre, where a self appears to be there but is not. And even then, naming is insufficient to endow the portrait with a self, or to retain the self within the portrait. For while the "image maker" may be present for the image that is made, he is also forever absent from it. The self stays with him, to the extent that he can hold and be held by it. Unable to exist in two states at once, it *cannot* inhabit the frame as it does the body (in spite of the latter's aspirations for transcendence).

Thus, the self-portrait is not merely selfless but is, more accurately, a *portrait of selflessness*. This is grounded in my recognition of my blackness, the sense that I inhabit a blackness that is subjected to the margins, but which does not insist itself *into* a center that has not been designed to accommodate it. Instead, it insists itself *as* center. The paradox of this self-centering is *archipelagic*, in that it renders the resulting image—the so-called "self-portrait"—a kind of visible impossibility, its assertion essentially negating the presence of the self it represents. In that central position, between *coming into being* and *being undone*, the self-portrait functions not as a proxy of the photographer but as a visible representation of a *void*: the inhabitation of an emptiness, a crowding of it, its suspension of time and space, a declaration of life in perpetual imagination of itself, an image of life in absentia. Lived, as it were, elsewhere. Beyond the reach of the frame.

The premise that the portrait has no self is also an admission of my own subscription to the idea of a self that can be possessed—that is, a self whose affect alone persists in the photograph, like a ghost in the medium. To speak of my self in relation to these portraits is to speak to archives and archetypes, to aspirations that linger at the core of the image and just beyond my grasp. It is to speak to the ineffable as if it were a presence I could behold. But it is also more than that. Equipped with and divorced from the terms of its own existence, the self-portrait is able to enact what I consider to be its fundamental advocacy—that is, its tendency toward remembrance *and* imagination, *held for* and *shown to* those who wish to make their presence known, and on behalf of those who may be absent, which will inevitably include the storyteller himself. By foregrounding the absence of the self with a visual projection of its nonpresence, the portrait argues for its own immortality—the mythical immortality of its mortal subject, that of the audience, and of the stories they have promised to tell and to witness.

There is, as I have said, no denying that a self was complicit in its making. But the endowment of a self that cannot be observed or measured is *not* a gift of the maker's intent or his influence. Quite the opposite, in that it is only in the *absence* of other words to name the character of the void that the self of the portrait is able to emerge, appearing to fill a vacuum caused by the inability of the maker to name what cannot be perceived, except by attempting to name what he has created—a "self" existing in name only, literally for want of a better word.

What better word is there than *self*?

This act of witness as faith lets us know of the inherent humanity of the maker (or, at least, his aspiration to it). But it does nothing for the photograph as a vehicle of meaning that is independent of the maker.

Imagine, then: the audacity of a thing to exist in spite of the logics that appear to contravene its production. This is an image. Now, imagine the materialization of what you have imagined. This, too, is an image. Imagine yourself, there, in it. Is there anything blacker than a thing whose obvious existence is founded on the idea that defies perception yet nevertheless demands that we look, and look for the language to say what cannot truly be seen, only felt and remembered as an impossibility dependent solely on your witness—your imperfect witness—for its reality? Is there anything more Caribbean?

No.

We—you and I—are on the outside of that.

Knowing it will occur has placed us in perpetual wait for|want of its perpetually imminent arrival.

I may be getting ahead of myself.

What does it mean to suggest a self-portrait may be made—that it exists, surely, but that it possesses no self that we can discern? It means that to attempt to regard a photograph of oneself is to embrace the paradox that *you cannot do what you think you are doing* and *you do not know what you think you know*. What to do, then, with the absence you observe, other than to embrace it for what you think it is, to subordinate yourself to the feel of quiet and noise that unfolds in spite of that absence, and to let the story be told?

It is, as far as I am concerned, a tacit continuation of my black fugitivity—rather than, say, of my being "captured." Its capacity *as a photograph* is an explicit embrace of the frame (qua frame-up) that rationalizes the subject *and* the subsequent fugitivity of the subject. One's awareness of the frame is a form of self-definition and a simultaneous declaration that what is defined cannot, in fact, be framed. Read this as a foreshadowing of a desire for freedom that can only be made in absentia as a fugitive "caught" in midflight. The freedom would already have occurred by the time you come to regard the desire for it.

We may conclude only this: one may *behold* the subject, but the subject will not be *held*. The subject—me, in this case—will resist it altogether, the experience of subjection *externally imposed* in favor of a subjectivity that is *internal* and *perpetually emergent*. What I am describing here is a transposition of presence. I mean to evade the subjection of being looked at but not seen. If I am not seen, let it be because *I* have evaded—and by evading I will have provoked an aversion of the normalizing gaze, an aversion to normalization altogether. This may be relevant as I move toward an allegory of this place and the people in it, notwithstanding the pathos I may have fostered of a fugitive Caribbean self held impossibly in portrait.

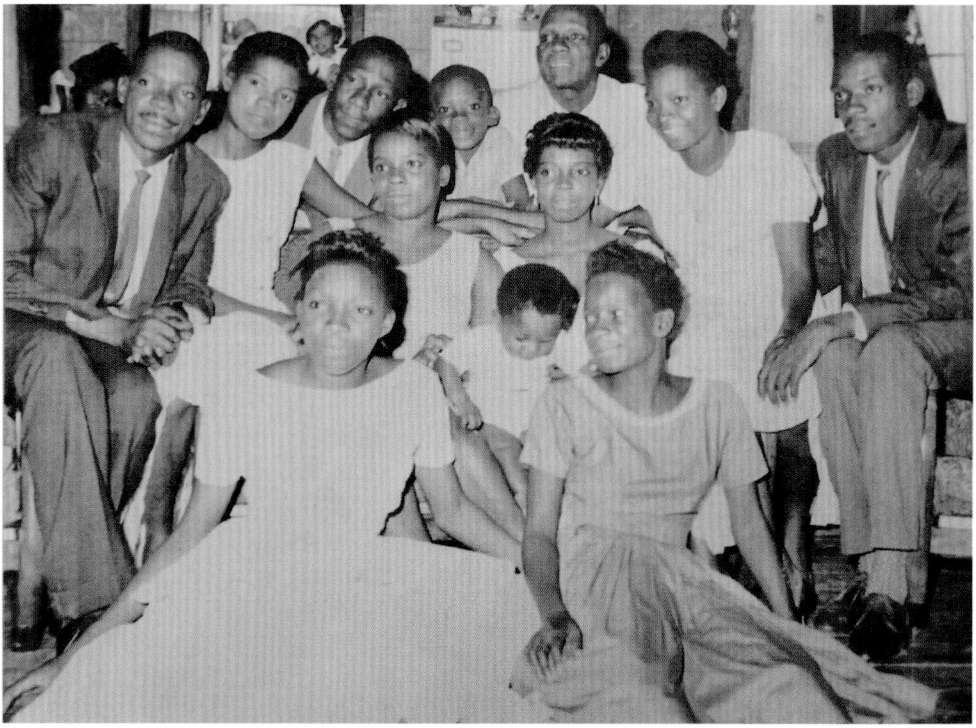

LOOKS

Here, then, is something meant to confound: a move closer, in words, to an imagining that is grounded in an allegory of my people and their tenuous constitution, a series of aversions that, in the end, constitute a way of seeing.

Here is a portrait of the Wrights, my mother's family, headed by Newallo John Wright, my mother's father. I am not *here*, yet. In 1961 my mother's family is not yet *mine*, not even in a symbolic sense. Still "subjects" of a Crown they have never seen, they become *my* family sometime after, in 1974, when they are all past this moment, memories in one way or another of their former selves. I only exist in the afterlife of the moment, my presence a fiction until my arrival makes it true. But this is a portrait taken as they approach the end of Colony, the beforelife of Independence that will occur the following year, in 1962.

Present, in a way, are:

Newallo John (NJ)
Frank, Lystra, Carl, Lennox, Jeanne, Collins
Marjorie, Maureen
Andre
Evelyn, Eva (who will be my mother)

They sit for what we know as a memento mori, a reminder of who once lived (there), for (us) who remain and sometimes return.[1] It is a portrait of presence

1 *Remember Trinidad when you are gone,* the image of colonial Trinidad says.
Remember your family. Remember us, Trinidad, your family, when you get there. Remember what we were and what you are. Remember here when you are not here. Remember and return. And remember even if you never leave here. Remember this place you never left, though everything and everyone will leave.
Even you.

but also a portrait of absence, of loss. They sit, widowed and motherless. Muriel, Newallo's wife, my mother's mother, had died some years before, in 1959. In retrospect, the scene appears to be a fiction because they had already begun to disperse. Marjorie and her husband Carl had already been married (the year after Mother's death) and were living somewhere else. On Coffee Street, maybe, or Hilda Lazzari Terrace. They nevertheless come "home" to sit with the others who will soon depart—

Maureen to New York,
Jeanne to Montreal, Toronto;

and who will later depart—

Evelyn to Caracas,
Eva to Toronto, Caracas, New York;
and who will sooner and later depart[2]

—returning briefly from their lives to a place that was, for some of them, a thing of the past.

In this way, the portrait is a fiction of a nonfiction. Not the making *as if* and *never was* as fictions do, but the re|making of *what was* (a family) in advance of *what will be* (their inevitable departures). The play of tenses leads to a contrivance: a return that occurs in advance of some later arrival after some have left (and left). A minority now remains: Lennox, Jeanne, Evelyn, and my mother, Eva.

The rest: *remains*, their remains (now) at rest:

Newallo John (d. 1988)
Frank (d. 1983), Lystra (d. 2011), Carl (d. 2008), Collins (d. 1965)
Marjorie (d. 2014), Maureen (d. 1997)
Andre (d. 2021)

For the moment, they are all alive. And all together. What I know and sometimes celebrate as the sculpture of their individual features—their looks—is softened now, as they sit encased in the living room, their subtleties simplified, their features and affects flattened into a map of a place I can never truly visit. Here, the past is not a memory but a thing that precedes memory.

What precedes memory? Call it, for now, *History*, a past before the past you know. Here, that history is a unification of lights and shadows flattened into the

2 . . . and depart.

single dimension of *family*—an archipelago of faces and bodies bound by their blackness in a sea of fabric, its folds and flows demarcated by hem and stitch, by the lines of its internal form, its long desaturated color, its onetime texture. Though it does not yet show them cracking or coming apart at the seams, their apparent "presence" is also a prophecy of an absence to come—theirs and, eventually, mine. No separation exists between them: hands fall into hands, shoulders join with knees, necks nestle against elbows, slender arms entwine. Held still, their faces resist the more conventional practice of photography as identification, gesturing in a way toward something that could be art—a gesture that, later transposed, will inform a method of making.

Taken together, it is like a curio, through and in which we can see the operation of an *exteriorized interior* (that is, the subject to be seen, *held* in view) and an *interiorized exterior* (that is, the object to make seeing possible, in which the *beheld* is held). Collected and held in the perpetuity of the frame, it is as if they had been hewn from the chalkstone of the Hill itself—San Fernando Hill. As if they hadn't gathered at the family home on Carib Street but *had been gathered* to produce a portrait, implicated in the fulfillment of someone else's vision. This is my mother's family further removed: a representation of a representation of a family.

To *see* them is to see what the photographer, Mr. Artiss, has made of them. It is to see yourself make a fetish of his fetishizing vision. It is to see the complicity of resemblance in the commission of this act. It is to see your history turned against you—weaponized, in a way—to see the unseeing of your family before they become your family. It is to see the unseeing of those you resemble, whose features you hold. Looking almost uniformly to their right, they are obscured by the intrusion of the photographer's direction of their gaze—a "Look over there, to your right, and smile just a bit"—that marks the portrait *as* portrait but misses the mark of the subtlety of self-possession and witness for which the form is sometimes known.

Here is a dis|possession—of selves, their containing bodies, their memories, of all the frame can hold—as they were directed to look *away from* the thing designed to look *at* them:

> wait a moment, be still;
> hold that stillness for as long as you can;
> hold it and hold your breath, try not to breathe;
> smile as you try not to breathe;
> look away—do not witness the taking of this moment of yourself as a photograph you will have to wait to see—miss the moment;

> be like sculptures of yourselves, perfect replicas of yourselves missing
> the moment, which you may later give as gifts of your black beauty,
> your beauty hung on walls, on a page, in an archive;
> stay there, *riiiiiiiiiiiiight there.*

See how the directions *misdirect*?

Their gaze is *not theirs* at all. It is *designed*—not the *looking at* that privileges the photographer's control of the scene, but a *looking away*, bearing the imprimatur of the photographer's control over the subjects themselves. An aversion. Almost uniform, they are not *themselves* at all but subjects *objectified* and subsequently arranged to enable the making of a portrait. But it is a portrait of a particular way of seeing—their absented presence no different from an absence. And seeing what? Like portraits themselves, they miss themselves at the moment of their objectification—their transformation from subjects to *subjected*. They appear to miss the subjection.

The moment itself is not theirs at all, but the photographer's. I arrive too late to know what *must* have happened for them. What they gaze at (the moment of the directed gaze) and what I seek from that gaze (an accurate transcript of that moment) are not *here* but elsewhere. To complicate the matter, I know the map is not a map at all, the archipelago only a metaphor. No *there* exists as a place for me to visit, not even in the materiality of this text I have always known: a *not here* (that is elsewhere) and a *no there* (that is beyond the boundary of elsewhere). It will confound because, of course, it is *meant* to confound, but see it as the logical extension of the *Nowhere* we encountered earlier.

We recognize the hegemonic demands of a prism acting with light on the body, imperial and postcolonial, as if its discipline were normal, as if it were as native as loincloth and feather. The point is clear: the photographer is looking for accessories to adorn the execution of a visual cause: *seeing* the subject. For which he has managed to make accessories of them—black curios, softened and polished, set to sit and smile just so in the frame. Hegemony portraited. Crown and Colony portraited. The end of Colony—*postcolony*, *neocolony*—and the coming Independence framed. Blackness framed. A family of Wrights disciplined. He has made what Barthes would call a *studium*, a collection of standardized meanings conveyed as an image, of light and chemical and paper convened to tell the story of their gathered bodies.[3] Even as a photographer, and mindful that my critique of the craft can undermine my own practice, I find these violations difficult to accept.

3 Barthes, *Camera Lucida*.

I want something else to be the case with my family's portrait—an idyll or a host of imperfections that are ours. There are several anomalies that together seem to form a visual counternarrative of the formality of encasement that we see in the genre. But they only amplify the photographer's control of form and his further subjection of bodies (and what they hold) to fit the dimensions of the frame. Look, for example, at the crown of NJ's head at the top of the frame, Frank's and Collins's missing shoulders on the left and right, Evelyn's fingertips at the bottom left. These may be minor, a simple matter of cropping, but I notice these missing parts of my family as if the portrait itself were a looted crypt: humeri, phalanges, and frontal and parietal bones of the cranium all missing. Skin, too, their dermal blackness removed.[4]

I want a nonfiction that is less fictionalized than the one I've come to know—an alternative to their dispossession, their explicit in|visibility. Too late for blame, and confounded, I find myself at a loss—a loss that is like a portrait, or the mystery of its paradoxical subjection. Too late to correct the portrait or sabotage its making, I am bound to consider its *affect*, toward a subsequent method of reading. To produce it, I conspire with the girl who will be my mother.[5]

In this portrait of her family, she is virginal and distracted. Her gaze is not a gaze, but a *look* held still, appearing as if caught. If "caught," it is between direction followed and direction ignored (look, for instance, at Lennox looking at us). "Caught," as we are all caught, between one thing and another, or before and after one thing or another. She is before the breakdown—before she is "not herself." No children of hers to speak of, yet. No child has come. None to mourn for never coming. No children of other women—all of them white—in her lap

4 I wonder, in terms of my own photographic method, whether the disembodied can be mutilated? This is, perhaps, an ethical question (of *should*) and an existential one (of *could*). In terms of nonfiction, I think there is a significant difference between the mutilation of a memory and the recognition of memory's mutability. This ought to apply to material nonfictions as well.

5 Not counting the children (two of whom are not members of the family but are adopted into the portrait), those "being taken" in|to the photograph are either complicit in the biography of the photograph they help to make or are conspirators in the undermining of it. That is, the subject in the photograph is either a saboteur or will, at some point, be implicated in the sabotage of the work of the image, turning it (however belatedly) to a purpose that will differ from that of the photographer. Given the form(ality), the posterity of dress and suit and tie, of polish and polish, I doubt the photographer would have wanted to craft an intimacy to ruin it—or to craft an intimate ruin from the outset, which I think is worse.

or on her shoulder or in her many stories of the perfect care they received, the benevolence of her employers.

Even *here*, in this portrait, she is *not here*.

And yet, she—this representation of her—is the major contention of the portrait—what Barthes might call its *punctum*—that both defines *and* ruptures its integrity. She has destroyed the photographer's intention out of reflex.[6] She is distracted, and her distraction attracts. That attraction is what makes the portrait what it is, taking it beyond what it was intended to be.

Moving outward from the point of impulse and her own volition, we can speculate that she is either looking at nothing, at Andre, at Evelyn, at Frank's hands (seen behind Evelyn's head, in the space created by Marjorie's lap), at Marjorie's lap (behind Evelyn's head, where Andre must have been at first), at Frank's knee, or at something beyond the frame (something *not here* in the frame, *no there* beyond what we can see). Maybe the yard, which I will come to later. We can speculate, but even the speculation leads to an impossibility: framing a thing we will never trace. Her look is *hers*, a thing we will never find. Perfectly fugitive—and, thus, free—her distraction undoes the hegemony of the form, its beautiful discipline.[7] It has transcended the archipelago, gone off the edge of the portrait, escaping the reach of history itself—a past with no future that breaks open to reveal a future with no past.[8] The portrait is both these things at once.

Her look is also a broken gaze. A break in form and a form of breaking—an *oramaclasty*. It sets me on a path beyond the portrait, toward the unseeable. The portrait breaks open, the gaze breaks into a look and gets away. But just as "talk does bring talk," my consideration of one image leads inevitably to my consideration of another. The face, as we say, *cyah hide*.

6 This is contentious enough to elicit some basic redress. Its work may be described as *a paradox of presence* in Caribbean and post-Caribbean thought, method, and practice.

7 If you feel yourself wanting to ignore it or wishing she had behaved like the others, or done what the others had done, or that her disruption had been detected as potential and that it had been resolved before the shutter opened, try to resist the impulse. It is a trap.

8 I'm thinking here again with Campt, who argues: "The grammar of black feminist futurity is a performance of a future that hasn't yet happened but must. It is an attachment to a belief in what should be true, which impels us to realize that aspiration. It is the power to imagine beyond current fact and to envision that which is not, but must be. It's a politics of pre-figuration that involves living the future now—as imperative rather than subjunctive—as a striving for the future you want to see, right now, in the present" (*Listening to Images*, 22).

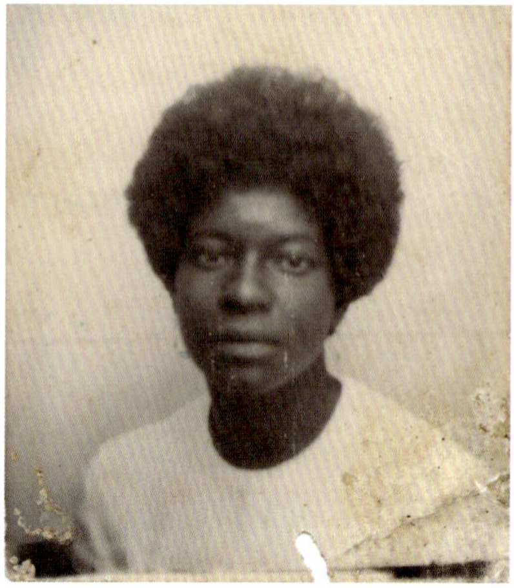

Treating the errant look as prodigal, I want to re|turn to the unsmiling face—prima facie—in an unremembered photograph of my mother. She is perhaps twenty-one here, grown but still bound to a certain yard, to the moss and the dirt, to the standpipe and canal, the sometimes wasted water that still conspires with the old theories of being, grounded into edifice and boulder and gravel and sand and dust. Like the photograph of her mother and her motherless family, this one is an impossibility: a shaft of light disturbed into a form. Arriving too late to witness her memory of its ascension to narrative (and then to meta-narrative), my encounter with this portrait is a walk into an empty room. The vacancy of her stare, the sloped shoulders of an exhaled breath, the exhalation held within the frame—each causes an echo, each echo amplifying my fear of a departure to come.

Hers.

She says she does not remember anything about it except what she can see—the weightless wig, the silvery ghosts of earrings hung, the ribbed top bleached bone white. Nothing else—and in that "nothing else" of *head* and *hung* and *rib* and *bone*, a memory of *tabanca* you might have seen before. Perhaps a sense of freedom that is not *freed* but instead is able to *free itself*.

It is the earliest image I have of her in a postcolonial state. But, marooned by her own forgetting, she appears as solitary and unknown as an island, an island that waits in vain for the eventual settling of its constitution, that waits to be held in somewhat sharper relief. On this island of her unremembered self, her fugitivity (while perfect) is moot, appearing almost perfectly framed, disengaged from the urgency of having to free itself from our view. It is untouched, in the way an unknown place—or an empty room—is untouched. *Innocent* only because we have never seen it, we do not know what there is to see. Lost in the gaze of this postcolonial version of the girl who would be my mother, we could miss the self-possession, that grasp of sovereignty mediated in relation to the archipelago of family, its belongings, its own mediated possessions at the hands and eyes of a photographer.

I am writing as if I know how to write about what I do not know, but each word is a performance (some a play and a pretense) of knowing. Thinking for a moment that I have arrived at this gaze as the necessary consequence of an errant look, I bring my learned assumptions to bear:

> *The consequence of "taking liberties" reminds us that the liberties that are taken do not themselves equate to liberation. It reminds us, too, of the constant work of liberation, where for liberty to remain, one must work oneself to ruin—to remains. What remains, then, is not oneself, but the consequence of that work, the effort held still as a portrait to be later held and beheld.*

This theorem is an aversion, how I attempt to corral what I think is my mother's gaze and where it comes to rest: with a cautionary tale meant to forestall the possibility of greater risk, the greater efforts of the mind such risks will demand. The truth of it has already eluded me, leaving only a cowardice that rationalizes. Thinking I have talked myself into an understanding of my mother's portrait, I manage to talk myself out of doing more to understand myself. Rather than surmise what the portrait itself can teach, as part of the growing anthology of faces and their looks (and my looks, as well), and choosing to fill it with my own anxieties, I have arrived at nothing new.

> Am I so desperate for the grounding of the familiar that I would construct merely an allegory of the Caribbean?
>
> Yes, of course I am.[9]

9 (See me scrambling for terms to explain my contortions, or to frame them.) But this is the limited and limiting action of nostalgia—as cliché as a wave reaching the *point mort* on the beach of the memory, beyond which is a trench whose man-made tides pull outward only to bring you back, exhausted. Breathless for meaning, you can miss that the pulling and pushing is self-imposed, that your exhaustion means only that you have not drowned and that your love of the sea is contrived.

The metaphor of (her) black Caribbean self-determination unfolds—is already unfolded, laid flat—and appears as plain and untroubled as any portrait I have ever seen. But it evades. I almost miss it. I almost miss what it means to break it open. Is there nothing beyond the photographer's subjection, beyond the witness of it, beyond the memory of that witnessing in our practice, beyond our own capacity for subjection? Is there nothing beyond the beheld whose gaze is held? Is there a letting go? A letting loose? A getting gone? A gaze we follow past ourselves, whose path we track and lose, whose obscurities insist beyond the self-righteousness of my Caribbean subjectivity, its perfect subjection? Something I have yet to see? I almost forget to ask. I want something new, to think what I have not yet thought of my family and my mother and, perhaps, myself.

Beheld in its isolation, we note that the portrait at best is *only* an island, its allegorical potential going no further than its borders. But the allegory of portraits as single islands and as archipelago is too obvious. One doesn't arrive at it but departs from it to arrive at some other place, some other meaning it has produced or helped produce. I don't mean to be prescriptive here. We remember the past of this gaze, don't we? The look? Yes. We remember its movement, its actions beyond our reach. The portrait is not only a prophecy of a break (and a fear) to come but evidence of a gaze whose nativity—whose native look—has not yet returned. It is, perhaps, also the realization that it will not. A portrait of an emptiness we recognize but do not know.[10] Here is a face that looks like mine, whose story I tell in the amplified absence of memory—my mother's partial memory of her former self. The un|making of constitutive texts and genres will lead inevitably to a "making with" that attempts to do what the look and the gaze have already done—that is, exceed the limitations of my self-making.

I will tell it as if it were a surd: an enacted absence materialized as a portrait that *says*, whose intention we do not see but whose meanings linger long after who she *is* becomes who she *was*, and the violation of referring to her in the past of someone else's vision is eclipsed by my desire to see her for myself—knowing and not knowing what, with all my seeing, I will miss.

But that alone can't do.

I feel that to be "taken on its own terms" is also a demand to be viewed *with*—that is, *in context* and *in parity with*—its antecedents and contemporaries, its known and unknown pasts. This gaze, for all its apparent vacancy, is what the obvious *punctum* of a breaking look was in the first portrait. It can best

10 You only *think* you know, my mother would say.

be seen, then, in relation to the look, centered as they are on the singular subject of the girl and young woman who would be my mother. Its affect appears transformed into something comparatively mundane, its details almost general, almost disciplined in its generality—the *studium*. But no, though posed as a *studium*, it too is a *punctum*. A disruption in its totality: breaking the form of the original look, breaking into a new version of what it was, breaking the trajectory of the photographer's intent. The portrait itself is a way of seeing that breaks into a way of being seen. Of course, this distinction poses no dilemma for those who miss the resemblance between one portrait and the other, who have no memory of the look that comes before it, the one that breaks things.

We remember, though.

Taken together, following some framing explanation, some more precise theorizing through which they may be more formally known, we will see that they are both *punctum* and *studium*, breaking their individual form with impossible speculation, breaking themselves open with un|remembered memory to do the oramaclastic work of Caribbean nonfiction.[11] Looking (as we are obliged to do) through the reflexive engagement with a broken gaze—the errant look of a distracted girl—to see the look itself that matures and comes to rest as a gaze that is held, that holds and beholds, we encounter a phenomenon designed to re|read what it becomes: a look of a future self gazing back at me—and maybe at us.

Maybe at nothing at all. This is method *materialized*.

Taking liberties with the form to "liberate" a version of my mother from the constraints of the frame—seeing her in and beyond it, then losing both her and her gaze—I am brought to the inherent paradox of the portrait where my impulse to liberate is undone. Taken in relation to the family portrait, this gaze is the biography of a past that is past, yet it argues for what all portraits argue: that it is a past *not yet* past, that (because it is not yet past) it should be taken on its own terms. It remains as it was because what it *was* is what it *has always been*: a moment passed, whose future is yet to come. Its singular relevance is not enough.

11 What is the term for the *punctum* that is a *studium*? There may be none.

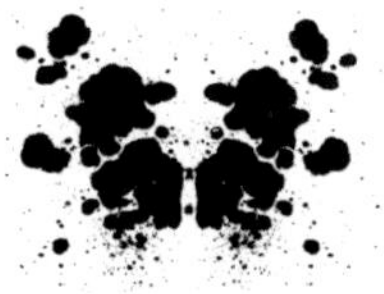

MOTHER

> "I could make you out of iron and make you walk."
> —Eva, my mother

My mother thinks she knows me.

Every now and then, and sometimes for no reason at all, she finds a way to tell the story of her decision to start me at school. This, for better or worse, is how she traces the provenance of my accomplishments. The logical outcome of this brand of provenance is a story I have heard many, many times. In this one, I am three years old and speaking in full sentences.

"Yuh sure?" I ask.

"Yes!" she would insist. "Full sentences, in perfect English!"

"I said, 'You see you?'" she recalls herself saying. "School for you! Down to Teacher Bailey!" School was the Clydesdale Private School, a collection of old desks arranged beneath the house belonging to a woman everyone knew as Teacher Bailey. She was "a short woman, with *dougla* hair, more gray than black, with a mole on her face, near her nose." This from my mother. I have forgotten her face.

I used to think the memory of my being stabbed belonged to a genre of memories of children lost or almost lost, that I shared aspects of that fate with my uncle Collins. But I was no panman. No child harbored enough of a grievance against me then to almost lose a blade in my heart—a pencil no more a knife to me than a pen was a sword.

Origins matter differently to those who make a mold of their children. A mold of a concept of "origin" in the shape of a child. I would wonder if I were her son or the prototype of a son—more the result of her tinkering and revisions, her alchemy and artistry. In her repetitions of this phrase, I am, perhaps, the blackness that is at the first *and* final stages of that alchemy, its discipline, its tenderness. After my refinement has cooled.[1] But she would never tell, saying only what she always says.

My mother thinks she has forged me—moves from tracing my origin to something more akin to techne, moves from locating her sense of my beginnings as an external phenomenon that occurs elsewhere to having the more internalized idea of her son being the manifestation of her own idiosyncratic design (making a son out of iron) and her ingenuity (making him walk). The execution of this design is alchemical. By making something of a human-made miracle|miracle made human, she takes and transcends the role of alchemist, ascending to something of a god made, like her son, in her own image.

I would say this is her composition of me as a *text*—her casting of me as a machine; the suggestion that I was not only (a) subject to being read, but that I could be a predictable (or at least "programmable") "model" based on her original design; her confidence to say what she knows, what she has done, and could (still, always) do; and from the vantage point of time and space away from her.[2]

I encounter an aesthetic of arrival—mine—by looking back.

I am what she would call "own way."

1 Turning black black black.

2 In a way, the affective resonance of "origin" begins to dissipate, becoming more "original" as it moves away from the ironic rigidity of origin.

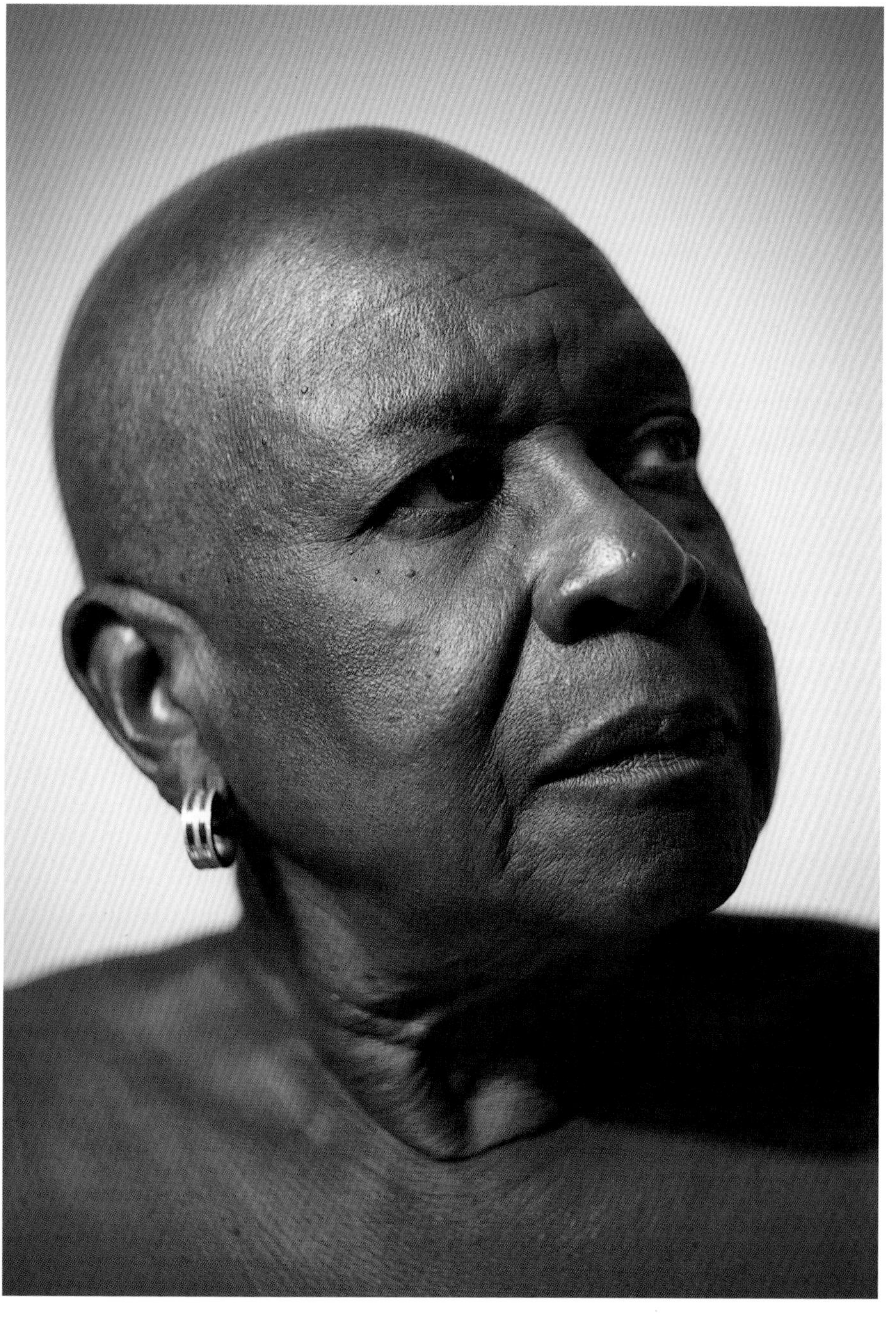

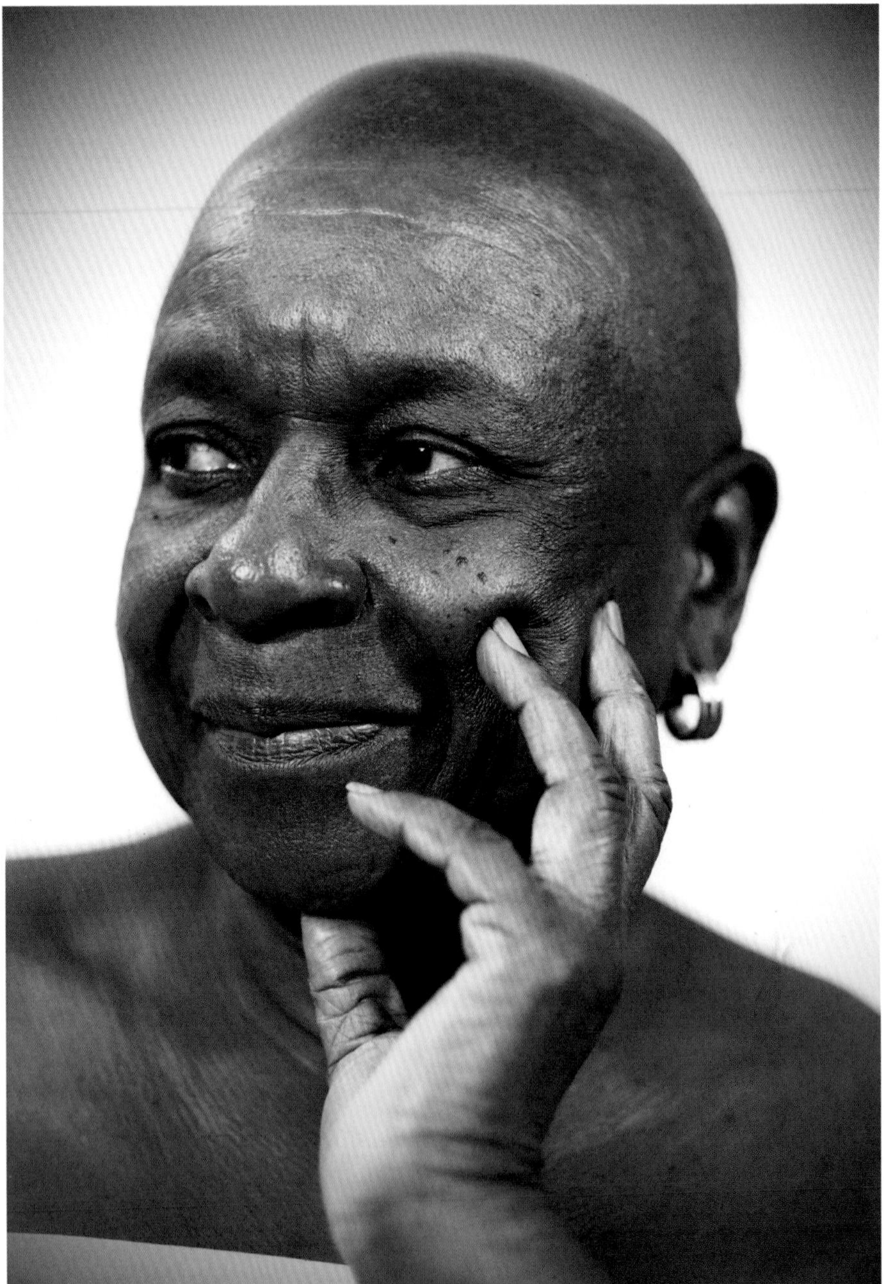

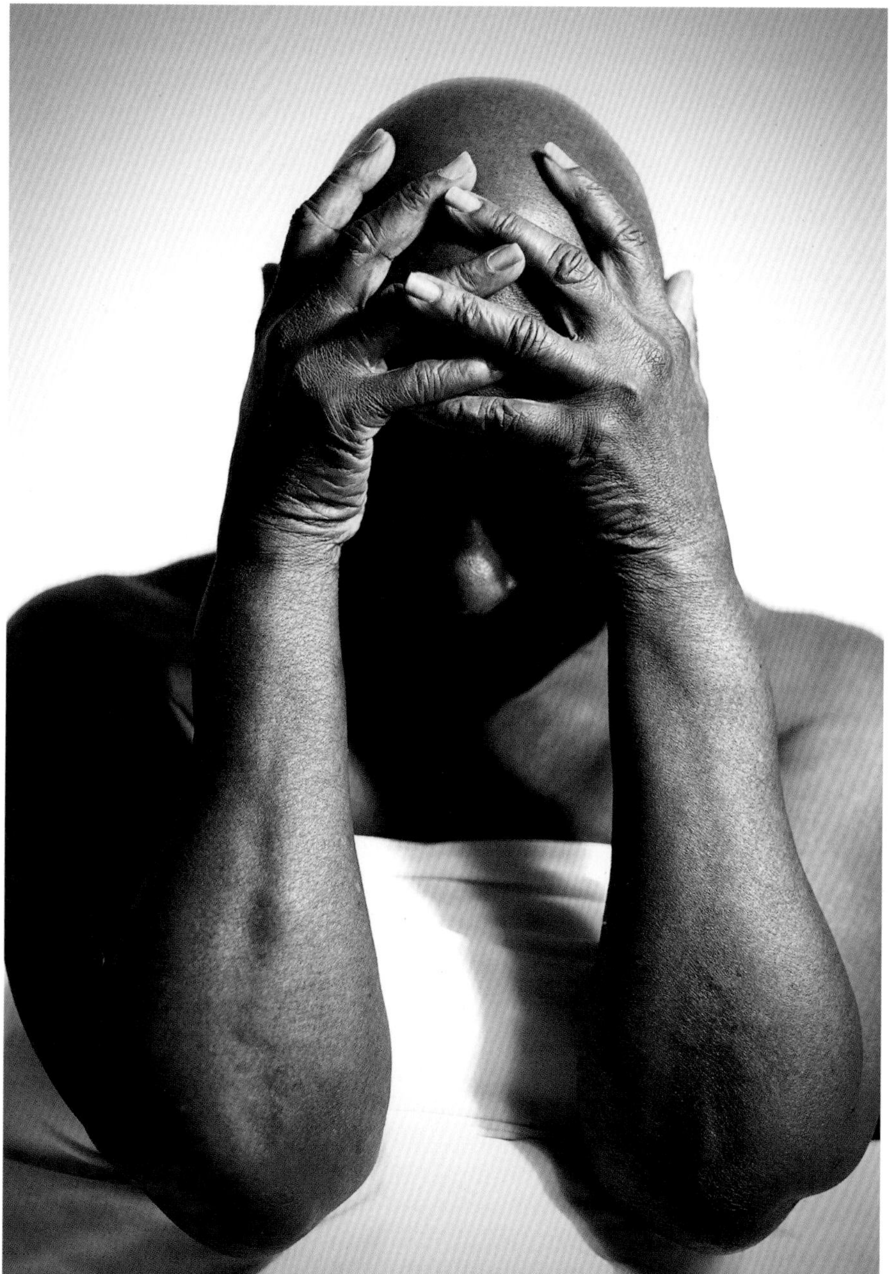

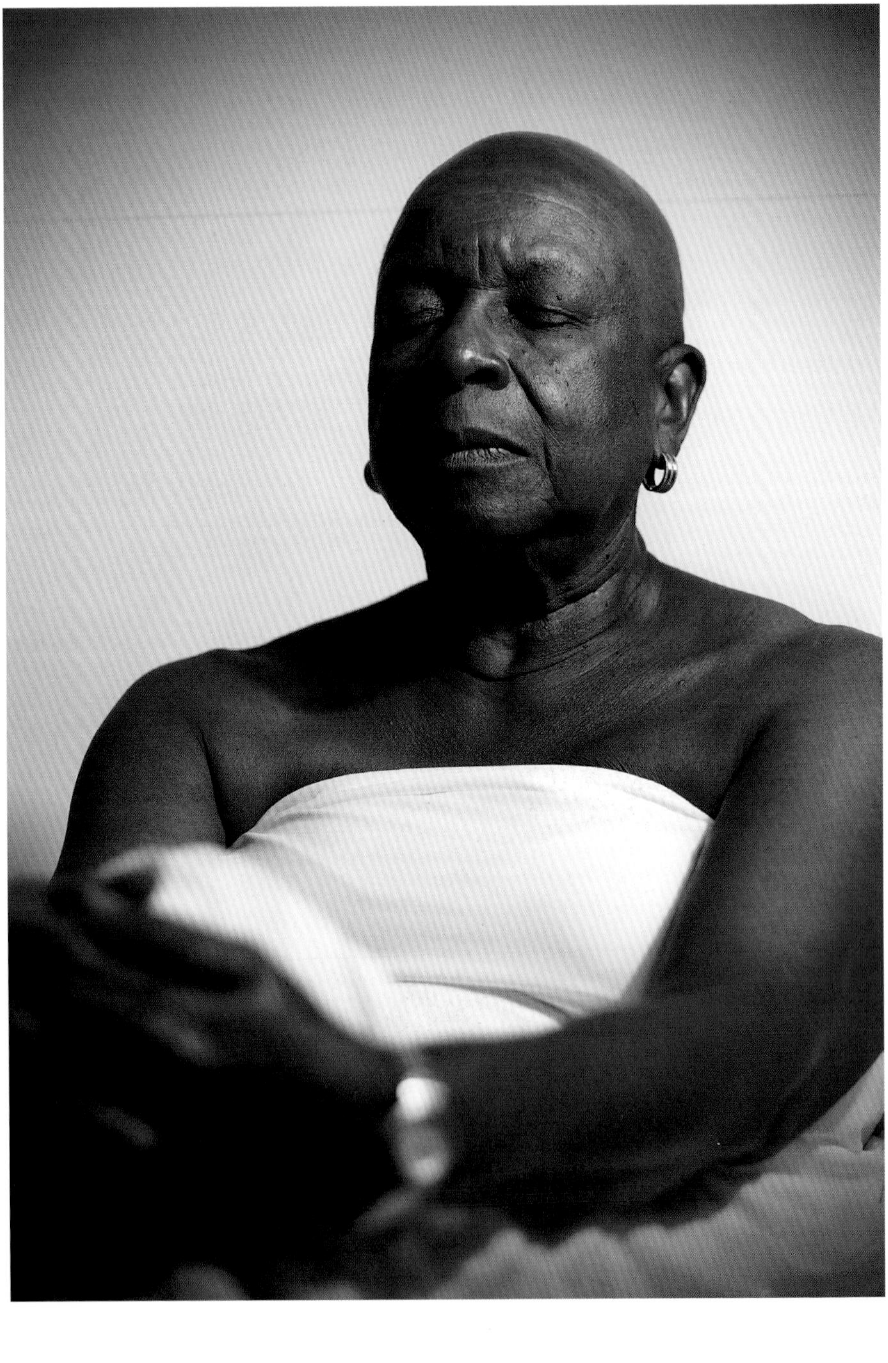

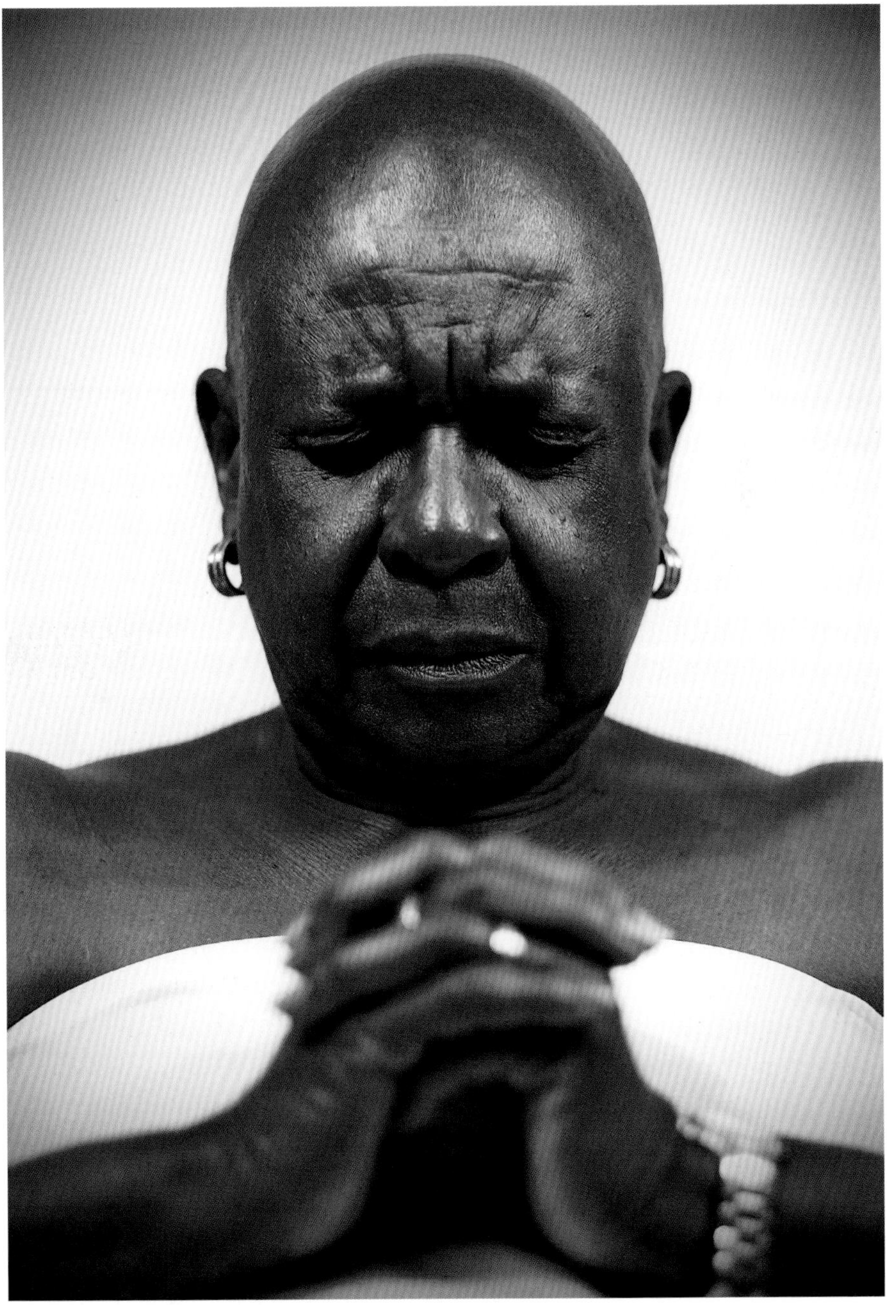

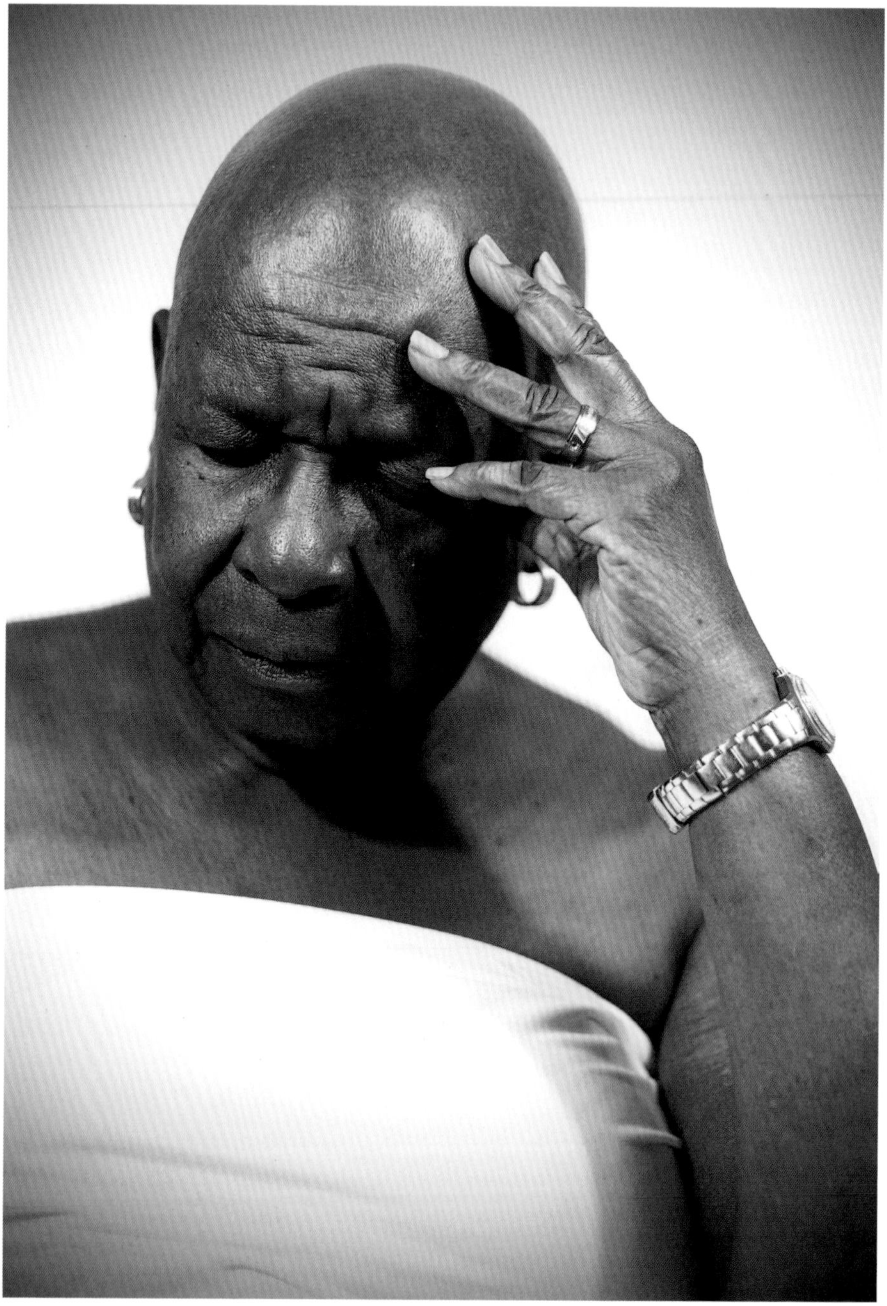

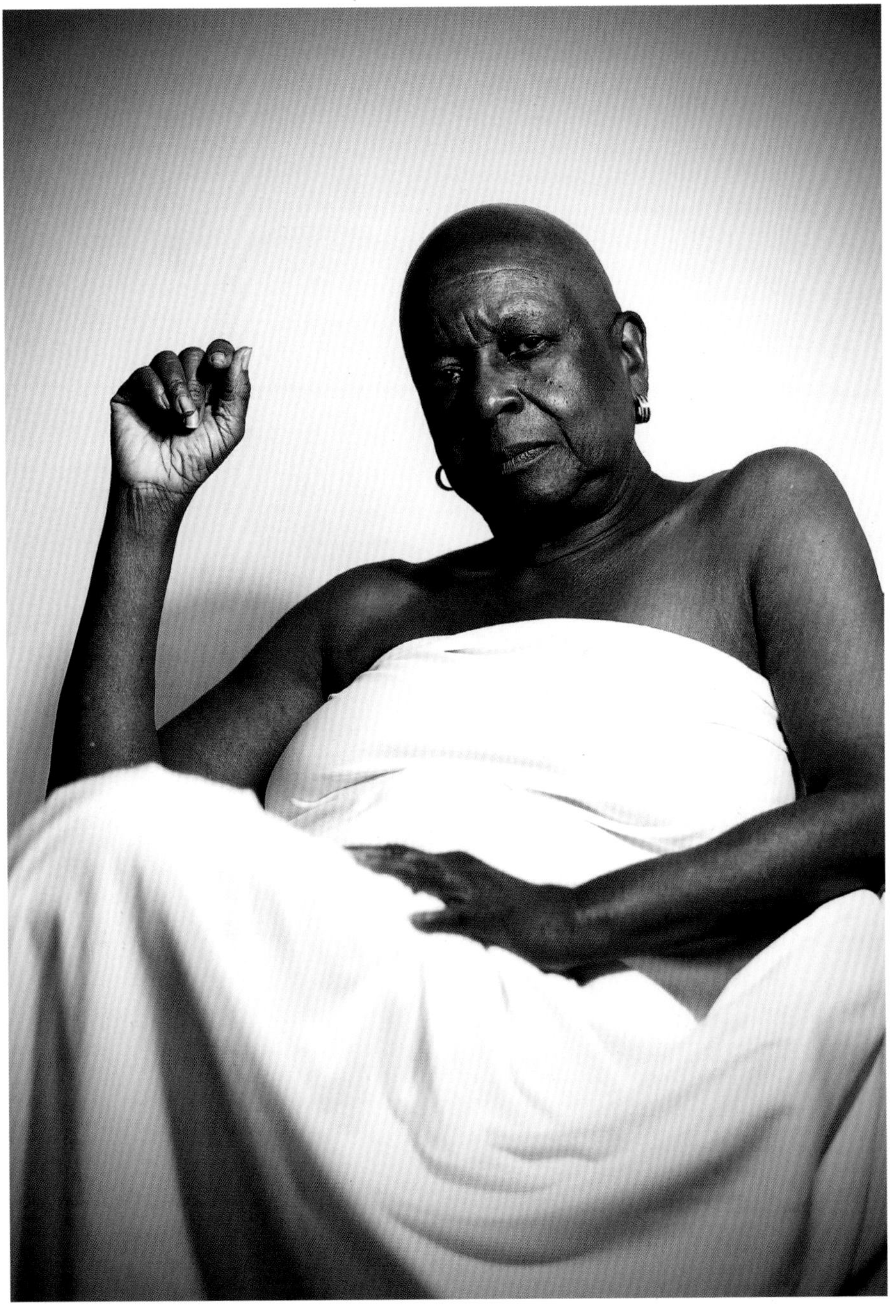

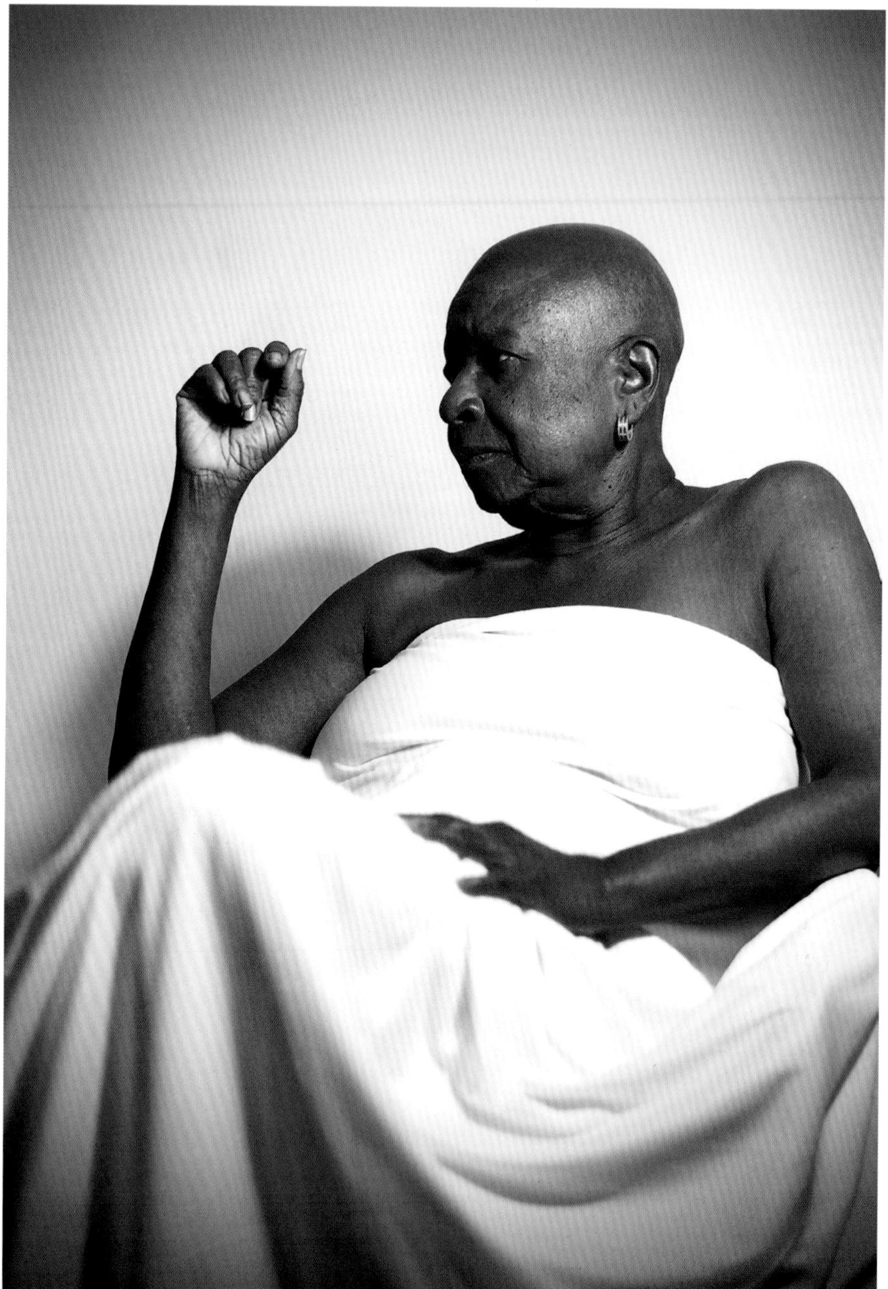

SON

For an only child, freedom is an illicit thing.[1]

It cannot be earned or won. It cannot be bartered for. Begging will not do because it will not simply be handed over just because you beg for it. It *has* to be taken—the tools, time, and materials, too; each must be stolen if they are going to be of any use. You could say that I was a thief, if that is what one would call a child who steals himself.

What else would such a child be called? Can he come of age of his own accord?

I wasn't exactly what the big people would call "own way." As far as they could tell, I was soft in the way my mother was soft, but wild ("Like your father," my mother would say, though at the time I had no way of knowing). An only child spoiled enough to get what I wanted but unspoiled enough to never lose myself in the asking (thieves must never be too comfortable with asking for things; asking corrupts). So while it was just a matter of time before I started walking to school without her, it couldn't happen soon enough for me. It had to be now. If not now, then near to now, or as near to now as I could get. I was eight. I must have been, because it was on my way to school the year before that she told me not to be afraid of the dead. My uncle Peter had drowned and been buried some days before that, and I was afraid he'd come back to haunt me.

1 I am my mother's only child and the oldest of my father's six. After me, there is Stefan, Ayana, Nicholai (newly deceased), Jovian, and Joel. Except for Stefan, the remaining siblings are with his wife Lynette, whom I was made to call Aunty Lynette. My grandmother Vena wanted us to know each other in spite of our parents, so I spent weekends on Charles Street, where my grandparents lived, and sometimes on Devon Street, where my father lived with his family. This was in La Romaine, a short distance from San Fernando. My aunt Michaelene would take me there. I don't recall ever leaving La Romaine as a child.

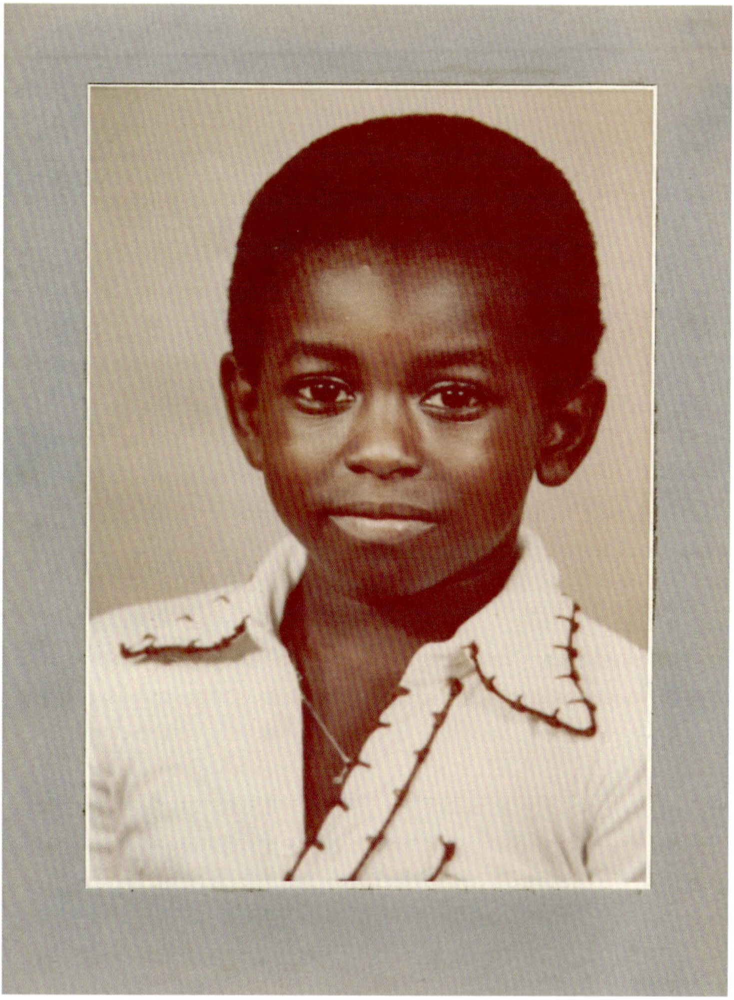

"I's not the dead you have to be afraid of, son. I's the living."

The lesson was a barricade, a guard against the afterlife. Whether it was weakened or reinforced when we tended to the graves on La Toussaint I couldn't tell, but its effect on me that morning was deep and comforting. Just after we passed Rambaran's Pharmacy and the stairs that led up to the tailor who made my pants, I had conquered a fear. My mother's certainty felt godlike. I basked in the freedom of it, knowing that nothing else mattered that day. Still, I was restless—anxious, in the way "own way" children can sometimes be. Emboldened by the prospect of owning my self, I was unconcerned that the living were any more dangerous than the dead, whom I no longer feared.

Soon, I was walking home with my cousin Richard (Lenore's son) or sometimes with Brewster, who looked to me like a Rodin might look to someone who's never seen a black man gleam in the Trinidad sun. I'd never seen a Rodin, so Brewster was the mold—a prototype model for a blackness I didn't yet have the language to admire or the tools I'd need to chisel and smooth my own body into an image such as his. I had no bronze, no body to speak of. (I hadn't yet lived enough.) And whenever I thought of him, it would never be as he was in that moment, walking up Carib Street with his nephew and me, but playing his six-bass, his arms stretched across the rack, midway between a B and an A, before reaching for a pair of Cs. He was contained within the colossal pans not so much as if they were a cell he'd need to escape but as if they were made of the same thing. There were some like that, who played as if they were tortured or possessed.

Others went in search of the unknown things their pans would yield. Dave, my father's brother, was one of them. My mother would tell me how he would bring her oranges from Grampadaddy's orchard in Erin and keep her company whenever he was in San Fernando, holding space and marking time for my father, whom I would only see some weekends. (He was a panman too, but he had always played a different pan, a different arrangement to a different tune. "Own way," like his son. In years to come and dissatisfied with his absence, I'd go in search of him.) Dave, because he was lighter on his feet, of a smaller frame than Brewster, flitted around his rack like a chikichong or a hummingbird, coaxing the thick sound out of his drums, dancing like an alchemist who'd discovered an elixir in the steel that sweated beneath his hands. He willed himself into the steel. The steel sang itself for him. I wished I could play like them, metal soldered to my bones. I had it in me, but I never made a note. And though I was born in the Year of the Bassman—1974—I was content to exist for a while in the shadows they cast. There'd be time, I thought, to grow into my body. And time enough for that body to grow into the six-bass I knew was waiting for me.

Time enough to step out of their shadows and into the light. But then I'd be home and Brewster and his nephew would continue on to Black Street, where they lived.

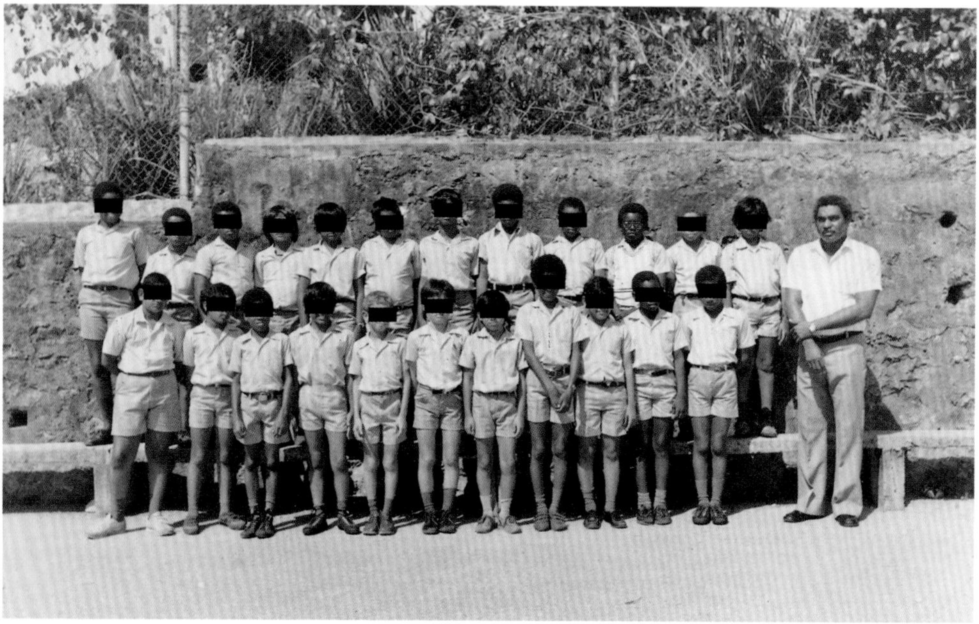

Going to school was a straightforward affair: my mother made sure I was hardly ever late. She'd be up long before me, preparing my lunch for the day, making sure my uniform was pressed and shoes polished before Aunty Lystra made breakfast for my cousins and me. They sometimes fell out, but never in the morning. *Get up, son. Time for school. Go and bathe.* The water was cold and woke me down to my bones because Alvarez, Aunty Lystra's man, hadn't yet put in the water heater like the one Aunty Marjorie and Uncle Carl had. Book bag packed and fountain pen filled, I left home fed and feeling every bit the official I was being groomed to be. I was destined to have my hands in the oil, my bloodlines corrupted throughout by it. If I had tried to run from the Browne in me that beat a path away from my father and his father before him, I would find my grandfather, a Wright, chief production clerk at Tesoro (Trinidad, Ltd.) in the oil fields of Santa Flora. He had positioned me in absentia, having already left the house on Carib Street to raise the sons—my uncles Curtis and Peter—he'd had with his second wife, Miss Pearl.

We all left through the back door. Passing through the front meant passing through the living room. That meant we would have to risk walking on the large rug Aunty Lystra had put there years before any but the oldest of us, her daughter Denise, was born. It was a memento, holding space for a vision she'd had of a snake coiled up on that spot. Aunty Lystra saw spirits, so as a family given to magic, no one challenged it—we just waited for it to come to pass, eventually forgetting. Still, we passed through the kitchen, through the yard (sure to say good morning to Mr. Gibbs and Mr. Phillip), and down the steps to Carib Street. Then it was off in our own separate ways.

Freshly pressed and polished, I must have smelled like a municipal office, brimming with the kind of promise that mornings alone could provide. I *Morning, Sir*red and *Morning, Miss*ed my way to school in a blur. But on the way home, the burden of my mother's expectations cast off somewhere in the schoolyard, I took my time and immersed myself in what I came to understand was the *feel* of the streets—my senses all conspired, rallying around my newfound cause. I suppose I blended in, my gray shirt matching the old asphalt and my khaki pants the dingy drains of a city that was not yet ready to be a city. It was still a town but with aspirations, emboldened by oil and other things. I was one of its sons, and I walked unclaimed and untouched through its streets.

I could have taken a 'Round de Town or Pleasantville taxi, and it would have dropped me off at the nine steps that led up to the yard. And I could go play with the other children who lived there, midway up the southern slope of San Fernando Hill, my own Olympus. But walking felt better to me than being crammed into one of those grunting Galants or Renaults that lined the curbs, smoking like workmen on a break. I preferred to count them as they passed, holding my breath as I noted the subtle changes in their designs and colors. They were always packed at that time of day with people who wore the full weight of the day on their faces, yoked across their shoulders, sliding down the lengths of their backs, their shadows dragging behind them like tired Moko Jumbies. Days so long their quick morning paces slowed to a hazy afternoon shuffle to the taxi stand and then, mercifully, to home. Sometimes, their children would be with them, younger versions of the day's successes and defeats, waiting for another taxi to come, or another. There was misery, it seemed to me, in every loose button, in every worn-out crease, in every stitch of a gabardine uniform. It was the look of people whose lives seemed to hasten an afterlife, pushing them steadily to the grave. Big people and their smaller versions, all of them old. Spending time each afternoon looking at my mother, between her long sighs and silences, I memorized the moles and new wrinkles that gathered where they always tend to gather, before she would pick herself up and join Aunty Lystra for a second shift at home. It was, I learned, the look of softness hardening.

On foot, the fastest route was to stay on the school's side of the street, past the Woolworth's and Republic Bank and onto the strip of an island that led to another island on the far end of the junction. On that farther island stood a clock, a cubist monolith that was always only sometimes right. But there it stood, a graying fulcrum of tenses and moods—where High Street, Mucurapo Street, Pointe-à-Pierre Road, La Pique Road, and Coffee Street all converged.[2]

The natural current of those streets could turn a child around and take him as far as Palms Club before he'd realize that he'd been drifting toward Vistabella. Or, maybe half-aware that he'd gone off-course, and that home was the other way, up The Coffee to Carib Street, he could tumble down St. James Street all the way to the wharf, where *corbeaux* jostled with pelicans and egrets for scraps from the day's catch before retiring to their respective roosts—the pirogues, eaves, and almond trees near the end of the wharf, by the old rail that ran up the coast to Port of Spain. He could so easily be lost, drowned, looking more like jetsam or driftwood at the end of the day than like a child. The circumstances of Peter's drowning stood as a warning for all of us: *friends will carry you, but they don't bring you back*. We all knew the story of how Miss Pearl almost gutted herself bawling for him and beating her chest on the shore of Vessigny Beach.

2 A generation removed, the policeman's gray
starched shirt, blue short pants, seem idyllic.
Nostalgia builds, calcified in mounds, in the heart's cave.

Patent leather belts can keep a king and queen in place,
we know, despite ourselves (who love them still).

It may be that glinting buckles shine the same
as Orion in spring—and that misfortune is an
equinox for a people. Still.

The sidewalk is a rough collage of faces,
aged ambassadors for frames too busy crossing
the junction to see its roads turn like the hands

of a clock with the passing day, the fulcrum
of a city that forgets to question itself.

To save my mother the news of another drowning in our family, and to save myself, I would cross onto the Promenade by St. Joseph's Convent, and take the side street along the high gray walls of the Cluny sisters' house. I would climb up and into No. 11, the decommissioned locomotive stationed behind Carnegie Library at the junction. (Both were monstrosities—steel and the memory of steel—dormant and immortal.) Climbing down from it, and flattening a juice carton or kicking a food box half-emptied by a vagrant sometime earlier, I would pass by Bobby, who sold ham sandwiches in hard-shell hops bread with ketchup and pepper from the body of a small onetime bus. Hollowed of its seats and steering wheel, its headlights popped out like the eyes of a sun-dried grouper.

"Aye, Small Man. Yuh good?"

"Yes, thanks. Yuh have Orchard today?"

"Yeah."

In his twenties at the time, he seemed to me a relic encased in that old bus, with its rust painted a light blue, its gaunt lettering. *Sandwiches. Juice. Coffee. Tea. Snacks.* The hops bread, set neatly in rows that depleted steadily, looked like young women's breasts. A single brown-skinned woman's breasts, perfectly and infinitely replicated in some local bakery—Attong's on Keate Street or Steve's up by Irving Park, where we would play before and after going for bread. Butter bread. Plaited bread. Hops. As Bobby made what he knew I'd come to get, he seemed to take no interest in encouraging my fantasy and handled the hops with the pair of tongs rather than with his hands, which were large and round. A good thing, I thought, because in his bare hands the young woman would have shrunk, becoming a girl. I bristle to think of it, now. His smile, which was warm, always seemed to cool a bit as he cut the bread open and arranged a few pieces of ham so they lay just over the edge. It came back as he dressed the sandwich: three or four circles of sweet ketchup, one smaller circle of pepper sauce that spread when he put the top of the bun on and wrapped it in rice paper, twisting the two ends.

"Here."

"Thank you!"

"Okay then. Reach home safe, eh, Small Man. Go home straight." Or perhaps he said, "Walk on the side, Small Man. Don't run out in the traffic to get bounced, you know."

I would already be eating, the sandwich halfway undressed, dripping on my fingers, its shell cracking like a mishandled artifact, the broken mold of a brown-skinned woman's breast in my hand.

"Don't make your mother have to look for you, all right?"

"All right."

Bobby was blacker than I was, blacker than Brewster's look of aged and polished bronze. His teeth shone like sun-bleached bone. From him, I learned to talk and listen to strangers blacker than myself, who could consume the severity of whiteness with a smile, whose smile was whiteness consumed. From him, I learned to trust the sensitivity of my tastes in public as if they were instincts: *this sweet, this salty, this warm, this will burn.* I learned to love each equally as they competed like words—sweet, salt, warm, hot—for my tongue's affection. My public tastes and discretions sharpened among strangers in the road. Particular strangers, posted like agents who'd been drafted by my mother or Aunty Lystra or by their brother Frank (who was an uncle but was never "Uncle Frank" to us), all lingered at waypoints along the route. Even the men who throughout the day would drink themselves sober at the bars and recreation clubs. They all knew my face, and that my face, like the rest of me, belonged to my mother, Eva. *A child*, they all would say, *lucky who look like the mother. Blessed*, they would say.

The drivers and their touts would stop their cars for me to cross.

"Hold on there, Small Man." And I'd look where they would look, learning to gauge the distance of oncoming cars. "Okay, go ahead now." Sometimes I cut across without their guidance, provoking them. "Aye, Small Man, what the ass you doing, boy?" *Sorry, sorry*, I would say, accepting the temporary demotion—from Small Man back to boy. But when the hustle was as much a prayer as prayers to those who feared the hustlers, forgiveness was easy, and my redemption among them was almost certain. I'd see them tomorrow and find again the Small Man I had lost between chrome bumpers and plastic-winged hood ornaments.

I didn't learn to curse on a gravel heap behind the old Licensing Office on Carib Street, walking home with E, who lived a little way away on Carlton Lane. But it was where my mouth would finally form the shape of words I'd heard for years. We climbed the massive heaps of cream- and gold-colored pebbles and watched our footprints crumble, the loose gravel erasing the records of our daily trespasses.

Say it.

Say shit.

Say fuck.

Say it.

(Say it, however hushed, and begin to understand what you've never understood: that your thoughts can take form in your mouth and then disappear. They will mean things, these things you say, but sometimes they will mean nothing. Big people do this, saying things they don't mean. They make promises. They lie. Say "fuck," and learn, for the first time, that your mother is not God—only *godlike*. She answers your prayers but sends her petitions upward on your behalf. Learn, for this first time in your life, that all that she can see does not always include you. Curse and learn to forgive yourself. Curse and learn, at last, to speak with an authority you had not earned but taken. You have crossed over into a slightly darker place, not yet lost, but "own way," a pioneer determined to stretch beyond your mother's reach, beyond the scope of her sight, outside the womb of her embrace. Those footprints, if she ever found them, would tell the story of her son so eager to be a Small Man, to bring himself into the world without her push. So curse, Small Man. Curse and go home.)

"Fuck."

Set atop these gravel mounds, the secret pacts of the falsely wayward children of single mothers would soon become the foundations of someone else's house, keeping their owner's secrets with greater intention, forgetting we were ever there. Or they would become a box drain, taking those secrets underground, flowing downhill to the grated sewers, grinding themselves smooth in the canals. Our secrets were our own, but we shared them with this not-yet-city of ours. Other secrets, not cast like these in random stone, we kept. If I had cursed myself on those gravel mounds, I'd never know. When the route you've taken to escape is a gravel path, try to take note—try to remember that you have always been a coming together, a gathering of cells, strands, organs, bones, ideas. You are an idea of a gathering that's come to pass.

"I going home."

E cut down La Coulee Street. I walked past a sentry sleeping at the gate to the Borough Yard. Other more and less wayward children—the Navarros, the Grants, the Babbs—would roam too, but we all went to different schools and wouldn't see each other until later. There was Coffee E. C., Anstey Memorial, Government School, St. Gabriel's, and mine: San Fernando Boys R. C. It was as if we'd been deployed, sent on a kind of reconnaissance mission to know the boundaries of our town, surveying its pulse and its architecture, retaining what we could of those perishable days.

All together, finally, in the late afternoon, we would play and play until the birds turned into bats.

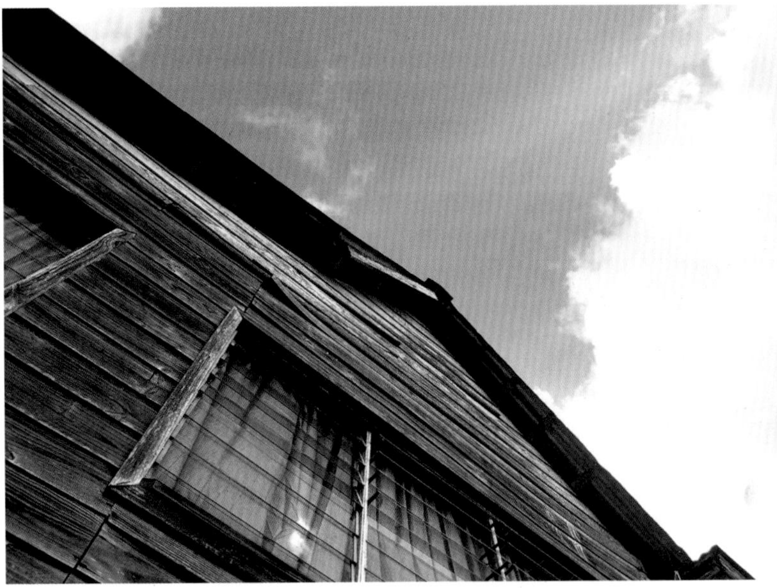

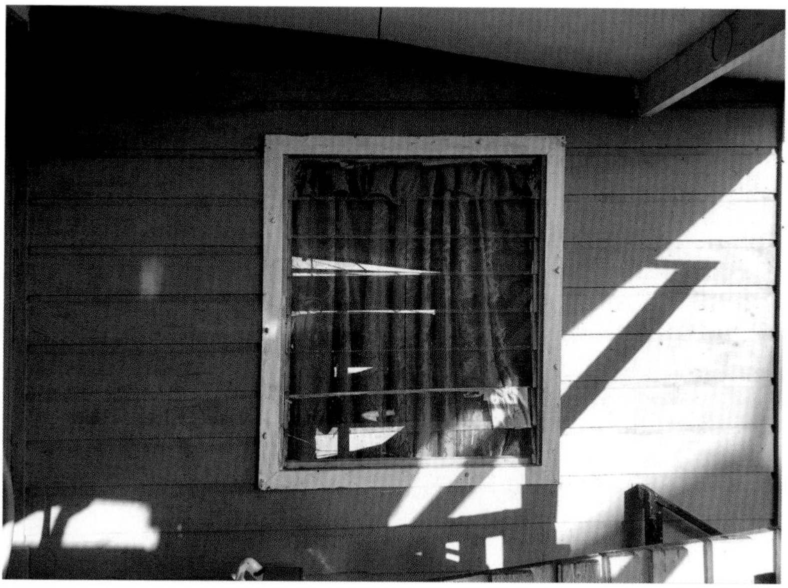

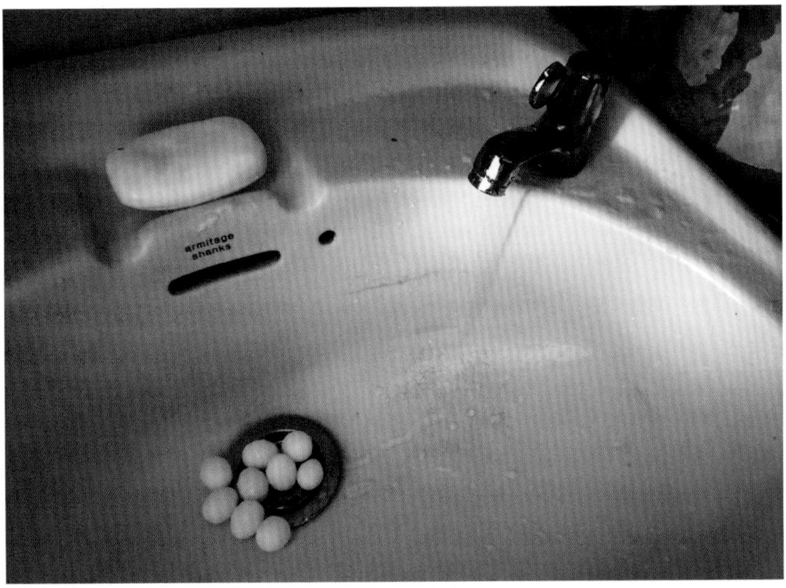
armitage
shanks

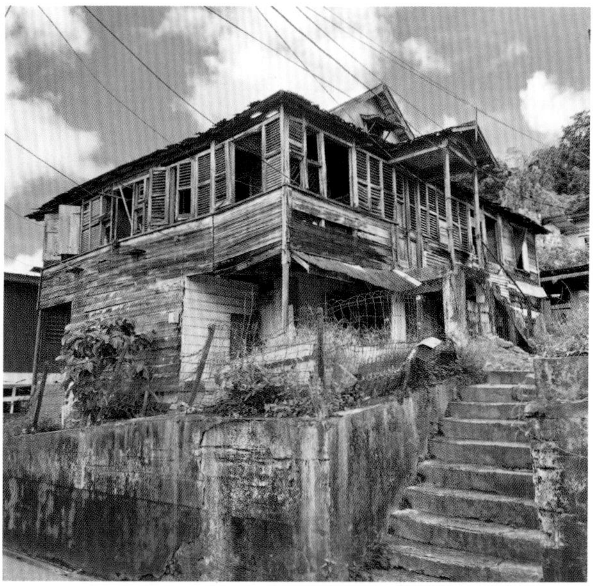

STORY | ING

Here is an image:
You will dare to tell an unbelievable story.
You are, perhaps, a child. Or, perhaps, you are grown.
Big, as we sometimes say.
You will nevertheless be chastised for telling stories, for "storying."
Lying.

This, obviously, will be the lesson:
A liar is a thief,
and a thief is a murderer!

You and I know you are none of those things—you never thief nothing, you never kill nobody. You only know that you tell a story, and that your skin is black, and your hair is thick, and your eyes are yellow where they should be white. If you fail to learn this lesson, you will be punished for it. You'd need to "hush and take your licks before you get something to cry for."[1] But understand. You will not be chastised for the liar you may be, or the thief or murderer you may become, but for something far simpler and far greater: the story you dare to tell, that you dare to tell it.

You will be punished not for violating the significance of a singular "truth" but for your refusal of its singularity for one of your own—*Whose truths?* You will never really be encouraged to ask. "Hush and take your licks" is how you learn method, your introduction to (the) discipline.

1 Related, by blood, to "Hush and let people like you."

Your accuser will not say this to you:

> It is because you are black, because when you are seen, you are seen as black, though never as black as you are. You are an unknowable mind and, thus, an unbelievable body. Your blackness is unbelievable. Your daring is an impossibility—a mythos that binds.
>
> *But ask:*
> Whose truths bind you now?

Your guardian, whom you will sometimes call
Mother, Mammy, Aunty, Tants, will not say this to you:

> It is because you are the story, a myth (or fragment of a myth) that others must sometimes struggle to believe, you are subject to a truth but not authorized to participate in its making. It is because the "truth" of your blackness—your black unbelievability—is that in this scenario you are, in fact, a fiction.
>
> *But ask:*
> Whose truths make a fiction of you?
> Whose truths lie?

Your jailer, whom you will sometimes call
doux doux, darling, cousin, enemy, friend, self, will not say this to you:

> It is because you are black that what you have to say will sometimes feel as if you were making something up that never happened, even if it has. It will feel like magic, pouring out of your mouth as if it were someone else's memory you had learned over time, perfecting the tricks and intricacies of its tones and pauses, its rising and falling, pouring out as if you had crafted a myth.
>
> *Ask:*
> Whose story?

Ours—yours and mine, or mine alone for now—offered in the dialect of witness and rupture. It is a version of *us* taking and making form in the dissipation of form itself. This is genre enacted beyond the mythical boundaries of its composition.

Simply put, the attempt at nonfiction by unbelievable bodies means the voice—whether singular or collective—that makes the claim of truth will *always* be read as unreliable. Not wrong per se, just unreliable. We "show up" for things and for people, insist our presence. But we are considered unreliable because we are, at base, *unbelievable*—in the sense that we are cast, as much by ourselves as by any other, as a people *not to be believed*. Try to refuse the outrage of this fact. Lean, instead, toward the strange authority it affords us, the unbelieved. Being unbelievable, we position ourselves for a particular consequence: the setting of conditions in which to make anew what *could be believed*: an *alternate* way of knowing. We would be positioned to determine and dictate ourselves *to* ourselves. The challenge would then be to believe such a thing is possible and that we have accomplished it, or that we will.

Let me show you what I mean.

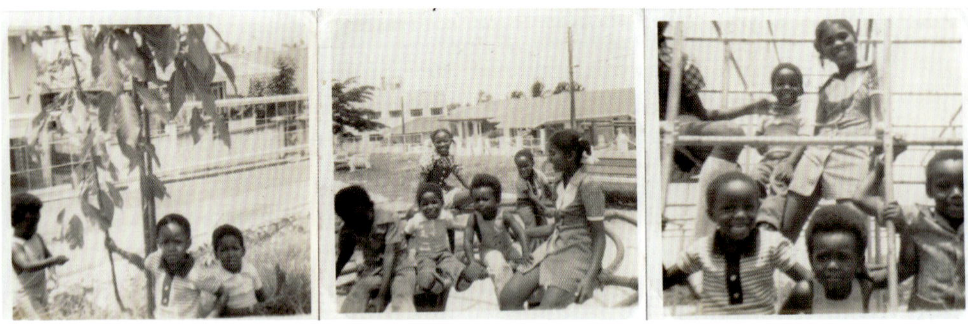

PANMAN

In 1974,
Antillean All Stars was Genesis.

And the road was the church,
the Savannah the cathedral.
Pan was praisesong and recessional.

In 1982,
Hillside Symphony was Revelation.

And people
of moments and movements,
of shame and spectacle, would sing.[1]

1 Sing a hymn to soothe your weary souls from the drudgery of everyday life. It will bring you peace, a peace you must also seek. You must go out in the road, put your hands up, close your eyes, breathe deep, and wine like hell. Even in the silence of streets you are afraid to walk, you will remember what it is like to feel. Wring the pan and drum from your spine, wring it from your shoulders. Wring out your heart. No one will stop you. Who will dare to tell you how to feel? Who dares to silence your grief? Or mine? We dance to save ourselves out of the abyss, chipping away at its walls.

On quieter days, I spent time with my friend G. Between me and G, I was the veteran. I'd touched a girl's bare shoulder as we searched the exposed parts of our bodies—hands, shoulders—for matching moles. I'd broken my wrist in La Romaine. I'd known more death, so I took it upon myself to be the leader in our pair. He came to live on the Hill a short time before, and I felt he knew nothing of the things I knew, the things I'd heard from my cousin and his friends, the games we'd played as children, the many things I'd done, and the secret things I'd learned to keep.

He must have had adventures on his own, but he didn't dally after school and was usually already home long before I got home, changed my clothes, and went up the Hill to play. We sat on the roof of Babb's abandoned house, climbing the bricks of the old pigeon coop like stairs and walking along the beams to the apex, sitting on the rounded ridge until our tailbones hurt. Two fledgling cussbirds, roosting as the others played. Perched there like totems.

Below us, there was a panyard—Antillean All Stars. Behind us, near the Carib House, was another—Hillside Symphony. One you could see from there, the other only hear. Depending on the time of day, it was difficult to tell which was in the other's shadow. One we would pass on the way to school, the other on our way to the shop. For us, they were one and the same. We knew the players. These were bands that, like all bands at the time, snapped up the badjohns before the jails could take them or after they let them out. The more respectable ones would take their leave from the Borough Yard or the office or the oil field to play the pans that, between the black gold, bureaucracies, and garbage, had defined the crudeness of their workdays.

I think of my uncle Dave,
the panman, who almost died in a fire.
I think of my uncle Collins,
the panman who died
and whose murderer did die in a fire.

I carve a route that leads—part by part, image by image, memory by memory—to my past. And to a past that was not mine, whose stories wait their turn like the restless players, their sticks drawn like daggers on the Strip before they climb the ramp to the stage and arrange themselves in formation to bombard the North.

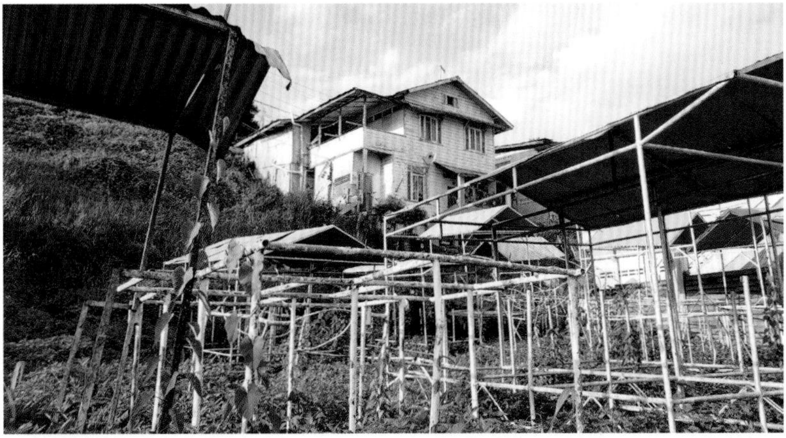

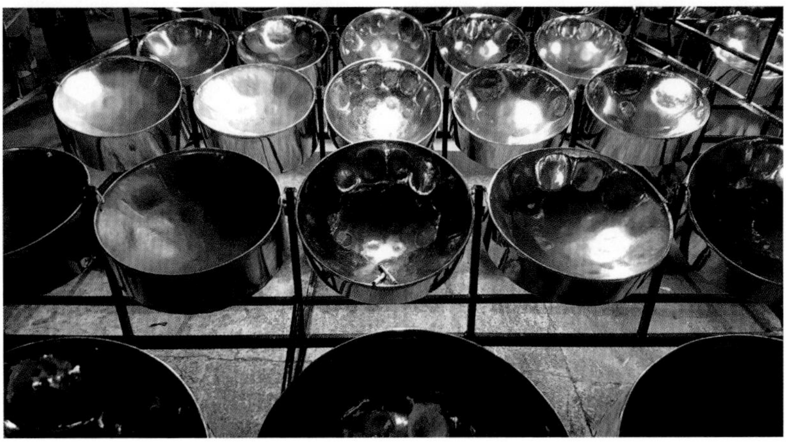

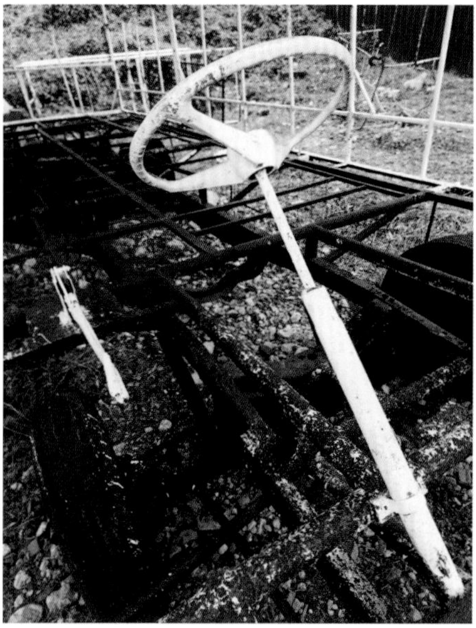

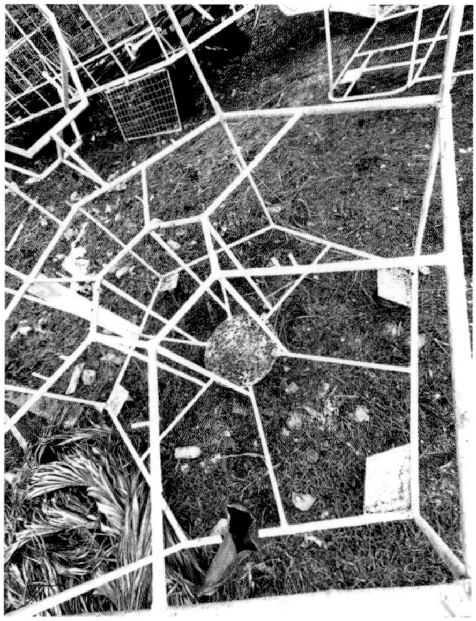

Here, for instance, is "Bass Man" (1974) as sound transcribed:

Peem Pom
Peem Pom pe teem
Peem Pom
Peem Pom pe teem
Peem Pom
Peem peem peem pom peem pom pom pom pom pom pom
(Repeat)

If you've ever seen a panman in motion, you would think you know what causes thunder and lightning. You would swear on graves that have not yet been upturned that you know where rains come from, what causes the breeze to turn frantic and furious, pelting galvanized sheets and planks like a deranged lover. You would swear, knowing that you should not. You would, calling the names of ancestors you have never known and feeling the subtle upwelling of nausea that begins at your navel and swirls upward to your chest in the preceding breaths, before bursting like the rain clouds you have learned, note by note, to summon—"man," here, as in humankind, exceeding gender, exceeding the absurdities of mortality and godhead. You would storm, almost compulsively, forgetting to seek forgiveness for the blasphemy, forgetting what blasphemy is at all when you realize that the music of this land of oil can only be played in the absence of the thing itself. The absence of Oil.

Music—pan music—is the absence of oil.

The music is prophetic because it is an ode to emptiness—to the return of emptiness, the open secret that what you hear can only be heard from the hollows, can only be known if the pans and barrels become drums, either casting off the historical narrative of their design or never being filled at all.

Empty.

Every interaction with this instrument is predicated on the perfection of emptiness—from the almost tribal clanking call to arms to the inaudible vibrato of the final notes that mixes into a grumble of imperceptible whispers, the sound of immeasurable sighs. The perfection of emptiness. *Playing pan*, then, is a method of emptying, of making space, of charting the void with sound. Each note is an enactment, an embodied intention directed outward. Take note of this latter state and what it must mean: that the sheer originality of this music is grounded in its abject refusal of the rigidity its instrumentation appears to embody. You find that the steel of these drums may be the most pliant element in the band, their bending into sound and light.

Or is it the panman and them? Turning emptiness into sound. Sounding sound into meaning. Meaning meant to be felt as if known. Known as if remembered. Are they the more pliant ones? Is their sound the navigation of loss, their music the perfection of it? The loss of what they play (since they do not always take note of their notes). Playing in acknowledgment of absence, their recognition of it. Playing, as it were, in absentia.

Pan, you will hear them say without saying, is the mastery of touch. They do not play as much as feel what must be played. They grope in vain for the sound. And though they would play year-round, their practice sessions would intensify as they neared the Panorama competitions. And though they learned the tune, it wasn't enough for them to simply play—they had to ignore the chalkboards and burrow deep beneath the notes. They had to play as if they could empty themselves into those drums—their tuned concaves were shallow, but you could see your face in them. They looked just like you: the people and the pans they played. Steel was their democracy, the panyard a republic devolving into desperation and chaos around sunset. Until, finally, the *clank-clank-clank*ing of the arranger's baton on the side of a bass quieted them all for practice as a band. A moment for a straggler to finish a phrase. A false start, another more insistent clanking, a curse, a caution. Then silence. Then the tyranny of noise pounded into music, its chaos refined. Between each act, our breaths stretched farther and farther out, for miles it seemed, across the gulf, almost reaching the mainland.

"I think I might have AIDS," I said, reeling us in.

"Eh heh?"

"Yeah, boy." It was the most likely diagnosis I could find for the subtle itch I'd felt in my groin earlier that day. But I might have said that I had skinned my knee, or that water was gone, or that there was another daytime blackout, and it would've been the same response from him, used as we were to any number of miniature catastrophes that kept us in place, marking us where we were. Perhaps we were all marked off, an area on a map of San Fernando, where the young inherited little more than the cynicism of their elders, testing their boundaries when they could. I had learned the area from my own explorations, but the lines were drawn long before I thought to find my way. Always part of a longer story. I scratched and then swallowed. The panyard grumbled.

It was a tell that I knew G couldn't decipher: the swallowed breath that said even the young have pasts, that we were younger once than we were in that moment, the memory that I was seven before I was eight, more in my mother's care than out of it. I think, perhaps, that is what makes a veteran: the acknowledgment of a past. Such pasts—those of the young, still so fresh so as to be mistaken for innocence—are easy to miss. The vulgarities, modulated in the not-yet-breaking voice of a boy who followed another boy, then led another, had no sting. So even when, a year or so later, after losing a fight in Mr. Taitt's Standard 5 class, I blurted out that another boy was a *fucking mothercunt*, the shock was soon forgotten.

If there was supposed to be something illicit in our shared virginity, I wouldn't have known. It wouldn't be the only thing, though, and passed with others in a rush. I didn't know that for a virgin to have AIDS, the matter would be less immaculate than my annunciation was likely to make it. And why would I? And what did it matter? The condition was still a mystery to us here. Still lesser known to G and me. Its causes, too, were more like myth, its ravages no more real to us than rumor. I knew as much about it as I did about the kinds of love that would be used to curse those who suffered. We hadn't yet learned to ridicule them, to glorify their slow withering and painful deaths as a kind of justice. For us, it was the aspiration, that tendency all children share: to live in want of adulthood and its vulgar pleasures, the pleasures of the announcement—the sure knowledge that we were adding to our own growing catalog of *I've done this or seen that thing, have touched that one or this one*—that was the mark of any grown-up person, even the forced-ripe ones like us. We were more thoughts than deeds, unafflicted in reality but afflicted nevertheless. And there I was: dying of a disease I didn't have.

In this part of my city, guilt was also the province of virgins—and its currency. It was known. If you've ever set your secrets in stone, you will know that they lose their density when they decompose or are ground to dust, and they rise up with the slightest breeze to dislodge themselves, betraying the (r)anchor of the moments that made them. On the surface, they shine, taking light and twisting it to their purpose. They burst, bringing up everything they—and you—have swallowed. Now, exposed like a wound to the light and open air, I felt my lungs displace the lies I'd told myself with the truths I'd forgotten how to tell, or was just too young to know, without the words to fill the silence in me that the act would create. Until my long breaths, punctuated by the hesitant arrests of my rib cage and diaphragm, reminded me. It was guilt, at first.

He played with my cousin Denise. Pan, nothing else. He wasn't what she'd call her "type." He looked more ancient than a Rodin, from a time before the perfections of physique. So his beauty felt worn, cracking in the dry air.

"Come, Small Man. I want to show you something."

"What?"

"Come nah? I'll show you. You 'fraid, or what?"

"No."

"So come, then."

He had been sitting on the couch in the living room but moved to the floor by the time I got close. He took my foot, caressing my ankle as he put it between his legs. "You feel that?" he asked, his touch careful, almost gentle.

"Yes."

He smiled. "Wiggle your toes." I did.

"How it feel?"

"Warm."

Warm. Because men whose bodies were made of bronze and steel would heat during the day and still be warm by evening. Because blood is warm. Because warm knows warm. I wonder how my feet must have felt in his hands. Aside from their warmth, I mean. Were they rough, though young, from running barefoot from the house into the yard and up the Hill, before being called back for slippers that would burst as we ran? Were my toes still free of fungus and chigger? Too absent-minded to notice, I wonder now if he had, careful not to run his fingers along my sole.

All of his limbs were long, as if he'd been grown to the size of a man and then stretched a few inches more in every direction—beautiful in the inhuman language of masks and sculptures. Even his neck was long. And when he swallowed, the balled-up bones in his throat would try to escape before relaxing back into place, infinitely accepting. I imagined that if I were that ball of bones, I would become stuck in his throat, choking him—stretched men do not swallow own way boys. Lodged in his throat now, I realize I wasn't a pioneer braving the rugged frontiers of my life but a refugee. Innocence was my native state, and I ran headlong away from its persecutions, crossing its borders every chance I could get, taking every chance I could, until I escaped into whatever unknown thing experience had in store for me. But I hadn't yet lived, and its language was foreign to me, its inhabitants strange.

I had rarely seen him without a pair of pansticks in his hands. Like every panman whose weight was weighed in steel, his sticks were a part of him, and when the tips of his fingers wrapped around their lower ends, his thumbs along their shafts, they seemed as light as hollowed-out bones until the blue rubber balls bounded off the six-bass, and the deep notes spread across the ground like an oil spill—notes you would feel rather than hear, not to be savored like those of a tenor or double tenor or cello but to be endured: the rolling, rolling notes, asserting themselves, insisting themselves. Sound, like marrow, filling him up. Empty-handed now, his long, bony fingers unfurled, he seemed out of place. Uncertain, except for what music he might have been playing in his head.

He was blacker than Bobby and taller than Brewster. In his yellow jersey and green sweatpants sitting near Aunty Lystra's brown rug, he looked to me like a deconstructed kiskadee, grounded and bereft of its fat, with only bone and muscle to hold him together. No longer given to flight, he looked almost constricted, swallowed and brought up. He looked like something to be pitied. So I pitied him. How else was I to look at a thing that looked as though it were about to die?

"Kevin, come." Denise called me, and I ran off toward the kitchen. My mother would soon be home. I didn't think to tell her when she came in that evening or any other evening. I hadn't been taught to view myself as prey, so I didn't know that I was in the presence of a man who thought he could consume me. I was never in fear of being disbelieved. The reason for that was simple: I never knew it was a story I could tell, or that I should. It was, perhaps, a deficiency, a lapse in my mother's upbringing of me for which she would receive no charge and require no absolution.

If I had been cursed by his touch, I'd never know. There was no hardness there. And yet, the polyester sweatpants didn't hide for me the truth that a man's balls would feel like no other thing than what they were. He left me there to consider the nature of intimacy between men and those who wished to be men. Was this how he rationalized his touch? Seeing me not as a boy but as a man, only smaller? A small man dislodged from his mother or a boy who had dared, however briefly, to give her up? I don't know why he didn't try to continue, but he never did. And I would see him from time to time, but he never came back to the house. Maybe I disappointed him, keeping for myself what power he'd hoped to take—that selfishness I cultivated in my own wayward practice of loving the world and everything in it. He never said. And what kind of man was he to give surrender to a child the way he had, to give over dominion to me in that way? That *I* should have pitied *him*? What traces of masculinity remained in him after pan practice that he would want me to help him revive? He never said.

Thinking I was free to curse, I thought for years that I'd cursed myself. It wasn't freedom but the illusion of freedom—and the curse, only the illusion of a curse. There had to be something more than that, I thought, something that freed me from the constraints of those illusions. But what was it? To whom could I turn for that answer, who would then free me in a way I hadn't known in my own mother's care? Could I turn back to my mother now, or had I gone too far, strayed too deep into that dark place, that there was no going back for me? I panicked. Had I become the friend that carried and did not bring back? (This is what guilt would make you say.) Or had I needed to find my own way back? To heal myself of a wound I hadn't inflicted?

For children, there are freedoms that come with speaking—from a mountaintop or a heap of gravel we will pretend is a mountain—without the fear of being heard. And then, there are those that come from not speaking at all, that reside at the base of your spine, in your throat, between your toes, tethered to the hope that what goes unsaid will be enough. Common in each of these freedoms is distance—the distance, for example, between the one who is free and his mother. He is not free, only freed into a kind of early ruin. And ruin, warm in the making, grows frigid even in the sun.

For me, it is all still there, behind the transparent louvers, behind the opaque curtains, that sense of ruin. There, infinite in its obstinacy, the looming lies of an obscene memory and a song I have learned to sing against it:

> I was not a victim,
> though victimized;
> or perhaps a victim,
> though not victimized.
> I string the polarities—
> noting nothing and knotting—
> then play them like a stolen lute
> against my skin.

Caribbean nonfiction is not so much about confession as the work of an already self-confessed truth in the life of a story that demands to be told; whether the demand is in the remembering or in some new articulation, you will determine for yourself. It is an art that asks, "Who do you think you are?"[2] Answer or do not answer, but know that *not* saying carries with it a greater tendency to *do*, bringing you closer to who you will|must be, though somewhat further from who you say you are. I want you to understand this. For it is this increased likelihood of doing, or daring to do that spurs me on—pushed as much by courage as by shame to engage vision with voice, and that voice with a body of its own—that is, a body that is more substantive than symbol that unfolds into

2 Also, more quietly, it asks: How do your truths arrive? Do they come to make archetypes of your former self? Do they release you now, like some errant memory? Or is it you who memorializes them?

symbol, but a symbolism more materially formed, that blooms out of the humanity where it has hidden for decades and into an infinite unknowing. A form that remains in the world, godlike in its distance from who I might have been and close to who I wish to be. Godlike, but human-made. A body one may see, whose meanings one may be inclined to envision.

And whose story you may be inclined to believe.

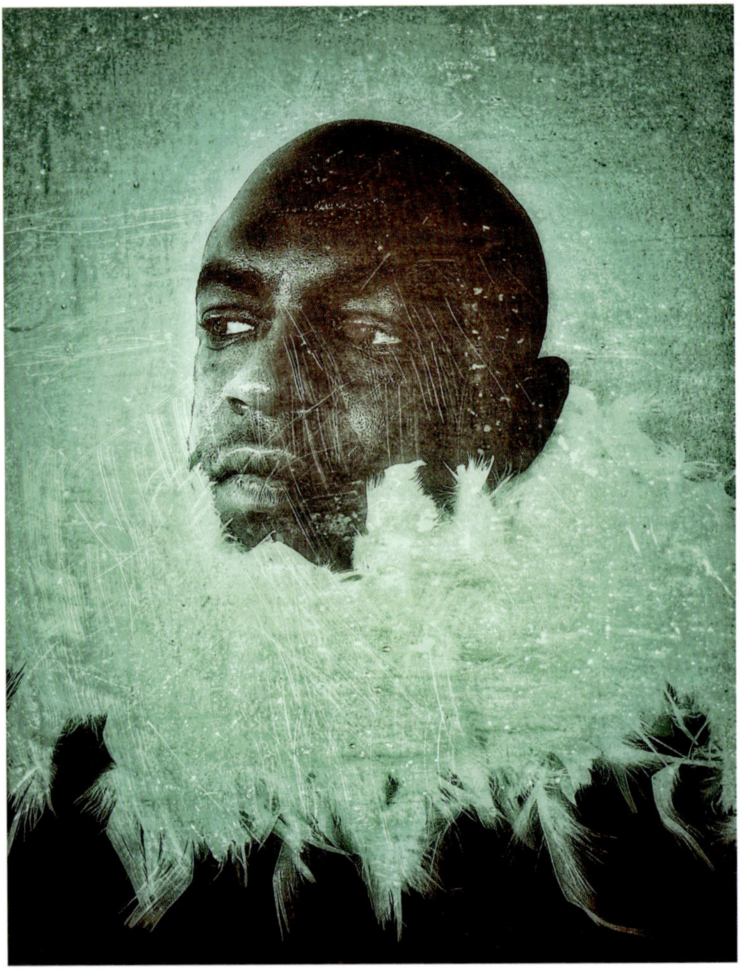

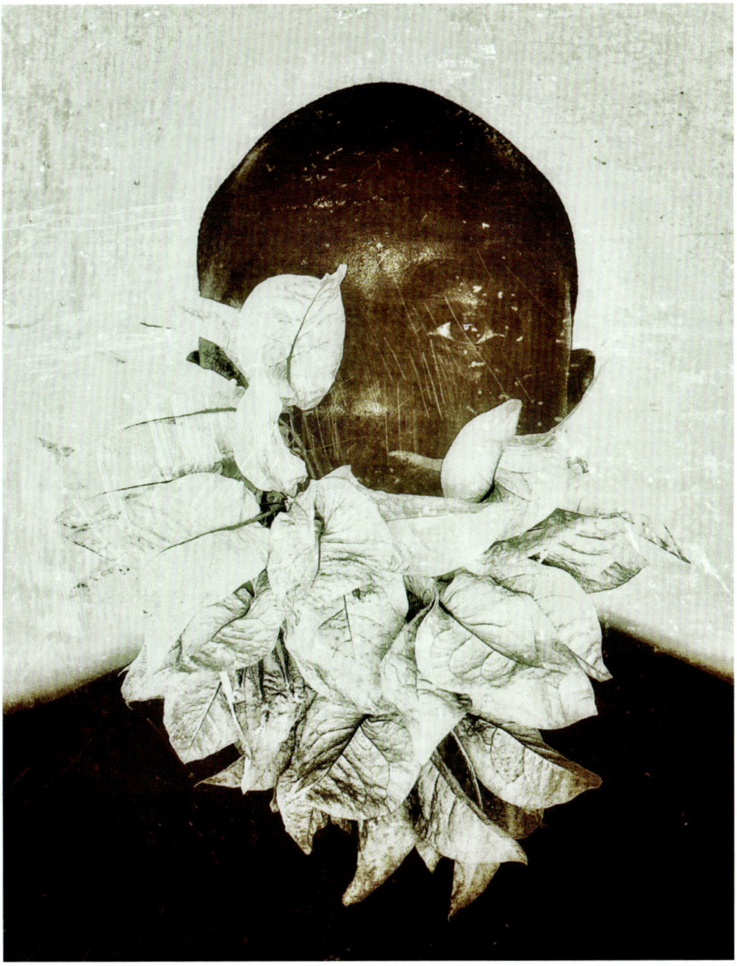

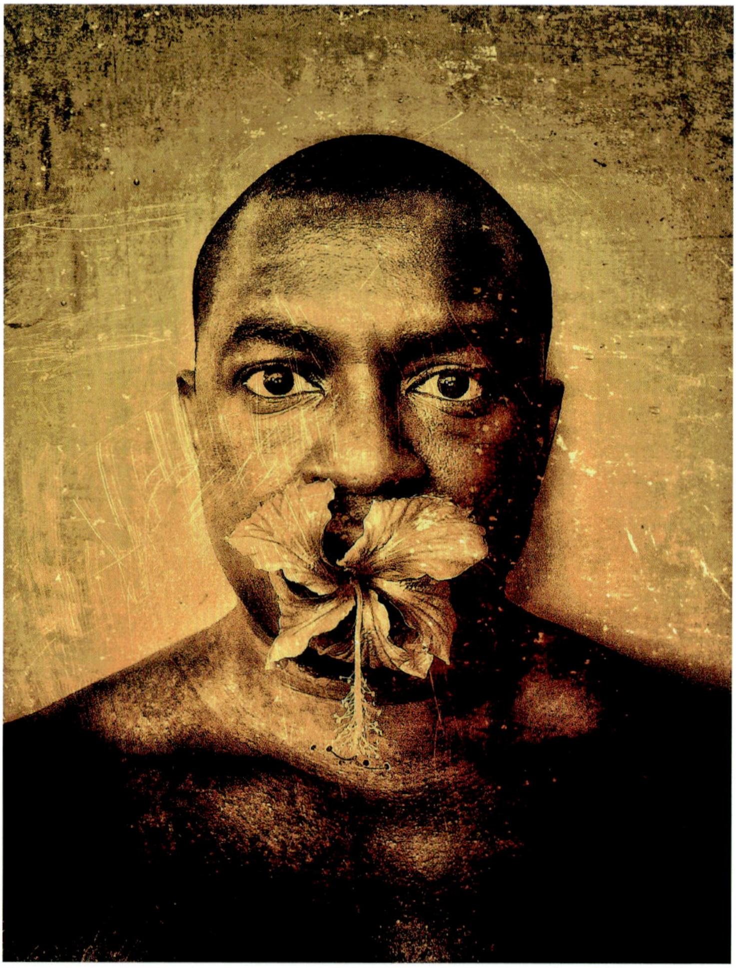

NAKED

In Belmont one night, after a reading of an essay
on Wilson Harris's *The Carnival Trilogy*, in a procession
of drumming and dancing through the narrow streets, a
former classmate tells me I was the first boy he saw naked
in the changing rooms at high school—his first naked boy's
body, that first witness of a nakedness other than his own.

We lose each other in the procession
(and again in the years that follow).

The drummers drum their hearts out into their drums in
the tray of a pickup truck as it inches along. People stand
by their gates and in their galleries, looking out, dancing in
their yards.

And the drummers drum their hearts out in the humid night, skin
meeting skin. Too late for the day's dust to rise, all is sound and street
and light, a flock of dancing blackbirds.

Later, I dance with a woman I have not seen in decades.
Each step is a "How have you been?"
and a "Where have you been?"
and a "What are the odds of this?"

And the drummers drumming.

FALL

Finally, at the annual high school reunion, you come to terms:

Student. Former student.
Athlete. Cadet.
Friend. Prefect.
Brother. Menace.
Some of these you were. Some of these you were not.
Because of your class, because of your lack of class.[1]

Men you once remembered as boys, you (having seen them) can now only remember as men—their boys' faces melted away in the memory, in life, hardened and softened with age. Shames and violences, too, have seemed to go that way (yet wait in the shadow at the end of the covered way for the last drink of whatever courage comes unbottled now to show themselves with bared teeth, with social drinkers' gums).

It is a smile, not a grimace, that says:

I forgive you.
I am forgiven.
I forgive.
I am not forgiven.

1 Who you have tried to be in all these years is wedged between these two: being and having not been.

A smile back that says:

I should have been
better.

The unsaid is often the most obvious thing. Presenting as a silence, the affect of its simplicity lingers like a *metaphysic*. To you, as to me, it may at first appear to be a missed opportunity. But it waits, haunts. The memory as an imagined object—doubly objectified—works beyond the words, makes room for their eventual arrival, though your body will sometimes strain beneath them.[2] At stake in this nonfiction, therefore, is the ability to articulate the unsaid, the withheld, knowing that words fail with pressure:

I am ashamed of what I have and have not withheld.

2 Sleep has been more difficult these nights; my hands hurt. My hip, too. I worry about what I can make with a troubled hip.

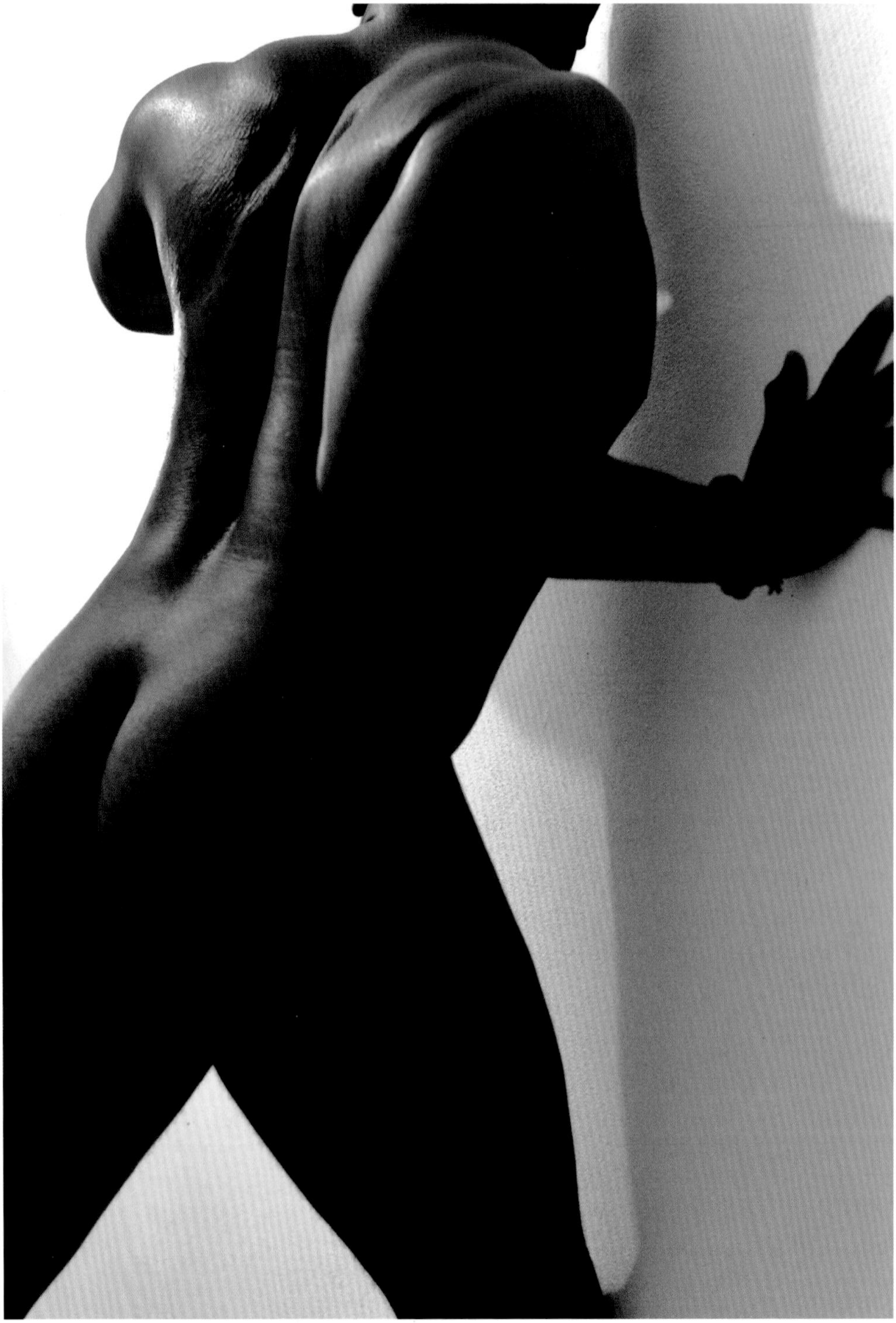

1985

I had already worn a perm to primary school by the time
my cousins told me that being at Presentation College
would make me into the bullerman or the faggot or the hen
or the pantyman or the tantyman or the macumé man all
boys who went to that school were destined to become.

I hadn't yet been touched on the ribs by a boy at school,
who would ask three years from now if I was yet broken
by the care of my grandfather. Not yet touched by a grown
man, who would see me broken by that care and three
years from now try to feed on me, his and his holy broth-
ers' divine appetites for breaking boys—and breaking into
them—already legend. Hadn't yet known the tenderness of
touch untethered to desire or known the undesired touch.
Not yet afraid, then unafraid, of touch and its genres.

Nor resolved to tease another boy as a means of saving my own savaged life, still afraid to say who it was that held me down and sodomized me at the house in Los Iros. Still afraid to say.[3]

I hadn't, by then, begun to refuse the fury I was supposed to embody, wrung almost dry of my self-disgust, almost dry of the bullerman or the faggot or the hen or the pantyman or the tantyman or the macumé man I was supposed to become.

3 *Sancte Michael Archangele, defende nos in proelio; contra nequitiam et insidias diaboli esto praesidium.*

1987

I had sought him out at the root, renaming his undeclared sexuality as a genus. He belonged to the family of animals related to myself as human but too different to be similar. He had not yet taken what little straw remained of my torment into the bathroom, not yet torn the place apart with sound, breaking before his voice would break. My rage had become his. And it rattled off the walls, and it soaked into the decades-old grout of the New Block. It sharpened the stale, rounded edge of urinals propped up like stained caskets at a funeral parlor for dead and dying boys, boys dying to be men, who looked for froth, whose shame was sharp and stale (a gilded pain returned to you like the fragments of your alma mater poorly sung).

1988

Not yet attuned to the leaving breath of a dying man, my grandfather Newallo, who had come home to Carib Street so he could wither and be laid in a kind of state near to where Muriel had once been laid—their bodies anchored, spirits sent along with prayer:

> O, Clement!
> O, Loving!
> O, Sweet Virgin Mary!
> Pray for us, O Holy Mother of God,
> that we be made worthy
> of the promises of Christ.

Not yet spat on by the Indian boy with money.
Not yet thinking I didn't deserve everything that was happening to me.

I had not yet used that pain as a key, not yet come out on stage as Hermes in the choir's production of Ulysses—where we all dared to be who we were and who we were not, dared to know empathy, to learn touch as something other than fear. Dared to know mercy as more than a game of twisted hands and knuckles intertwined. I had not yet burst onto stage, gilded and scarlet, caped and painted, to free the hero from Calypso, who was played by such a lovely girl—a soprano. Not yet forgotten my lines, not yet found my place, pretending to be a god (to be that much more the man I might become). Not yet broken, my too young heart not yet open. No trapdoor in the stage. Nothing looming in the wings.

I had only returned some years before from my own inhumanity, my animality as a collared beast at the hands of the dean of discipline, Mr. J, my black rabidity too black for the classrooms and "out of bounds" corridors. But not too black for the thick black strap he put around my neck to lead me out of class, parading me along that same corridor, exhibited like some mythical thing he'd caught in the act of being a black boy. It was a cared-for thing, the strap—I could smell the saddle soap, its unsaid stories about the bodies of other boys. Its cared-for leather black like me.

1988

What manners—"mannersing"—make us "man"?
Make us human enough?

Like prayer.[4]

4 I *am* human and enough.
I must (still) say this until I remember.
Remember, too, that it wasn't my animality that was being collared, but my black daring, my uncollared origin. There were other boys celebrated for their ability to embody a superior animality. How many beasts had we known? How many horses galloping up the track? And fish? How many had risked drowning even after the brown-skinned boy was pulled out, his head golden with mud from the unfinished hole? Perhaps if I were a better animal, of better breeding, I might have fared better, been added to a "better" house. Either way, I dared to be from somewhere else, where the audacity of origin is not celebrated, where our colored bodies would need to be collared. I had acted contrary to precedent, as if I had none.

1989

I had already liked the pretty boy because he was as pretty as the girls in the choir whose sense of class was always an octave or two above my own. Prettier than most, though none so pretty as the too-black girl who, the following year, would save me. Like a vacant *soucouyant*, my desire to be around beauty was a mask. A skin, poorly worn for a song of passing time too briefly sung. We have aged more beautifully.

I had strained to make the descant notes, scraping the sound from my throat—a belted note. Not liking the un-pretty one at first, but loving and envying him later for how he learned to be liked for what he could do: bake a cake, talk shit with a straight razor's edge for a tongue, or with heavy hands pretend a kind of strategic mediocrity that would ensure his acceptance among those of us who would not do better or did not have to.

Playing dead to catch *corbeaux* alive,
to feed them cake.

Only after would we hear about the athlete—a "boy's boy"—who wanted his attention most among us, who would beat him up for telling us about it. We might have loved him more because of that.

The clichés bind. And blind, as you must know. I was never
far enough outside the frame of patriarchy to think myself
a man. Only now, my black humanity seen|seeing through
the relic of the beast I was supposed to be, do I make of
my lowered eyes and open hands an apologia, only now
do I sense (in every sense) the origins of my tenderness to
achieve a more human pitch.

As if my heart were an unbroken drum.
My tongue tuned, as if it were a pan—
as if I were made of iron and made to walk.

Perhaps—in the peem pom peem of some earlier run—you
can hear the repudiation of self-contempt stripped bare of
the willingness to punish without mercy.[5] Perhaps by daring
to court further damnation by embodying the iconography
of his inherited angst—in the making of godlike things—
the erstwhile sinner will say, "I am human and enough.
Enough, at any rate, simply to say that I am human, and
then to act accordingly."[6]

5 *Santimanitay*: *sans humanité*. In Trinidad, the term is used to mean "without mercy," but that is a loose translation.

6 I am reminded by Zakiyyah Iman Jackson that I am not in competition (or even conversation) with the likes of liberal humanists who went to great lengths to "humanize" blackness (*On Becoming Human*, 2020). *Humanize* it only so they could place it below whiteness, closer to the animal—closer, still, to the mythical, the supernatural. In these pages, nothing haunts you, as long as you know the *douens'* bones require no correcting. Here, serious talk does sound like laughter, or like birdsong. To some other subhuman animal who, by their very nature, would not "know better," I suppose it must be a privilege to be "accepted," included in a version of universalism wherein we are cast as human beings, while not being quite human enough. I am not part of that equation. If I am thinking about my animality at all, it is as a pretext to a humanity that is mythical and elusive, that cannot be held. This is less a question of mastery of my humanity than it is a question of surrender, which is to say that I surrender to the question of what it means to be human without being compelled to provide an answer; I surrender to the modes of this being without being compelled to note the consequence of its many undulations, its moods, its temperatures that shift like thermoclines at Grand Anse or Las Cuevas.

To act accordingly, and to say,
"I should have been better.
I know that."

To say,
"My hurt should never have been yours.
It should never have been at all."
I am forgiven. I am not forgiven.

FORM

One

From:
(a) Common Entrance

To:
1E, Presentation College, San Fernando[1]

1 The doctor's son
The nurse's son
The teacher's son
The contractor's son
The businessman's son
The khaki boy from Los Iros
The dark brown boy from New Grant
The dark brown boy from Marabella
The red red boy from England
The black black boy from England
The brown boy from the States
The white boy from Canada
The white boy from Point Fortin
The white boy from Pointe-à-Pierre
The black boy from Carib Street
The boy who vomited every day
The boy who hardly spoke
The boy we called a girl

Only some remain(ed).

High,
high above the dusted field, like a *corbeau* whose
deep-whistling wings buzz the solitary radio antenna,
high above the quarried face of silt and shale,
a black boy whose name I remember
has launched himself from a trampoline.

He is not just flying but in flight—at the core of it.[2]
He is, to me, a rare and fragile beauty.

Extending his spine[3] and limbs,
his pointed fingers already long,
he appears at first to soar—a sonnet of a boy,
stretching out, out beyond himself,
                                        into a freed verse.

I am holding my breath[4] as he twists,
unheld, in the thinning air of my memory.
Inching ever nearer the sun, he does not melt,
                                        pointing fingers,
                                        pointed toes,
                                        his pinions steady.

2 What exists at the core of *flight* or any action, for that matter? Is it the intention?

3 I am not yet envious of his, as my own has not yet failed. No scar yet. No numbness. I am decades younger, in awe in another time—another century.

4 The breath, held throughout, is an act of faith.

Two

Behind me, there is the Hill

Where a girl I'd never kissed would
sing a song to me. "Calypso Music,"
by David Rudder.

Before we kiss, I answer every
question she asks: "Yes, my love
(I never knew till then),
I can hear the distant drum."

She hums a second verse
in perfect pitch, harmonizing
between breaths—mine, then hers.
Our breathing is a shared lyric.

Yes is the answer to every question.
Her skin is so soft, incomparably
black.

I think, later that evening, that
there is a song I would never sing
to her.

"Lorraine" by calypsonian
Winston "Explainer" Henry is
about a man who dreams of
leaving his beloved in New York as
she sleeps. Driven almost mad
by his *tabanca* for the experience
of Carnival, the singer arrives in
Trinidad, immersing himself in
every scene, losing himself in
everything but his beloved. In the
song, he twists time, inverting
the order: as the song begins, we

learn that he leaves before she wakes, returning in verse—in what we learn is either his memory or his imagination—to tell her not to grieve his absence, and why.

Taken a slightly different way, his arrival is a projection, a fantasy of arrival and its fundamental inconveniences:

> He has not left.
> He loses her before he leaves,
> losing her infinitely.
> He is still losing her.
> His arrival is an infinite loss.

How many times have we spoken to sleeping lovers, punctuating their breathing with our questions, with our complaints and anxieties? The song itself is an account of *tabanca*, a recounting of a dream that (at least within the boundary of the song) occurs between the singer and his sleeping lover.

In reality, you could say, he may never leave, only wish to leave. And wish to arrive. She is, his lover in this song, asleep as he struggles with his resolutions that do not ever come to pass. He wants to leave, but either does not or cannot. Perhaps he wants to leave but needs to stay—stay grounded, as it were. Impossible to tell.

Nevertheless, the *tabanca* is self-inflicted, enabling us to see how the complexities of arrival—of coming and coming again—are acts of the will.

The singer is "showing us a form"[5] by appearing to show his lover a form—the anticipation of arrival before leaving, even if the leaving does not occur. He wants to leave but cannot. It is a situational impossibility, crying because he cannot leave. It is also a dream, an aspiration, written and sung in the language of *tabanca*, to which we are sometimes compelled to dance.

Failed love abounds.

5 "To show a form" is, in the vernacular, to make an argument. Argument is the form, the phrase a device through which that form is shown and, possibly, seen. "Seen," here as in "understood," not merely perceived. In the way Rastafarians would say "seen" when they sit and "reason."

Three

Behind the Hill,
there is the serpentine
stretch of road
that leads to the yard
where I grew up.

The girl I'd never kissed is
a woman now. We take the long way
to the lookout at the end of
Ambard Street, where we could see
the whole of this hypertensive city,
and (before the song she would
sing and hum to me) listen to its
grumblings in the night like a
record playing past its grooves.[6]
Beneath the noise, we hardly hear
the "old lady sugar" of our
remembrances, the creaking of
our own settled joints.

When the random easterly blows
in on us from the gulf, I shake
and recall lighting deyas along the
concrete wall that led from Babb's
house to the lookout's edge.

The pungent carbide smoke and
bamboo at Christmas and New Year's.

6 "What Caribbean city is *not* hypertensive?" D asks, when I first read this to her. We laugh. I's true.
"Who listens to records now?" we ask, as some vintage reminder comes up alongside to answer.

The jumbie bird over Delraj's house,
over Babb's, Brother Austin's, Uncle
Babsey's.

Over ours.

Behind him, the city,
exhausted, sprawls out
like a scandal.

Then there is Paradise,
a cemetery.

Then there is Paria,
a gulf.

La Toussaint.

Four

We have been gathered for a gymnastics display—a show of our understanding of *form*, the conscious motions of our bodies in space. The saints of every house are out:

Andrew.
Augustine.
Barnabas.
Bede.
Gregory.
Winifred.

La Toussaint.

Too afraid to try the apparatus, I roll poorly, then rejoin the line—our monograms, received too late for machine-stitching and secured instead with shining safety pins, flap like little flags in the breeze. We are boys, but because we are just out of primary school and still wild, we are also the beasts and fledglings of a new state—assuming a new form—standing like browned and blackened pylons, draped in white. Like the ones you see that would plot the points of the former jetty near the wharf at Flat Rock or back near the old facilities building at Portsmouth.[7]

His ascension and descension are an act of will. His flight and landing are a gift—his descent is not a descent but a *coming again*, a return from his suspension in midair. I see him decades later at the Tabernacle in London. I am there to read and exhibit images from a book I have written, and he and his husband have come to see it.[8] We speak humbly of the marvelous things he and I have done, but I say nothing of the roles of his hands and feet and spine in these things. We embrace and part after a few hours.

What manners have made us "man"? The cliché binds, of course. And yet, in midair, he was a form I had never seen and that I had longed to see. I never

7 There, a girl I wished I'd kissed has moved on with her life—gone from there, I think.

8 The woman who once called me an ocean has also come. She has written a book about blackbirds and has sent me a signed copy for my birthday. "For the graves, the houses, the sea . . ." Our tropes intertwine.

tell him as plainly as this: that his flight was what emboldened me as a child, walking only inches above the ground, to tell a grown man leaning like a fixture into a wall on Coffee Street that his public urination was unacceptable, that he should pick it up—"pick up" what he had dropped, re|collect what had flowed out of him. Holding himself partly in hand—inches above the ground—I knew he could only ever be some of what he must have thought himself to be.

A rare and fragile thing is black beauty that its apparent disposability is a deception, couched in the presumption that whatever it entails will present itself again and again—different every time, every time a little better than before. A rare and fragile beauty is the form that is shaped like a black boy in the sun—a black boy who flies so near the sun, so near the argillite face of this Hill that when he descends from the height he has created from his own insistent gravity, he is no longer a boy, but a full-grown man in the eyes of boys still too afraid to use the apparatus. The world in which he sets his feet has changed. *He* has changed it.

Five

To ask if you see what I see is to know, already, that you do not, that you cannot, and that you must instead imagine, that you must draw on your own memory to see mine. Your memory, or your imagining of it, must precede my own. And yet, the clichés of black manhood bind. *Safety. Terror. Loss. Grief. Love. Flight.* This is how we matter. *Mattering*, here, not as mere practice, but as *method.* A method, in a way, for arriving at a memory of touch, through which we see ourselves—and see ourselves *in* and *through* each other.

It encapsulates an act of faith, in other words, in the concept of flight as (well as) the expression of memory—of memory as repetition (as remembering). *Memory*, as more than a strategy of identifying with or making an appeal to the ability of an audience to respond to familiar things—or, to respond familiarly to things which may not be.

What manner of man am I? What manners make us "man" in a way that matters? Manhood, I learn perhaps a little late, is nothing to be feared. Even if this fearful thing is in me, even if it *is* me. In the end, it may be nothing at all but a genre of touch, a breath one holds and lets go. I think, now, that it is enough to see a black boy go from god to man, to see that black man fly to think better of myself, to parse the myth of my own animality and name myself man—incomparably black—who listens for a song he may never hear.

> A song.
> A bruise, as with a flower.
> A scratch, as with a thorn.
> A wound, as with feathers.
> A sense of myself taking form.

It is, I think, enough to be shown a form to see what there is to see, and what truths lie beyond its boundary.

Six

To be "shown a form" is to have the rhetor (speaker, artist, performer, etc.) provide deliberate access to the very formulation of his intent as it coalesces into an act. It is an invitation to witness how a thing *comes to be*—and how it comes to be entirely about itself, almost (auto)biographical.

An essay on form, "Calypso Music" is not about calypso as a genre but about the music of calypso itself—a song about sound. As such, it doesn't fit within the structural conventions of calypso but engages freely within and beyond the form. Rudder doesn't simply break form but bends, twists, stretches it. He does this to reveal what he suggests is at its heart—a spirit, a memory, a vision. In fact, by the time we hear the song, he has *already* deconstructed it, its conventional aspects dissipated and reconstituted as a thesis on (let us call it) the psychosomatic nature and affect of the music, rather than a more structural forensic study of the form itself—a *thesis* on the rhetorical work of feeling that is embedded within and simultaneously transcends the form.[9]

To demonstrate this, Rudder goes beyond the form into something that invokes the music of calypso without subscribing too strictly to its conventions: the song is about sound, a praisesong dedicated to the *pathos* of the music itself. By shifting the focus from form to the affect of its content, Rudder slips the constraints of form altogether for a more abstract and exploratory discussion of what calypso music was, is, and will be.

We first encounter calypso as an abstraction that coalesces in the form of Rudder's voice and self-awareness—he is a "seed" germinating from the archive of tradition. He names early calypsonians Neville "Growling Tiger" Marcano, Raymond "Atilla the Hun" Quevedo, and Theophilus "Mighty Spoiler" Philip, who moved from the *lavway* form (common among the *chantwells*) and contributed to the shift from single-tone to the more melodic double-tone (ballad) calypsos in the early to mid-twentieth century. Present, too, are Raphael "Roaring Lion" De Leon, Philip "Lord Executor" Garcia, Rupert "Lord Invader" Grant, Egbert "Lord Beginner" Moore, Fitzgerald "Mighty Terror" Henry, Aldwyn "Lord Kitchener" Roberts, Slinger "Mighty Sparrow" Francisco, and guitarist Fitzroy Coleman. Rudder also pays homage to Fitzroy "Lord Melody" Alexander in his more subtle reference to "the spirit of the melody."

Alternate title: "Rudder's Calypso: A Break in Form to Show (a) Form"

9 To hear it in the way I refer to it here, it must be sung to you.

But note that while he appears to be embedding himself in an overwhelmingly masculine tradition, he is also departing from it and moving toward something else—"a brand-new discovery"—that relies on an original composition to increase the probability of moving the audience. Departing from what is *formally* known (calypso as genre), he invokes what is *formerly* known (calypso as music). That is, he shows us a form that doesn't merely seek to contradict the validity of the calypso but transcends it in order to demonstrate a more nuanced understanding of the affective potential of the music. That potential is transcendent, taking a path through memory—what is remembered, what is forgotten—until it ascends. Listen for when, following his mention of Spoiler's trademark "Ah wanna fall," Rudder insists, "Ah wanna rise!" To emphasize the shift, there is a change in key. In fact, the *tonal* change complements the *structural* changes that have been occurring all along. There is a sense that the song is coming apart by design. The varying meters of the opening lines in each verse seem to emphasize this even further.[10]

The form he had established to describe the history of calypso changes repeatedly, coming apart with every revolution. But its revolutions also reveal the very thing that form tends (however unsuccessfully) to corral: a Caribbean futurity that, despite its overt masculinity, appears (to me) to be feminine in origin. The opening lyric is a question that refers to the sound you have just heard: a bouncing drum, a melody that laughs, revealing itself before the utterance that will describe it.

You are being called and reminded of having been called: "Does the rhythm tell you 'come, come, come'?" Acting as *chorus*, the backup singers respond on your behalf: "Yeah, yeah!" If you can hear it, you will know why yes is the answer to every question and why a thing you never knew will suddenly seem like something you have always known. If you can hear it, you are closer than you think to seeing what he intends. You *are* being seduced—you already know that. But you are also being called back, called home, called to remember what you have been missing, to remember what will seem like a "brand-new discovery" but will be ancient, preceding word and thought and tradition. Preceding *form*.

10 And, perhaps further still, we might recall Walcott's homage to this very line in "The Spoiler's Return." It is a fall, as with the original, but one that is uttered from the afterlife, as a damning commentary on contemporary Trinidadian society. The fallen know best how to recognize the circumstances of their damnation—and the misery of a nation that seems to have damned itself.

Rudder is playing a *mas* here, one you are invited to hear as well as see, to remember as well as understand. But he is not masking his intention at all.[11] Nothing is amiss. No trick is being played. Nothing has been hidden—in fact, what appears opaque or obscure is more likely because we have not seen it, but it rests out in the open, in plain sight, like a city you hardly see *even* as you go about the business of living within it. As listener, you get to see what he's saying, see what he says the sound is doing.

Its roots extend from the natural environment into the more organized realm of cricket, and we see the syncretization of the percussive rhythms of the *tamboo bamboo* compared to the legendary skill of West Indian cricketer George Alphonso Headley. The references stretch from sport into an intricate series of literary allusions. Can you hear "the lyric and the melody that sending yuh soul to the boundary" and fail to think of C. L. R. James's *Beyond a Boundary*? Do you return to the mention of Spoiler through Walcott's "The Spoiler's Return" and find providence or parity between Walcott's "I decompose, but I composing still" and Rudder's "real jamming start and today we jamming still"?[12] Will you finally go looking for your old, dog-eared copy of Earl Lovelace's The *Dragon Can't Dance* to confirm your feeling that Philo, the calypsonian, is a reference to Spoiler, whose return Walcott later dedicates to Lovelace? Then, feeling your way through the sonic-haptic experience of bongo and *tassa* drums, do you notice the vernacular indictment of empire ("bassa bassa") with scant regard before arriving with Rudder at a conclusion that is utterly visceral and untranslatable?[13]

Wo yeah yeah, wo yeah yeah, wo yeah, calypso!

11 Try to remember that one is not necessarily the other, in spite of their shared etymology. Mistaking one for the other is how you trick yourself into thinking you are hiding what is, in fact, clear as day.

12 Or do you stretch a bit further to reference its connection of Spoiler's aforementioned fall to Rudder's "The Hammer" since Walcott's Spoiler gives that message to Desperadoes from Laventille? You might say you know what causes thunder when you hear Rudder's tribute to Rudolph Charles.

13 Though not named in the song, the drum given prominence in the discographic data is, in the fact, the Log Drum, played by master drummer Jajah Oga Onilu. Rudder refers instead to the bongo and *tassa* drums.

Do any of those things occur before we realize that this song is doing more than it appears to do? What manner of masculinity is the performance whose thesis is "rooted deep within my Caribbean belly," whose "discovery" is grounded in mystery? You "shake like a Shango," but "[don't know] why it is yuh shaking." Both the shaking and the not knowing, Rudder insists, are calypso music—its essence.

In the end, you find that it is as ethereal as an easterly wind blowing in from the gulf, on which laughter is a drum, breath a lyric, and love a melody sung to a restless city.

A song about sound that sounds like love—love of form, love *as* form—to me.

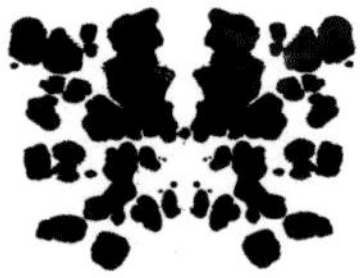

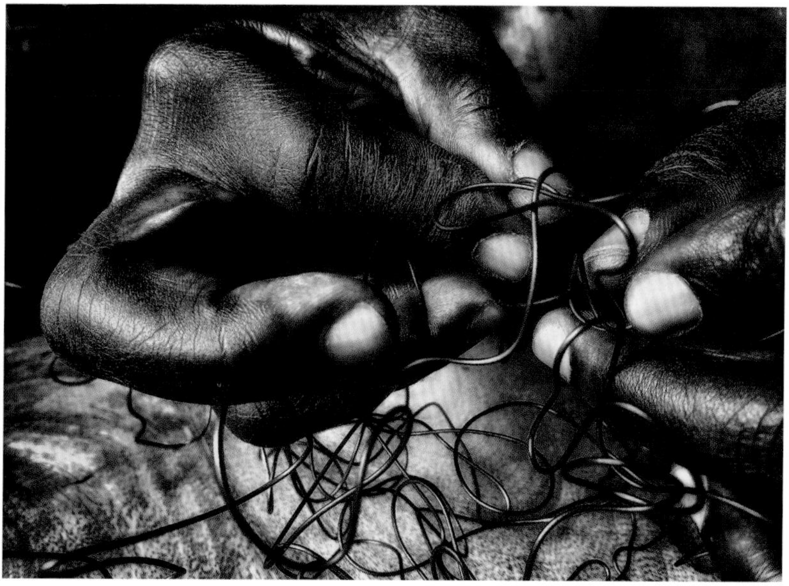

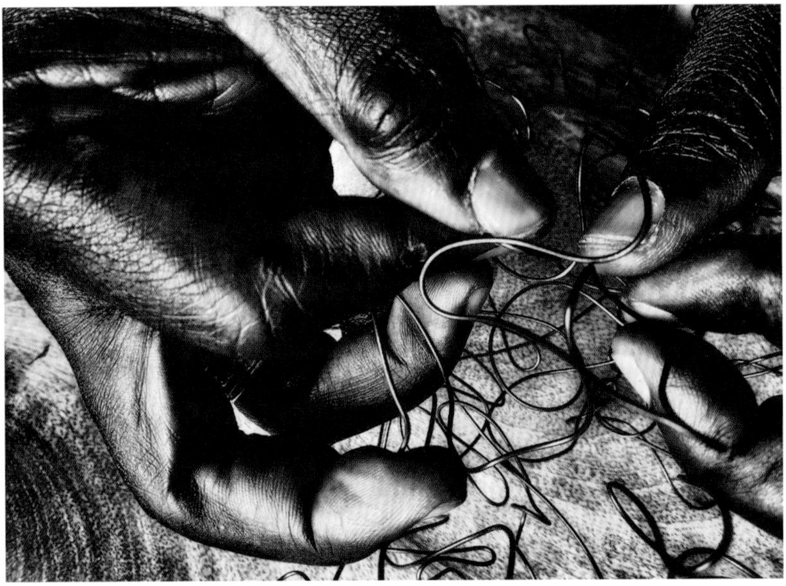

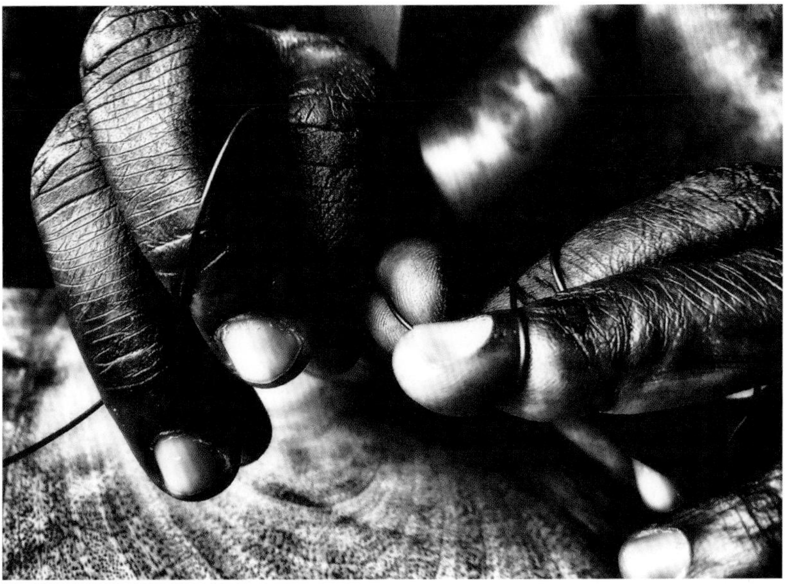

TECHNE

Not bleeding at sunrise is *art*.[1]

What do I know of wire bending,
of dressing wood?

Only the face I make as I bend it,
barehanded, pausing to see if I've cut myself
on the ends, along its frictioned lines.
The steel is "dark annealed" but rusted after years in my cupboard.
Stored away, languishing.

Only what I can grab from the mill,
the obvious splinters, the flaws that show up too late, coaxing the obstinate
blade to yield to the grain.

Only that my hands hurt when I sand, only my gradually loosening grip.

Only myself bending toward one or the other.
Only that I am my mother's son.

1 From "Morning Coffee," an unpublished poem I shared with Conrad Mercier, my high school English Language and English Literature teacher—and form master. 2001, I think. Emphasis is Mr. Mercier's.

Only that in these bindings, I am also bound. In these contortions, I trace the wringing of my wrists. Though at times it will appear as if I have the privilege of a sustained exclusivity—as if anything could be mine long enough to claim "I" and "me" and "mine"—it is only because I am the only son of my only mother. And my onlyness is a promise of kinship to come. Kinship, here, is the longing for touch.

What do I know of archipelagoes?

Only that they are a notion of solitude turned inside out, the materialized myth of place whose Obeah of singularity is turned inward. Only that it is a space to ask whether it is possible to look at oneself from the inside, from the position of subject. Only that with wire and wood, with skin and finger, bone and nail, with that which is surrounded and that which surrounds, unbinding is the work.[2]

Only that I am looking out for you so we can be unbound, waiting like freedom for you to arrive.

2 I used to think my hands were small for a Browne, too meaty for a Wright. I have always been a Browne, just with smaller hands. Like my mother's. Not as small as my mother's but smaller than my father's. Smaller, still, than those of my grandfathers, Newallo and Radcliffe. I realize these are the luxuries of a mind that had never had to wonder where its hands belonged, leaving space enough for the realization that "legacy" is not so much made as borne in the restless motion of memory, held in story. What appears to be crafted, then, is a realization remembered: a truth that lies motionless at first, then turns and returns.

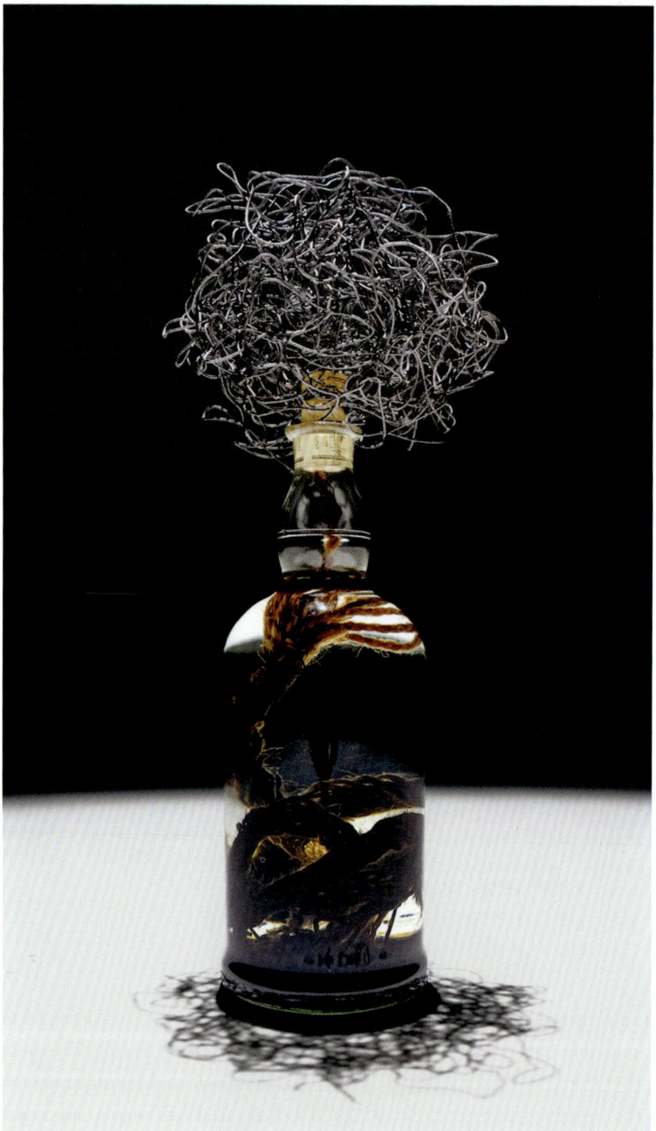

UMBILICI

Umbilicus No. 1

Of what am I descended if not unburned oil?
If not some inverted *marronage*,
whose foreshadowing is of an undiscovered memory
bottled up?

Where on earth is my navel string?
Where is it buried?

The once inhabited womb is not an emptiness
but the memory of embodiment—perpetually *re-embodied*.
The body, unredacted, is the womb's memory.
I am the memory of my mother's labors.

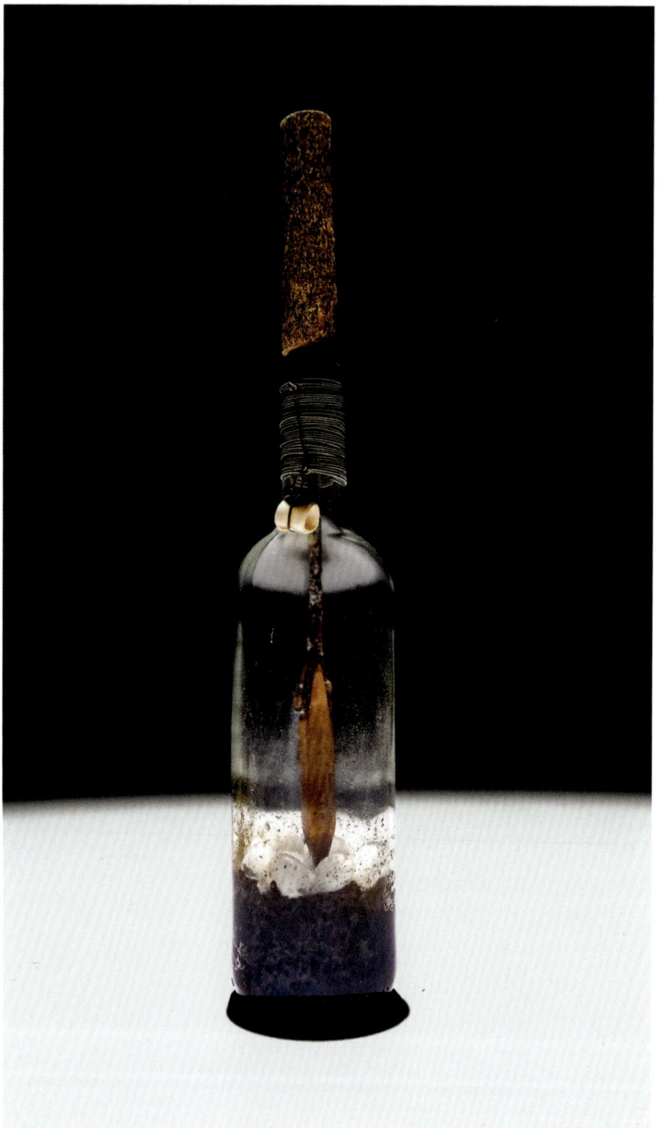

Umbilicus No. 2

The *phallus* is a pretense,
appearing as if it is not
centered on itself, aimed
at its core of stone and
dirt—the whiteness of
the stone, the blackness of
its coffee earth. Seeking
no womb, its suspension
is permanent, its reflexivity,
however bent, is unbroken.

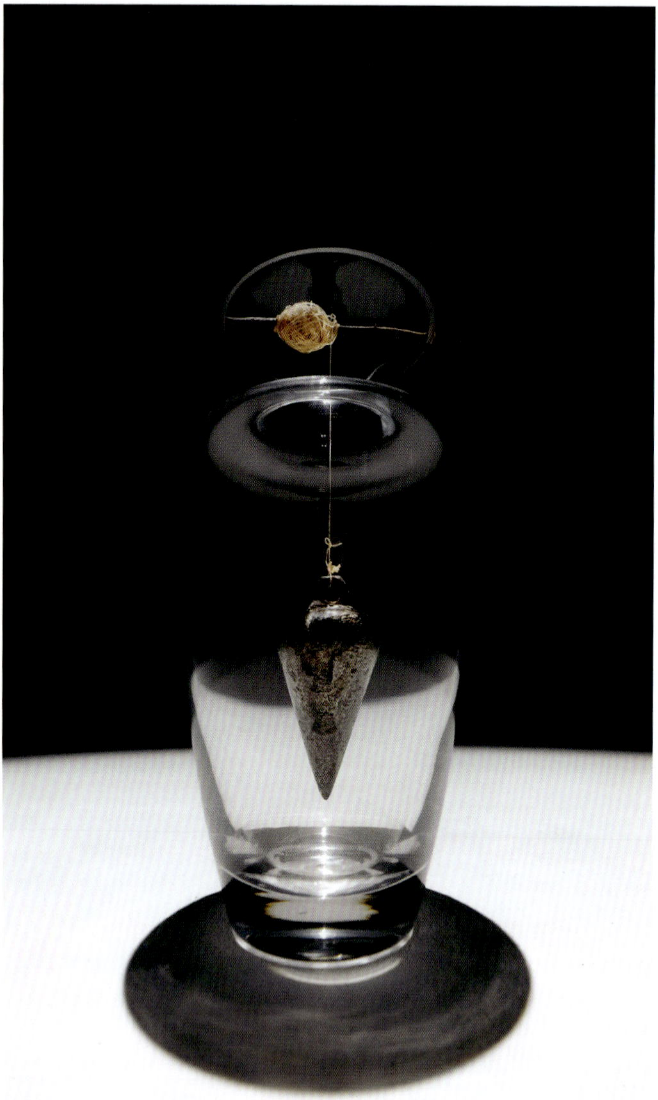

Umbilicus No. 3

Tangled fishing line to catch no fish.
Broken guava stick held
across the mouth, bitting the chasm
in which the bolted head of a plumb weight
waits (and wades when the water moves it).

We are all subject to gravity,
bound to it as to the grave.

These *Umbilici* are renditions of the will to live, of black life cast momentarily as|in the inertia of suspended intention. Their assemblage is the path of sound—of an utterance—on its way to becoming subject(ed) to light:

> a series of intentions subject to light,
> subject to be seen,
> their internal subjection subject to witness.

An oramaclastic assemblage that passes for seeing.

See something tender in the residual dust that gathers on the brass, their still, unanchored questions, their untrawled utterances, their quiet hemorrhage, their singular *marronage* upward, inward. See in the refracted rounding of the rusted hooks that rest too easily on the coffee grounds and sugar, where I might, at first, forget about the rope pictured best in the early morning or late afternoon.

It is a witnessing.

Remember "witness"? How it reminds you to look inward, and to look back? Looking in *is* looking back—it is studying the hook once lodged between unknown ribs, its point that would stretch and tear the spine, the unseen and unforgotten skin, the serpentine nature of handmade rope resting half-suspended in oil, turning gradually darker, until it is as black as the sugar and coffee dregs. Black as memory. Black as the past. Invisible. Settled in its shallow depths.

Something must carry you, or bring you (like water, like knowledge).[3]

What has borne you?

What has brought you to this place—right here, or to wherever you are?

In a sense, the *Umbilici* were all bound to be biographical, but they are also a projection—the projected biography of an unbinding to come. Their assemblage is archipelagic—appearing to undo themselves. What do I mean by this? I mean their design is oriented toward the eventual dissipation of their form. Their coherence is a dissolution of my intent.

3 Depending on how that bearing is achieved, or accomplished, you may arrive at an angle, with a peculiar orientation that marks you for life. But also as *alive*.

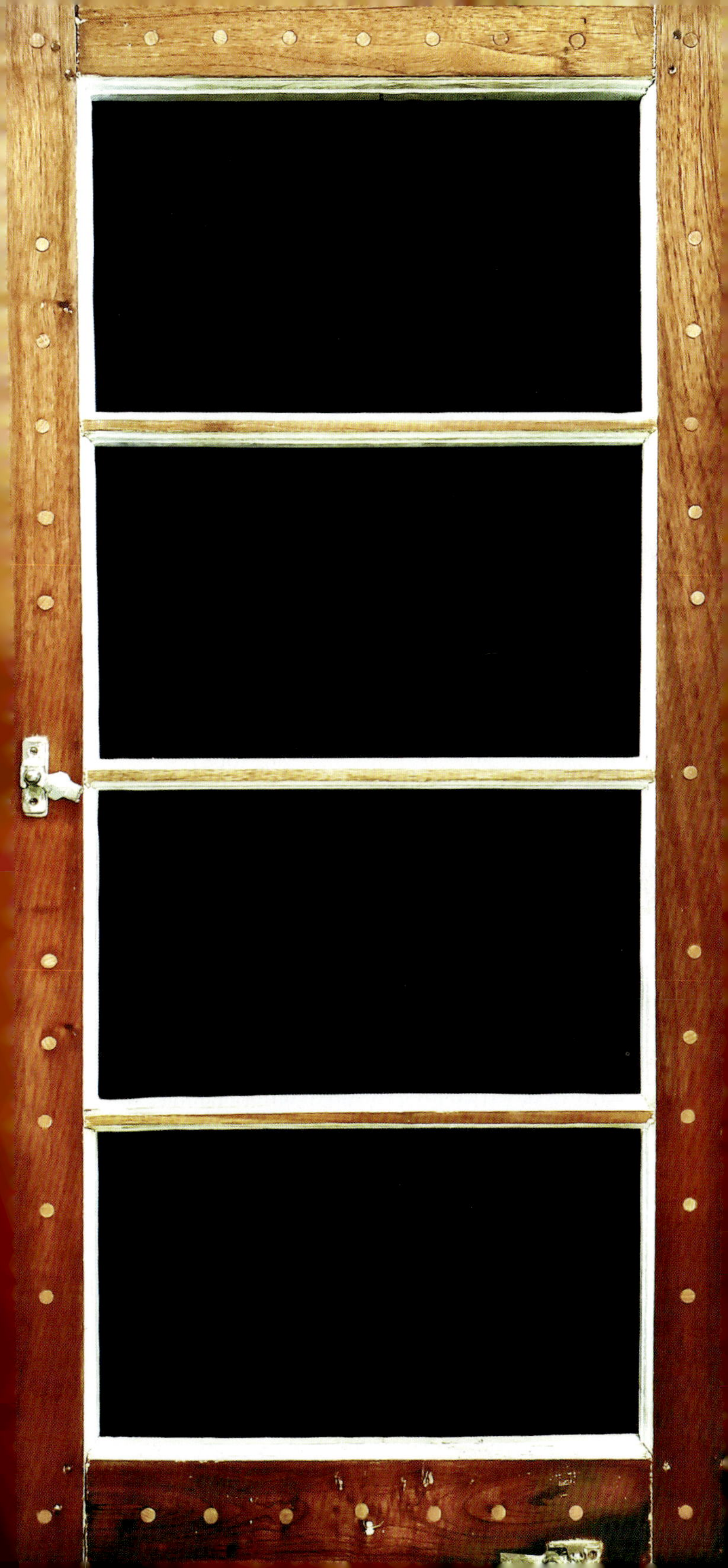

CHARLES STREET

I

We sit, almost huddled, like a shrine on the porch
until, at last, you embrace the utility of your gift
with tempered Hog Plum and Pommecythere,
no witness to remnants of Carambola left to settle unchecked
in the ghetto of a favored glass.
You have not fallen into disrepair, my love—
not cracked into a barricade
—though the lines gather near the vestibule
around the abandoned hermitage of a mouth.
We do not linger like words that have lost their place in a language,
no dust or cobwebs in our laughter,
but move now to measure the space between said and unsaid,
like unsent letters, left folded beneath the clothes and the camphor.
Soft candle. Rose water. Talcum. Needles. Pictures.
And we, the remains of settled joys, rise up to settle again like dry grass.
From growing envy, disturbed by some common bird,
we learn to reconcile, where pains take shape.

II

Wait a moment.
Watch the children walk by the house,
their necks not yet strained with age, and turn
to look half-cocked past the frosted panes.
Good night.
Good night,
good night.
Who is it that broods and hums like an ancient hymn
in the darkness now, what rusted screw
from centuries past now holds those windows in place?
Now, with slighted reverence,
they summon near the old parlor like pothounds, who plot
your death without conversation.
Had they caught the scent of your anguish,
got some rumored news of your surrender,
heard you were dead, that they show such interest
and seek your corpse for evidence?
See how the errant, unsaid good nights turn indigent
and loiter near the shadow now for your scraps?

III

The house plays like a broken music box.
This roof, like a sieve for day's lights and
odd rains to leave their dregs, for splinters and nails.
Rippled, galvanized rust, battered poinsettia paint.
Then, the applause of shades rising, of rain stretching
across the floor of this house where everything is old.
Curtains, hems stained and withered, look like the old Hill from here.
Inconsistent floors hold the singular tempers of a gulf.
You must be more than effigy.
Hidden, it is still possible for you
to move about this haunt and be the living
history of this place you love out of habit.
Where you—mad, ungracious miser of our frailties,
genius, mother, a soul's jealousy—live.[1]

1 The thirty-nine lines in this poem are embedded in the sealed holes that line the border of *Charles Street*—one line to a hole. The poem was originally written in 1999 but revised in 2021. The revision was transcribed onto a strip of brown paper, then cut (as seen in the accompanying image), rolled, embedded, and sealed. The window frame is one of four I found at Talparo junction, Trinidad, in 2017—after a talk on *kalinda*.

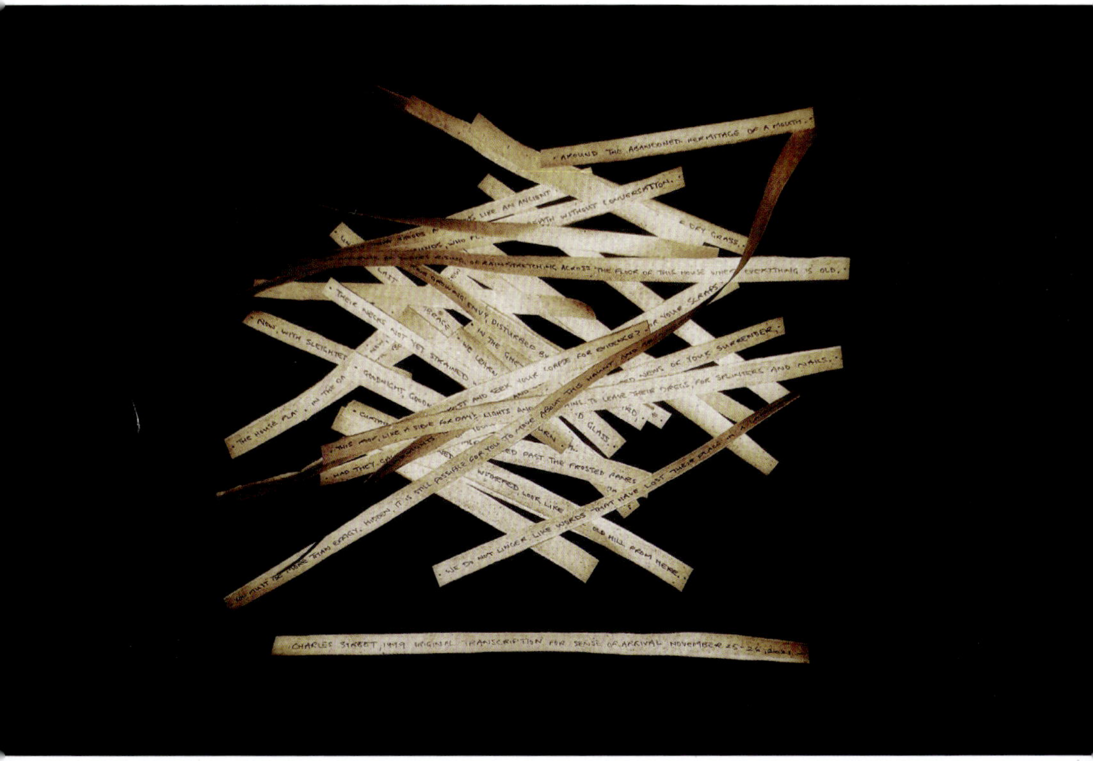

AROUND THE ABANDONED HERMITAGE OF A MOUTH.
DRY GRASS.
WE DO NOT LINGER LIKE WORDS THAT HAVE LOST THEIR PLACE
CHARLES STREET, 1999 ORIGINAL TRANSCRIPTION FOR SENSE OF ARRIVAL NOVEMBER 25–26,

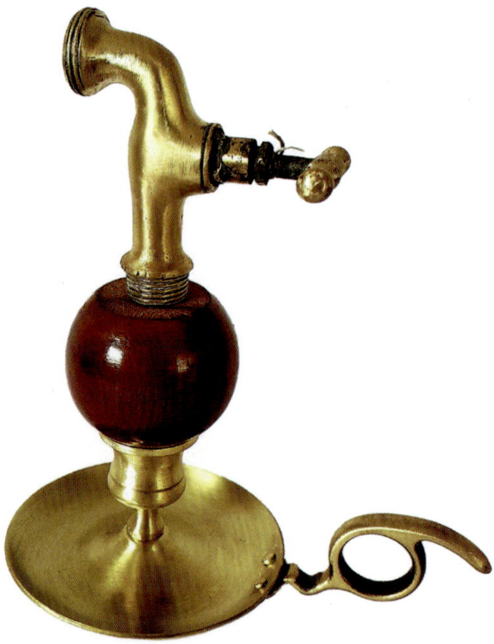

ANIMÆ

There
behind the house on Charles Street,
and then around the front, walking slow until
she is out of sight   and sound,

Miss Louise
an old Spiritual Baptist woman,
will announce the things she has made by hand—

Sugar cake,
Tambran,
Toolum.

Her voice is a bell.

Sugar cake! Tambran! Toolum!
Sugar cake! Tambran! Toolum!
Sugar cake! Tambran! Toolum!

Sug . . . ca . . . Ambra . . . Oolu
Sug . . . ca . . . Ambra . . . Oolu
Sug . . . ca . . . Ambra . . . Oolu

Alternate title: "A Black Boy Considers His 'Place,' Recalling That Art, as He Thinks He Has Perceived It, Is a Form of Ruin"

Uh . . . Aye . . . Ah-ah . . . Uh-uhm
Uh . . . Aye . . . Ah-ah . . . Uh-uhm
Uh . . . Aye . . . Ah-ah . . . Uh-uhm

Pampalam! Palam! Palam! (as a bell)
Pampalam! Palam! Palam!
Pampalam! Palam! Palam!

. . . ! . . . ! . . . !
. . . ! . . . ! . . . !
. . . ! . . . ! . . . !

Her voice setting, setting until it fades
into an evening of sugar cake pinks and slightly sunburned whites
and of peanut brittle golds and shadows,
and of glittering *tambran* ball browns
and their blacker brown seeds, into a night the taste of longing, the color of toolum.

On a night the color of toolum, my grandmother Vena said to me what she'd hoped I would never do. A night of molasses and grated coconut, rolled into imperfect spheres and left to cool on the linoleum counter, the black that isn't the black of Butler's statue at the junction in Fyzabad (his face and hands the same oily black of his suit, his beard the perfect white of his shirt), but the more complicated black of the oil field workers who call each other "Comrade" on the picket lines and at funerals, the black of her skin as we lean, street-lit, on the banister at the house in La Romaine:

"I doh want you digging holes for a living."

I have taken this to mean different things at different times:

> 1999: Your grandfather, father, uncles, and cousins all share an affinity for oil and its pleasures. You see what it has done to them. Remember what happened to Dave. That is not for you. Look at your hands. Those hands are made for other things. Do other things.
>
> 2004, mid-October: Do not fall into the traps of

your profession. Do not set traps for yourself, or for others. Do not play tricks with what may be your life.

2004, late October: Clumps of heavy mud thrown into her grave as Dominic, the youngest son, plays parang and we dance at her gravesite like we danced those nights before. I danced like a blackened dervish. Like an old top in the yard. I never mastered the flick of my wrist to get a top to dance.

But I danced.

2011–14: Come home . . .

2017: Come home. Your family needs you.

2020: Leave. Wait.

2021: Wait.

2022: Leave.

I have defied her many times.

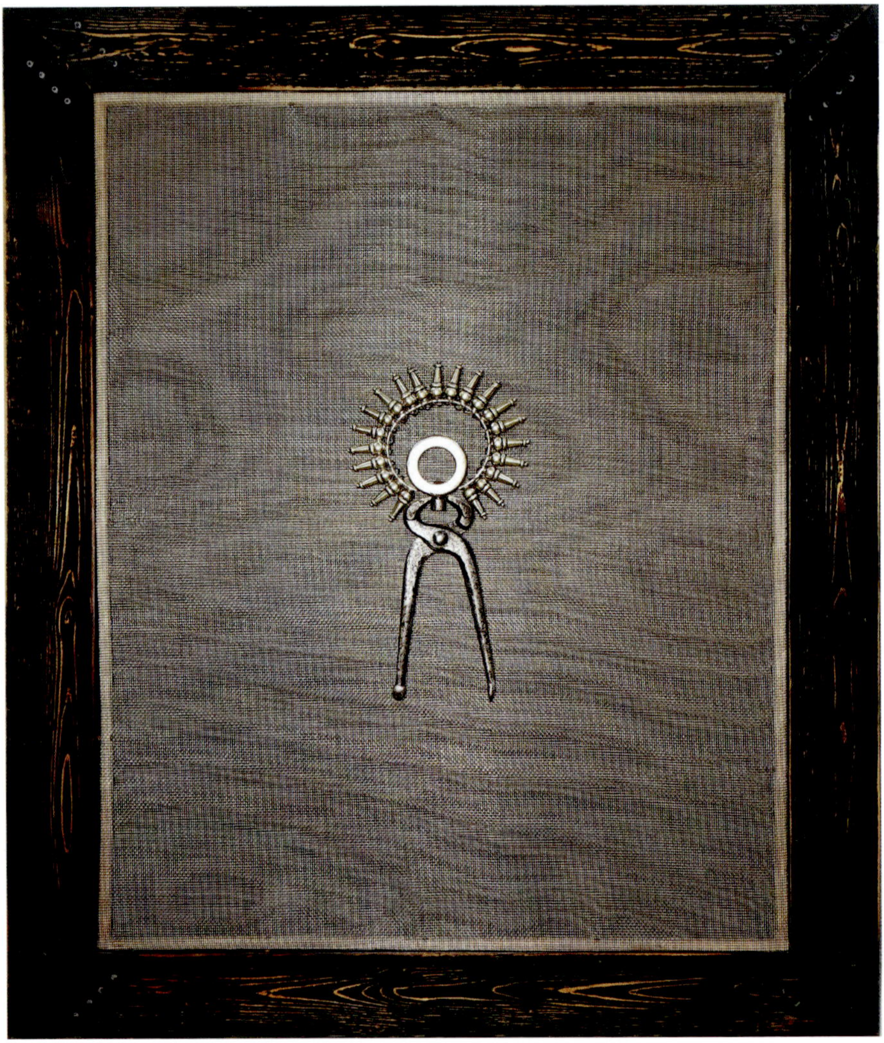

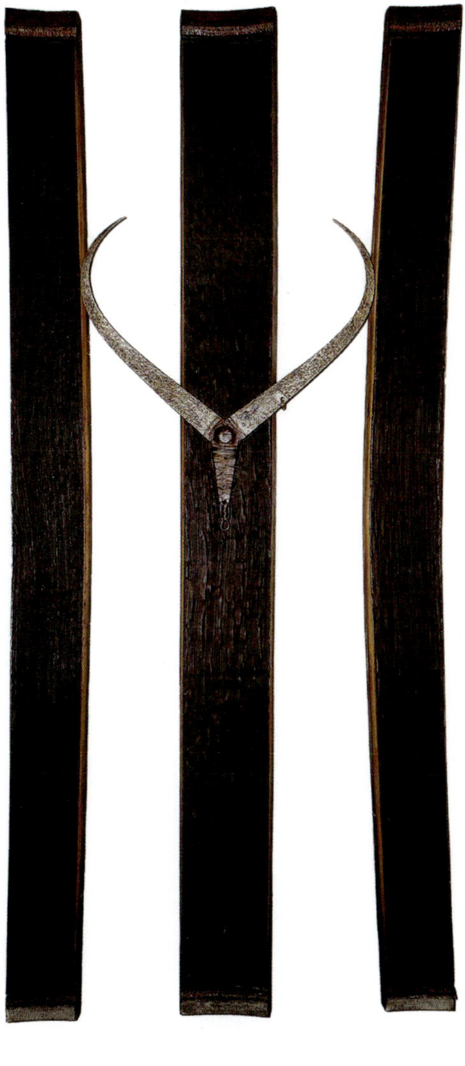

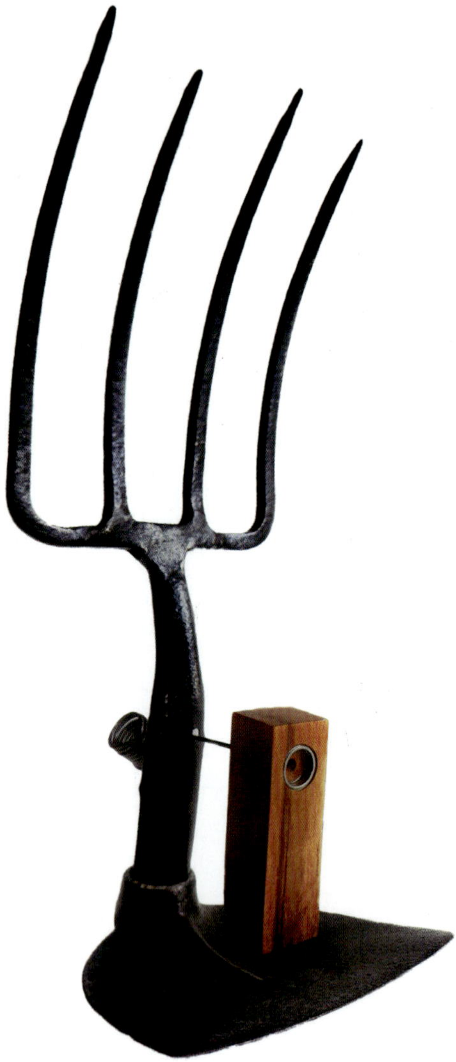

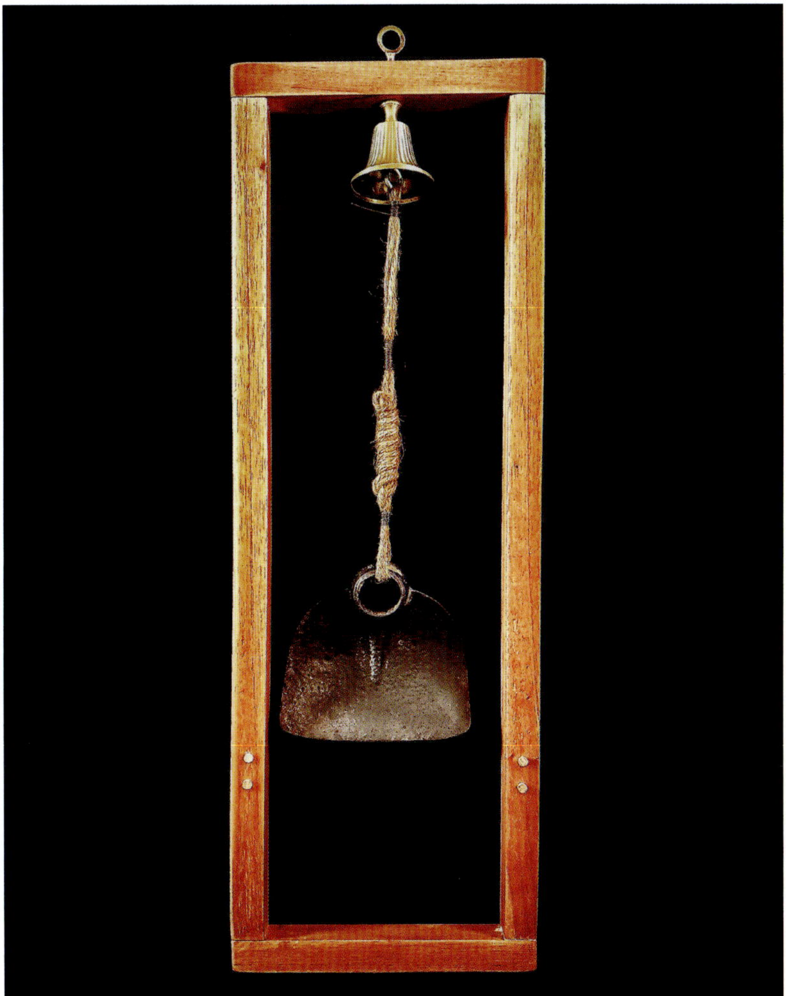

Though it is bound to come apart, memory is not a ruin—it will not rust or rot, in spite of yourself and your forgetting. It will be the same blackened green of the canals behind the house in La Romaine, the same old water that swirls until it runs from mud to silver-gray to glass glittering in the shallow. And an old woman's brown skin sugared and salted in Carenage and San Fernando, water- and evening-cooled on this island, will hold its shape. If it is like anything at all, it is an utterance cast into the infinite, unlistening cosmos. No expectation of a response, no flinching lip or rolled and batted eye moved to tear. Instead, the dasheen bush will inch upward from the drain before it bursts: massive, heart-shaped, open like the aftermath of an Independence Day fête.

I safe here.
I home.

I remember Vena.[1]

1 Be patient with the memory of things that remind you of people. It's not that they mean to mislead, as people sometimes do, but that their angles—the subtle, unsettled ones—are sometimes given to mild exaggeration, to story. Like the acute angled lies of an infinite drunkard who, whistling "In and out the Dusty Window," stumbles up and into an open door. Or like the obtusion of his senses, the gulf that grows between what is touched and what is felt. Or like the settling angles of the dust that rests on his forearm as he tries to set his story straight, falling asleep before he could finish. He will wake soon enough. And then a different spoon will knock a different bottle. A different hand will rest on different skin. A different window in a different yard. Remember: one is always as unhinged as the other. One is always breaking, the other creaking in unison with the termite-ridden jamb.

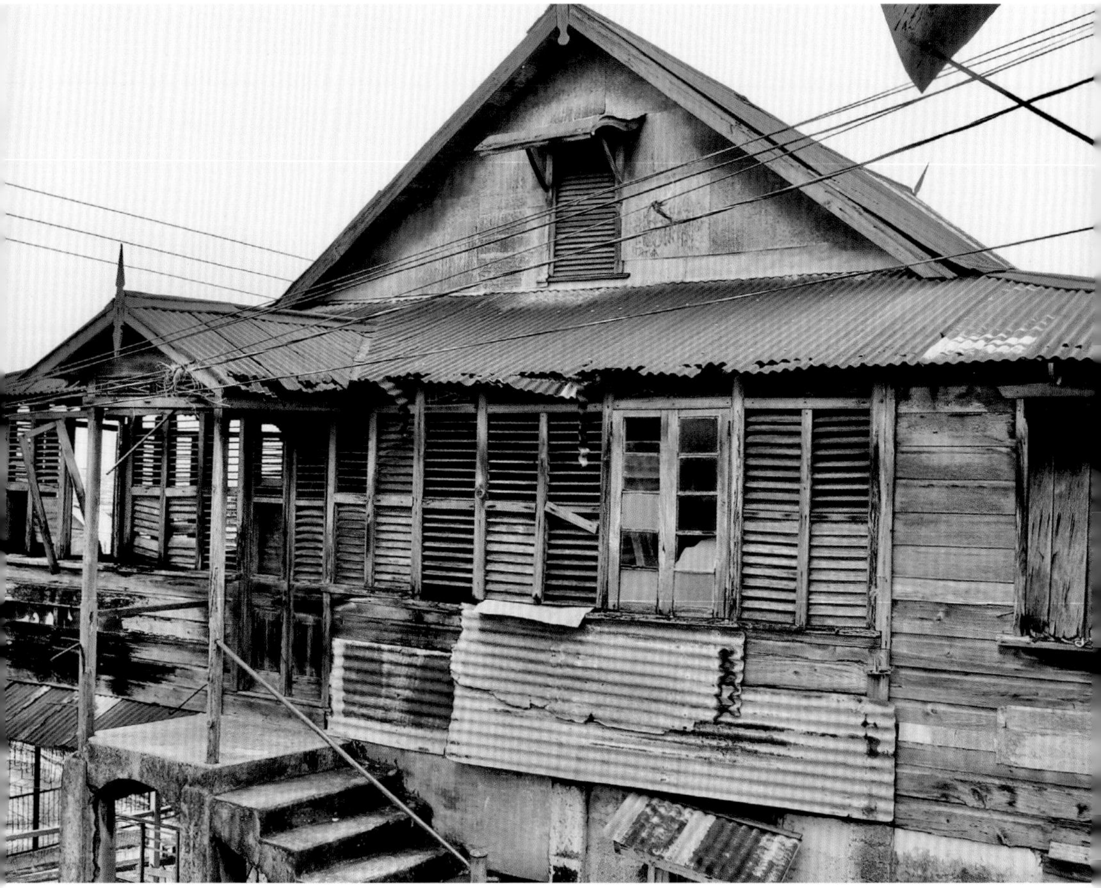

YARD

Out.
In.
One's relation to a yard is infinite.

To those passing eastward up Carib Street in San Fernando, the starkness of its retaining wall is an abruption—where (one might suppose) the quarrying of the Hill had suddenly stopped and houses took root in the unforgiving rock. Only someone scouring the foxed and dusted archives at City Hall would want to take it for the footing of a citadel. Only for a moment, though. The illusion of one abandonment will come apart before the truer story of its vacancy takes its place. *True*, that is, until a break in the wall reveals a set of laventillian steps—steps that, even for us, to ascend would be to descend. It must, to the passing glance, be more so the ghetto, as buildings grow from their barrack yard beginnings to stand in each other's way, obstructing the views of those inside of them. But, for those who stayed—who were born and grow and die there—the act of "looking out" is really "looking in."[1]

It is a negative space.

How do I say "This is not depravity," that "it is not deprivation," in a way you would believe? Only to say "This is what we mean when we say the yard is home." Home as I have already described it, as in neighborhood and city and nation is home. Yes. But not only that. *Home* as in the phenomenological reality

Alternate title: "Moving Simultaneously toward In|Exteriority and Ex|Interiority"

1 Across the street, Jackie (a second cousin) looks out for a while, then retires to the chair in the gallery. Then, again, gets up to address the unruly curtain. She notices me and waves. I wave back.

of Caribbean presence—that is, the experience of simultaneity, of being both here and there, out and in.

This is the yard—the archetype of an outside that was the world for us when, too small to go anywhere else, we could go no farther than the steps.[2] Before we could go into the outside world of the yard, the outside was first an extension of the inside we knew. Now, it is also *yard* as trope and repository of motion and the stretching of space over time, the transposition of being here and there. *Yard* as transcendence beyond the very concept of boundary. *Yard*, too, as rhetorical device. And as artistic method. This should come as no surprise. Our earliest experiences of perspective arrive in the shape of structures that hold us.

Yard: as|in the sense of a Caribbean imaginary that is, let us say, obliquely opposite to its origin in the memory. A perspective.

And in this yard, from this perspective: this house. This is not the house I grew up in but the house I grew up around. I grew up, you could say, mostly on the outside of it. It was left to Brother Austin, my mother's uncle.[3] It is, too, something of a self-portrait in the sense of being an image of my perspective—that is, me seeing this house from just outside the house I grew up in.[4]

There are other houses in the yard—Uncle Babsey's house, to the right of the frame and up the Hill, where he lived with Miss Phyllis and their granddaughters Arlene and Angeline. Arlene died young. Aunty Daphne and Mr. Joe lived in the house to the front, left of the frame, with her daughters Lenore and Dianne and her son Ken, who whistled like a bird in my mother's memory. Across the street, farther left, the house belonging to Tanty Van and Mr. Cecil. And ours (which I will come to in a moment). Aside from mine, I only know these houses from the outside—as enclosures of spaces I could only imagine. I must have gone inside, but the details of that are gone. I have nevertheless allowed myself to be fascinated by this one. Not so much a home to me as evidence of an enclosed space and of its enclosure simultaneously subjected to light—the prismatic action of light acting on what is visible to tell the story of what is not. I mean to treat enclosed space as a material concept, and to treat the memory of that space as a material expression of a Caribbean imaginary. By which I mean

2 N 10°16'41.8", W 61°27 '27.9"

3 I've only ever known it as his, where he lived for a time with Miss Claire and their children. They left before I was born, and only Brother Austin remained.

4 Think of it in the way one thinks of reflections, in which you see a version of yourself that you cannot actually see—what you see is not yourself but a representation whose truthfulness you come to trust over time, naming what you see as *you*.

the material action of being Caribbean and of making Caribbean things—the practice of nonfiction toward the making of art.

Regarding the imperative of this nonfiction to direct the narrative inertia of an image toward some solid distinguishable form, I have thought about the language of the first spaces I had ever known: their tilts, their lilts and lisps, their petrified stairs, their oxidized accents, their eaves, dropping here and there off the edge of the gutters like gossip, their empty, off-center attics, the glint of their tarred and stone-weighted roofs. Somewhere in these houses, between their weathered jalousies, their arthritic hinges, their skins oversweetened with old lady sugar, their crawling vines that smother, and their cupboards and drawers: a language, a rhetoric of Caribbean being that invokes. Call it a creolization, if you like. But note that banging galvanized sheets have no dialect we can distinguish. This is design that exists out of spite and in spite of itself: the treatment of space as a concept that may be subject to creolization but that transcends the very notion of it. I'm referring here to the epistemological transposition of space and material to un|make and re|make meaning as phenomena: objects gathered like curios on the page, on a shelf, in a room.

> Ask: What is the invocation that echoes in our galleries,
> runs up and down the steps, troubling its partitions, the
> weathered edge of aggregated brick, the waning in the curl
> of broken fretwork?
> I will say, blackness, of course.
> Mine, but it may as well be yours.

To make the photograph, I stood where my mother is sitting in another photograph of family (that is as much a fiction as anyone might contrive about family—the one we come to believe is a nonfiction, an assemblage of onetime truths dilapidated now into myth—nonfiction, we know, is felt in the scramble, the desperation and absence). You see her there in the back row, sitting (and looking out) to the right. I am there in the photograph too, sitting next to my restless cousin Noel (Aunty Evelyn's second son), beneath my aunt Lystra's wing. Brother Austin's house is to your left, across the expanse of the yard that is also to your left. Denise (Aunty Lystra's first daughter) and Rachael (Cousin Lenore's first daughter) are looking down into it—it is outside the frame. They are framed within it—framed, more precisely, within the space just outside the house that is framed within the yard. I stood there, in that space once held by my mother, steps away from the space I once held.

Like the photograph of our extended family pressed into an uneasy tableau on the steps of 16A, the story of one house is a foil for a story in a house you do not see. It is, in a way, a refraction of an intimate space that exists obliquely opposite to it.

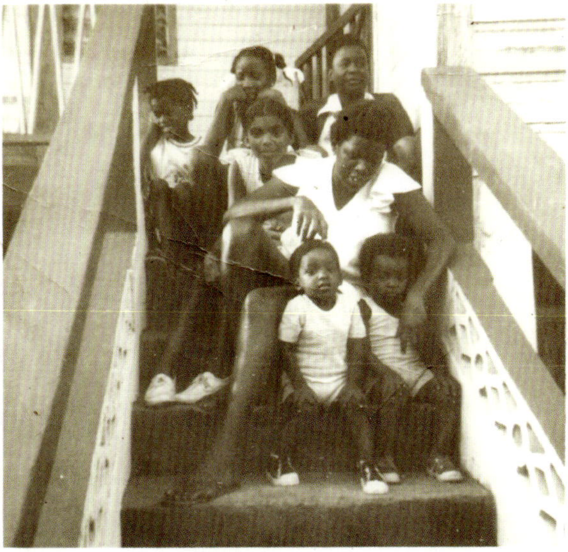

Ask: What is obliquely opposite to intimacy?
And I will say: An interlocutor
suggesting with looks what remains unsaid
between one and the other.[5]

What more need be said that can so clearly be seen?

For one thing, the story of a house beheld in this instance for what it has in common with bodies and for what, in its objective materiality, it is able to do that our bodies *cannot* do: be regarded, for once, without the overweighted violence of memory that threatens to obscure our black subjectivity.

5 The "unsaid" is not "unsayable" here. It is more of a "talk some, keep some"—that is, not what I am unable to say but what I will not say, a crafted silence that I will break only to say, "Look at my mother. And then at me, many miles away from her."

It is still standing, though its insides and outsides are even older than they once were, less romantic. Less given, as ruins sometimes are, to romanticism. It is more of a vagrant now, outpaced by a city eager to outrun itself. It is not inhabited by ghosts, though the man named "Moco" who lives there now could be called a Jumbie. He would laugh if I were to say that to him, knowing that I invoke those spiritual stilt walkers who, even in my adulthood, cause wonder and awe. "Moco," whose name I never knew.

We pass each other in the yard, "Whapm now?"

"I dey, wi. Just cool."

"Yeah."

"Yeah."

Never mind who says what to whom, who calls or who responds. What more need be said in the commoning space of the yard, where one's voice bears no greater sovereignty than another's? Instead, let time pass. What we think of as time (past, present, future) is also a record of the senses giving account of themselves, such that our knowledge of the *when* of what we experience is based solely on the *what* of it that remains. The present is known through the senses, the past resonates as a sense remembered, and the future is imagined as a result of those remembered things—that is, their memory of what was sensed. Asking you to imagine with me is also asking you to remember.

If it is too soon to imagine all of this, do what I have done: just let time pass and come back when you're ready. I will do the same thing. Eventually, having given some definition to the frame of the yard we inhabit, I will come back to see what there is to see, to return the absent|ed bodies to it—like the former bodies and bodies formerly known as "cousin," and "cousin," and "self," shown here as a singularity perched between the *here* of home and the *there* of the yard, on the cusp of inside and outside.[6]

Let time pass, until who we *are* becomes who we *were*.

Let us meet on the other side of it.

6 See how "to come back" is not always the same as "to return." Sometimes, "to return" is to "bring back" or "to be brought back"—that is "to bear" and "to be borne."

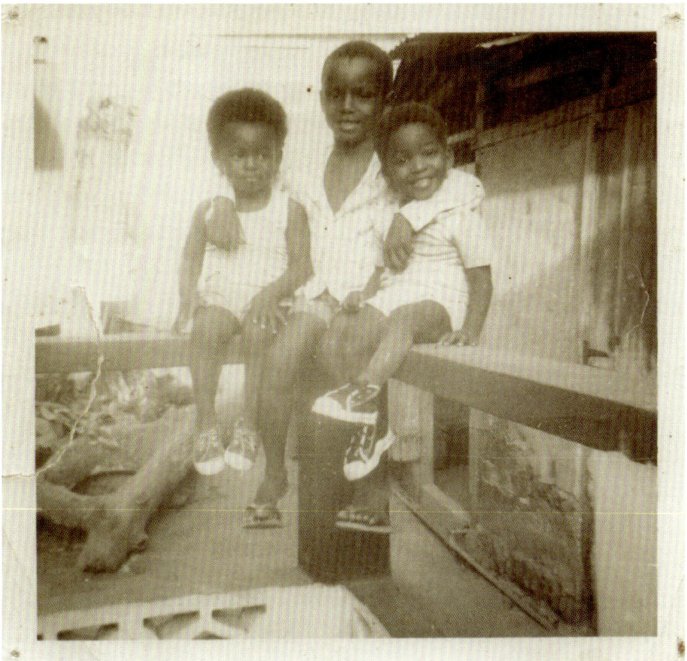

There, better now.

Now, with my eyes securely lashed, I take the walk into a former life. Black as I have always been—almost unheld by light—I find no conqueror imposing on this sprawling tide of my past. Nor any Castilian god and his cholera, nor restless galleons, but speckled fowls that come to roost in the zaboca tree. I sit in the yard where I was born, grew up, and died. (I only say I must have died because I have learned to wait like a ghost for something to happen. But I am still alive.)

Now, I sit like a sentry, looking out for what internal disruptions emerge. I talk with my cousin Dionne about the loss of Noel, breaking the monotony of my singular presence with the viscerality of an unspeakable memory. Our words come bounding from slender necks of the *petit quart* bottles to swirl like an enchantment (the secret words we know but do not utter), or like Sunday market mothers who negotiate the wooden stalls with shining skins, their salt and water turned to oil. What was it that has brought me back again to haunt myself, to risk tarnishing things about myself that appear too clean? A story of presence on this bleached-stone hill, lightening like long-buried bones the things we keep that cast vaulting shadows on our passing days.

We almost miss it—ourselves aging. We almost fail to see that this yard of ours is a negative space. Negative not merely by obvious circumstance but by design—it is *not* what it holds, *not* what we are inclined to see when we go out into it. Out in the yard, we only see what the yard is not: a house, a series of houses bound together by design, people bound within them, a method wherein the bound may be unbound.[7] We almost fail to note the tyranny and beneficence of the ordinary: that this yard, while an outside, is also an inside. It *holds*. One is always *out in* the yard.[8]

Already elsewhere. In this yard, a batallion of restless jack spaniards hang honeyless in the eaves, and our shared irreverence for what can do harm bears no burden of ritual beyond our hardened tongues, knows no blind baptismal acceptance of those who have crossed the waters from there to here. Here and there—as still as a portrait in that *hereness* and *thereness* of the yard—we almost fail to note ourselves, our own ignominious passing from day to day that can grind us both to dust that blows, light as light, in and out of the yard, the space between us passing like time.

In truth, I am only saying this to make some sense of absences—absences I have known, absences I have not known—that feel like home. The memory of home that feels like blackness, like Caribbeanness to me.

My blackness is a manifestation of the yard.
My Caribbeanness is made in the yard, made of the yard *itself*.

7 *Design* not only as object but as the conjuring of a space for them to be, enabling the materialization of intention and the inhabitation of those who intend.

8 One doesn't just look "out" but looks "out into" the yard.
One doesn't "walk out"; one walks out "and into" it.
And "going out" is also "coming in."
And "going out" is also "going in."
One "goes in" to "go out."
One "goes in" to "go in."
And so on into the recursive absurdity of daily life, the strange and awkward conjugation of space, and our places within it.

ORISA

I find myself at a crossroads:

Asking you to see the abstraction of a blackness that is also Caribbean is asking you to know what cannot be known—to see what is typically not seen. This is an act that resides in the province of feeling. It is, for us, a reminder that Caribbean nonfiction, if it is to be understood at all, will demand its own imaginary. At the heart of this imaginary, and its corollaries of corroding memory, perishable materialities, and unreliable action, is a question: How do I make the unseen seeable and maintain its obscurity?

Imagine the out|in as a treatment of space over time, coming out of those houses and into the yard, out of your mouth into the world. Imagine it as a presence. *Presence*—mine, yours—that is an imposition of the will. *How* we come to matter.

Imagine enclosed space as a material thing—stone, perhaps, or wood or sugar or salt. You can imagine these things because you have already turned inward from the din of the city to see what there is to see between us. You have been imagining all along. You are in the gallery of the house with its windows closed to the muffled sounds of passing things, the comings and goings of people you know and do not know, the barking dogs, the morning whistle (gone quiet now, like the flame at the refinery in Pointe-à-Pierre).

Imagine the reconfiguration of memory as the too-familiar tropes of Caribbean being—house, root, and sea, for instance—that present themselves in material ways, *as* material. Not just the built environments but the environments we build—named in this lesser capacity as *Art*.

Dedication: For Black gods felt, known only in passing.

Imagine *Memoria*, an early manifestation of the yard, but now tethered to *Xangô*. It is a monolith in each instance, but only incidentally. It exists in relation to the bedrock, and is as much an inside as it is an encapsulation of the outside.

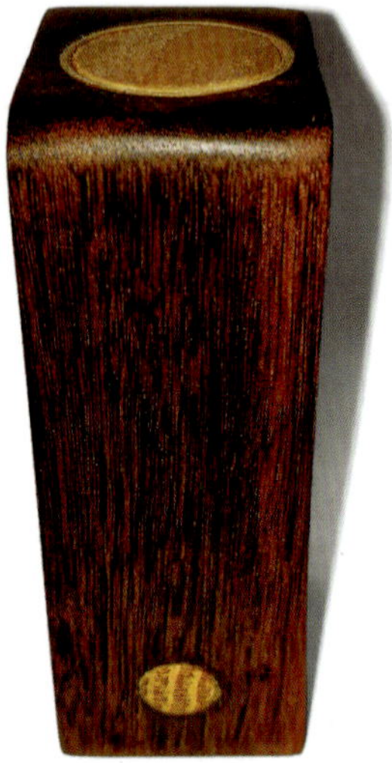

Pulverized stone from San Fernando Hill fills the smaller hole near its base. The hole at the top is hollow—a reflection on how the negative space may be materially represented and internalized, held in secret like a scroll, or like silence. Like a breath is held.

Imagine things made to catch the memory of breath now presented as an object or as light, the "memory of breath" unfolding as an instance in our long engagement with enclosed space—the space outside of us brought in—and then out again. The act of Caribbean *being*, presented as an object that has been subject to the will—subject, that is, to a desire *to be*.

Caribbeanness as a phenomenon of presence.

A presence that is more than a foil for nostalgia, which is only the absence of remembered things. A presence that declares, "I am not what you surmise, but something different, something obliquely opposite to what you remember. You may recognize me—recognize yourself in me—but I have changed, gone some distance from what I was and might have been."

This is a move toward method—*nonfictional* method—to articulate a presence that is enacted as|an absence, a collection of absences. This relates not only to material that doesn't exist or exists in absentia or out of sight. Nor does it relate to the people whose presence may be so taken for granted that they *appear* absent, but to the imperative of *making* in the apparent absence of the materials we may need (such that what we make may even appear to have been made from nothing). It is the imaginary materializing, hardening into conceit: a daring, in the blackness you may see and the blackness you may not see, to be called *Caribbean*.[1]

What I mean is what I have said.

The memory of presence is not only absence but also the enactment of an intention to return (and return)—the imminent arrival of an outcome yet to be seen. And what is that outcome? Say it is an arrival we can take for granted without having to explain why it has occurred (though we may be compelled to do so, from time to time).

This is conceit. But more than that, it is in the construction of the supernatural—or representations of the supernatural that are not themselves supernatural—that I emphasize my humanity. The very act of producing representations of the supernatural does not presume a supernatural creativity but rather articu-

1

Exinteriority	Inexteriority
ex|interiority	in|exteriority
ex: not merely	*in*: not merely
an exteriorized interiority	an interiorized exteriority
but that which	but that which
was formerly interiorized	may not be exteriorized
not essentially *exterior*,	never been *exterior*,
just no longer *interior*	but not essentially *interior*
by being, in part,	by being, in part,
the memory of exteriority that	the aspiration—that is, the wish
once was	to be
temporal, read through the lens	*spatial*, read through the lens
of an obliterated	of a yet unconstituted
time	space
—a "onetime"—	—a "nonspace"—
that is, a time that no longer	that is, a space taken up by an
exists	object

|

It binds and undoes, like an archipelago is bound and undone.
The notion of a space, the notion of a time.

lates the limitations of a humanity that is, in and of itself, simply human. What more need be said, be done? For the unbelievable body, the unbelievable mind, the unbelievable story, the answer to that question is, obviously, more. More until we do not need to argue for our humanity or be questioned for expressing it.

Here, only impermanent things are named after gods. Named, as it were, for what I do not *know* (but nevertheless feel), for what comes before naming:

Esú, Oshún, Ogún, Xangô, Yemaya

Naming what *cannot* be named, for what can only be known in passing.

Omitting, too, what *cannot* be omitted, in which there are only traces of what has passed.

Remember spirit?

Do you see the fence of Esú's ribs,
its visage of forgotten pressures,
its junctions and linearities exposed?

Touched along the sanded wound,
the piece appears to sing.
Its singing distracts.

Its stillness is a wardance.

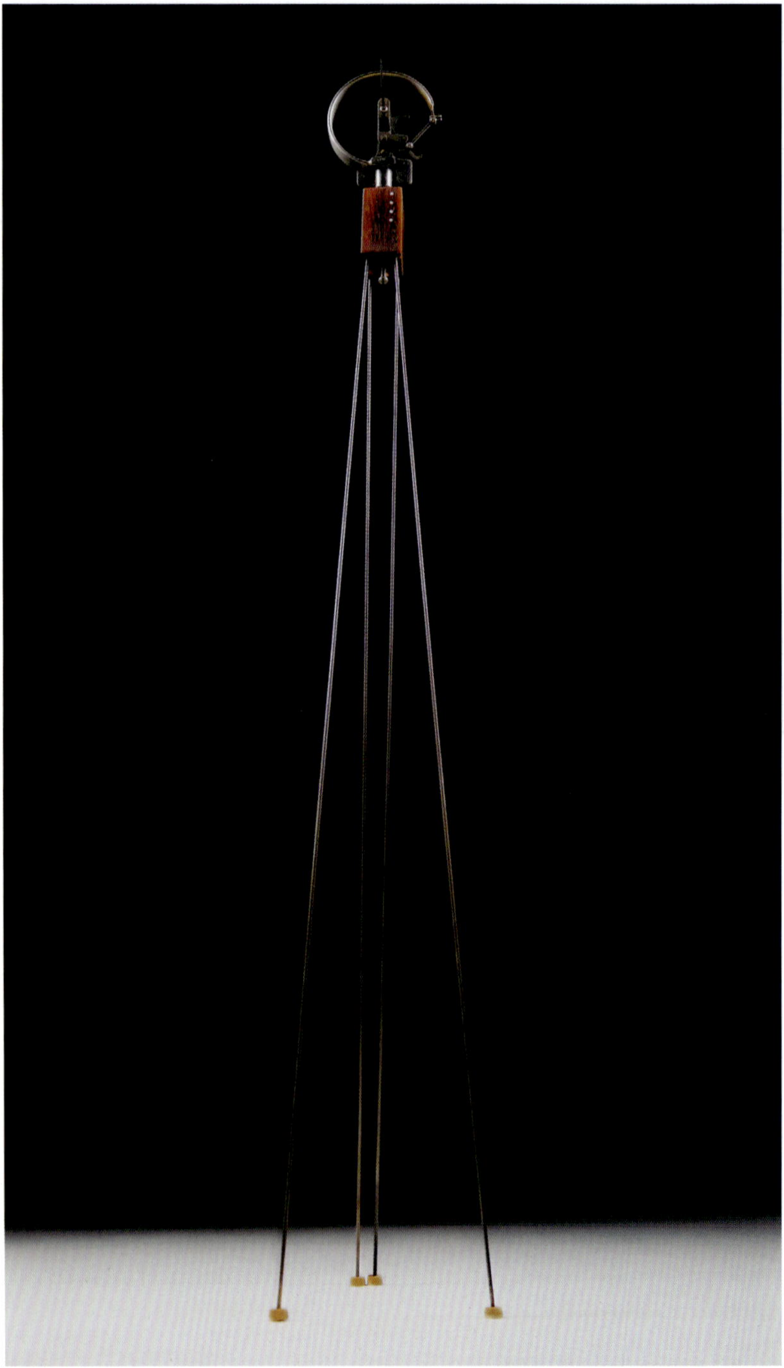

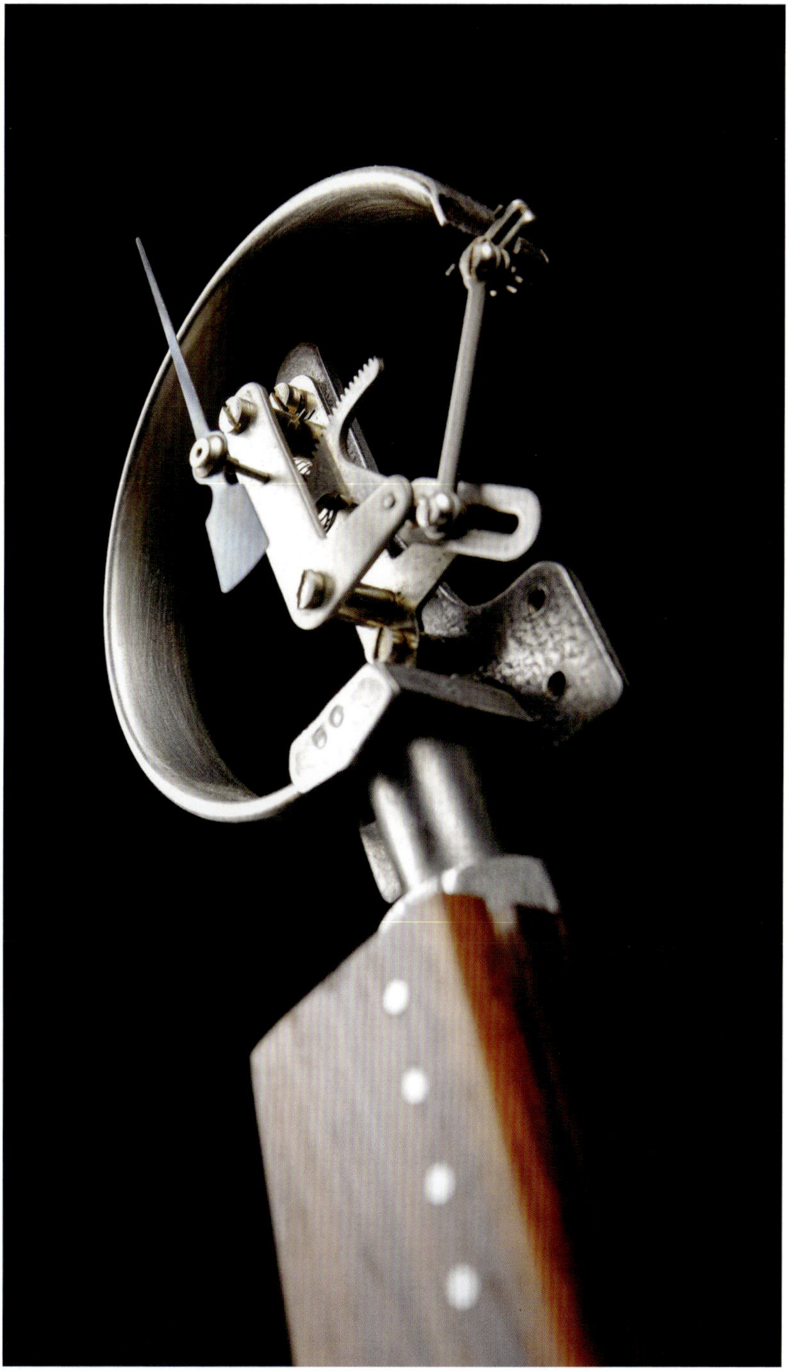

Oshún, its memory
of a confluence—watered down,
dried up—is now an anticipation
of water to come, will dance
or appear to dance,

its trembling legs
become still before long,
each moving through its paces,
evading fugitivity itself,
like a portrait,
like my mother's gaze.

The sweet single-mindedness of water.

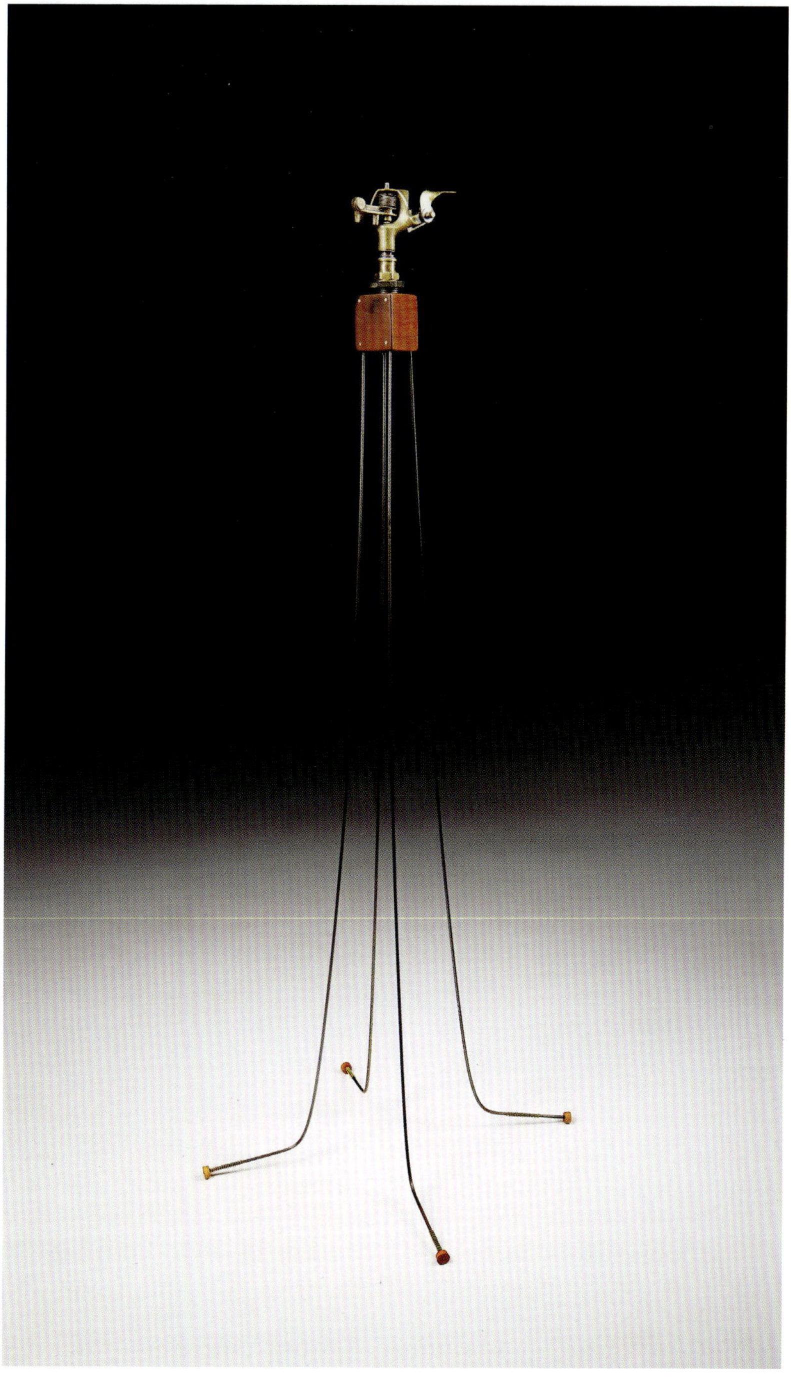

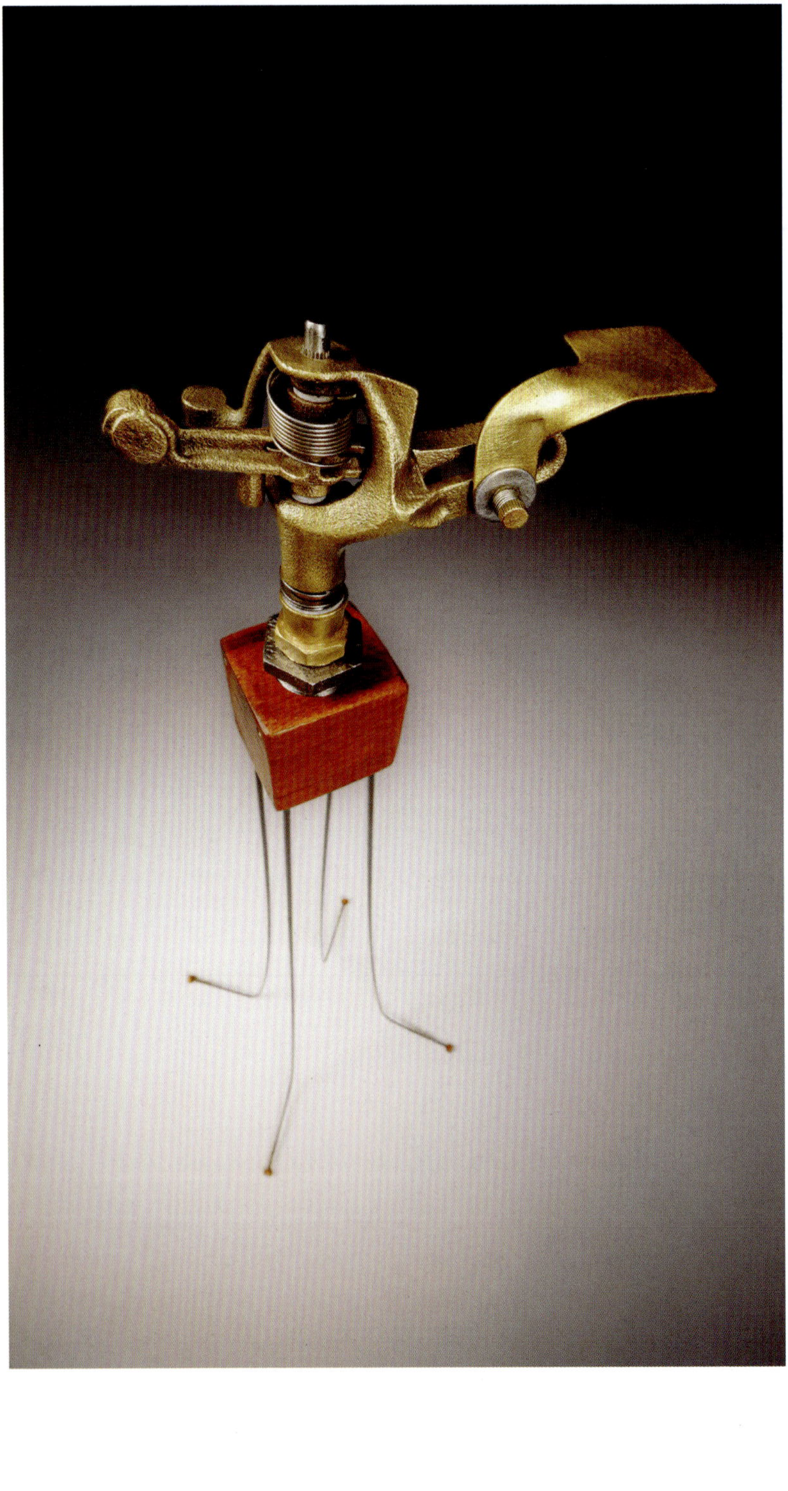

Ogún asks: "Am I a blade pointed
skyward in the reeds, having freed
myself—freed to stand in wait for
those who would seek and find
me?

Or, have I not freed myself at all,
nor been freed, and stand in wait
for seekers and would-be finders?"

Ogún answers, will rock and appear
to rock, a blackened blade and
broken stone inside of it, sealed
with a section of steel.

Ogún answers without asking.

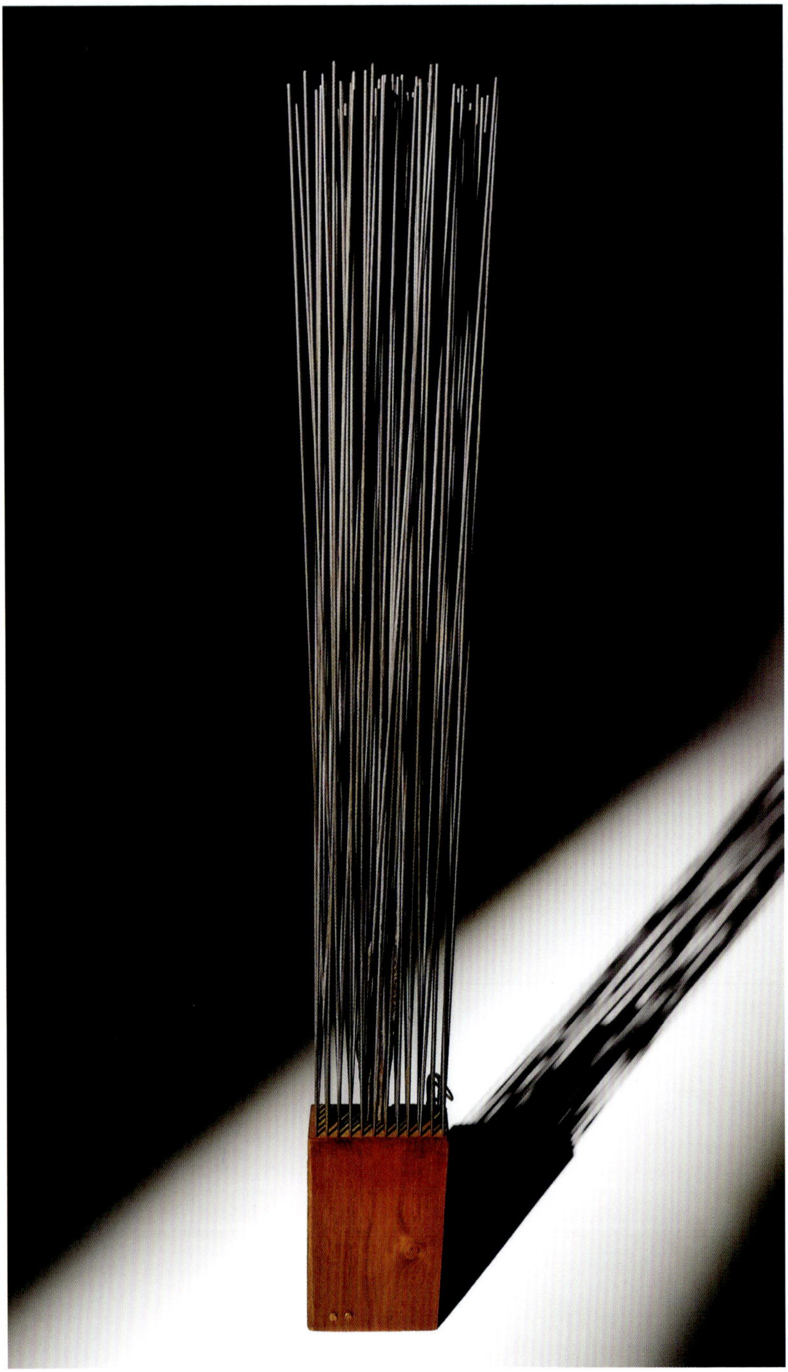

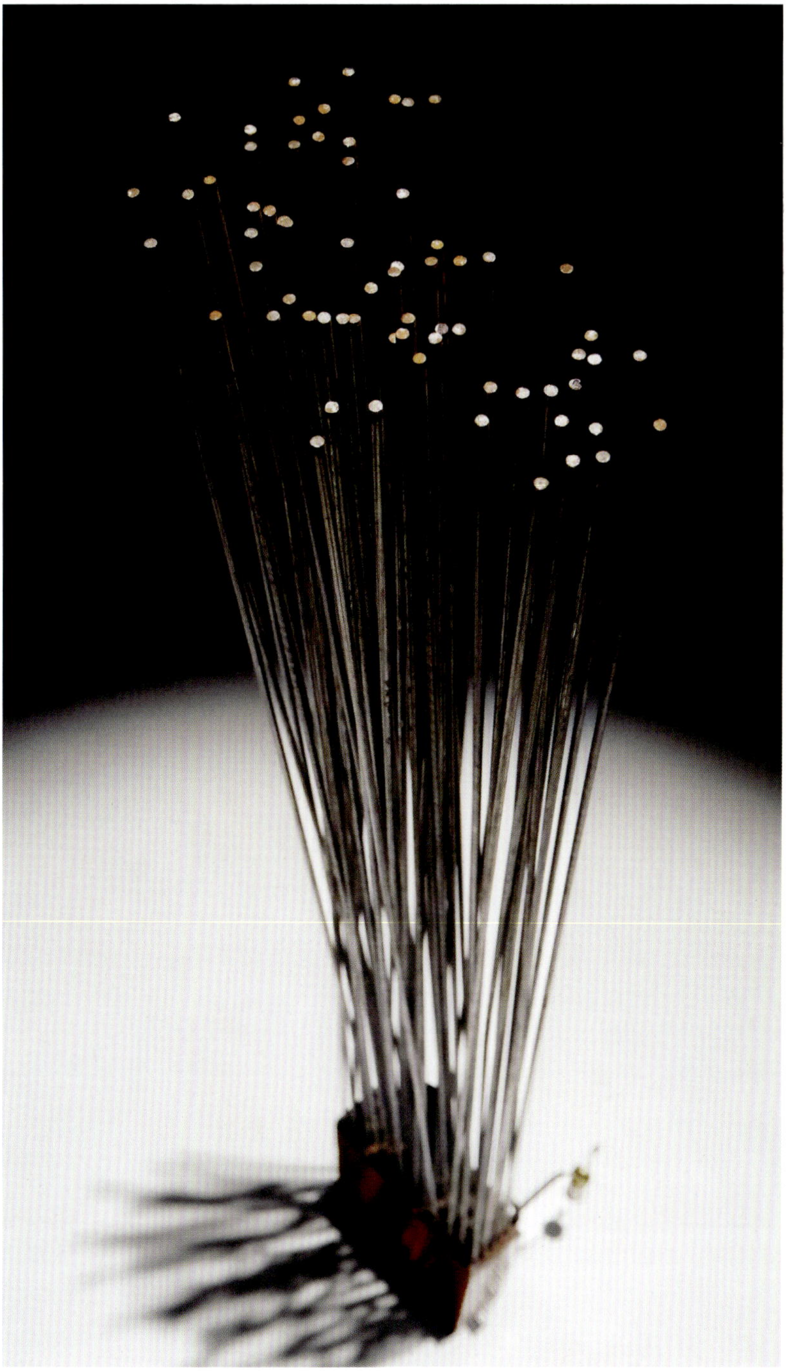

Xangô, nodding if touched,
a battalion of nails turned inward, hovers
(like a "Pain Tree") above the void at its base—
a revolt moving up through the valley.
Nodding at its now voided use
of permissions and pleasantries,
tethered to memory,[2] to the waiting weight
of its unswung blow.

Its head, a mace.
Its heart full of sand.

2 To *Memoria*.

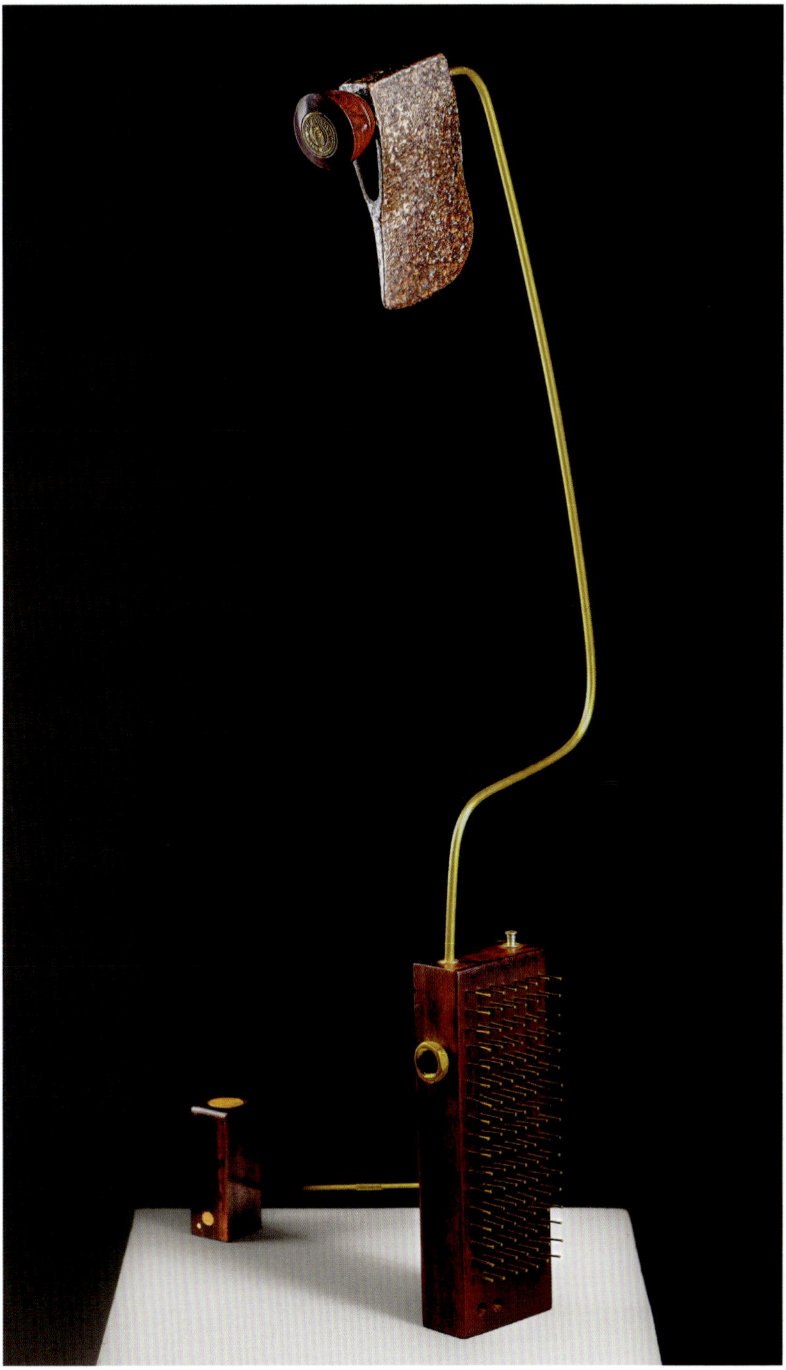

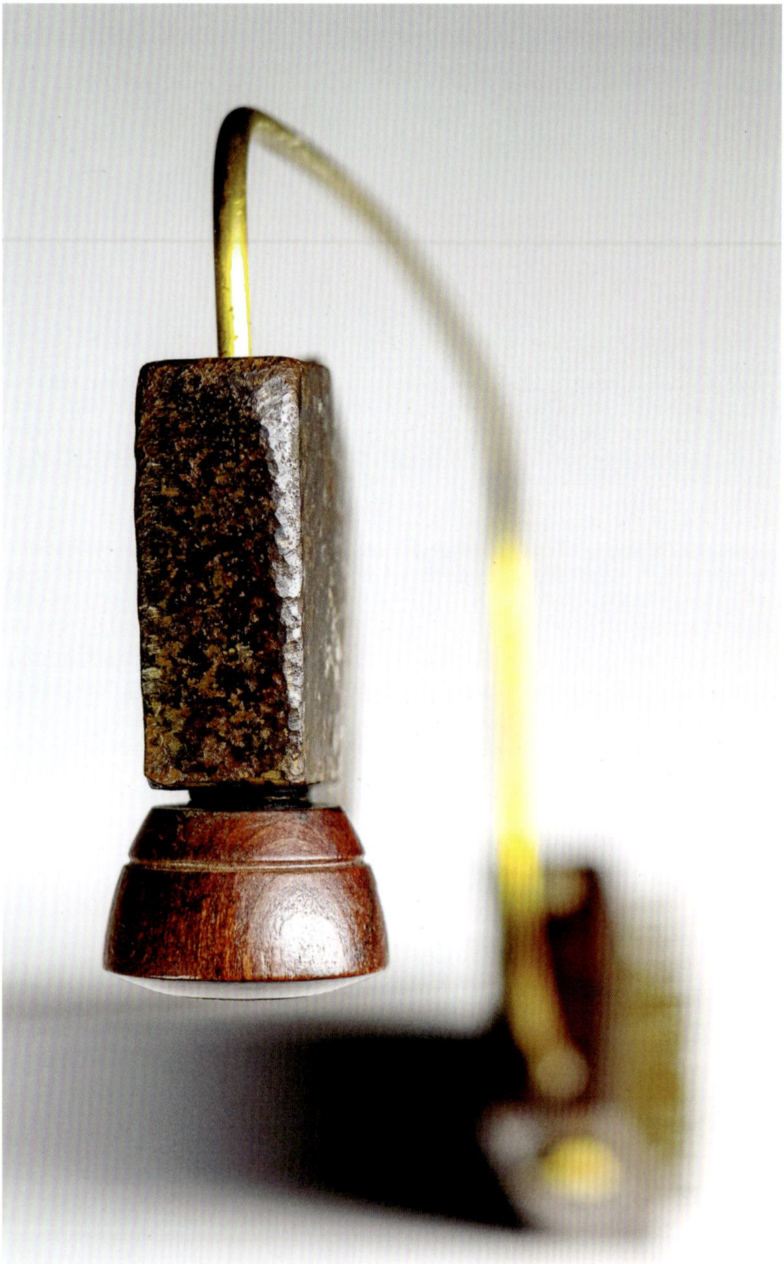

Yemaya, if mishandled, betrays its form,
coming apart at the crown, at the couplings that
marry teak to steel to brass, its structure dissipating.

And at its base, a wooden vault—a gift from a love who
once called me "an ocean of a man"—in which
I keep things I hope will not disperse:
a bois canot leaf
a miniature of Lakshmi
a silver soap dish that grays
a bottle with my mother's grayed hair
a bottle of sand
a bottle of liquor—mixed spirits
a teacup
a piece of blackened driftwood
a stone the texture of ore
a thimble of sea salt.

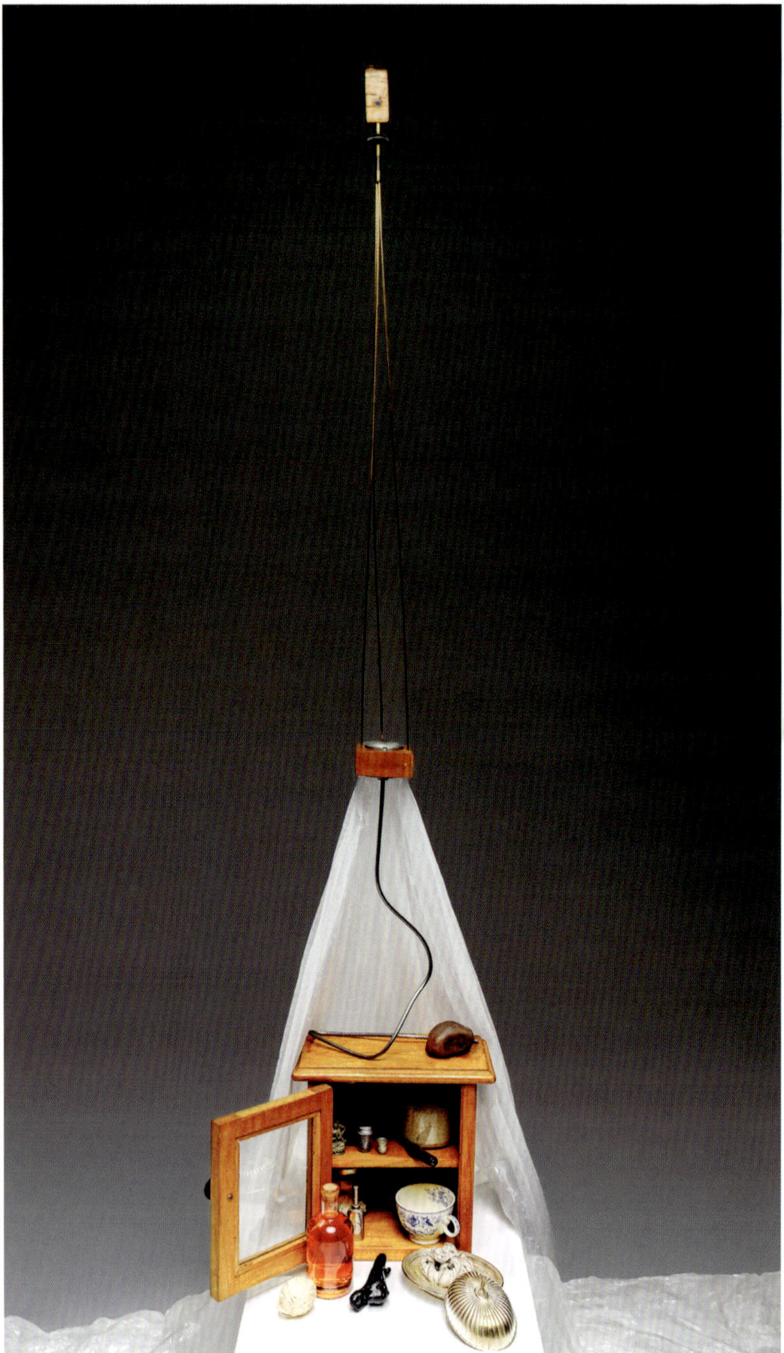

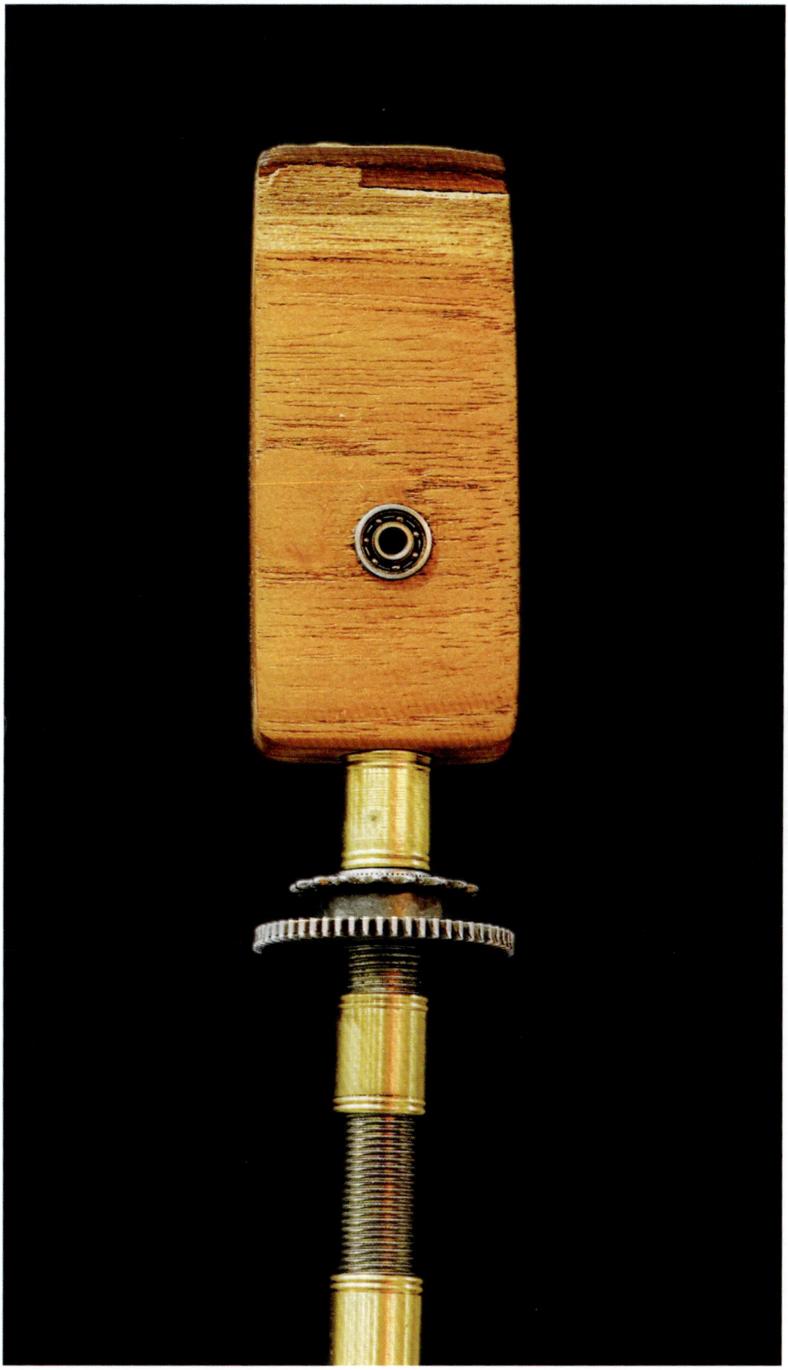

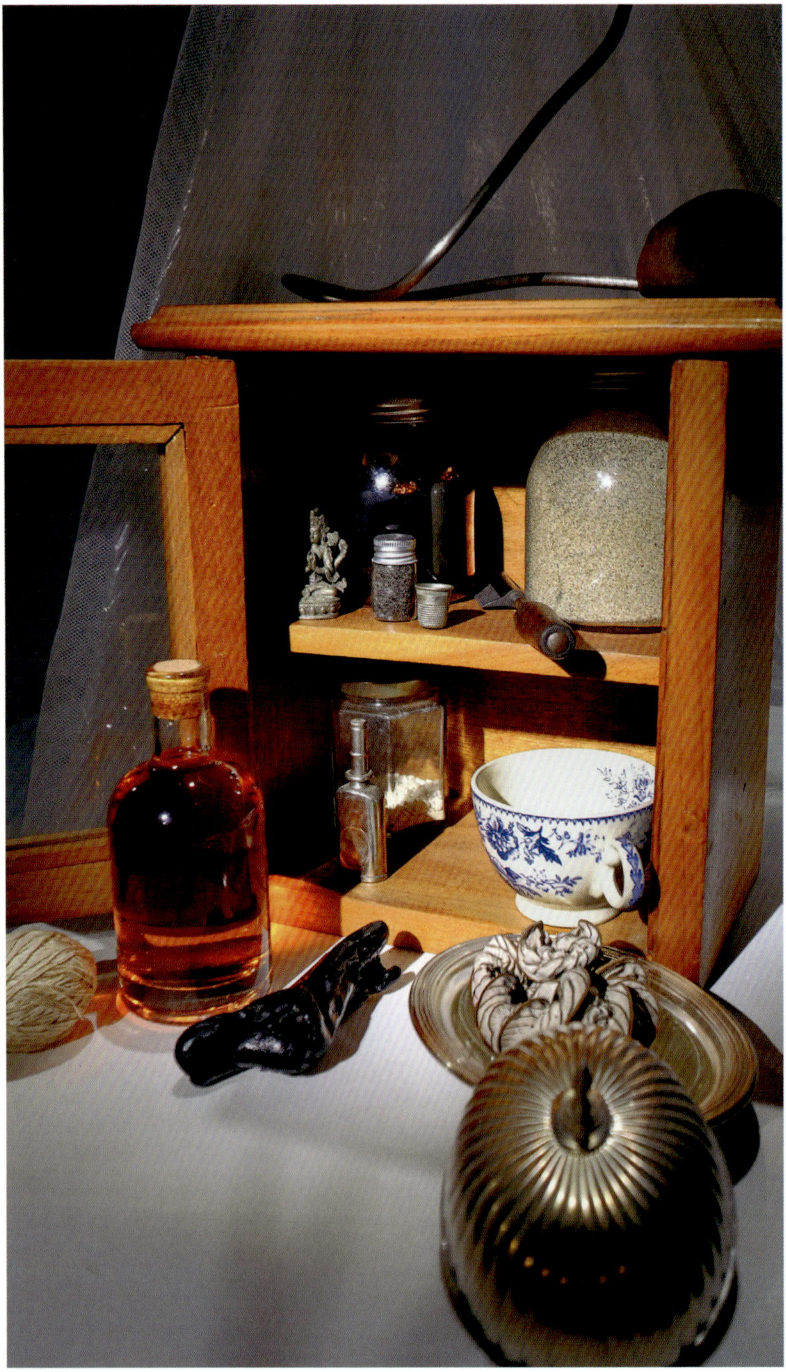

Have I gone too far?

In spite of our well-earned beliefs, I think we understand that the notion of a god is as literal as the notion of the ineffable and the immaterial can be. The literal is *immaterial.* The material is *symbolic.* As such, the *incorporation* of material|ism is more the insistence of a humanity that is able to not only conceive the ineffable and immaterial as an embodiment and embedding but (more specific to my concern) devise material evidence of process. Black potentiality and creativity are therefore taken as self-evident, their existence and significance not up for debate.

Putting aside for a moment the fact that there is perhaps no greater declaration of humanity than the creation of a man-made god—or of a godlike thing—the *Orisa* augment the implicit declaration of their presence with a declaration of explicit impossibility: an articulation of the ostensibly inarticulable idea that the abject refusal of an inevitable black precarity is not merely observable, but that its fullest expression of refusal will be something we cannot know but feel. It is, to me, divine—divine in a way that cannot be held. The material is only a symbol of that feeling, my material imagining of that feeling *as matter.* A matter, that is, of character. *Ethos,* if you like.

Matter, *holding place* for a mattering to come. *Ours.*

This idea is rife enough with abstraction: the use of materials emphasizes the limitation of symbol that already precludes a presentation of the literal body. But consider how the abstraction might feel

> in your hands,
> along the side of your face,
> how its burning, its old grease, its rust might smell.

If it is an appeal, it is one that has to do with form in a general vernacular sense, and with specific ones, as well—of knowing, sharing, and keeping knowledge. It is an appeal, additionally, to engage with the idea that what is *known*—inscribed on paper, embedded in the wood, and sealed—may not be for sharing. Not always, at any rate. But that is the obvious thing. Rather than rely too heavily on their interior machinery, I have elected to disassemble them by hand, refusing the presumptions of their "usefulness"—that is, their usefulness with regard to what *could have been* their potential usefulness to me now (as with the projector) and of how *they might have been* used (as with the pressure gauge in *Esú*). This is a treatment of method inherited from my mother—though my iron is already made, though none walk.

You see it, too, with the *Animæ* I have made from my grandfather's tools:

> the fork and hoe in *Patria*;
> the fulcra of *Sola* and *Caroni*, their orders of
> genesis and revelation lost in the mesh and
> the sweetened smoke;
> the hoe in *Caribea*, its suspension revised for
> rest, its bell silenced . . .

In each precedent, a *license*. *Authority*, if you should require it.

And where disassembly was neither possible nor required (say, as with the elementality of an axe-head in *Xangô* or the single blade in the rods|reeds of *Ogún* that insist on being seen in plain sight), each of them stands waiting, like an open secret, to be seen.

Like the house, the story of the *Orisa* began as a foil for a yard I no longer see, except in memory. Not just the single yard on Carib Street but those on Charles Street, Turton Street, wherever I have had the privilege of a yard, or the privilege of missing it—the nonyards of the Bronx, of Brooklyn. Less obvious is that each of these *Orisa* is an expression that is spoken *and* unspoken, written *but* unread, read *yet* unrecited at the end of the Caribbean—at its ostensible *edge*. As such, they draw directly on my understanding of the limitation of symbol, and the limitations of material to do the symbolic work of naming what cannot be named.

SURD

Blackness is a surd.
Caribbean blackness is a surd.
They go without saying . . . [1]

Have you ever been seen and not seen in a single glance? Seen and not seen even in a long, studying stare? Has your illegibility ever felt like freedom? If so, it will make imagining easier. If you have been seen and not seen, you already know what I mean when I say that your blackness is a surd.

I have, for some time, been embedding scrolls of paper in small pieces of local wood—apamate, carapo, greenheart, mango, pomerac, roble, and teak—which I have called *Surds*.[2] I will not say everything I have embedded, but there are love notes, dedications, incantations. To know what I have kept, you would have to destroy them.[3]

They are encapsulations, too, of the memory of breath, which I have designed as a series of spaces—a sense of space whose meanings are withheld. What

Alternate title: "On the Materialities of Quiet and Absence"

1 What is the path of sound? You know, knowing us, that "saying" is sometimes silent. Sometimes unsaid, though sounded by the breath. Saying, for us, is sometimes perpetually un|said. Not unsayable. Not silenced, just unsaid.

2 In phonetics, a surd is a sound that is uttered with the breath and not the voice: e.g., the phonetic sounds of *f*, *k*, *p*, *s*, and *t*. In mathematics, it is an irrational number or value that cannot be further simplified into a whole number or integer. Its irrational form is its simplest: e.g., Ö2 or Ö3.

3 This is hypothetical, of course, but it prompts additional considerations that are, I feel, more generative than my idiosyncrasies. I hope they are not destroyed.

does this mean? In short, it is a reflection on interiority and on an internalized exteriority—notions of inside and outside you might have first encountered in the house and in the yard. The encapsulations demonstrate both how the object encapsulates the idea and how the idea encapsulates the object. Each is an end in itself. Each is a space I have designed, a kind of place, a making of meaning, which I draw from various preoccupations. Some I share, others I keep:

Burial
Prayer
Secret
Return
Sex
Conspiracy
Grounding

In them, we encounter a paradox in the practice of memory and nonfictional art: a materialist approach to essaying that insists *form* is also the *disruption* of form—the *disruption of the form of the thing itself*, as well as the *concept of form*, the concept of its apparent *originality*, and (this may be worse) its *origin*. The question of disrupted origins may matter most for those of us whose province has largely been the imagination, the imagined, and the imaginary. Or for those of us who dare to matter here, taking in the finitude of our coasts and the temperamental infinitude of tides as we contemplate the provenance of our expressions and the meanings that endure.

Provenance is a question of method—a method of determining origin, or the condition of being (an) original. The details of that origin are not always relayed in original ways but the opposite: like the original, the story of its origin is remarkably rigid. You see the paradox, of course: origin grounded in rigidity; rigidity meant to affirm the veracity of origin, preserving and authenticating it, keeping it in a kind of stasis. This particular story—call it the *Surds*' "origin myth"—is hardly supposed to change.

Besides being a thing that is not subject to change, the origin's existence—its movement in time and in the memory from the moment of conception—is constrained, the narrative of its beginning remaining more or less unchanged in the telling. The rigidity of this "unchanging story" is one that is, and is supposed to remain, *as original* as the thing it represents. The changes, should they occur (and they do always occur), are supposed to be minimal, as long as there is that measure of fidelity to the origin. A thing is "original," in other words, according to a series of enduring designs—its "originality," ensured by design, is encased within a story whose design is meant to endure in spite of its re|iterations of origin that are, in fact, rather unoriginal.

Now, consider that what endures in this series of *Surds*—the myriad interactions of wood and metal, object and image of object—is designed to work *against* the viewer's tendency to interpret what they see. It defies its origins, actively disrupting its provenance. Its iterations—from *No. 0* onward—bear this out, repeatedly. However certain it will feel in your hands, however sure it will appear to the discerning eye, it will offer no certainty. Do not let this deter you. It is only a reminder of the harm conceit can do.

Pick them up.[4] Set them down.[5]

What we encounter with the *Surds* is an object whose existence is meant to illustrate the affect of shifted space—a shifting of the shape of space—rather than the mere consequence of what filling space might entail. The notion confounds (because it is meant to, I suppose). The creative disregard of discipline unbinds. Until such time as they are given a form and you hold them for yourself, let them also be a symbol of innumerable consequences held in suspension in the imagination—the *not yet, but will be* of black freedom. Not merely beheld but withheld until your arrival makes it real. Put differently, what we see is not what we think we see but is, instead, a conspiracy of expressive form, in which the components of that expression are collectively "liberated" from reception itself, resisting witness—even the witness of its maker. *Original*, in a way.

4 Easy, easy.
5 Gentle, gentle.

You have been prepared for this.[6] Though, I still wonder if I could persuade you that these spaces (can) actually exist for us, or whether you will believe they ought to be read (if at all) as pure fictions that come about as the result of a desperate imagination—an ever-aspirational *Imaginary*—and our very Caribbean tendency to craft spaces like these that do not exist. *Unreal places*. If I could persuade you, I would argue that they are the materialized forms of archipelagic thought, that their apparent fictionality operates as a conduit to their essential nonfictionality. We would then be faced with what it looks like to create something out of nothing—and then append degrees of nothingness to these things we've created without negating their existence altogether.[7]

6 Prepared, too, by the preceding passages, which demonstrate a form of surdic writing, diverting your gaze from what may be considered the "subject": the origin of the *Surds*. You will note, for instance that while I have not divulged the origin myth (beyond their basic material composition), I have nevertheless begun to discuss an engagement with them. The implicit argument is that the origin myth is *not* essential to the affective experience of the *Surds*. To make less of origin is to make space for arrival to occur. Its myth endures and is unessential to our engagement and interaction with it.

7 Are you thinking of archipelagoes?

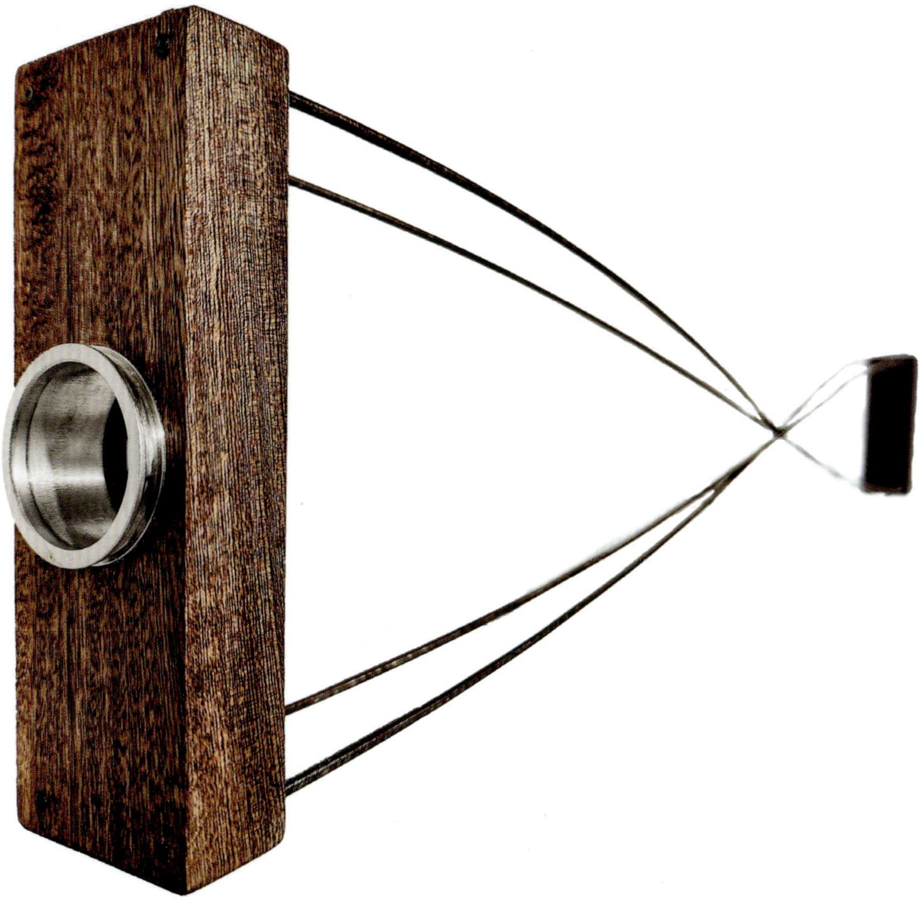

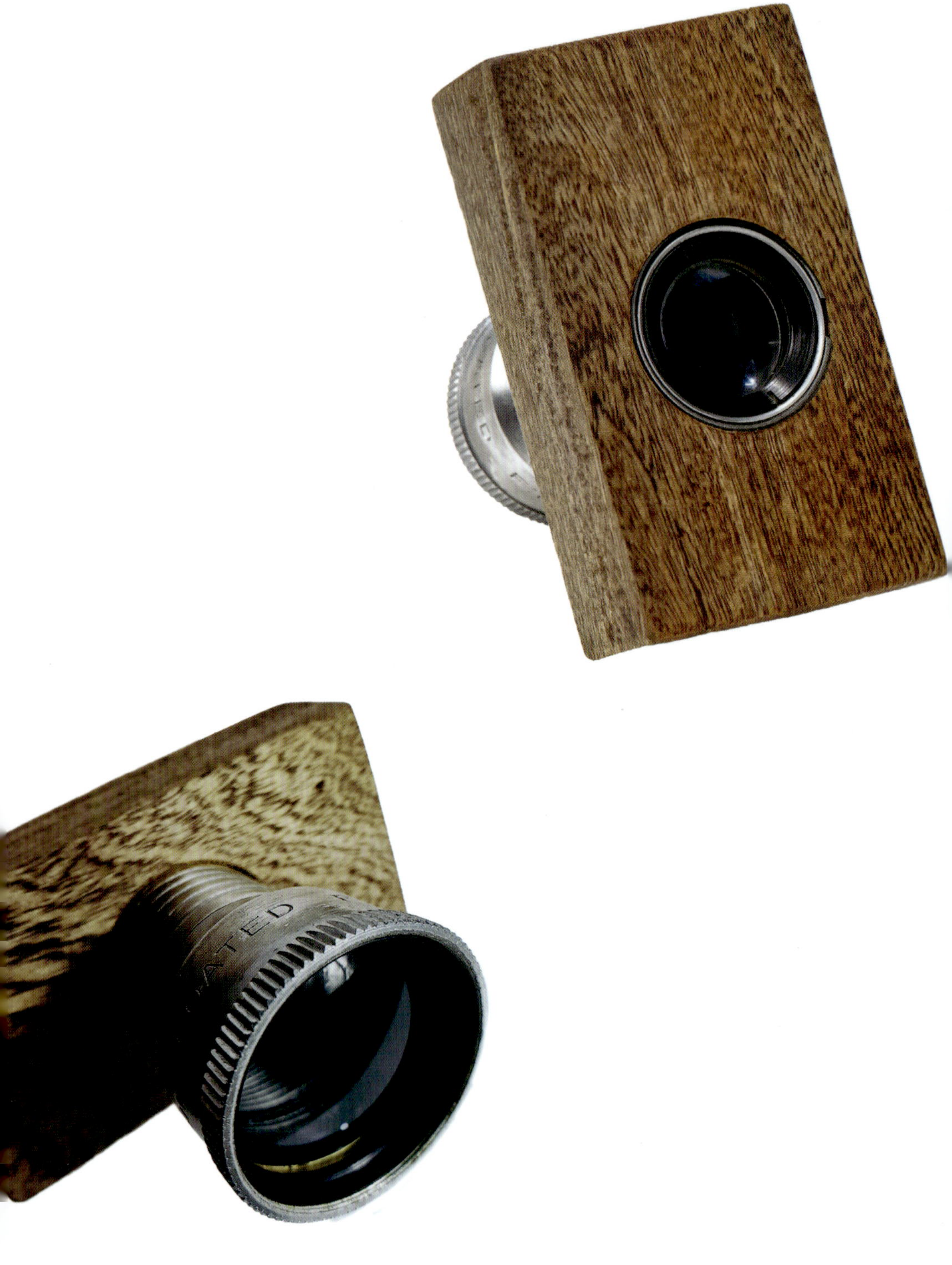

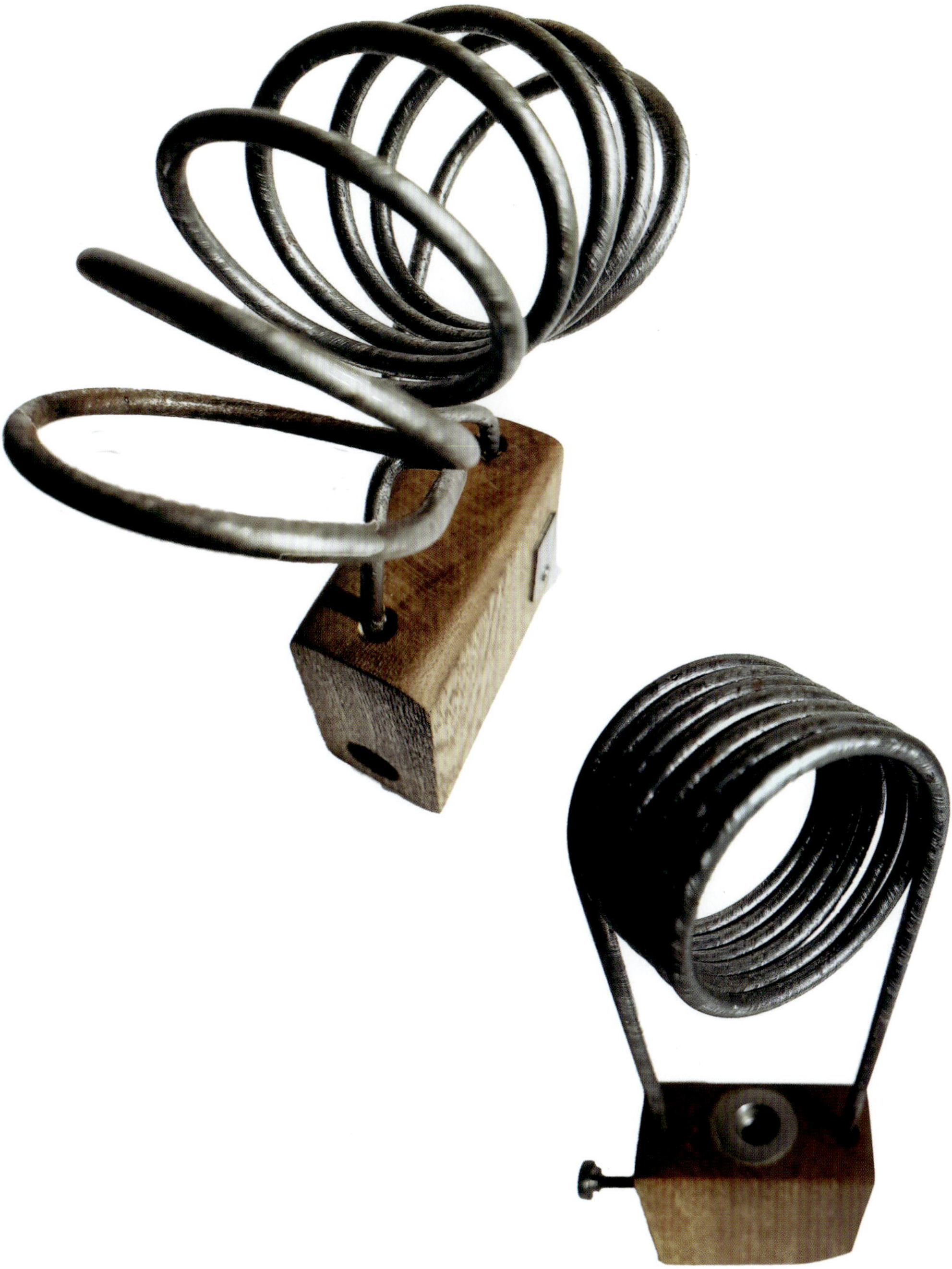

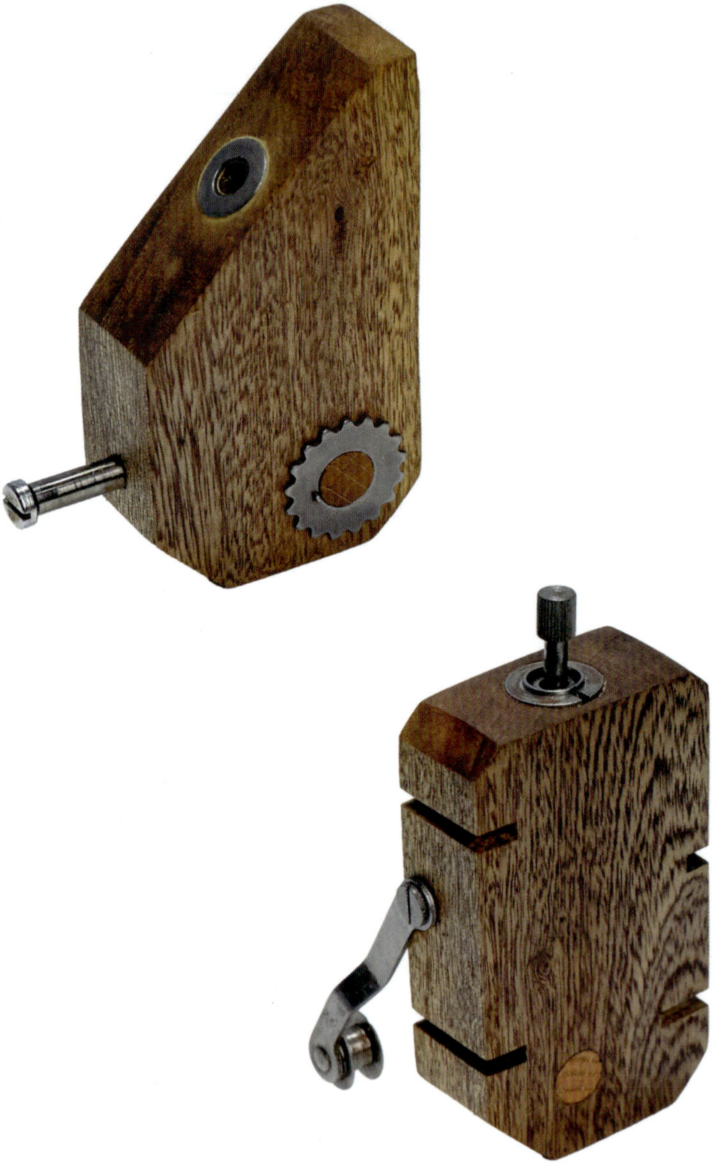

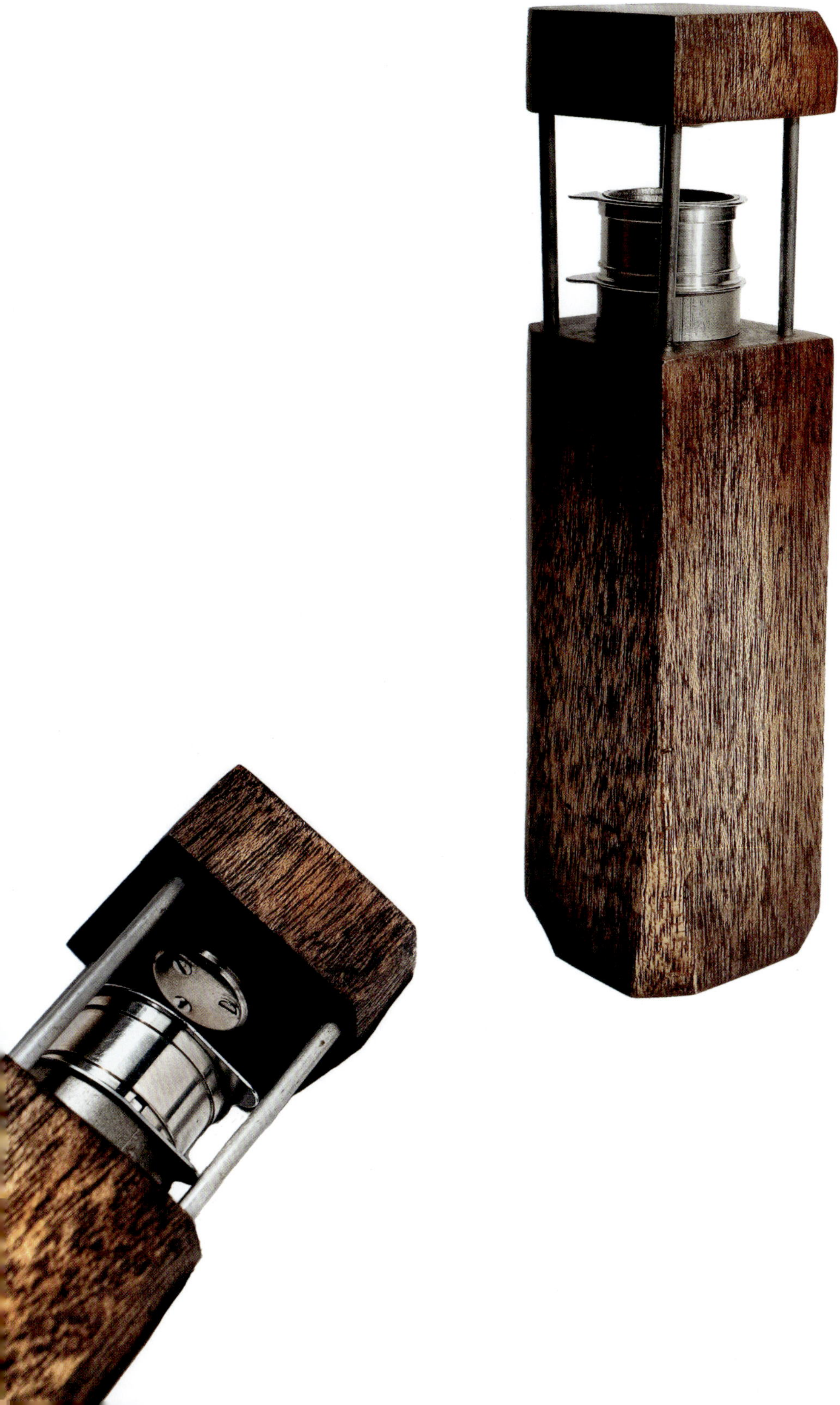

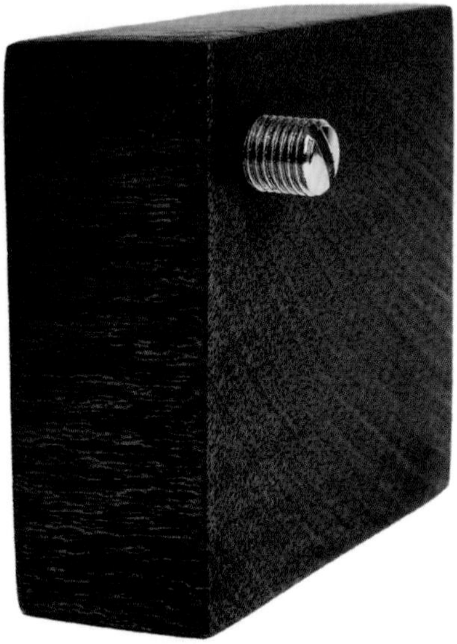

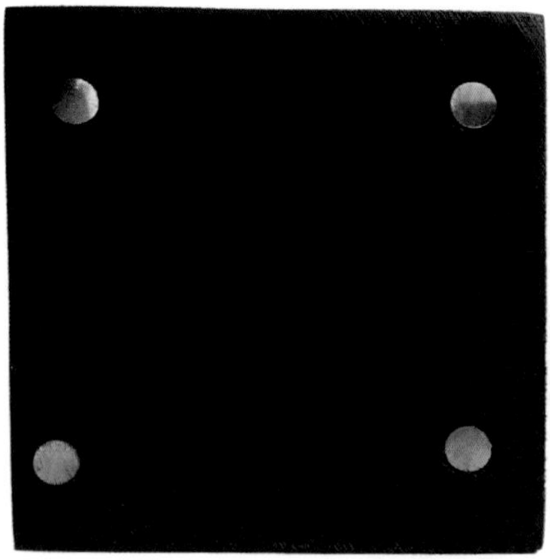

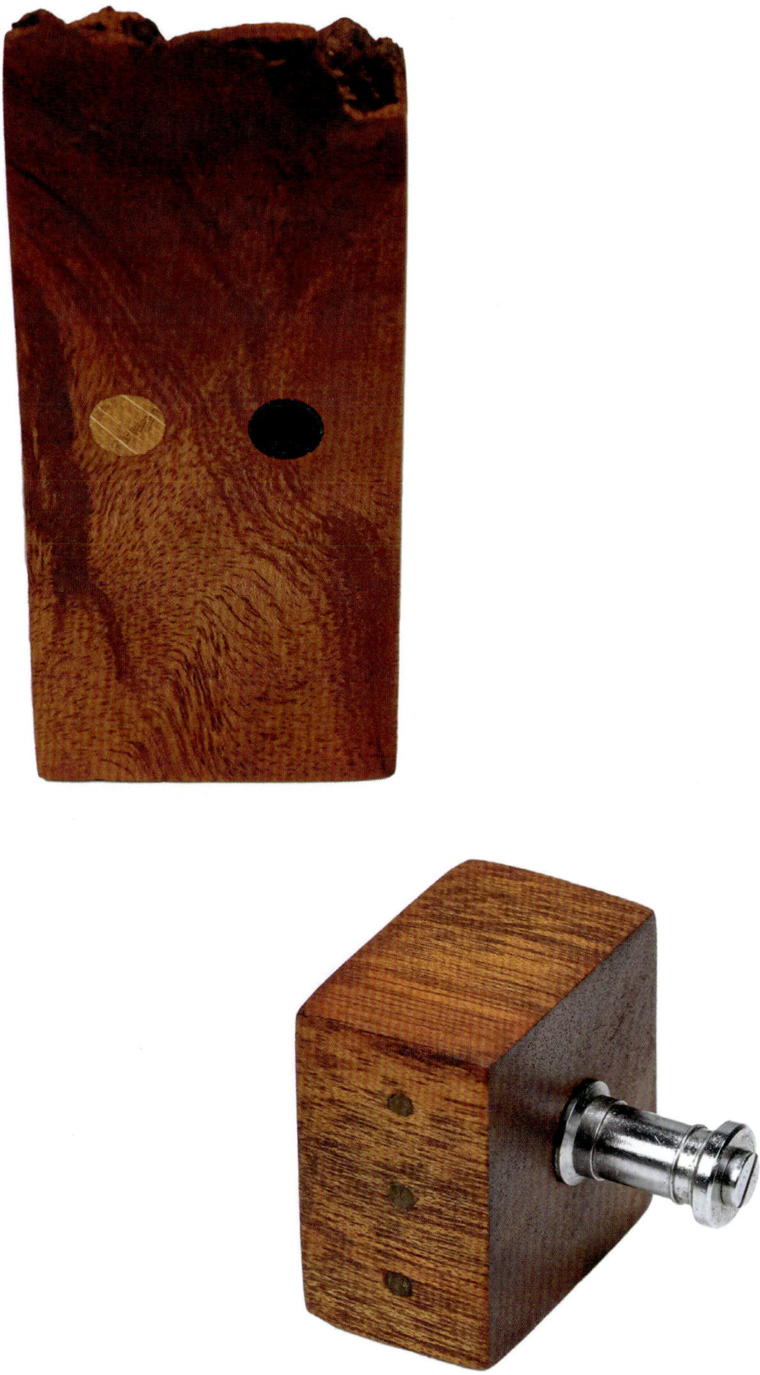

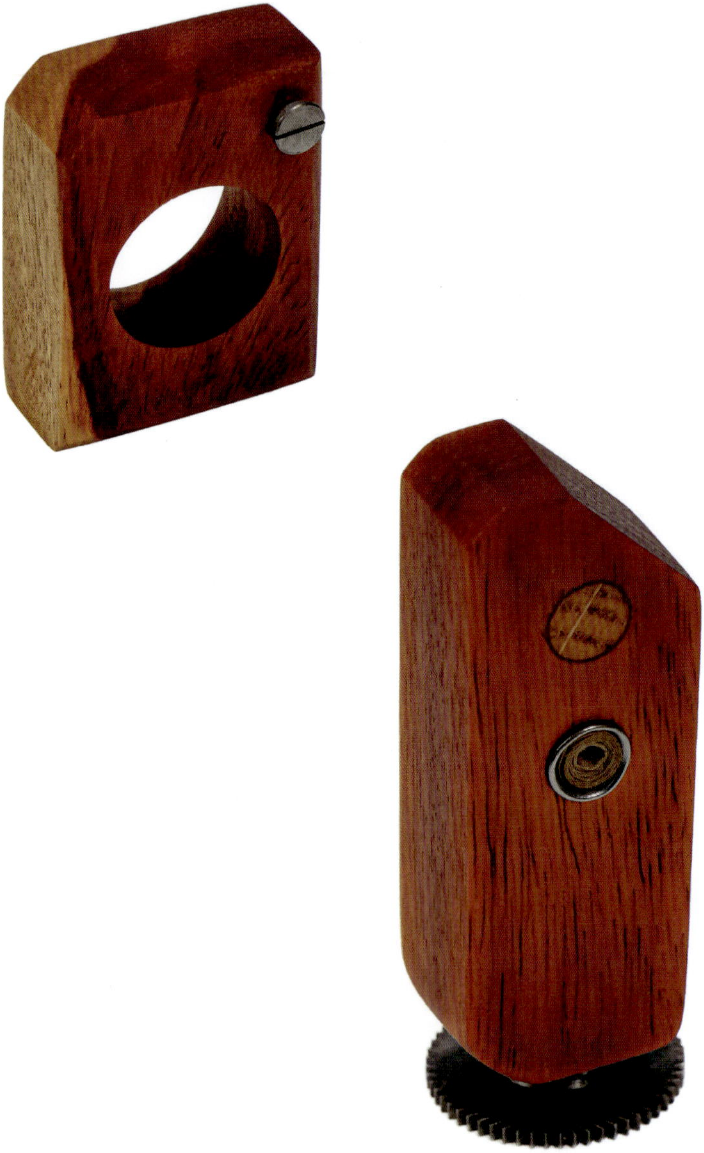

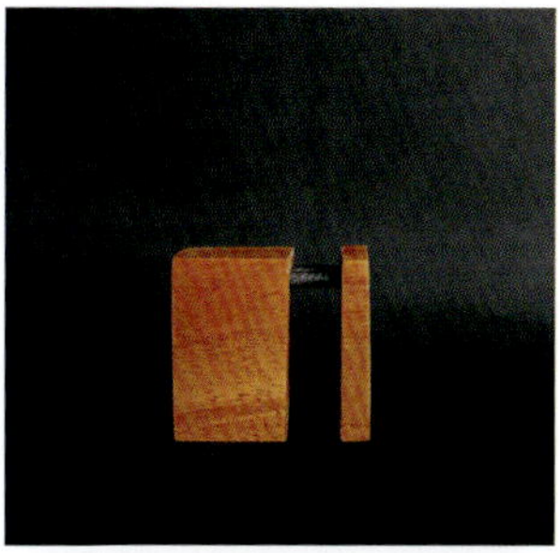
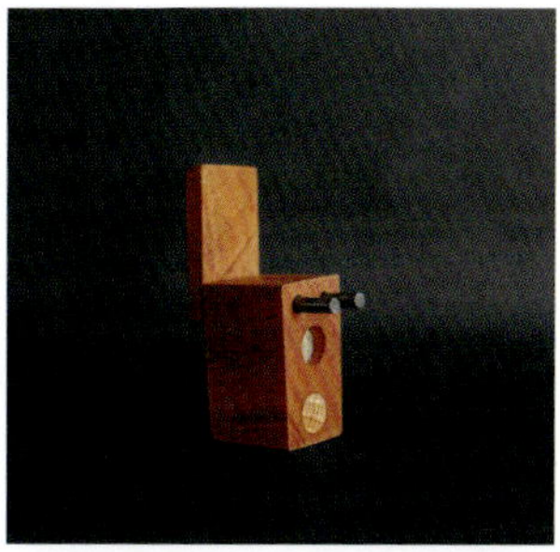
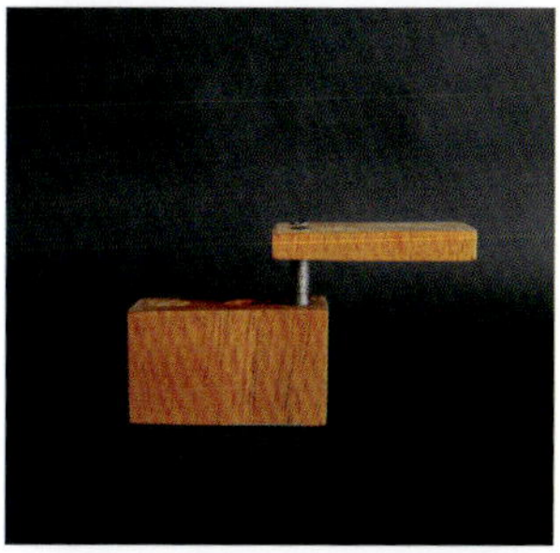
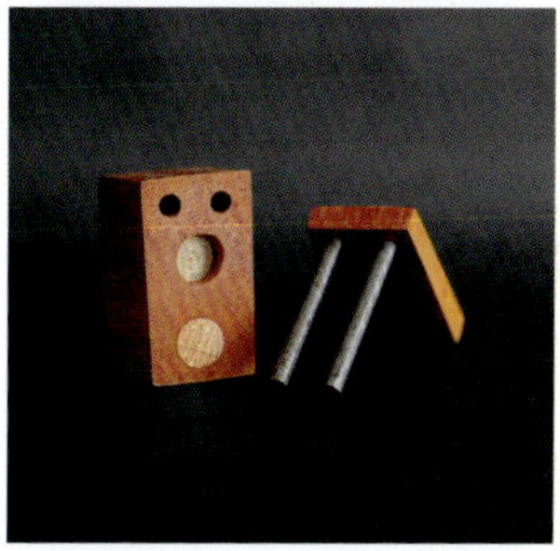
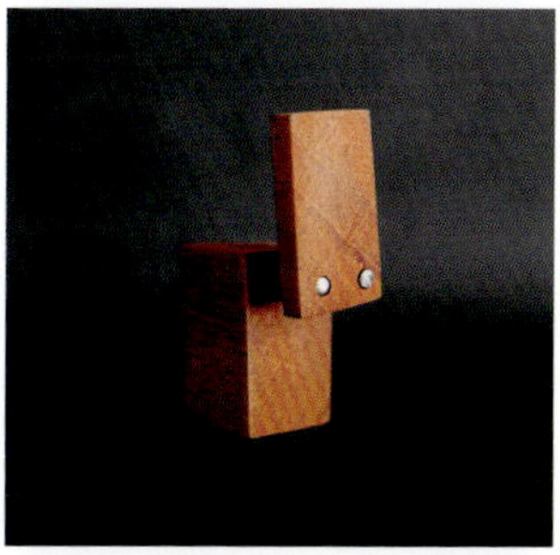
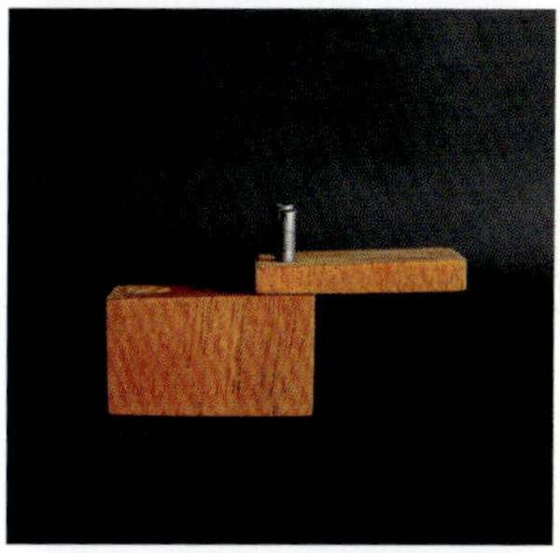
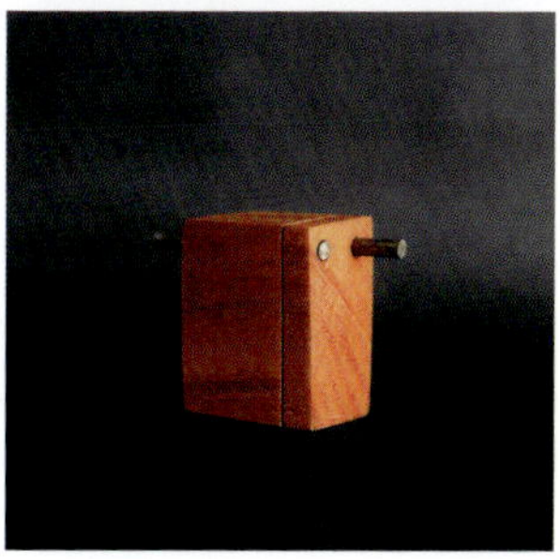
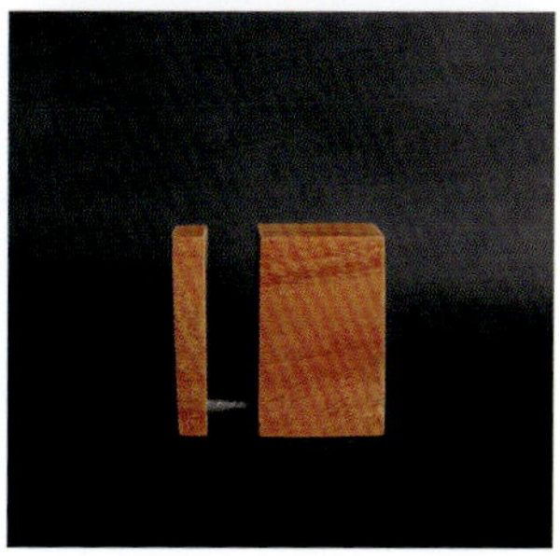

Whereas the *Orisa* seem to emerge from a somewhat identifiable rhetorical situation—that of the yard and its abridged history, the gauntlet of family—the *Surds* are a different matter. Even if they appear to be made of the same or similar matter, their fragmented iterations matter differently, responding not to any situation in particular, but rather functioning as the representation of that situation's absence *and* the absence of words to describe it. Their imperfect absence is obscure—that is, the affect of their total invisibility is *obscured* by their materiality, a *presence* that is an *absence* in material form. Like the fugitivity of a self-portrait, these *Surds*—while mediating and, in some ways, refusing the enduring suggestion that there is nothing there—also deliberatively flirt with the question of "What if there were?" An activation of *nothingness* and *nowhereness* that occurs in advance of the eventual inhabitation of space by a "who" that we may not really know or a "when" that we may not be able to name. They evade—their evasion is unavoidable. This is their design.

You see them, but only ironically, missing their angled meanings, missing what lies behind and inside of them—paper, my mother's hair, my grandfather's hair, other things. Their obscurity is amplified by the materiality of what you cannot witness—not just obscured from view but deliberately hidden away from you. Like knowledge is sometimes hidden away—in the "talk some, keep some," it is what is kept. (Like rhetorical intent is sometimes withheld and depends on the clarity of its ethic for the eventual shape of its consequences.) The obscurity of an apparent presence only further obscures, simultaneously amplifying the absence of what we do not see. They symbolize multiple absences that are meant to resonate but whose very absence precludes the likelihood of resonance beyond, say, the flash of its image on the page—like a portrait, in the sense of light passing through that offers a glimpse of its collision with an object.

The *Surds*, then, are the materialization of emptied space (different from the negative space of the yard) in the sense of space having already been vacated and having had nothing said or written about it. (The fact that I am writing now is an obvious contradiction and violation. The fact that I use parts of a projector, re-presented as a former conduit to light that is now only subject|ed to it, only emphasizes this notion of light having passed through.)

Caribbean people recognize this paradox—we can live out our entire lives without ever having been seen. Looked at, certainly, but not seen. As such, what we observe in the *Surds* is a disjunction, for they are essentially "outta timing" or *akairotic*, existing as an attempt to resist even the space—the ambience—they so obviously fill. If they "say" anything, it is "Do not say anything, as nothing has been said, only perhaps a sounding that is unvoiced." If forced to say—or be—anything other than what they are and are not (an absence, a materialization of vacated space), we will find that they are an expression that means to undo itself. Like a redaction whose negating function is, first and foremost, self-negating. Like an archipelago. Their self-negation is inherent to their subjectivity—my subjectification of them—as I devise a sense of a blackness that can undo itself but is also beyond anyone's efforts to undo it.

There is no *codex*, no special marker for what lies buried within them. No shrines or monuments for their martyred meanings. No manual—what has been made is manual enough. You must forage in the field laid out for you, marking for yourself the ideas that matter, which neither time nor death have erased. In the space they have cleared, roam barefoot or on hands and knees, with eyes opened or shut to find what may be there, all the while accompanied by the obscurities created when light illuminates only the edge of some dangerous outcropping, some pitfall, some "thing" you thought you knew.

Meanings linger in the penumbral space. Questions come and go. Mine, for the moment, is this: Where does "originality" manifest other than in the symbolic and material interaction between our temporal understanding (evidenced in the recognition of things that exist) *and* our spatial engagement (evidenced in what has been created)? This may seem like a binary opposition of "space-time" or "question-answer," but it is not that alone. Note the almost imperceptible flash of a pause between the asking and the answering that binds the question about the made thing to the resolutions of its maker, binding the story that is being told to its teller, binding the time for telling to who (in time) will take up space to tell it.

Take, for example, *No. 7: Polyptych of an Infinite Arrival*, a series of topological iterations. It is a riddle, an embedded "if now was then, and then is now" impulse that turns and returns and upturns, whose design invokes the Carnivalesque ethos of the Pierrot Grenade, or "Grenadian Parrot."[8] Known for its deliberately confusing speeches—a series of spells cast with misspelled words—this *mas* is an indictment of *mimesis*, for it is in what it appears to say that what it means (to say) is embedded—it is in the performance that the performer is most and least himself. And who is someone when they are least themselves? I think you know.

8 The title is a derogation, of course—a reminder of how well we sharpen our tongues and teeth against each other.

Each topological iteration is an "original" expression of the *Polyptych*'s shifting significations—or *isomorphism*—which occurs by being manually shifted, its components (wood, steel rods) reconfigured into "Horse," "Dragon," "Douen," "Moko Jumbie," "Coffin," and other unnamed ideas. Ideas materialized for the eye and the hand.[9] Its topology, which (eventually) operates beyond the reach of language, suggests a repetition with difference that reinforces the symbolic material work of Caribbean nonfiction and one's hands in the mediation of its meanings. As a *Surd*, the Pierrot-cum-*Polyptych* exists here as a consequence that follows (and, as such, can be traced back to) the design and delivery of an agenda that is ultimately unvoiced. A body that is not the body but an *embodiment*, its articulable humanness implied in the series of reconfigurations that come to define its character.

Look.

Look as if you were listening to its speech—its implied *speechifying*. The Pierrot is a rebuke, a mockery of pretense itself, but not necessarily of the pretender—*all* are welcome in the Carnivalesque.[10] Even its silence is multidirectional, as integral to its performance as breath is to the performer. The Pierrot isn't critiquing the intellectual per se but the performance, the tacit treachery of intellectualism.[11]

We recognize this behavior because we have, at one time or another, been forced to twist ourselves *and* our language|s in knots to disentangle the discursive threads of our obscured origins, only to locate a source that may be no deeper than the unbound breath, no more mysterious than a shrug. We sometimes concede. But I am showing you these things because I want you to know that I am not making too much of arrivals—that I cannot.

When I think I may be close to a grand declaration of what arrival must be, what Caribbean nonfiction must do, words fail (or we fail each other). Words

9 Less so for the ear and nose, not so for the tongue.

10 In *Tropic Tendencies*, I suggest that the Caribbean Carnivalesque is "the premier act of rhetorical (re)invention and the critical response to the shifting situationalities of everyday life—[it] undoubtedly forms the basis of all dialogic performances related to the region and its descendants. . . . From the initial attempts at utterance to the phenomenon of cybernetic disembodiment, the carnivalesque will stands out as a predominant feature and a necessary impulse" (Browne, *Tropic Tendencies*, 12).

11 Its relevance may be traced even further back, to the intent that prompted its exigence: to *instruct*, to *demonstrate*, and to *remonstrate*; to *show a form* and to see that form dissipate.

fail, and language—its more awkward "languaging"—is an acknowledgment of that failure.[12] Its "success," recorded in our erstwhile proficiencies, is merely the perfection of that failure. And understanding, however perfect(ed), will always be incomplete because it emerges from that failure. It will never be *quite* enough. It is a familiar tautology. Their inadequacy has meant for me that they have and will always be either subject to an image or an object, or they will have the image or object be subjected to them, through explanation, explication, analysis, or theory. Do you see the inevitable breakdown of this notion? The negative space suggested by the impending ruin? The echo it yields, leading to what will be the challenge of method, its dissipation?

In these works that have survived the gauntlet of my ineptitude and have (over the last few years) come to address the various urgencies for which I believe arrival is oriented, we are invited to consider whether they have a role beyond function, a role closer to a *purpose*.

What is the material purpose of arrival?

If you ask, I would say that it is to open space and shift it, particularly when words fail (as they inevitably will). In such a way, I think the unsaid work of the *Surds* may be cast farther ahead of me, beyond the reach of my own experience, held in suspension until such time as it is given a form, like what I have shown you here. Its obscurities are a map I have used, a schema for knowing my place, while its contradictions have equipped me with the means of forgetting, forgetting my "place" altogether—and opening space when and wherever I can. In the end, the inherent liberatory characteristics of these works may as well be no one's—neither mine nor yours—belonging nowhere, except as a thing in and of itself. *Nowhereian*, in a way. When you get to them, make of them what you will.

By then, I will have had my chance.

12 Remember that point about language: at its best, it must function to make itself obsolete, to facilitate meaning that is beyond its capacity. Done well, it is bound to fail.

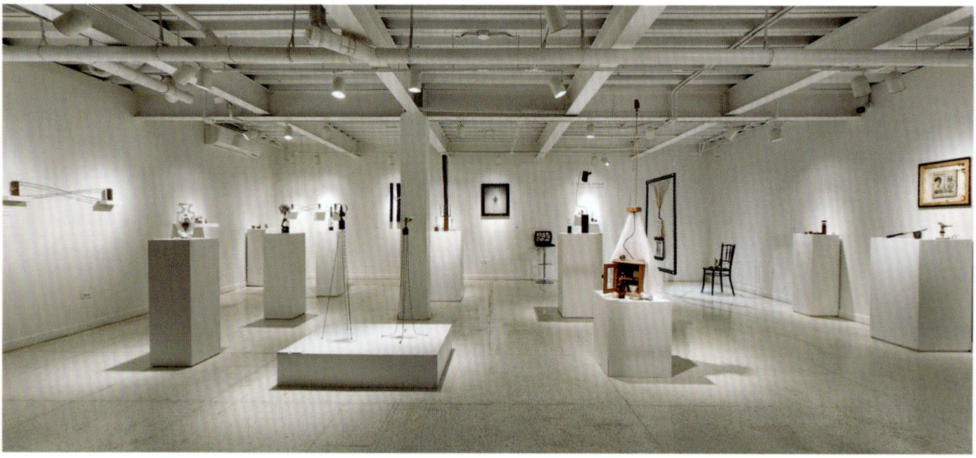

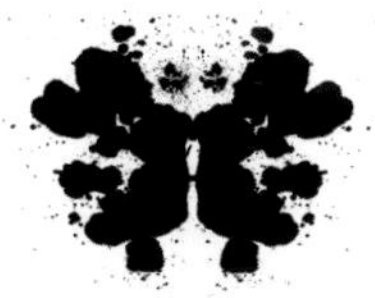

. . .

You may not have been
coming apart all along.

But an echo will
burst from the gullet
of your eventual arrival,
a whisper bottled up like ink.

Spilled. Poured.

Dissipated.
Designed.

Alternate title: "On Things That Are (Not Yet) What They Will Be"

Our stories come and go like dust. Legacy is whispered, clean clothes cover dirty ones, and we do not all learn the provenance of every particle, lest we find some darker part of ourselves in the stories we uncover. This is to be expected. In memoir, and nonfiction more generally, the remembered act and the act of remembering are finite. Though we may wish for timelessness—not of ourselves but of our work, that it will be seen, read, remembered—we do this knowing that we ourselves will not last nearly as long as the work.

The inherent finitude of the act precedes the memory of the act itself and the unmeasured potential of its symbolic representations. Before being applied to meanings that exist beyond the body, perhaps we will understand that the act of remembering is as finite as the act it is intended to memorialize—delimited, as it were, by the very impermanence of the body, the pointed ends of nerves and fibers and veins. In moments of anxiety and self-doubt I may have overlooked the significance of this ephemerality, but I know that it leads to a more ethereal sensibility—since, having souls and spirits or being made of stardust, we are fundamentally ethereal beings, in spite of the interruption of a finite life.

The act of remembering in an ending world—or a world whose ending appears to have been accelerated—shortens the shelf life of symbols that, when placed against or alongside the original, seem trite. We, too, seem to shrink in the face of time at its end, of memory at its end. Facing the imminent obsolescence of memory, the distance between the act and its remembrance is shortened out of urgency. Nevertheless, because its form and content cannot be empirically observed, we understand that the objective representation of memory is an impossibility.

But what can we make of—and in—this precarious *now*? What is the work of memory and making in catastrophic times? Where is the urgency of memoir, and nonfiction more generally, to be found if not in the skin or in the encounter with what rests just beneath it, carried around like an idea whose time is yet to come? Where can we begin if not in this gone-too-soon act of remembering?

Well, here: Whereas we might argue that fiction can offer an untrue projection that leads to a deeper truth, nonfiction is concerned here with the crafting and gradual coalescence of truths grounded not in the fact(icity) of memory but the truth of it. This is one of the tensions of an art that turns on itself like an inkblot to challenge its in|consistencies.[1] Though an obvious oversimplification, it is sometimes as if fiction wants me to imagine a tenderness that was never there, while my sense of nonfiction compels me to attend to the tenderness I have found.

To claim a Caribbean nonfiction is to concede, at the very beginning, to the mutable nature of its expression—in book form and in forms that exist outside of the book. It is to concede to the *affect* of things that are *here* and *not here*: presences, absences, absented presences. It is a *sense* of a nonfiction whose shapes continually shift—a desire to shift myself, and to have you and time and space and text shift with me. Think of this as an initial conceit that is adorned in a series of insecurities—that of artist, imagemaker, author—all of which will evolve into a vision|version of human as opaque as the Sahara-dusted cities that we must see from up close to really *see*—to see what will, at times, be obscured by feeling, by what we are inclined not to *know* but to *sense*. To sense "making" as a deliberate form of human being, and to sense the text—the thing deliberated on and subsequently "made"—as being *having been*. Proof, that is, of a humanity that nevertheless persists.

An arrival that is, as I have said, infinite.

1 I am not equipped to debate truth as a concept, least of all the truth of arrival in words alone. Nor do I have the time. My laboring breath reminds me of the hourglass in my chest. I am concerned, rather, with the extent to which the adjectival and adverbial form—call it the characteristic *realness*—have any bearing on the meanings we allow ourselves to make and the stories we allow ourselves to tell.

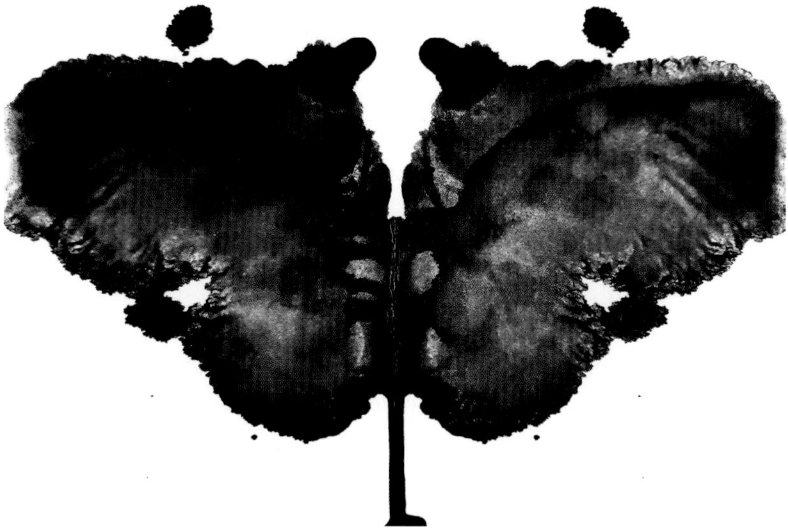

Our pessimism is tacit, as I have said. But it is not beyond the material, discursive, and affective reach of our creative tendency toward sabotage, which may involve sabotage of methods themselves, as well as the processes they inhere, what we make and subsequently unmake. Take the following, which, for the sake of way-finding, can be read as exemplary "process-states" of human being that lead to forms of being in what may still be considered the modern age: Capitalization, Colonization, Industrialization, Automation, Digitization, Conscientization, Intelligization (narrow, general, super). The litany grates. The point here is that *none* of these is human—patently *nonhuman*, in fact. Notwithstanding our perhaps necessary forays into posthumanism and transhumanism, because these "process-states" insist fundamentally on capital, my feeling is that they can only yield forms of what might be called *nonhuman being*, tending eventually to a state that is, in fact, *inhuman(e)*.

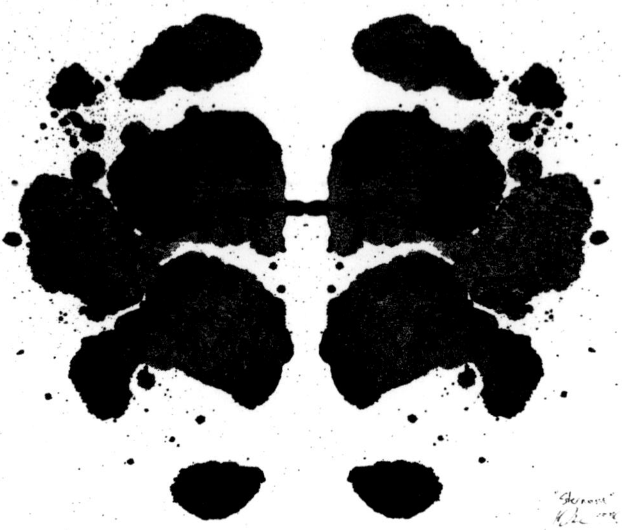

These are *absences* of the human, which are based not just on human absence but on a conceptual absence of humanity that is itself based on a singular, explicit preoccupation: the awareness of human finitude, specifically the fact that human beings (as individuals, persons), human beings (as a collective, as people), and human beings (as concept, "a people," "humankind," "humanity," etc.) will die. Die off, die out, be allowed to die, be killed—a *humanness having been*. The various instances of this terrible awareness—their genocidal shadows that stretch centuries-long across the expanse of human being—are not ours alone to contend with, but we have our own copy to read, as the saying goes, our own copy to write.

Insofar as we are inclined to embrace the irony of an afterlife we may never get to experience, we may conclude that we exist contrary to the infinitude of arrival. But this is not to be despaired.

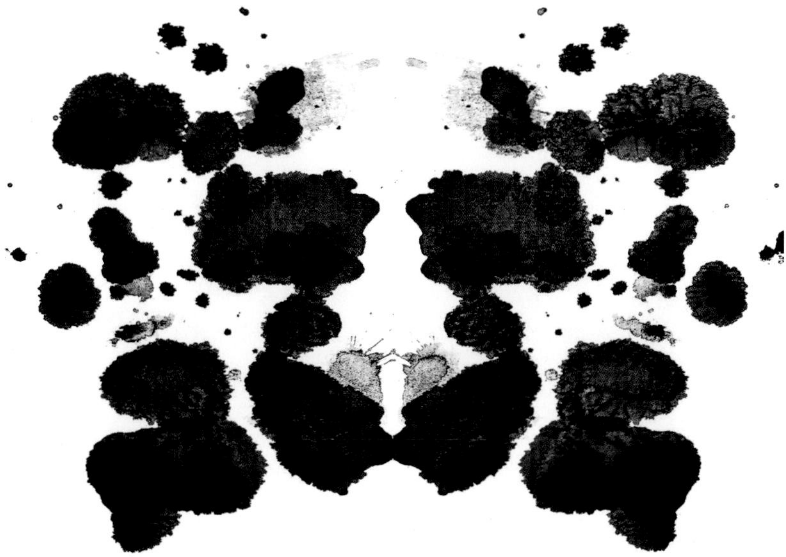

Yes, the ironic optimism of these nonhuman|inhuman "advances" touches, I suppose, on the point of being at the height of aliveness when facing death, the idea that one would have to be alive to witness the end of life—no point of life is more absolute than the moment of death, no power over life greater than that, no achievement higher than the obliteration of humankind—the obliteration would be proof of our potential at its zenith. Achille Mbembe makes this point much more effectively in *Necropolitics* (2019), and the idea unfurls (beautifully, terrifyingly) into an analysis of power's force and affect on bodies and the spaces those bodies inhabit. But as I think about the ostensibly finite approach to an infinite arrival, that point has proven obstinate: absolute life as|is death. I doubt we need it emphasized that such a life is not the life we envision as part of our everyday. And yet, repercussions of that absolute life still resonate as an enticement to that elusive afterlife, resonances we are able to experience or observe as memory, as imagination, as spirit. Though, we may never be inclined to ask to what end—and whose.

Whatever life—or life as|in death—may be, my concern is how ours might be experienced in forms other than the ones we have become accustomed to, and in terms we recognize. Because, indeed, we have conceived of them. Made them out of what we have brought and what we have found. This, then, is the situation—already so normal(ized) as to hardly register as rhetorical, let alone necessitating rhetorical attention. But it is also a reminder, increasingly insistent, that no age has reckoned effectively with the disposability of black, brown, indigenous, and (yes) white bodies. No empire will volunteer itself on our behalf to correct this unreckoned reality, each with its long history of misery, violence, and death. We learn that no government forged in the image of empire is bound nor will bind itself to that reckoning. And that literally, from time to time, it is we who must contend with what it means to exist in a world designed for increasing degrees of absence, the deliberate "absenting" of bodies and what bodies can do.

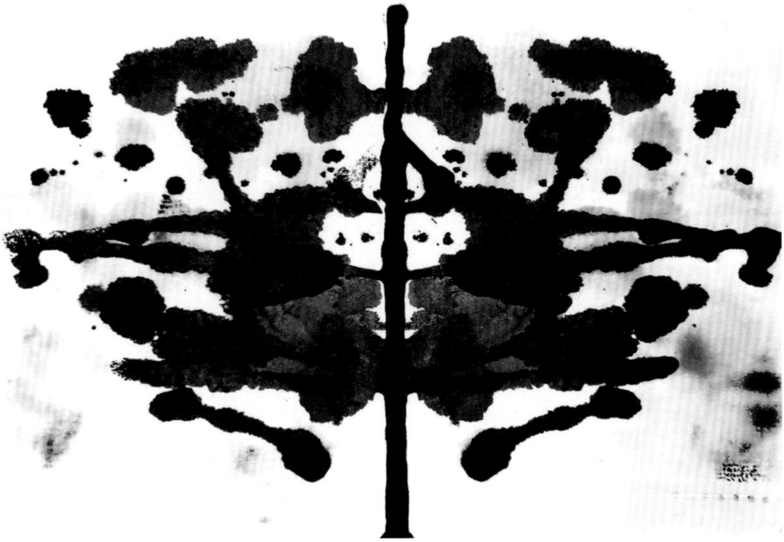

The notion of absence as nonhuman|inhuman being is a gesture—perhaps a promise—of the inevitability of "no people." The insistence that *here* is, in fact, peopled by "nonpeople," which is to say, not peopled at all. *Empty*. Not just decolonized but *uncolonized*. Not just uninhabited but *uninhabitable*. The end of all power, even that which is intended to bring about our absence to ensure its own continuance. We are still here, though. And yes, I know: the insistence of the human—myself, you, my people, who are particularly but not exclusively black—into this nonhuman and increasingly inhuman dynamic feels like a cruelty, like a reification of the violence and wretchedness of human life.

But it doesn't have to be that. It can be other things, made into other things.

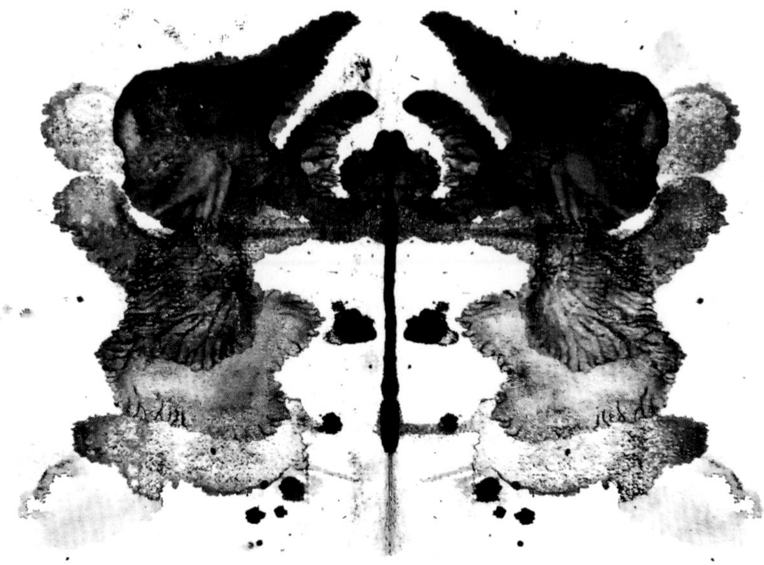

We who know better—that we are people and already endowed with spirit, memory, and imagination—are able to see what is happening here: that the promise of this world and its genres and subgenres of modernity mean to refuse life. *All life*. In the interim (while we are still here, and to the extent that we are inclined to pay attention to the operation and actualization of these process-states, and to then refuse them on the basis of our basic humanity), we learn what it means to exist in this *here* that seems destined (or designed) to become a *nowhere*. Notwithstanding our obvious endangerment, it is still a "nowhere we want to be." We are able to say, "We belong nowhere," without irony. We will know what that means, having already navigated the mystery of the archipelago's unrealness to arrive here.

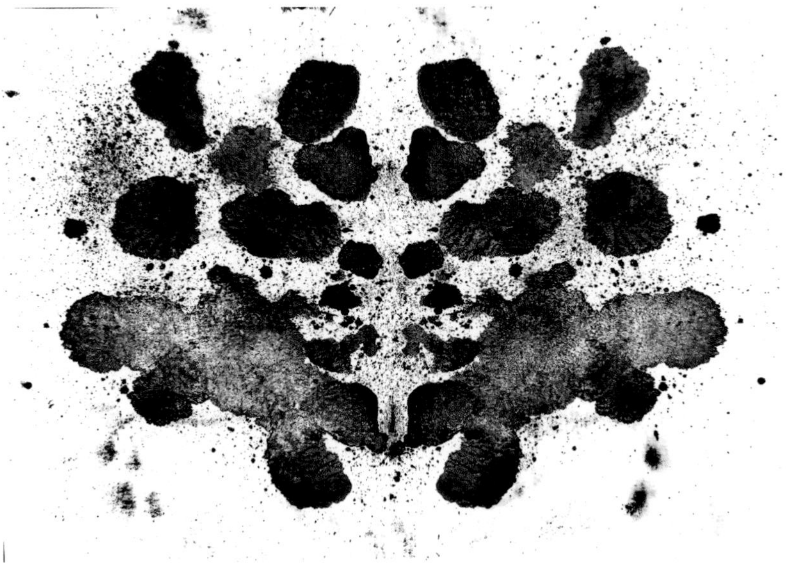

More crucially, and having rejected the refusal of black life as the only outcome, we see that we are not just able but obliged to put our Nowhereian sensibilities to practical use—that is, toward our insistence on presence in this relentless absenting, our insistence on humanity in the face of this nonhuman|inhuman logic and its processes, in the face of its abject inhumanity. Obliged, in other words, to orient ourselves to the more "democratized" emptiness of the nowheres newly at our disposal—the nowhere of "digital space," for example, and the virtual "no-bodies" whose artificial intelligences have already been transposed, their motives already having transcended the boundaries of the archipelago—of all their respective archipelagoes. By "no-bodies" I mean those who, by their very existence, threaten the logics of reality itself, let alone the rhetorics those realities enable.

That is, if such things, in spite of their material impact on the bodies who do not inhabit that same digital space, could be said to have a self, or we the rhetorical capacity to identify them—and with them.

Inevitably, the question of *who* we are as "a people" will lose significance because we will find that being Caribbean will not be enough. The *Caribbean*, as a concept more than a region, will not be enough—it will not hold, nor will it hold us. In truth, it has not held for some time. To some, the revelation will feel, at first, like prophecy fulfilled—an *ent ah tell yuh dis place unreal!* finally coming to pass. But it will not be a prophecy, only a revelation: not only that my people exist but also that we matter *beyond* what we have tended to believe. That we are, in fact, unbelievable.

We may still find ourselves mired in the reality of everyday life and may never be compelled to make new ways for ourselves. But we know this is not the worst thing that can happen to us, only proof that the "better to come" may not look the way we expect it to look, that *we* may have to *look* differently, or elsewhere, to see what difference—these different things yet to be seen—might yield.

You will find me here, in any case, at the end of this too-short season of action and abstraction, no longer in a place where the imaginary merely remains "imagined" but where it is positioned for the mundane experience of blackness as breath, with breath as uncontested space, as evidence of sovereignty reconfigured as something like freedom, evidence of a path toward it. You find me immersed in the dynamics of infinite arrival, making space, bound equally in memory and imagination, in the stillness and silence of the image, in the scent and feel of the object, in the tenuous subjectivity of Caribbean being.

SENSE

In *The Blue Clerk* (2018), Dionne Brand describes what I think is an obvious thing. It is born, as you might expect, from an impossible thing, and moves to the obvious with the characteristic ease that makes the work both infinitely accessible and inimitable. Following the title of the opening poem, "Stipule," a definition of the title itself is offered:

"A small leaf-like appendage to a leaf"

Before you get anywhere at all, the definition bids you go back—return to the title, confirm what has been defined. Then, when you think you are ready, continue. Try to stay inside of it, breathing it in.

With a recognition of natural process, the nature of process, and their implicit relationships to structure and logic, the definition pauses abruptly. But it teaches: the stipule is "like" a leaf but not a leaf, not the leaf to which it is appended. Not yet. This poem has not yet begun. This poem—named for a thing that is simultaneously a thing and not yet the thing it will be—is not yet a poem.

It is on its way, though—it *coming*.

As it leads you over the blank sliver of the page, from the epigraph to its first line, the prophetic work of the poem becomes a bit clearer. It is a line in time-lapse. A disjunction houses the impossible thing, at first, that is shaped into a splice. Then (when shaped by Brand) it is "spliced" in the place we are invited, but not compelled, to look: at the end. You may not see it unless you look for it. Who looks for splices at the beginnings of poems, at the ends of lines? But there it is. You may want to call it other things, but it is what Brand says it is: a stipule, a thing existentially spliced between the "like" that it is and the "as" that it promises to become:

"I have left this unsaid. I have withheld. What is withheld"

"What is withheld"—this very series of words—is a stipule. See it? The impossibility of an "unsaid" that is said? The restatement of the "unsaid," dually confessed as a withholding let loose on the line? The stipule *itself*, compounded by the confession that absolves it? The "I have withheld . . . what is withheld" looming in the ether of the epigraph? Not yet having departed "like," we do not arrive at "as" by the end of the line but here, at:

"What is withheld"[1]

It is neither a question nor a statement but an ending interrupted by its antecedents. The rhetorician in me wants to call this an *enthymeme*, but it is not that—it only appears to be, making plain what appears, at first, to be withheld. What I have withheld is that I am terrified of the thing that afflicts me, calling me to account for thoughts of my own mortality. That is what a tumor is, isn't it? Protruding like a horn above my left eye, encroaching on the orbital rim, threatening my vision, making a cuckold of my vanities. An ugliness inside of me. When a piece of it is cut out and cross-sectioned for a second biopsy, I see that it is a type of black—a type of blackness—a bloodied beauty against the stainless blade. Now, it is as familiar to me as the limers on Coffee Street, who check their Play Whe ledgers like actuaries.[2]

I have written a memoir of Caribbean blackness as a sense and an anticipation, a parable of waiting and of wanting that is grounded neither in terror nor in peace, nor in anything absolute. And I have made things—objects made from the assemblage of other objects—that are each complete.

And I have withheld.

What I have withheld

is what I have failed, until now, to admit:

that the practice of nonfiction, while "a genre of being human," is also a practice of restraint, an art of withholding derived neither from fullness nor from

1 Brand, *Blue Clerk*, 3.

2 Play Whe is a numbers game that is more than a game. A game of dreams for dreamers. Numbers and caprices. Feelings. Senses. *Corbeau* is 11, in case you wonder. *Dead man* is 4. I play those whenever I play, which is not often.

the lack of it, but from the need—my need—to extract only some of what has remained within.

> A what has remained within that says, in sum: Tell me again about how secrets are kept. About the hidden ways of knowledge. And about the codes of unsanctioned conduct.
>
> Tell me again about the action of unmovable things designed to gesture to the past, how you have made them move, made them envision a future.
>
> Then take a breath. A black breath—held and unheld—that sustains.
>
> Take a breath, then make a beautiful thing—a space for the continued empathy of Caribbean people, who are beautiful but not beautiful alone.
> Nor always beautiful together.
>
> Make a thing that cannot hold the unholdable pathos of your Caribbeanness, a thing that is, for you, like the banded belly of your grandmother—or mine.
>
> Make a thing that cannot hold you. Let it take you through grief. Grief is only a waypoint. Pain is unavoidable, but it is passing. Not just pain in the abstract but a constellation that gathers at the joints when we make things and dare not to rest without thinking too much about what we have done.[3]

3 *Think*, your remembering muscles will say, *but not too much*.

> Then say, having moved yourself, what arrival will be. Say what it has been. We arrive at a thing that, as far as you and I are concerned, is already here. Our process—the afterlife of thought—will be its recursive consequence, the fact of it already here by the time we arrive.
>
> (The consequence of a before that unfolds into an after.)

And so it will be that, with deep intention, we set about doing precisely what we have come to do: compose ourselves, take liberties, and make our way as we go, with arrival occurring not merely as a matter of some errant consequence, but as a consequence of matter itself.

ARRIVAL

Arrival: a turn (here, as in what one "makes")
: making a turn (to come again):
the coming again (from the turn
made)
: a revolution (what one makes and
has made)
: a departing (in infinite revolutions, arriving
infinitely)[1]
: a reach (as in, We eh reach yet, eh.
But we coming.)

An opening (here); a *Krik*[2]
: a body (here, oneself,
but also one of work, of labor)
: a deliberative opening of the
labored body (illicit, eliciting,
unbelievable, unbelieved) that is
antecedent to the forensic dissections
of its meanings, an opening up
antemortem, an unhinging (here, of parts
of the body):

1 Do you know *douens*? Do you have them where you are? What are your myths of an embodied arrival that mimic return, making one infinite and the other impossible? Mine, I have heard, run in the forest—and, lately, across the labored breadth of the page.

2 Remember?

feet at the ankles (a douen);
mouth at the lip and jaw (a kiss);
eyes at the lids (a dream);
fingers at every carpal turn (a touch).

In *A Sense of Arrival*, I have turned inward to gauge for myself the degrees to which Caribbeanness will lead to areas of new understanding. I have concerned myself, so far, with matters of who we are to consider what might become of us, to imagine what we might be inclined to make of ourselves—and *for* ourselves. The obvious essentialism of these concerns is provisional. That is, it is intended to achieve a very specific goal: mapping a moment in contemporary Caribbean intentionality and articulation. It is, at its most basic and its most complex, a rhetoric and a composition, a philosophy of Caribbean rhetoric. But only nominally, strategically. The attempt speaks, no doubt, to the desire I have harbored for a kind of *ontogenesis*—a Caribbeanness *rethought*, rather than more familiar ontological preoccupations. I mean to arrive, in other words, at "who we mean to be" instead of return to "who we have been." Shouldn't we all seek to liberate ourselves from immutable formations, from frames that do not shift? How else to imagine freedom? How else to enact it? It is also to reinforce for us the need to not only see ourselves in and through others, but to see the Other as clearly as we see ourselves in and through them.

In truth, I am reaching for you—to arrive, you remember, is also to reach. If you come apart from time to time, I will come apart with you. I will break beautifully with you, our pieces resting motionless in some future hand, diminutive as sand, or ants that stop to ponder the distended bird-pecked belly of a mango in the yard. Sometimes you are where I want to be: sitting near what was a jetty at King's Wharf in San Fernando. Time has long claimed it for itself, leaving us here like castaways to mind the eroding shore, to see and not see the galvanized sheets that betray their vanities, rusting the colors of copper and bronze, to walk past the split wood and broken stone, and to see the bones of fish and cat and dog turn a blinding white in the abandoned terminal at Plaza San Carlos.

I have been waiting for you.

Is that you on the horizon? Around the corner by the shop? Up the Hill? Dancing like a blackbird on the tension lines? Is that you between the forgotten innocence and the half-ripe conscience, between the pleasures taken past their primes? It might just be you.

It might just be you, here to show me what this thing will be in the end.

Come, sit.

And if you ask why I would want you to see yourself as separate from the archipelago, however momentarily, I would say,

> "Because arrival demands and is also departure—we've known this all along.
>
> "Because arrival at what it can mean to *be Caribbean* depends as much on a departure from what it has meant.
>
> "Because you are neither your navel string nor the place where it is buried, nor the fish you have eaten or failed to eat, nor the song you have sung or failed to sing.
>
> "Because Carnival is not enough—not *nearly* enough—we've known this since the Proclamation of 1884 that banned our black, embattled bodies.
>
> "Because to see yourself as separate is to see *yourself*. To see yourself in relation—your being as a relating. It is also to see the archipelago in relation to your impending arrival. By which I mean the view of arrival as an expression of and embrace of a Caribbean futurity that is not immovably anchored in the Caribbean nor reducible to a single individual. It is an act of precarious sovereignty, just before that sovereignty dissolves.
>
> "Because arrival is a beautiful thing—dangerous, endangered—that we have conspired to make divine, a thing we have dared to name "beauty," a beauty we have made that is something more than a memento of our black Caribbean life, a totem of our insistence on living in a world that cannot love (us).

"Because arrival is not merely the recognition of the constancy of our precarity passing like a breath into the ether that we may be inclined, now and again, to sense, but *sense* itself. Breath itself.

"Because arrival is the blackest thing I have ever known, the most Caribbean thing I have ever seen."

Why else?

As for me, I'm sitting at a rumshop in Paramin, and at the edge of blue and gilded waters at Grand Anse, and near the egret-laden acacia trees at Brimstone Hill, and on the rocks at Blanchisseuse and Matura and Toco and Castara, and on the steps at Sacre-Coeur, and on the eroding road in Guayaguayare, and on the cliff at Ambard Street, and in the yard on Carib Street—

where all I have is an idea—a sense—until your arrival makes it true.

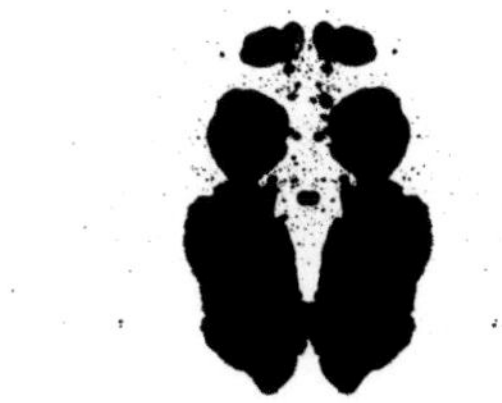

FIGURES

Surd

. . .

ACKNOWLEDGMENTS

To
Eva Wright, my mother
for breath and for sight,
for form and for memory,
for courage,
for language,
for love.

To
My sister, Ayana
My brothers, Stefan, Jovian, Joel,
and Nicholai (d. 2023)
for one reason alone, in spite of our distance.

To
Dawn Cumberbatch, "The Original"
for everything I cannot name.

To
Christina Sharpe
Dionne Brand
Elizabeth Nunez
Saidiya Hartman
Tina M. Campt
M. NourbeSe Philip
Sylvia Wynter
Audre Lorde
Earl Lovelace
Derek Walcott

for your knowing work,
for every knowing word—the elegant singularity of letters,
for writing impossible things,
for crafting life—black life, Caribbean life—out of impossible things.

To
Ayanna Lloyd Banwo for Yemaya's chest, for the sanctified *corbeaux*.
Richard Lessey for your flight and your landing—your decades of grace.
Mel Gabriel for sitting with me—and *for* me.
Lorraine Charles for a harmony whose resonance has no finer acoustic than your voice.
And for chartreuse.
And, of course, for red.

To
Joshua-Michael Charleau for splitting the daylight.
Rasheed Hosein (d. 2019), for the robber's barrel and its sight.
Anique Jordan for playing white and being black, unwretched.
Alexie Lexington Joseph for your blonded beauty.
Stephanie Kanhai for splitting the darkness.
Amanda McIntyre for your light that needs no filter, your joy.
Nykimo Nicholas for calling me to see you barefoot.
Andrew "Kutu" Sanoir for swallowing the fire whole.

To
Brian Adonis
Miguel Ayres
Rene Farrow
Kenwyn Findley
Naitche Sanowar
for brotherhood.

To
Jason Audain
Rondel Benjamin
Vaughnette Bigford
Roger Bonair-Agard
Leroy Calliste (d. 2022)
Janice Derrick
Nehal El-Hadi
Karlene Francois
Melissa Harper
Che Lovelace
Steffano Marcano

Joan Morgan
Grace Ngugi
Marsha Pearce
Jamie Philbert
David Rudder

for reading, for looking,
for talking, for listening,
for reaching out, for answering,
for giving ground, for taking time,
for making space.

To
Isabel Brash
Martin D. Mouttet
Geoffrey MacLean (d. 2024)

for welcoming me to Medulla Art Gallery, Trinidad, where the *Animæ*, *Orisa*, *Surd*, *Tabanca*, and *Umbilici* series were so beautifully exhibited.

To
Elizabeth Ault, Benjamin Kossak, Lisa Lawley, and the entire production team at Duke University Press. You all have been a pleasure to work with. Elizabeth, thank you for seeing the beauty of this book from the beginning. The anonymous readers, especially, who saw what I could not—and then took the time to show it all to me. What a gift it has been to think—and to grow in my thinking—with you.

To
Collin G. Brooke and my colleagues at the Department of Writing Studies, Rhetoric, and Composition at Syracuse University.
Our doctoral students. In particular, Karisa Bridgelal, Urmi Parekh, Abigail Long, Brenna Tellames Williams, and Curtis Jewell. I am so honored to work, think, and learn with you.
Kristi Johnson, without whose masterful assistance *A Sense of Arrival: An Exhibition of Essays* at Medulla Art Gallery could not have happened.

To
All whose names I may have omitted, it is as I have said: I have written a sense of you into the grammar and tensing of this book—your influence appears on every page. For that, you have my deepest gratitude.

Thank you.

The publication of this work was supported in part by the Faculty Creative Activities and Research Grant awarded by the Office of Research in Academic Affairs, with additional support from the Office of Academic Affairs and the Department of Writing Studies, Rhetoric, and Composition, College of Arts and Sciences, at Syracuse University.

SOURCES

Discography

Brown, Dennis. "How Could I Leave." Single. Kingston, Jamaica: Joe Gibbs Records, 1976, vinyl.

Black Stalin [Leroy Calliste]. "Caribbean Unity (Caribbean Man)." Track 2 on *To the Caribbean Man*. New York: Makossa, 1979, vinyl.

Bob Marley and the Wailers. "Redemption Song." Track 10 on *Uprising*. Kingston, Jamaica: Tuff Gong, 1980, vinyl.

Explainer [Winston Henry]. "Lorraine." Track 4 on *Man from the Ghetto*. Brooklyn, NY: Charlie's Records, 1981, vinyl.

Jackson, Millie. "If Loving You Is Wrong I Don't Want to be Right." Track 1 on *Caught Up*. New York: Spring Records, 1974, vinyl.

Knight, Gladys. "Midnight Train to Georgia." Track 1 on *Imagination*. New York: Buddah Records, 1973, vinyl.

Lord Kitchener [Aldwyn Roberts]. "The Road Make to Walk (on Carnival Day)." Single. Chicago: Jump Up Records, 1963, vinyl.

Mighty Shadow [Winston Bailey]. "Bass Man." Single. Brooklyn, NY: Straker's Records, 1974, vinyl.

Mighty Shadow [Winston Bailey]. "Pay de Devil." Track 1 on *Dingolay*. Barbados, Kisskidee Records, 1994, vinyl.

Roaring Lion [Raphael De Leon]. "Papa Chunks." Track 1 on *Vive Le King*. Barbados: Ice Records, 1995, compact disc.

Rudder, David Michael. "Haiti." Track 2 on *Haiti*. London: London Records, 1988, vinyl.

Simone, Nina. "Ne me quitte pas." Track 1 on *I Put a Spell on You*. Amsterdam: Philips Records, 1965, vinyl.

Simone, Nina. "Sinnerman." Track 9 on *Pastel Blues*. Amsterdam: Philips Records, 1965, vinyl.

Videography

Philbert, Jamie J. *Bound: A Free, Spellbound, Humming*. University of Limerick Irish World Academy of Music and Dance, 2022. Vimeo video, 5:32, https://vimeo.com/781949227.

Philbert, Jamie J. *Patterns of Freedom*. University of Limerick Irish World Academy of Music and Dance, 2023. YouTube video, 7:49, https://www.youtube.com/watch?v=ivoYMHz16m4.

Rudder, David Michael. "Calypso Music." Performed at the 1987 Calypso Monarch Finals, recorded by Trinidad and Tobago Television, 2007. YouTube video, 9:04. https://youtu.be/8lJFxF_iNDY.

Bibliography

Barthes, Roland. *Camera Lucida: Reflections on Photography*. New York: Hill and Wang, 2010.

Bénitez-Rojo, Antonio. *The Repeating Island: The Caribbean and the Postmodern Perspective*. Translated by James Maraniss. Durham, NC: Duke University Press, 1987.

Blake, William. *Milton: A Poem in Two Books*. London, 1804–10.

Brand, Dionne. *The Blue Clerk: Ars Poetica in 59 Versos*. Durham, NC: Duke University Press, 2018.

Brand, Dionne. *A Map to the Door of No Return*. Toronto, ON: Doubleday Canada, 2001.

Brito, Renata, and Felipe Dana. "Adrift." *Associated Press*, April 12, 2023.

Browne, Kevin Adonis. *Tropic Tendencies: Rhetoric, Popular Culture, and the Anglophone Caribbean*. Pittsburgh, PA: University of Pittsburgh Press, 2013.

Campt, Tina. *Listening to Images*. Durham, NC: Duke University Press, 2017.

Césaire, Aimé. *A Tempest*. Translated by Richard Miller from *Une Tempête* (1969). New York: Theatre Communications Group, 1997.

Glissant, Édouard. *Poetics of Relation*. Translated by Betsy Wing. Ann Arbor: University of Michigan Press, 2010.

Hartman, Saidiya. "Venus in Two Acts." *Small Axe* 26 (2008): 1–14.

Jackson, Zakiyyah Iman. *On Becoming Human: Matter and Meaning in an Antiblack World*. New York: New York University Press, 2020.

James, C. L. R. *Beyond a Boundary*. 50th anniversary ed. Durham, NC: Duke University Press, 2013.

James, C. L. R. *The Black Jacobins*. New York: Vintage, 1989.

James, C. L. R. *Minty Alley*. London: Secker and Warburg, 1936.

Lovelace, Che. *Che Lovelace: Paintings 2004–2008*. Trinidad and Tobago Art Series. Port of Spain, Trinidad and Tobago: Robert and Christopher, 2008.

Lovelace, Earl. *The Dragon Can't Dance*. London: André Deutsch, 1979.

Mbembe, Achille. *Necropolitics*. Durham, NC: Duke University Press, 2019.

Naipaul, V. S. *The Loss of El Dorado: A History*. London: André Deutsch, 2003.

Sharpe, Christina. *Ordinary Notes*. Toronto, ON: Knopf Canada, 2023.

Spillers, Hortense J. "Mama's Baby, Papa's Maybe: An American Grammar Book." *Diacritics* 17, no. 2 (1987): 64–81.

Stedman, John Gabriel. *The Narrative of a Five Years Expedition against the Revolting Slaves of Surinam*. First Edition. London: J. Johnson, St. Paul's Church Yard, and J. Edwards, Pall Mall, 1796.

Stothard, Thomas. "Voyage of the *Sable Venus* from Angola to the West Indies." In Bryan Edwards, *History, Civil and Commercial, of the British Colonies in the West Indies*, Third edition. London: printed for J. Stockdale, 1801.

Strauss, Benjamin, and Scott Kulp. *Sea-Level Rise Challenges in the Caribbean: Data, Tools, and Analysis for a More Resilient Future*. Princeton, NJ: Climate Central, 2018.

Thistlewood, Thomas. *The Diaries of Thomas Thistlewood, 1721–1786*. Thomas Thistlewood Papers. James Marshall and Marie-Louise Osborn Collection, Beinecke Rare Book and Manuscript Library, Yale University, New Haven, CT.

Walcott, Derek. "The Schooner *Flight*." In *Collected Poems 1948–1984*, 328. New York: Farrar, Straus and Giroux, 1986.

Walcott, Derek. "The Spoiler's Return." In *Collected Poems 1948–1984*, 432. New York: Farrar, Straus and Giroux, 1986.

Wynter, Sylvia. "Rethinking 'Aesthetics': Notes towards a Deciphering Practice." In *Ex-iles: Essays on Caribbean Cinema*, edited by Mbye Cham, 237–80. Trenton, NJ: Africa World Press, 1992.

Wynter, Sylvia. "Unsettling the Coloniality of Being/Power/Truth/Freedom: Towards the Human, after Man, Its Overrepresentation—An Argument." cr: *The New Centennial Review* 3, no. 3 (2003): 257–337.

INDEX